Beyond the Basics
A Resource for Educators on Sexuality and Sexual Health

3rd edition

Action Canada
for Sexual Health & Rights

Authors
Makeda Zook
Karen B.K. Chan
Frédérique Chabot
Brittany Neron

Editors
Ani Colekessian
Sandeep Prasad

Illustrator
Alex Hutcheon

Designer
AN Design

Online and print production
Autumn Corvus

Action Canada for Sexual Health and Rights
251 Bank St., 2nd Floor
Ottawa, Ontario K2P 1X3
Canada
Tel +1 (613) 241-4474
info@sexualhealthandrights.ca
www.sexualhealthandrights.ca

Forewords

What do you wish you'd learned in sex-ed? That's a question that we at Action Canada for Sexual Health and Rights have been asking throughout the preparation of the third edition of *Beyond the Basics*. It's a question that we can't ask enough because everyone seems to have something to say and the answers are highly revealing. Sexuality education in Canada (when taught) remains highly varied between school to school, even teacher to teacher. And for the most part, it's a couple of lessons on anatomy and risk.

The sexuality education I received in school 20+ years ago wasn't much different. We learned about body parts and how they functioned—all scientifically accurate and generally useful to know. Then there was the cautionary tales of "risky sexual behaviour," mostly focused on the STIs we could contract if we had sex. I remember a video with a line about anal sex being inherently riskier than vaginal sex. None of what I learned prepared me for being a queer youth trying to navigate complex emotions, attractions, and relationships with peers. The sex-ed I received didn't seek to break down problematic aspects of my school environment, where homophobic comments, body-shaming, and sexist jokes were commonplace, and where dominant and constricting notions of masculinity flourished.

Under international human rights law, we all have a right to *good quality* education. There's a lot that is included in that concept but all too rarely do parents, governments, and the education system see sexuality education done well as being part of that. *Beyond the Basics* takes an approach that is rooted in *comprehensive* sexuality education—seeking to move the bar beyond anatomy and risk, to ensure students are better prepared to lead empowered sexual lives where they feel comfortable in their own bodies, can exercise their right to bodily autonomy, and are equipped with the skills to challenge oppressive gender norms. The comprehensive approach fosters cultures of consent, respect for diversity, and critical thinking skills, some of the most valuable things that students can learn in school, which also happen to be some of the hardest things to teach.

In *Beyond the Basics* and the Online Hub, educators will find the tools and information they need to bring comprehensive sexuality education alive in their classrooms. Educators are the crucial vehicles by which young people can realize their right to comprehensive sexuality education—*Beyond the Basics* is dedicated to them.

Sandeep Prasad (signature)

Sandeep Prasad

Working in the area of health requires a special kind of "bifocal vision" (the concept of "bifocal vision" in this context was first shared with me by Dr. Peter Selby, to whom I am grateful for the term). One lens must always be focused right up close on the individual in need of help, the single person who requires information or support or some form of intervention. But at the same time, there is another lens that must focus the big picture, in which social change and population health, not just individual health, is the goal.

With this educator resource, Action Canada for Sexual Health and Rights is exercising bifocal vision. One lens is focused on educators and young people in classrooms all over Canada and beyond: these pages offer a very concrete and helpful resource to the front line. The book is a toolkit for promoting health through individual level behaviour change. It is well-researched, evidence-informed, and easy to use. Comprehensive Sexuality Education (CSE) can positively impact people's overall health and well-being throughout the lifespan, and resources like this can therefore make a difference to thousands and even hundreds of thousands of individuals in their personal and sexual health over many decades.

But there is another lens to this work, one that is sharply attuned to social change at the highest levels. This lens focuses on the values that drive Action Canada's policy work and its advocacy for stronger CSE curricula across Canada. One of the strengths of CSE as an approach to sexual education is that the connections between systemic forces and individual health outcomes are made. This is the work that connects the structural drivers of health to individual experiences. Challenging systemic oppression and body shaming; demanding public policy that supports consent, healthy relationships and resiliency; all while keeping one eye firmly focused on the individual in need of education. *That* is bifocal vision.

As a family doctor, I am deeply supportive of *Beyond the Basics* and the many educators who will use this book. As a mother, I am grateful for it. Whatever is being discussed in the schoolyards and the basements of the nation must be put into context by educators who have the resources and skills to communicate with young people at every age and stage. We are lucky to have them.

Danielle Martin MD, MPP, CCFP, FCFP
Family Physician
Vice President, Medical Affairs and Health System Solutions
Women's College Hospital
June 2017

Acknowledgments

We are incredibly grateful for the support of the following people and organizations that have made the production of the third edition of *Beyond the Basics* possible:

Jolanta Scott-Parker, Ash Hunkin, Alexander McKay (Sex Information and Education Council of Canada, SIECCAN), Shane H. Camastro (Native Youth Sexual Health Network), Beck Hood, Piper Kearney (intersex activist), Celeste Orr, RJ Jones, Shannon Sloane Mulligan, Kim Snider, Kelly-Ann Ryan, Jennifer Henry, Elena Young, David Udayasekaran (Planned Parenthood Toronto), Ariane Wylie (Planned Parenthood Ottawa), Bianca Stortini (MD, FRCSC), Julie G Thorne (MD, MPH, FRCSC), Scott Anderson, Camille Arkell, and David McLay (CATIE), Bev Chernos, Abigail Kidd, Erika Shaker, Emily Turk, Meg Saxby, Hannah McGechie (Ten Oaks Project), Roberto Ortiz and Matt Harding (MAX Ottawa), Adrienne Silnicki and Amelie Baillargeon (Canadian Health Coalition), and all Action Canada for Sexual Health and Rights staff members (including Sarah Kennell, Meghan Doherty, Tara Henderson, and Darrah Teitel).

A final thank you to all our partners, allies, donors, and supporters that we've had the pleasure of working with over the years.

Table of Contents

CHAPTER **O**

Introduction

—

O.1 PURPOSE AND PRINCIPLES

Sexuality is an integral part of being human. It is a complex set of personal, social, and spiritual experiences that go beyond sexual activity. In other words, sexuality is not just about what our body does and what we do with our bodies, it is how thoughts, fantasies, desires, beliefs, attitudes, values, behaviours, practices, roles, and relationships are experienced and expressed (WHO, 2006a). Sexual health is one aspect of sexuality and a key component of overall health and well-being.

Sexual health is defined by the World Health Organization as "a state of physical, emotional, mental and social well-being in relation to sexuality; it is not merely the absence of disease, dysfunction or infirmity. Sexual health requires a positive and respectful approach to sexuality and sexual relationships, as well as the possibility of having pleasurable and safe sexual experiences, free of coercion, discrimination and violence. For sexual health to be attained and maintained, the sexual rights of all persons must be respected, protected and fulfilled" (2006a).

Sexual health requires a comprehensive understanding of sexuality, which is why *Beyond the Basics* takes such an approach to sexuality education. As an educator, it is important to discuss sexual health in the context of a person's entire self and experience of the world. The comprehensive approach is also in line with the 2008 Public Health Agency of Canada *Canadian Guidelines for Sexual Health Education*, which consider sexual health a key component of overall health and well-being.

Comprehensive sexuality education recognizes sexuality as an integral part of being human and includes the ways that sexuality is expressed, manifested, and impacted by emotional, social, cultural, physical, psychological, economic, spiritual, political, and economic aspects of an individual's life (UNESCO, 2009). It provides a holistic understanding of sexual health. In this way, comprehensive sexuality education considers how sexual health is related to **human rights**, gender norms, emotional, psychological and spiritual well-being, civic engagement, and the social determinants of health (environmental, political, and economic) (ISHC Working Group, 2011). *Beyond the Basics* provides educators with tools, such as activities, information, resources, and reflection questions, to implement and integrate the principles of comprehensive sexuality education into classrooms across Canada.

Working in concert with the *Canadian Guidelines for Sexual Health Education, Beyond the Basics* supports access to effective, evidence-based, developmentally appropriate sexual health education that provides relevant information and skill building opportunities necessary to enhance sexual health and well-being (Ophea, 2013; Public Health Agency of Canada, 2008; Sex Information and Education Council of Canada, 2010; Society of Obstetricians and Gynecologists of Canada, 2004).

Sexuality education is often taught as part of physical and health education in provincial and territorial curriculums across Canada. All provincial and territorial ministries of education have set out mandates or expectations for the provision of sexuality education in schools; however, the extent to which different ministries of education provide specific learning activities that correspond to their teaching guidelines or curricula varies considerably. Updates to provincial and territorial curricula often also lag behind social and technological changes that impact sexuality education.

Beyond the Basics has been designed with the dual purpose of providing school-based educators with learning activities that are consistent with the most up-to-date provincial/territorial mandates for sexuality education and community-based educators with a range of learning activities for comprehensive and high-quality sexuality education.

Guiding Principles of Comprehensive Sexuality Education

The new edition of *Beyond the Basics* was inspired by Action Canada for Sexual Health and Rights' commitment to supporting access to up-to-date, evidence-based, and comprehensive sexuality education and sexual health services in every community.

The content of *Beyond the Basics* was created to reflect the principles within the Public Health Agency of Canada's *Canadian Guidelines for Sexual Health Education* (2008) and international guidelines for comprehensive sexuality education (High-Level Task Force for ICPD, 2013; ISHC Working Group, 2011; UNESCO, 2009).

Beyond the Basics is informed by and intended to promote the following principles:
1. Comprehensive sexuality education emphasizes the self-worth and dignity of the individual.
2. Comprehensive sexuality education empowers people to make decisions about their bodies, gender, sexuality, and reproduction that are right for them and make sense within their own lives.
3. Comprehensive sexuality education encourages critical reflection and developing critical awareness of the ways that norms around gender and sexuality impact people's lives.
4. Comprehensive sexuality education encourages people to foster cultures of sexual respect and gender equality.
5. Access to comprehensive sexuality education is a basic human right and being able to exercise and realize **human rights** is an integral part of sexual health and well-being.
6. The goals of comprehensive sexuality education, which are:
   a) To assist individuals in developing skills, a healthy self-concept, respect for others, peer support, non-coercive and rewarding relationships, and the ability to exercise self-determined decision-making related to sexual and reproductive health.
   b) To assist individuals in developing skills to avoid Sexually Transmitted and Blood Borne Infections (STBBIs), sexual coercion, and unplanned pregnancy.
   c) To encourage the development of critical thinking and analysis around social norms related to gender and sexuality.
7. Comprehensive sexuality education includes the ability to make informed choices about sexual and reproductive health and behaviour. In order to make informed choices, individuals must have access to evidence-based and comprehensive sexuality education appropriate to their age, stage of development, and learning styles.
8. Comprehensive sexuality education must be sensitive to each individual learner's beliefs, values, culture, religion, and spiritual practice.

9. Comprehensive sexuality education should reflect and be informed by the principles of non-discrimination, human dignity, fairness, **equity**, and **human rights**. That is, education should not discriminate on the basis of race, religious and cultural background, ethnicity, physical/cognitive ability, or other such aspects of human diversity. It is equally important that sexual health education not discriminate on the basis of individual differences related to sexuality such as **gender, gender identity, gender expression,** and **sexual orientation**.

0.2 CONTEXT AND CHALLENGES

Sexuality education does not take place in a vacuum. Sexuality is a fundamental part of being human and, in this way, sexual health education takes place across all contexts of students' lives: the classroom, the family, the community, wider society etc. The *Canadian Guidelines for Sexual Health Education* (Public Health Agency of Canada, 2008) specifically note that sexuality is shaped and influenced by biological, psychological, social, economic, political, cultural, ethical, legal, historical, religious, and spiritual factors. It is important for educators to recognize that the ways in which each student internalizes, interprets, and acts upon what they learn and experience in the classroom is an interplay of all of these factors.

There are a wide range of factors affecting young peoples' sexual and reproductive health that educators should become aware of in preparation for teaching sexuality education. Among them: the social determinants of health, sexual coercion and assault, and the impact of information technology (e.g., the internet, social media, texting, and communication apps) on the ways that young people learn about and experience sexuality.

Sexual health is significantly influenced by broader societal determinants of health. A **social determinants of health** perspective recognizes that factors such as income, race, immigration status, gender, sexual orientation, housing, access to social services and supports, level of education, social exclusion, and access to health services, among others, are important factors for determining the health of populations (Raphael, 2009; WHO, 2008). Socioeconomic factors are also specifically linked to negative sexual health outcomes such as STBBI rates (Dean & Fenton, 2010; Public Health Agency of Canada, 2013). Being aware of how social determinants of health impact the lives, sexuality, and sexual health of students enables educators to provide sexuality education that is sensitive and relevant to the lived realities of their students (for more information, see module 2.4).

As an educator, it is important to be aware that sexual violence affects people of all ages and backgrounds. Please proceed with the understanding that any student may be a survivor and/or witness of sexual violence and that discussions on this topic can be upsetting, overwhelming, or triggering. (For more information and resources on how to manage this within a classroom setting, see modules 1.3, 1.6, and chapter 8).

It is difficult to know exactly how many young people in Canada have experienced sexual coercion and assault (note: sexual assault is a legal term that includes offenses involving the sexual abuse of children). While it is estimated that fewer than 1 in 10 sexual assaults are reported, the available data suggests that more than half of all sexual assault victims are under the age of 18 and 25% are under the age of 12 (Brennan & Taylor-Butts, 2008).

The almost universal use of digital technologies such as the internet, social media, texting, and communication apps has had a powerful transformative impact on the way that people in Canada learn about and, in many cases, experience their sexuality. The popularity of digital technologies has important implications for young peoples' sexuality. For example, while the internet gives young people easy and anonymous access to information about sexuality and sexual health, not all of the information available on the internet is accurate.

The internet has made it easier for young people with diverse gender identities, gender expressions, and sexual orientations to build community across physical distances through the sharing of personal information but at the same time, personal information shared online can be used against young people and shared through social media, possibly leading to sexual coercion, assault, and bullying. It is important that educators are aware of the online social context that plays a new and changing role in students and young peoples' sexuality education and sexual lives. (For more information and resources refer to module 5.7 and chapter 6).

0.3 SEX POSITIVE SEXUALITY EDUCATION

Historically in Canada, school-based sexuality education has often been an exercise in risk management. Activities and programs were designed with the primary objective of preventing young people from becoming sexually active, becoming pregnant, or engaging in "risky" sexual behaviour. This was often accomplished through implicit or explicit fear tactics that cast sexuality in a negative light associating sexual desire, intimacy, and pleasure with negative outcomes such as unplanned parenthood, social stigmatization, and infection. Critics of these types of sexuality education programs have labeled them as **sex negative** and pointed out that such approaches distort and obscure the life enhancing and enriching aspects of human sexuality. Sex negative approaches to sexuality education may lead students to tune out important health messages because of what young people may perceive as an endless stream of warnings related to their sexuality. Taking a **sex positive** approach to sexual health education means that the enriching aspects of human sexuality are celebrated and consent, pleasure, and well-being are emphasized.

Sexuality education that provides adolescents and youth with information and skills that contribute to the development of equitable, mutually beneficial relationships and recognize that sexuality can and should be a source of pleasure within those relationships will resonate with and engage young people more effectively. This does not mean that sexuality education should ignore potential negative outcomes of higher-risk sexual activities but it does mean that this information is contextualized on a continuum of risk, while emphasizing critical thinking, personal awareness, and sex positivity. (For more information on how to teach sex positive sexuality education, see module 1.2).

A risk management and sex negative approach to sexuality education focuses on what makes sexuality "bad" or "something to fear" instead of acknowledging the positive aspects of human sexuality. This is particularly the case when it comes to youth; young people are often perceived as being risky, naïve, and/or deviant when it comes to most aspects of life, including sexuality.

The concepts of **resilience** and **empowerment** are important to consider when teaching sexuality education. They can support educators in learning how to meet young people where they are at in their lives from a strengths-based perspective. A **strengths-based perspective** recognizes that young people are resilient, strong, capable people with contributions and experiences worth listening to. This approach to teaching sexuality education helps ensure that young people are motivated to act on the information they are being taught. (For more information on youth resilience, empowerment and how to be a youth ally, see module 1.7).

O.4 AN INFORMATION, MOTIVATION, BEHAVIOURAL SKILLS APPROACH TO SEXUALITY EDUCATION

While providing students with relevant and important information about sexuality and sexual health is a step in the right direction, providing information alone is not enough to empower and inspire students to adopt behaviours that support their sexual health.

The activities in *Beyond the Basics* encourage both critical thinking and awareness, as well as specific skill development. For some topics and activities the objective is to encourage critical thinking and awareness but not necessarily promote the adoption of specific types of behaviour. For others, the objective is for students to develop specific social and behavioural skills related to their sexuality (i.e., setting boundaries, communicating about consent, or negotiating condom use with partners). One commonly used model for achieving the second objective is the **information, motivation and behavioural skills (IMB) model**.

The IMB model is a useful and evidence-based approach to ensure that young people have the motivation and skills they need to assess information, think critically about how it is relevant to their lives, and carry out decisions that make sense for them.

The IMB model has been proven to help students go from receiving information to implementing it. It is described in detail in the *Canadian Guidelines for Sexual Health Education* (PHAC, 2008) and asserts that sexual health education must be based on three essential elements:

- Information: helps students become better informed with information that is specifically relevant to their sexuality and sexual health needs and is easily translated into the desired behaviour.
- Motivation: provides students with opportunities to become motivated to act on the information they have learned. Sexuality education can address factors such as emotional motivation (comfort levels), personal motivation (attitudes and beliefs), and social motivation (peer norms and social supports).
- Behavioural skills: assist students in developing the specific practical skills (e.g., negotiating condom use) needed to act on information and awareness, to perform a behaviour, and to build the confidence to do so (PHAC, 2008).

The components of the IMB model form the basic information and skills necessary to facilitate and support individual empowerment. "Information" provides students with critical thinking skills needed to develop self-awareness and critical reflection. "Motivation" helps students move from critical thinking to action by providing incentives and reasons why taking action is important to their lives/realities. The development of "behavioural" skills assists students in figuring out how to most effectively act on the information provided and awareness gained. Many of the activities in *Beyond the Basics* are informed by the IMB model. As an educator, it is recommended that (where appropriate) you teach sexuality education from the IMB model.

0.5 USING BEYOND THE BASICS

The intention of *Beyond the Basics* is to provide educators with information on sexuality and sexual health that is accessible, comprehensive, and accurate. *Beyond the Basics* offers the tools to reflect on assumptions and biases and teach young people about sexuality and sexual health from a sex positive perspective. The activities in each module help move students from information to analysis, empowerment, and eventually action (e.g., intervening when witnessing sexual violence in module 8.5) or a subtle action (e.g., developing a healthy self-concept in module 5.3).

Recognizing the time pressures that educators face, *Beyond the Basics* is written to easily move in and out of chapters, modules, and activities that suit the particular age, maturity, and trust in each classroom. Each chapter provides a short introduction with reflections for educators. The modules within each chapter include activities related to the overall chapter theme.

Levels
Each module specifies the general age group that the activities are appropriate for. Activities are categorized into levels 1, 2, and 3.
- Level 1 corresponds to grades 1 to 5 and ages 6 to 11
- Level 2 corresponds to grades 6 to 8 and ages 11 to 14
- Level 3 corresponds to grades 9+ and ages 14+

Most chapters cover content that is appropriate for all three levels. Some activities offer optional modifications for younger or older students. There are also activities with basic and advanced options based on the level of trust and maturity in the classroom.

Layout and Logic of the Book
Each chapter covers a broad topic and is divided into modules that include an introduction and an opportunity to dive more fully into content through interactive and reflective activities. Some chapters contain educator resource modules, which are an opportunity for educators to build on knowledge gained in the introductory modules. It is strongly encouraged that you read the introductory module of each chapter as this will provide a foundation and understanding of how to approach the topic area.

Each activity-based module includes "Big Ideas," "Cross-Curricular Connections," and a list of "Materials." The Big Ideas section is intended to orient educators to the main ideas of the module. The Cross-Curricular Connections are lists of subject areas in which the activities can be taught outside of physical health education. The Materials section indicates what is needed in order to facilitate the activities within the module (this section will often refer to student handouts, Educator Resources, and Educator Answer Keys that are necessary to complete an activity). All student handouts, Educator Resources, Educator Answer Keys and Resources can be found on the Online Hub at www. beyondthebasics.online or in the *Beyond the Basics Companion Book*. Other practical tools for educators include important terminology (highlighted in bold throughout each module and defined in the definitions section of the book), "Quick Tips," and important background information or context that we call "You Should Know."

Each chapter in *Beyond the Basics* builds on the content of the one before. It begins with more practical teaching tips for educators, then moves into values that guide the book and create the foundation for comprehensive sexuality education. From chapters 2 to 10, *Beyond the Basics* builds critical thinking and awareness skills in students' understandings and experiences of the world. Students learn how to apply necessary skills into their daily lives, both inside and outside of the classroom (including online). Towards the end of the book, more specific, technical, and legal information is given around topics such as sexual assault, contraception, and STBBIs.

Evaluation

Classroom teachers may be responsible for assigning grades to students for the following modules. There are some activities in which assigning a grade will be easy but due to the collaborative and exploratory nature of most activities, this is often not the case. Because *Beyond the Basics* is not modeled after a single curriculum, it does not provide any specific evaluation tools. We recommend that evaluation methods be chosen based on provincially set best practices and at the teacher's own discretion.

Continued Learning and Educator Support

Information on sexual health and best practices for teaching sexual health are continuously changing with new developments and norms in the areas of activism, social movements, communication, media, and information and digital technologies. In the same way, how we teach sexual health is forever changing. In order to most effectively adapt to the fast paced nature of change, Action Canada for Sexual Health and Rights has created an Online Hub for educators using *Beyond the Basics*. The hub provides an online community for educators with up-to-date information, resources, and a forum to ask questions. Educators can access the Online Hub at www.beyondthebasics.online.

The Online Hub or the *Beyond the Basics Companion Book* with accompanying student handouts, Educator Answer Keys, Educator Resources, and Resources are meant to be used alongside *Beyond the Basics*.

CHAPTER 1

How to Guide for Educators

1.1 CHECKING IN WITH YOUR VALUES AND ASSUMPTIONS

As people living in the world, we all carry with us a specific set of values that are at times visible or explicit and at other times invisible or implicit. Educators are no different and just like all people, navigate and understand the world through a particular set of values, beliefs, and assumptions. There are many different factors that influence what a person's values are, including cultural contexts (e.g., family cultures, peer cultures, and school cultures) and religious contexts that a person grows up in and is exposed to.

Often the values, beliefs, and assumptions that individuals hold will go unnoticed and unchecked until we come face-to-face with a different set of values and beliefs that encourage us to re-evaluate our assumptions about what is normal, what is right/wrong, and about people themselves, based on their different identities and experiences.

Across Canada and within any urban or rural area, there is considerable diversity among students. This diversity manifests in a variety of ways such as diversity in family cultures and structures, diversity in values, diversity of sexual experiences, diversity in language, etc. It is important to recognize that a diversity of experiences, identities, and values exists within any classroom and that differences in values is to be expected and embraced through classroom discussion on sexuality that is appropriately facilitated (for more information, see modules 2.1, 2.2, 2.5, and 2.6). Before facilitating classroom discussions on sexuality and sexual health, it is helpful to reflect on your own values and to check in with your own assumptions about who is in your classroom, the families that students come from, and how students feel about themselves and relate to their own sexuality. Checking-in with your own assumptions allows you to be more responsive to the discussions and dynamics of your classroom as they happen, rather than assume and anticipate what will happen.

What does it mean to "check in" with your assumptions?

Everyone has assumptions. It is not negative or positive to have assumptions; however, assumptions can cause negative, harmful impacts on those around you if left unchecked. To check in with your assumptions is a process of self-examination. It involves recognizing that while something may be the "norm" or true for you, it may not be the case for everyone else. It is also a process of making space between the assumptions you hold and how you choose to (or not to) express them. When this space is made, it becomes easier to reframe an assumed "fact" that is rooted in your own experience into a respectful/appropriate discussion.

Check in with your assumptions...

About Families

- Some students live with their family, others live with a guardian, in a group home, foster home, or shelter.
- Some students have one parent/guardian, some have two, some have more.
- Some families have parents who identify as LGBTQ+.
- Some students come from a divorced family and may or may not have one or more step-families.
- Some students are parents.
- Some students are not biologically related to either parent.
- Some students are a result of assisted reproduction technologies.
- Some students come from loving families; some do not.
- Some students come from emotionally, physically, or sexually abusive homes.
- Students have diverse cultural and religious beliefs, which are not necessarily apparent.
- Some students have little or no personal freedom; some students have little or no supervision at home.
- Some students are unable to discuss sexuality and sexual health with their families.
- Some students openly discuss sexuality and sexual health with their families.

About Bodies

- Some students have little or no idea about how the body works, including sexual functioning.
- Genitals are diverse and most do not look like those depicted in textbooks and diagrams. Some students have ambiguous genitals; some are **intersex** (for more information, see modules 3.1 and 4.2).
- Some penises are circumcised; some are not. Some vulvas have been cut; some have not (and it may have included the labia and/or the clitoris) (for more information, see modules 2.2 and 4.2).
- Genitals do not dictate what someone's **gender identity** is; someone's gender identity does not dictate what genitals they may have.
- Some students who appear very large or very small are entirely comfortable with their bodies.
- Some students have visible disabilities; some have invisible disabilities.

About Gender and Gender Identity
(for more information, see modules 3.1, 3.7, 3.8, and 3.9)

- Some students are questioning their gender identity and this may not be physically apparent.
- Some students will identify with a gender other than the sex they were assigned at birth.
- Many students will identify as women/girls and men/boys; some students will not. Gender is an internal sense and is not binary (e.g., trans, androgynous, gender fluid, and an endless amount more).
- **Assigned sex** is not the same as gender identity.
- Some people might use different words for their bodies that more comfortably reflect their gender identity.
- We cannot make assumptions about a student's gender identity based on the way they look, dress, act, or by their name.
- Some students have rigid ideas about **gender** regarding roles, norms, rights, responsibilities, and potential aspirations.
- Some students' families have rigid ideas about gender regarding roles, norms, rights, responsibilities, and potential aspirations.

About Sexual Orientation
(for more information, see modules 3.1 and 3.3)

- Some students identify as straight, or heterosexual. Some students identify as lesbian, gay, and/or bisexual; some as queer; some as **two spirit**; some as pansexual; some as asexual; and some may be questioning their **sexual orientation**. Sometimes these identities get shorthanded as **LGBTQ+** and **queer**.
- Some LGBTQ+ youth do not reveal their sexual orientation to others, including family and friends.

YOU SHOULD KNOW

Gender identity refers to an internal sense of awareness and is not something that is physically visible. Gender expression is the way someone publicly expresses their gender. You cannot assume someone's gender identity based on the ways they express their gender.

- We cannot make assumptions about a student's sexual orientation based on the way they look, dress, or act.
- Students who are "out," or who are perceived to be LGBTQ+, may not feel—or be—safe in their school. We cannot assume whether a student is "out" by the way they look, dress, or act.
- Sexual orientation, like gender identity, is an identity that must be self-defined and self-disclosed.
- You cannot assume a student's sexual orientation.

About sexual activity

- Some students are sexually active; some are not. Some students who are not currently sexually active have been sexually active in the past.
- Sexual activity describes a wide variety of experiences. It includes and goes beyond vaginal, oral, and/or anal sex.
- Some students may have experienced pregnancy and you cannot tell this only based on who has decided to parent.
- Some students have experienced non-consensual sexual activity (e.g., sexual abuse, sexual assault, and sexual coercion).
- There are limitless ways that survivors react to, cope and deal with experiences of sexual violence (for more information, see chapter 8).

Educator Reflection Questions
About Families

- Were there any statements that surprised you? Why or why not?
- What does your family structure look like? How has this influenced the ways that you see and experience the world around you?
- What was your family's culture like? For instance, did your family openly talk about emotions, and/or your day? What did privacy mean in your family? What was easy and what was difficult to talk about within your family?

About Bodies

- Were there any statements that surprised you? Why or why not?
- When you were the age of your students, what did you know or not know about the ways that bodies work? Where did you get information about the ways that bodies work? How and why do you think this has changed for you over time?

About Gender and Gender Identity

- Were there any statements that surprised you? Why or why not?
- What is your gender identity?

- Have you ever had to think about your gender identity? Why or why not?
- What kinds of gender norms had an impact on your life and self-concept as you were growing up?

About Sexual Orientation
- Were there any statements that surprised you? Why or why not?
- What is your sexual orientation?
- Have you ever had to "come out"? Why or why not?

About Sexual Activity
- Were there any statements that surprised you? Why or why not?
- Think back to when you were the age of your students, what was your knowledge and experience on sex and sexual activity like? How do you think this will inform the way that you teach topics on sexuality and sexual health?

1.2 CREATING A SEX POSITIVE, ANTI-OPPRESSIVE LEARNING ENVIRONMENT

When teaching the sexuality and sexual health topics presented in *Beyond the Basics*, it is important for educators to create a safe learning environment for their students. Creating a safe learning environment includes actively working towards taking a sex positive and anti-oppressive approach to teaching and learning. Part of learning how to be sex positive and anti-oppressive is learning the ways that you might be knowingly or unknowingly contributing to sex negative attitudes about sex and human sexuality or supporting oppressive learning environments.

This module provides information for educators on what **sex positivity** and **anti-oppression** are, why these are important for a safe and effective learning space, tools to operationalize these values, and questions to reflect on the extent to which you are already teaching from these values.

What is sex positivity and why is it important?

Sex positivity embraces sexuality with the view that the only relevant concerns when it comes to a sexual act, practice, or experience are the consent, pleasure, and well-being of the people engaged in it or the people affected by it. In other words, sex positivity places no moral value on different sexualities or sexual activities. It helps us set aside our judgments and make room for the diversity of human sexuality. It is important for educators to embrace a sex positive teaching style because educators are more likely to listen and facilitate discussions on sexuality and sexual health from a non-judgmental place, and in turn, students are more likely to feel comfortable asking questions, clarifying their own assumptions, and ultimately receiving and retaining more accurate information (Oliver et al., 2013).

Sex Positivity Tips and Tools

- Check in with your assumptions about who your students are and what their experiences might be (for more information, see module 1.1).
- Frame each activity and topic in terms of consent, the well-being of those involved, and pleasure (for more information on consent, see modules 8.1, 8.3, and 8.4).
- Consider your students from a strengths-based perspective, recognizing that each brings expertise, intelligence, and ideas to the topics covered in this book (for more information, see module 1.7).

- Frame human sexuality in terms of something that is normal and not something unusual or something to fear.

Look through the topics covered in each chapter and the material covered in each module, ask yourself: Which topics am I comfortable teaching and which am I not? Why am I comfortable teaching some topics and not others? Does it have to do with a lack of information, a fear of not representing the material well because it is outside of my experience, or do I hold particular values, beliefs, and/or biases about the content?

Educator Reflection Questions

- What values about sex and sexuality did you grow up with? Where did these values come from and how have they changed over time?
- How do you define healthy sexuality?
- On a scale from 0 to 10, how comfortable are you talking about sexuality and sexual health with your peers? With your students? If these answers are different, why is this the case?
- How comfortable are you addressing students' questions and concerns related to sexuality and sexual health? What learning and/or information and/or supports do you need to seek out in order for you to feel more comfortable addressing students' questions and concerns?

What is anti-oppression and why is it important?

Anti-oppression is the recognition and active dismantling of systems of oppression. In teaching and learning environments, oppression can manifest itself through inaction, action, and unchecked assumptions made by peers, teachers, and administration (Kumashiro, 2000). Anti-oppression includes a recognition of the ways that oppression and privilege based on dominant forms of power structures affect the lives of everyone. Anti-oppression rejects the idea that most people are either oppressed or privileged and instead recognizes that different aspects of our identity overlap and intersect to create experiences of both having access to power and being oppressed by power. For example, a cisgender, queer, white, able-bodied woman may experience oppression in the form of homophobia and sexism but will have privilege in terms of not experiencing racism, transphobia, or ableism. (For more information, see 1.2 resources).

Developing an anti-oppressive teaching practice goes beyond the idea of accepting diversity. It recognizes that human diversity exists within a system that privileges (in both material and symbolic ways) certain

YOU SHOULD KNOW
Kimberlé Crenshaw, legal scholar in critical race theory and black feminist thought, first coined the term "intersectionality" in 1989. Intersectionality refers to the ways that oppressions do not exist separately from each other. It is a way of understanding the experiences of oppression as intersecting and overlapping.

identities, social locations, and life experiences while actively marginalizing and oppressing others. Anti-oppression works to identify that which is marginalized and that which is normalized, who benefits and why (Anti-Oppression Network, 2011).

Developing an anti-oppressive teaching practice and learning environment for your students is not just a one-time event or something that is limited to sexuality education, this book, or even your classroom in general. It is an ongoing, life long commitment to learning about the ways that you may unknowingly (and knowingly) contribute to upholding structures of power and to continually challenge yourself to change and confront the manifestations of those power structures (Fithian & Moyers, n.d.). Anti-oppression is not something that can be learned by reading one chapter of a book or attending a workshop. It requires ongoing learning, listening, and non-defensively receiving feedback on ways that you might be re-enforcing systems of oppression. This is by no means a comprehensive workbook on anti-oppression but it does provide a starting point for unlearning and challenging oppression in its many forms.

Anti-Oppression Tips and Tools

- Consider the power relationship you have as the educator within a classroom: What kind of power do you have as "the expert"? Consider ways that you could invite students to think about how they are experts in their own lives/experiences.
- Avoid making generalized claims about groups of people, instead use words like "some" or "many."
- Understand the difference between impact versus intent of your words.
- In your classroom, consider how generalizations, certain words, and/or perpetuating myths and stereotypes may have a negative impact on your students, even if that was not your intention. (For more information, see figure 1A).
- Avoid getting defensive. One of the quickest ways to shut down conversations is to become defensive. If a student challenges you on an idea presented in one of the activities, pause, take a deep breath, ask yourself why you are feeling defensive, and recognize that while you are having a reaction, your role as an educator is to facilitate learning among your students. Some of the best, most indepth classroom learnings can come from difficult discussions. Taking a deep breath helps ensure that you are responding to the student instead of reacting.

Figure 1A: While the intent was to water the flowers to keep them healthy, without knowing how much water to give, the flowers were over-watered. This has negatively impacted the now wilted flowers.

Educator Reflection Questions

- Have you ever had to actively think about any aspect of your social, cultural, political, religious, economic, physical, sexual and/or gender identities and/or experiences? Why or why not?
- Have you ever been discriminated against because of your identities and/or experiences (either visible or invisible)?
- Have you ever been given an opportunity not based on merit but based on who you know? How did you react and what emotions did it spark?
- Have you ever been denied an opportunity and/or service based on your identity(ies)? How did you react and what emotions did it spark?
- Have you ever been made to feel invisible or without anything to contribute in certain environments or social situations? How did you react and what emotions did it spark? Why do you think that this happened?
- Think about your teaching experience to date, has there ever been a time that you did not take action when you heard something oppressive, offensive, and/or discriminatory being said by another educator, staff member, or by student? How did you feel afterwards?

- Think about your teaching experience to date, has there ever been a time that you took action when you heard something oppressive, offensive, and/or discriminatory being said by another educator, staff member, or by student? How did you feel afterward? What kinds of supports were in place to make it feel possible for you to take action?

1.3 CREATING A SAFER SPACE FOR LEARNING

Educators and students need to be invested in the process of creating a safe, positive, supportive, and comfortable learning environment. Learning how to identify your own values, check in with your assumptions, and develop an anti-oppressive and sex positive teaching practice is an important first step in creating a safer space for students to learn and engage in course content. Learning how to support students in both proactive and responsive ways is another important aspect of ensuring that the classroom is a safe space to learn, ask questions, and reach out for support.

Safer Space Guidelines

The creation of safer space guidelines is a useful way to set up any classroom discussion about sexuality and start any of the activities contained in *Beyond the Basics*. Safer space guidelines are a living document that outline how to treat one another in the class and how to engage with subject matter in a way that is respectful to everyone in the learning environment. Setting up these guidelines is especially important when teaching sexual health because many of the topics may feel personal, private, difficult, embarrassing, and/or taboo to students. Safer space guidelines attempt to provide all of your students with safety, support, respect, dignity, and confidentiality.

The actual content of the safer space guidelines will look different depending on the age group(s) you are working with, the maturity level of your students, the closeness of your class, and how you decide to come up with the guidelines. If you already have a set of ground rules that you use to guide classroom discussions, it is recommended that you revisit and expand on these as you prepare to teach sexuality education. The modules that you decide to facilitate may also require some modifications to best support your students in their participation of activities and engagement with topics.

For younger students (level 1), you might choose to create your own guidelines. You may also choose to create guidelines with input from your students.

Examples of student guidelines
- Practise respect towards yourself (this could look like checking-in with whether or not you want to share something personal in front of the whole class, whether you would rather ask the educator privately, or write it down anonymously).

- You may be really excited about learning something and/or participating in an activity, while excitement is great, try not to interrupt or talk over other students and the educator.
- You may want to laugh and giggle at some of the content and while this is okay, laughing at what another student asks or shares is not.
- There is no such thing as a silly or "stupid" question.
- If something personal is shared within the class by your classmate, do not talk about it with people outside of the class unless you get permission from your classmate.

With students in middle school or high school (level 2 and level 3), it may be most effective to create the ground rules together. Creating the ground rules together ensures more buy-in from the class because the ownership and responsibility of the content is shared by everyone in the class (educators and learners).

Ask the students what they think would make learning about sexuality and sexual health more comfortable for them. Some may say they do not want to learn about it at all. Think of this as an opportunity to talk about the importance of comprehensive sexuality education and learning about sexual health in school (for more information, see modules 0.1 and 0.2).

If you decide to co-create the safer space guidelines with your students, here are some examples of what to prompt them for:
- Practise respect. This includes not using sexist, racist, homophobic, transphobic, classist, and/or ableist remarks, language, and/or slurs. (For more information on how to interrupt this kind of language if it comes up, see modules 1.2 and 1.5).
- Try not to interrupt or talk over others. Allow people to finish speaking.
- If you do not agree with someone's opinion, do not criticize the person; comment on the opinion.
- If someone else in the class discloses something personal, do not repeat it outside the classroom.

Individual responses to difficult material and trigger warnings
Sexuality and sexual health material can provoke emotional responses in students. These emotional responses range from happiness to relief, excitement, embarrassment, sadness, anger, stress, and anxiety. As educators, it is important to be aware of the range of emotional responses that the content in *Beyond the Basics* might provoke. Emotional responses can be triggered for a variety of reasons and while it is

important not to assume the reasons behind an emotional response, it is equally important to allow students to safely leave an activity if they become overwhelmed, **triggered,** and/or upset.

 Trigger warnings can be useful for flagging that some of the content covered in sexuality and sexual health education can be difficult to talk about. While it is sometimes important to talk through challenging material, it can also be very emotionally upsetting to a student who has personal experience with the content and/or has experienced a trauma related to the material being covered. For instance, students who may have experienced and/or witnessed prior (or ongoing) sexual violence may have an overwhelming emotional response (including flashbacks and ongoing memory replays) to content. This may or may not be obvious or visible. Providing a trigger warning ahead of teaching the course content allows students to assess for themselves whether or not they are feeling emotionally and mentally okay to participate in the discussion/activity. For example, in advance of the lesson, educators may let students know that a difficult topic will be discussed. The educator can describe in broad terms what the nature of the content will be and give students the option to leave the class in a discreet manner. It could also be the case that a student may not want to leave the class until they are getting closer to the point of being triggered or are actually triggered. Another scenario could be that a student wants to take 5 to 10 minutes to leave the space and then come back once they feel ready. As an educator, you need to be okay with and aware that any of these scenarios may happen. You should also make sure to promptly check in with any student who leaves the class and make sure that the student is followed up by a support person at the school. Ensure that the school's support people know that a difficult topic (such as sexual assault) will be taught in advance of the planned lesson. Ideally, a support person would be easily accessible and on call for any students choosing to leave class and seeking support. While much of the content within *Beyond the Basics* may be considered sensitive (due to taboos around sexuality and sexual health), not all of the content requires a trigger warning. Trigger warning icons are included at the beginning of each module that could be triggering and particularly difficult.

YOU SHOULD KNOW

Sexual violence affects people of all ages and backgrounds. Please proceed with the understanding that any student may be a survivor and/or witness of sexual violence and that discussions on this topic can be upsetting, overwhelming, or triggering. Acknowledge this at the beginning of every session and allow students to discretely take space if they need. Do your best to keep discussions focused, open, and respectful to everyone.

Educator Reflection Questions

- Think about a difficult experience that you have had to deal with in your past. Perhaps it was challenging, perhaps it was traumatizing, perhaps it was overwhelming, and/or perhaps it was stressful. Think about the way that difficult experience made you feel afterward. Now ask yourself: How do I react now to people talking about an experience or subject that is similar to the difficult experience I had in the past? What strategies do I currently use to deal with my reaction? What is something that other people can do to support me in my reaction?

- Do you as a person and as an educator value process over product? For instance, when you are leading a class or an activity, are you more concerned with taking the time to set up a discussion or do you rush towards the end in order to maximize your time and the amount of information shared with students? Think about it and make either a mental or physical list of the pros and cons to both. For instance, ask yourself: Why could it be important in terms of the students' learning and safety to take time with the process of a lesson and activity? Why/when might it be important to ensure that more time is spent on specific products and learning goals being met? What is in the best interest of the students? How can I effectively balance product and process?

- Think back to a time when you introduced an emotionally difficult concept in one of your classes (maybe it was talking about the Atlantic slave-trade, war, genocide, colonialism, or imperialism, maybe it was about a fictional story with difficult content, maybe it was a science lesson on cancer). How did you approach the lesson before, during, and after? What, if anything, would you do differently after reading this module?

QUICK TIP

Place a closed box with a lid in an accessible spot within your classroom and indicate that if students have questions related to sexuality and sexual health, they can anonymously write down a question and place it in the box. Explain that you will not answer questions about your personal life and if you have a question involving violence and/or abuse that it is best to approach you after class to speak privately. Pick 2 dates a month that you will set aside in order to answer questions received. Once questions are answered they will be shredded to protect the anonymity of the student.

1.4 LANGUAGE USE

Language is powerful and the way we use it is important. Language can (intentionally and unintentionally) communicate our assumptions, values, biases, and judgments. Language communicates to others whether or not we are a safe, approachable person and whether or not we are worth listening to. It is important for educators teaching sexuality and sexual health to become familiar with how to use language that is safe, open, friendly, accepting, and accessible to the diversity of students within their classroom.

Reclaimed Language

Just as language is powerful, it is also political. Reclaimed language is one example of very political and highly charged language. Reclaimed language is language that has been used at some point to hurt, shame, discredit, and/or discriminate against a group of people and has since been reclaimed as a political act of resistance and defiance. It is important to note that while reclaimed language may be used in a positive, empowering way by some groups of people, it does not mean that it is widely accepted in every circumstance. It is important to use the utmost caution and care with reclaimed language. This is true whether or not you are a part of the community or an outsider to the community that has reclaimed the language as a political act of resistance. This is because there is usually a diversity of opinions within the community about when it is and is not appropriate to use reclaimed language. Reclaimed language can still be very hurtful to some within the community and as an educator it is important to air on the side of caution and not use reclaimed language if you are uncertain. Likely, you can find another, less charged word to describe the same thing. For instance, if you are uncertain whether or not to use the term **queer,** you can use the acronym, **LGBTQ+** instead, being mindful of the fact that the word queer refers specifically to sexual orientation and may not include some letters within the acronym (e.g., transgender).

Gender Neutral Language

Often the language that people use by default is unconsciously gendered. This is partly due to the fact that in the English language, gender is framed as binary from the singular pronouns most commonly used (e.g., she/her and he/him) to the ways that we gender sexual and reproductive anatomy. When teaching sexuality and sexual health, it is important to become aware of the ways that you may unconsciously be

YOU SHOULD KNOW
The word Queer was historically used as a derogatory term for people who either were or were perceived to be LGBTQ+. In recent years, it has been reclaimed by some people within the LGBTQ+ community as a way of self-identifying and as a political statement against the oppression to which they have been subjected. With any kind of reclaimed language, it is important to use caution when using the word and this is especially the case if you are not part of the LGBTQ+ community. Refrain from using the word to describe someone else's identity, unless they have used queer to identify themselves.

using gendered language. Do your best to change the habits of assuming **pronouns** and gendering certain experiences based on assigned sex (e.g., always using the term woman when referring to pregnancy or assuming that it is only men who use condoms).

In *Beyond the Basics*, we strive to use non-gendered names and language. When describing anatomy and sexual activities, we use language in a functional way. For instance, we consciously refer to anatomy without gender (e.g., people with vulvas, people with vaginas, people with penises). With the recognition that terms used to describe gender identity, gender expression, and sexual orientation are constantly changing and evolving, for consistency throughout the book, we use the LGBTQ+ acronym. We endeavour to use this acronym and other versions of the acronym as appropriate for the specific concept under discussion. For instance, if we are referring to sexual orientation, we might use LGBQ and if we are referring to gender identity and gender expression, we may use the umbrella terms of trans and/or transgender. (For more information, see chapter 3). Using gender neutral language ensures that all students, no matter their gender identity, gender expression, or sexual orientation, feel supported and included.

Bodies, Bodily Functions, and Sexual Activities

It is common for people in general, and students in particular, to use slang words and nicknames to describe body parts, bodily functions, and sexual activities rather than use the anatomically correct language. Often, people do not know what the anatomically correct terms are. The reasons for this are multiple and include many people being taught from a young age that it is not polite or appropriate to talk about body parts such as genitals and/or erogenous zones and/or bodily functions. From this belief comes either silence or nicknames that are used in place to talk about bodies and bodily functions. As people move through adolescence and start to discover bodily changes and engage in sexual activities, this silence and/or nicknaming may translate into shame and negative self-concepts about their bodies and sexuality. This is why it becomes important to use and teach anatomically correct language. While this is important, it is also important to recognize that non-binary and transgender people might use different words for their bodies that more comfortably reflect their gender identity.

YOU SHOULD KNOW

The LGBTQ+ acronym includes gender identities as well as identities related to sexual orientation. Fully spelled out the acronym contains: lesbian, gay, bisexual, transgender, and queer, with the plus indicating more identities such as asexual, intersex, pansexual, two spirit, and questioning. It is important to note that even though the LGBTQ+ acronym is used as a way to shorthand queer and trans identities, sexual orientation and gender identity are two separate types of identities. The umbrella term "queer" does not include all identities within the LGBTQ+ acronym. People who identify as intersex may not include themselves within the LGBTQ+ acronym.

Educator Reflection Questions

- How comfortable or uncomfortable are you using anatomically correct language to describe body parts, bodily functions, and sexual activities?
  - What words do you most commonly use? Do these words change depending on your audience? If so, why do they change?
  - What kinds of information, motivation, resources, and/or support will it take to ensure that you are able to comfortably and confidently use the anatomically correct names for body parts, bodily functions, and sexual activities?
- Growing up, what were your norms and family culture around naming (or not naming) body parts and bodily functions? For instance, did you openly talk about bodily functions (like urination and defecating)? What kinds of words were you taught to use to name your body parts?
- Can you think of three examples of gendered language that you use everyday?
  - Using these three examples, can you think about ways to reframe your language and remove any assumptions or reference to gender?
  - Can you think of words you regularly use that already do this? (For instance, maybe you already use the term "partner" or "spouse").
- Have you ever used reclaimed language to refer to yourself/self-identify? How did it make you feel? How does it feel when someone who is not part of the same identity uses the reclaimed language to refer to you?

QUICK TIP

Do not assume the pronouns that someone may use based on how they physically express their gender. Always ask your students and regularly check in with them as people's preferred pronouns can change from day to day, week to week. (For fun and easy ways to encourage pronoun check ins in the classroom, see chapter 3).

1.5 RESPONDING TO DISCRIMINATION, HARASSMENT, AND BULLYING

As an educator, you are in tune with each student's learning needs and your responsibility to meet those needs. An important part of meeting learning needs is ensuring your students' safety and well-being so that they are more mentally, emotionally, and physically prepared to learn.

Students look to you to set an example in terms of the kinds of behaviours you role model and allow in your classroom. Students who are marginalized, oppressed, and who may feel disempowered are relying on you to respond to discrimination, harassment, and bullying both within and outside of the classroom. Their safety within their learning environment depends on the explicit and implicit support you give them, including the group norms you establish, the language you use, and how you communicate knowledge.

The ways that you respond (or choose not to respond) to oppression, discrimination, harassment, and bullying indicates to your students whether or not you are an adult that will be supportive and can be trusted. It is your responsibility to lead by example within your learning community. This includes immediately responding to discrimination, harassment, and bullying as you see it unfold and/or are told by a bystander that it is taking place. Your response will inform the tone, group norms, dynamics, and atmosphere of your class, what is and what is not acceptable and how you are or are not a trusted adult and authority figure.

The ways that you model responsive, supportive behaviour become extremely important when teaching sexuality education due to the sensitive and often charged nature of class content. The previous modules (1.1, 1.2, 1.3, and 1.4) outlined some of the ways that you can proactively create a learning environment that is safe and supportive to the diversity of students' identities, social locations, and lived experiences. This module outlines ways that as a teacher, you can effectively intervene and respond to any bullying, harassment, or discrimination that may come up in sexuality education.

Discrimination

Discrimination refers to actions or decisions based on prejudice about a specific social group/identity. Discrimination can be subtle and it can be overt. It can include granting or denying benefits, favours, attention, and/or access to a social group/identity. Discrimination often involves

stereotyping. It can involve both "positive" and "negative" stereotyping of someone who is part of and/or perceived to be part of a particular social group. Discriminatory behaviour can also be backed by harassment and bullying on an individual and an institutional level.

The first step in responding to discrimination is being able to identify the ways that you might consciously or unconsciously discriminate against someone based on **prejudice**, values, assumptions, and biases (for more information, see module 1.1). Conscious forms of discrimination are often more easily identifiable. Unconscious forms of discrimination are not only subtle but can also be automatic. As an educator, pay attention to how you and your students react to certain people and situations and the use of language to discriminate in subtle and overt ways (for more information, see module 1.4).

Discrimination and prejudice can also manifest as less obvious forms of social exclusion and teasing. Try not to fall into the trap of rationalizing a student's behaviour based on what dominant society prescribes as "normal" for certain genders (e.g., avoid the "boys will be boys" mentality as this not only reinforces gender norms and scripts but also validates the psychological and physical violence that can be a part of these behaviours (for more information on gender norms and stereotypes, see modules 3.4, 3.5, 3.6, 3.7, and 3.8). Even if what is seen as "normal" is considered to be a positive characteristic, labeling an entire group of people as "athletic" or "good at math" can be harmful as it places people in boxes that are restricting and not representative.

How to Respond Tips and Tools

- Making mistakes is okay. You and your students are human and it is normal for people to make mistakes. In fact, making mistakes is how we learn. It is not the mistakes that matter but the ways that we respond to and deal with the mistakes we make. As an educator, you may feel pressure to not make mistakes in front of your class because you are supposed to be the "expert." But part of role modelling positive behaviours with your students is about acknowledging that we all make mistakes and then demonstrating how to deal with them effectively. This includes:
  - Recognizing that you have made a mistake and apologizing either publicly or privately (for more information on apologies, see the video by Chescaleigh *Getting Called Out: How To Apologize* in the resources section);
  - Clearly stating how you will go about correcting your mistake;

- Remaining accountable to yourself and the person/people your mistake may have harmed by following through on correcting your mistake; and
- Asking the person/people who were most impacted by the mistake what you can do to further support them.

• Learn the difference between the intention behind your words/actions and the impact that your words/actions may have on individuals and/or entire groups of people (see figure 1A).
- The impact of your words and/or actions is more important than your intention.
- While the intention of your words/actions may have been good, their impact might be harmful to someone else. This harm is what needs to be addressed to work towards ending discrimination.
- If someone tells you that the impact of your words/actions was harmful and discriminatory, listen to their experience without interruption or defensiveness.
- Regardless of the intention behind your word choice, recognizing the impact that your words have on an individual and/or an entire group of people is key to moving into a meaningful apology and dealing with discrimination head-on.

• Practise non-defensive responses when challenged about your own assumptions, prejudice, and biases. Here are some strategies for non-defensive responses:
- Pause. Take a deep breath. Remember that the person is challenging an action and/or behaviour that can be changed and does not reflect a challenge to your fundamental being.
- Put yourself in the shoes of the person impacted by your assumption, bias, prejudice, and/or mistake.

• If you witness and respond to discrimination as a bystander, challenge the behaviour (not the person) in a way that is non-reactive and promotes open dialogue and learning (Fithian & Moyers, n.d.). Here are some strategies for non-reactive responses to witnessing discrimination:
- Interrupt the behaviour as soon as possible. Clearly and calmly state why you are interrupting the behaviour.
- Ensure that students know why the behaviour is unacceptable.
- If you are not sure exactly why the behaviour is unacceptable, do your research and come back to the students with a prepared discussion about why it was discrimination.
- Avoid saying "because it's the rules." This kind of response will not encourage behaviour change as it provides no reasoning or motivation as to why it is important.

- Think of yourself not only as an educator but also as a learner. Actively working to challenge discrimination is a process that requires openness to continual learning about discrimination that is both happening and being challenged at institutional levels. Learning about what is happening in the wider world is one way to ensure that your individual actions/inactions do not reinforce institutional discrimination. And keep in mind that best practices for individual responses to dealing with discrimination are also constantly changing. Below are some tips about how to be an active, ongoing learner:
  - Read the news, refer to blogs, and scan social media for new information (Anti-Defamation League, 2016).
  - Consider yourself a learner when confronted with a situation that you are not sure how to deal with. It is okay if you do not know how to respond. Consult with other educators who might have more knowledge on challenging discrimination.
- Turn instances of discrimination into moments of learning for everyone involved. For instance, instead of focusing on the target of the discrimination, create space for a conversation that examines the ways that different kinds of discrimination are interconnected and how discrimination affects everyone in different ways. Some suggestions about how to do this:
  - Instead of preaching about why discrimination is unacceptable, try approaching it as a conversation. If you do not feel equipped to have this conversation, reach out to other educators and community organizations that may have more capacity and knowledge about how to effectively and appropriately have this conversation. Part of being a learner is recognizing (and being honest about) when you have a gap in knowledge.
  - Use one classroom period to discuss the topics and themes at the root of an incident involving discrimination. For instance, if the discriminatory behaviours involved homophobic language used by a group of students in your class, do research on why the language being used was homophobic and then engage students in a discussion about the power of language. *You can ask them what they thought the words meant and whether or not they knew the impact that the words could have.* (For more information on language use, see module 1.4).
  - Ask students to privately reflect on whether or not they have ever overheard and/or been the target of language that impacted them negatively. Ask them to privately reflect on whether or not they felt that this language was discriminatory and why.

Harassment and Bullying

Harassment and **bullying** have gained more attention in schools and online due to a number of cases in Canada and the United States where bullying and harassment (especially gendered and sexual harassment/ violence as well as homophobic, transphobic, and sexist bullying) have led to suicides and large scale violence. As a result, there has been a plethora of literature written on the topics of gendered and sexual harassment and bullying, as well as how schools, teachers, and peer bystanders can respond to all forms of bullying and harassment (see work by Saewyc, 2011; Poteat & Espelage, 2007; Gruber & Fineran 2007, 2008; Meyer, 2008, 2014, 2015). Educators have an incredible opportunity to help stop individual instances and patterns of bullying and harassment as they are considered by students to be in positions of power and authority.

How to Respond Tips and Tools

- If you witness or suspect harassment or bullying, address it promptly with the students involved (if appropriate and necessary, involve the school administration, parents, and community organizations).
- For school-based educators, speak to your school administrators about the anti-bullying policies of your school and work with administrators, parents, and community organizations to develop integrated responses.
- If a student approaches you with concerns of harassment and/or bullying that they are witnessing, or are a part of either at school or online, take the following measures:
  - Take the student seriously and;
  - Ask questions and;
  - Let the student know what your school's policies are around confidentiality and;
  - Work to advocate for them and;
  - Inform your supervisor/administration and investigate the situation with the help and support of a school social worker, counsellor, guidance counsellor, and/or administrator.

If you see discrimination, harassment, and/or bullying happening...

- Interrupt the behaviour(s) immediately and address it either on the spot or at a later time (if more appropriate) (Fithian & Moyers, n.d.).
- Identify the behaviour(s) as discriminatory and explain why (do not identify the individual as inherently bad, instead focus on the behaviour) (Fithian & Moyers, n.d.).

- Acknowledge the behaviour(s) as something that is unacceptable in your classroom or the learning community as a whole (you can refer to your school's anti-discrimination and anti-bullying policies) and work with your class to come up with group norms and strategies that critically examine why challenging prejudice and responding to discrimination is something that protects and ensures everyone's safety.

Educator Reflection Questions

- Have you ever been the target of and/or affected by discriminatory attitudes and behaviours? How did this feel? What kinds of supports did you have (if any) to deal with, process, and respond to this discrimination? If you did not have support or did not know where or how to find support, how did this feel? If you did have support, how did that support feel and why do you think that you were able to access support?
- Have you ever been the target of bullying and/or harassment? What was the context and at what age did this happen to you? What emotions and responses did this experience provoke? What kinds of supports (if any) did you have in place to help you through this time? If you did not have support or did not know where or how to find support, how did this feel? If you did have support, how did that support feel and why do you think that you were able to access support?
- Have you ever witnessed or been told about bullying and/or harassment that was happening (either to or by a friend, colleague, and/or student)? How did you respond? How did it feel to respond the way you did? Reflecting on the incident, can you think of any other, different, ways that you would respond now?

Reflecting on your answers to the above questions, how do you think you could best support a student who is dealing with discrimination, harassment, and/or bullying?

1.6 FACILITATING SENSITIVE ACTIVITIES AND RESPONDING TO DISCLOSURE

The activities in *Beyond the Basics* include thoughtful personal reflections for educators and students, group brainstorming, critical thinking, group presentations, case studies, and role play. *Beyond the Basics* includes a mix of activities that cover interpersonal as well as intrapersonal learning. The reason the material is presented in such a way reflects the sensitive subject matter. As an educator, it is important to account for the strong opinions students will have, formed by deeply personal experiences. Students will need to explore their own thoughts privately, as well as discern what and how they want to share in larger group discussions. While instructions are provided on how to facilitate each activity, there are some general considerations to be aware of when dealing with sensitive, personal subject matter. (Information below adapted from Moore & Deshaises, 2012).

- Be an active facilitator, not a passive one.
  - Interrupt comments that are inappropriate and/or discriminatory.
  - Challenge any stereotypes that come up in an activity.
  - Make sure you understand the substance of a student's comment by paraphrasing back to participants what was expressed. You can use language like: "What I am hearing is _____" or "Am I understanding your idea correctly?"
- Clearly communicate learning objectives and provide a clear focus for any discussion.
- Prepare yourself to encounter views different from your own and instead of avoiding emotionally tense or charged discussions, help direct students' learning towards processing and critically reflecting on the big ideas in each module.
- Get curious about your students' views of the world.

Role Play Activities

Role play activities are an extremely effective form of learning that help students develop empathy, reflection, and critical thinking skills. Role-play goes beyond asking students to retain information and moves them into thinking through what information means in relationship to their own lives. While it is an effective learning tool, there are risks to consider when facilitating role play activities with sensitive subject matter (despite the potential for deep and powerful learning). Role play activities ask learners to take on a particular problem, scenario, and/or identity and to act out potential realities, responses, and/or solutions (Harbour & Connick, 2004-8). Sometimes embodying and acting out a particular scenario can place students in a vulnerable and/or personal position. Role play activities can also quickly move from "play" to "reality" without the educator realizing. This is often the case if the educator does not know the students well enough or lacks awareness of existing peer relationship dynamics among the group. Educators that know their students well can more easily avoid grouping students with complicated relationship dynamics that are directly related to the topics under discussion. Educators new to a classroom and without the opportunity to develop relationships with students or understand the group dynamic should approach role play with the utmost care and caution.

Role Play Tips and Tools

- Ensure that the objectives of the activity are clearly communicated to students (the objectives of each activity are stated at the beginning of each module).
- Provide clear roles for students (with clear parameters). Ask students to take the role play seriously; ensure they know that their role is not to make other people laugh or to reinforce stereotypes by being over-the-top.
- Before engaging in role play, ask students to privately (or in a small group) brainstorm a list of stereotypes associated with the role they are playing. Then ask your students to consider ways of role playing that do not reinforce stereotypes that may be harmful to people in the class.
- Do not be afraid of disagreement or debate among students. Disagreement can be a point of entry into learning and hearing stories that come from a diversity of experience. Effective and appropriate facilitation of disagreement looks like:
  - Everyone's voices being heard in the class.
  - Continually steering students' disagreements and debates back to the macro-issue instead of allowing disagreements to get personal by commenting on an individual's character.

Disclosure

Although many of the activities are designed in a way that limits the need for students to publicly disclose personal information, students will sometimes feel comfortable enough to disclose personal information during an activity and/or discussion. Students may also feel comfortable enough with you as an educator to approach you after class with information related to a personal matter or concern in their life. Sometimes the subject matter of a lesson can bring up something that the student did not know how to deal with alone or something that they were trying to create distance from or trying to forget.

For younger students (level 1) disclosure might come in the form of a funny story about themselves or about their family. Pay close attention: it might be a revelation about violence they have experienced or witnessed—emotional, verbal, physical, or sexual.

In the case of violence, the educator needs to believe the student, acknowledge what they have disclosed, and treat what they have said with the utmost importance, care, priority, and respect. From the beginning, be sure to outline the limits that you have in terms of keeping their confidentiality (refer to your school's confidentiality in the case of disclosing violence and abuse). It is important for the educator to let the student know that they cannot promise to keep a student's disclosure confidential.

For older students (level 2 and 3) some of the issues that they may disclose in relation to sexuality education include (but are not limited to):
- Gendered harassment
- Sexual cyberbullying
- Bullying and harassment more generally
- Risk of/being homeless
- Mental health struggles
- Questions and/or concerns about alcohol and drugs
- Discrimination at school and/or at home
- Questioning gender identity and/or sexual orientation
- Violence at home and/or with an intimate partner
- Non-consensual sexual activity or sexual assault
- Fear of pregnancy or confirmed pregnancy
- Fear of a sexual transmitted and blood-blood infections (STBBI)

1.7 YOUTH RESILIENCY AND HOW TO BE AN ALLY

There is a tendency for young people to be portrayed as naïve, untrustworthy, incapable, vulnerable, weak, in need of adult protection, susceptible to misinformation. This perception of young people is based on stereotypes and assumptions about their capacity, capability, and resilience. Evidence shows that when adult allies work towards empowering and engaging youth and when young people are given responsibility, trusted with information, and valued in terms of their ideas, opinions, and contributions, they are better able to integrate learning into their lives and move into action, including individual behaviour change (Kennelly, 2009; Jennings, et al. 2006; Oliver et al., 2013).

The chapters, modules, and activities in *Beyond the Basics* are written in a way that sees young people through a **resilience** lens and supports their empowerment. The activities are designed with the underlying assumption that youth are resilient and capable. In other words, they are not victims and/or vectors of disease; they are able to absorb and integrate information into their lives and have ideas, opinions, and life experiences worth sharing.

Youth resilience is simpatico with the concept of evolving capacities of the child, as enshrined in the *Convention on the Rights of the Child*. Evolving capacities is a concept that recognizes that children are active agents, bringing knowledge and capacity to decisions regarding their lives and autonomy, while at the same time being entitled to protections relative to their lives and maturity. A report produced jointly by UNICEF and Save the Children describes enhanced capacities as something that is acquired through experience, cultural context, and daily lived realities: "as children acquire enhanced competencies, there is a reduced need for direction and a greater capacity to take responsibility for decisions affecting their lives" (Lansdowne, 2005, p. ix).

Interacting with youth from this lens of resiliency gives young people the space to explore and take ownership over the kinds of information that they want and that are relevant to their lives. It allows young people to feel trusted and understands that they are already navigating through the world and life, with thoughts and opinions that matter.

Adopting this view of young people allows you as an educator to work towards becoming a youth ally. Allyship is something that has been written and researched about extensively and comes out of movements for social change and intersectional anti-oppression frameworks (for more information, see module 1.2). Becoming and working towards being an ally to youth is a continual process of listening and being able to take direction and cues about what is important and relevant to the lives of youth. Being a youth ally also means believing young people and being willing/able to advocate for them. Advocating on behalf of young people becomes very important within the formal education system as there are often multiple structures of power that must be navigated in order for youth to make change, find referrals, and get information relevant to their sexuality and sexual health.

Allyship Tips and Tools

- Have posters in your classroom with language around a "youth bill of rights" or "knowing your rights" (for more information, see modules 2.2 and 2.3).
- Refer to 10.7 resources to help youth identify local youth-friendly health and social services, and post a list of these services somewhere that is accessible in your classroom (so that your students can access it anonymously).
- Have a question box that is always at your desk so that your students know they can ask questions anonymously. Set aside time every week to look through the box and answer questions that come up.
- Ask students what they think. Take the time to talk with students and listen to students about what it is like to be a young person today. Some examples include:
  - What are their biggest concerns?
  - What are their biggest stresses?
  - What do they want to learn in relationship to their sexuality and sexual health?
  - What kinds of resources and information are they looking for?
  - Where do they feel like they are lacking knowledge and what is most relevant to their lives?
- Many of the activities in this book give students the opportunity to speak from their own experiences, recognizing that they are the experts of their own lives. You are invited to use these activities as an entry point to figure out what topics your students are most and least concerned with and tailor your lesson plans accordingly. Listening to youth and then taking the information they give you to make changes to how and what you teach is one way of building trust and practising being an ally.

Educator Reflection Questions

Think back to when you were the age of your students.

- What do you remember life being like?
- What were your hopes, dreams, biggest concerns, and biggest frustrations?
- What were you worried and/or stressed about?
- How did the adults and people in positions of power/authority treat you? How did you relate and/or respond to the adults in your life?
- Were there ever times that you wished that you were listened to more? How did you feel if your concerns, ideas, and/or opinions were not thoughtfully considered or taken seriously?
- Did you have any recourse available and/or accessible to you if you felt like you were wronged, harmed, and/or not taken seriously?
- What did you find the most helpful way an adult could support you in a time of uncertainty and/or crisis?
- How did you feel if an adult in your life assumed that you were naïve or untrustworthy, and/or incapable?

How do you view the young people that you work with now?

- What are the similarities and what are the differences you see between what life was like for you as a young person and what you understand life to be like now for youth? Do you think that life is harder, easier, or just different for youth now?
- In what ways did you or did you not consider yourself to be a resilient youth? In what ways do you witness your students as resilient?

CHAPTER 2

Sexuality, Human Rights, and Values

2.1 INTRODUCTION

There are always underlying values when it comes to **sexuality** and information on **sexual health**. Even when information is presented as "scientific," what is shared and with whom, what is included or left out, and what is defined as "normal" or healthy, are all rooted in certain values.

Canada is a diverse society with respect to culture, ethnicity, language, and religion, and in a host of other ways that often contribute to some very different beliefs about sexuality. As a diverse and democratic society, equality and respect for others are foundational to all of our freedoms, including the freedoms of thought, belief, opinion, and expression and the freedoms of religion and the right to participate in cultural life. The Canadian Constitution, particularly the *Canadian Charter of Rights and Freedoms*, reflects these principles and upholds the belief that diverse communities and values can coexist and flourish.

While many **human rights** are enshrined in the *Canadian Charter of Rights and Freedoms*, the *Universal Declaration of Human Rights* (adopted by the United Nations) contains a more comprehensive list of human rights, which are applicable in Canada and throughout the world.

In preparing to teach sexuality education, it is important to know how human rights relate to sexuality and sexual health, to know the ways in which human rights (as related to sexuality) are and are not always upheld in Canada, and to ensure that the human rights of all people in your classroom are respected and upheld (for more information, see module 2.2).

What does all of this mean for sexuality education in the classroom? It means that as an educator, you cannot tell your students what to believe but you can invite and encourage critical reflection as well as expect students to apply human rights principles (as enshrined in the Canadian Charter) into classroom discussions on sexuality. These principles include the basic values of equality and respect for others.

As an educator, it is up to you to do your best to foster and reflect these principles in the way you structure and develop classroom activities (for more information, see chapter 1). The activities in *Beyond the Basics* reflect the principles within the guidelines for **Comprehensive Sexuality Education** presented in module 0.1.

Educator Reflection Questions

- Are there any topics/subjects (outside of sexuality education and the topics covered in this book) that you were nervous about teaching? Why? What did you do to prepare yourself to teach them? Can you apply any of these strategies to the topics covered in this book?
- Have you ever encountered a friend or loved one who had different beliefs regarding sexuality? If so, how did you work through your differences? Did you use any of the basic principles mentioned in this module, such as honesty, equity, fairness, and respect? If so, which principles worked well and why?

Big Ideas in Chapter 2

- Sexual health is influenced by social factors as well as individual factors. Understanding both and how they interact with one another is essential to developing a holistic understanding of sexual health.
- In Canada, there are a diversity of values related to sexuality. Conflicting ideas, values, and opinions may emerge within the classroom. While this is expected, it is important to understand conflicting values within the context of human rights in order to cultivate respect and challenge hate.
- Sexual rights are human rights; they are enshrined within the *Universal Declaration of Human Rights*.

- Our values are influenced by a variety of sources, including parents, peers, and the media. It is important to know, understand, and be able to articulate how your personal values may look the same or different from these sources in order to make decisions regarding sexuality that are right for you.

HUMAN RIGHTS VIOLATIONS

(for more information on trigger warnings, see modules 1.3 and 1.6)

2.2 EDUCATOR RESOURCE: SEXUALITY AND HUMAN RIGHTS

Human Rights are...

- A set of freedoms and entitlements that belong to every individual simply by virtue of their being human.
- Universal, meaning that they should apply to everyone regardless of who they are and where they live.
- Rooted in the notion that every human being is fundamentally equal to every other and is as valuable to society as every other. Thus, every human being is equally deserving of being treated with respect and dignity and should be provided equal opportunity and be free from discrimination.
- Involved in and touch every aspect of life; they are interdependent and interrelated to one another. For instance, realizing the human right to health is impacted by and depends upon the right to seek and impart information and the right to safe drinking water.
- Enshrined in the *Canadian Charter of Rights and Freedoms*. The *Universal Declaration of Human Rights* contains a more thorough list of human rights, which are also applicable in Canada and throughout the world (for more information, see 2.2 resources).

Sexual Rights

Sexual rights are the human rights of all people to have full control over and to decide freely upon all matters related to their sexuality, reproduction, and gender, including sexual and reproductive health. Sexual rights entail a set of individual freedoms and entitlements as well as government obligations to respect, protect, and fulfill these rights. Sexual rights are fundamental to living with equality and dignity, free from discrimination, coercion, violence, and harm. The realization of sexual rights is essential to all human rights, to empowerment, and to freedom. Table 2A presents the nine human rights that are directly applicable to sexuality and reproduction as well as examples of violations of these rights. It is important to note that while this table includes the sexual and reproductive rights that all of us have by virtue of being human, this does not mean that these rights are always upheld. It is the unfortunate reality that many of the examples of violations occur on a regular basis throughout Canada. In the sections to follow, there are more in depth examples of human rights violations that are normalized through medical practice (e.g., unnecessary and non-consensual surgeries on infants with intersex traits) and through criminalization (e.g., denial of confidentiality and the right to safe work in the case of HIV testing and sex work).

Table 2A

Human Right	Examples related to Sexuality and Reproduction	Examples of Violations
Equality and non-discrimination	You have the right to access evidence-based, good quality, culturally safe, accessible, and relevant sexual and reproductive health care services (and health information) on an equal basis as others and without discrimination or stigma of any kind.	Not being able to access sexual health care based on your age and parental consent. A health care provider refusing service to patients without a health card. A health care provider refusing to provide sexual and reproductive health care relevant to sexually and gender diverse young people. Health care facilities not providing physical access to services and the appropriate equipment needed for people with physical disabilities. Unequal geographical distribution of sexual and reproductive health services and related costs for travelling to access services.
	You have the right to be treated fairly, with dignity, respect, and professionalism, and without judgment by all health professionals and throughout your interactions with the health system regardless of race, pregnancy status, immigration status, HIV status, gender identity, sexual orientation, income, age, religion, sex, education, physical or mental abilities, or other reason.	Health care providers treating people who have had multiple abortions with disrespect or denying them services. Health care providers treating sex workers with disrespect by denying them health services or making them complete mandatory STBBI testing. Health care providers denying people living with HIV health services and/or stigmatizing them in their efforts to access services. Health care providers refusing to provide health care services to someone they have labeled "overweight."

Human Right	Examples related to Sexuality and Reproduction	Examples of Violations
	You have a right to obtain legal recognition (identity documents) for changes to your gender identity, name, and pronouns. You also have the right to be referred to by your name(s) and pronouns that align with your self-identified gender identity without having to obtain legal recognition.	A physician and/or psychologist refusing to write and sign a letter in support of sex designation changes on legal documents to reflect a person's identity, name, and pronouns. Health care providers and educators refusing to use names and/or pronouns that align with someone's self-identified gender identity.
Freedom from torture, cruel, inhumane or degrading treatment or punishment	You have the right to access health care free from abuse, coercion, and harm.	Being denied health care services such as abortion. Health care providers giving patronizing, degrading lectures to sex workers about sexual health, sexuality, and the work they do. Medical professionals conducting non-consensual intersex surgeries. Health care providers forcing/coercing sterilization, abortion, and/or pregnancy. Health care providers abusing patients during labour, including delivery in handcuffs, being strapped to beds, forced C-sections, and/or the denial of pain relief during delivery.
	You have the right to pursue safe and fulfilling sexual and romantic relationships, free from abuse, torture, coercion, punishment, and/or degrading treatment.	Being sexually assaulted by a partner. Experiencing intimate partner violence in sexual and/or romantic relationships.

Human Right	Examples related to Sexuality and Reproduction	Examples of Violations
	You have the right to live free from all forms of violence (sexual, social, physical, economic, verbal, environmental, and psychological) inside and outside of romantic relationships.	Having to endure female genital mutilation.
		Having to live with the knowledge that the person/people who assaulted you enjoy impunity for sexual violence.
		Being harassed and/or bullied online and/or at school.
		Being pressured to engage in non-consensual sexual activity.
	You have the right to express your sexuality without fear of experiencing violence.	Being punished for public displays of affection with someone of the same-sex and/or same gender identity.
Privacy and confidentiality	You have the right to confidentiality from health care professionals (within legal limits).	A health care provider talking to a young person's parents about the fact that they are sexually active or disclosing their HIV status.
		Not being brought to a private area for the collection of evidence by a health care provider after a sexual assault.
		A health care provider refusing to provide care after a sexual assault unless the assault is disclosed to the police.
	You have the right to maintain privacy and confidentiality of health records (within legal limits).	A health agency sharing sexual health records for marketing or profit purposes.
	You have the right to share only the information you wish to share with health care providers.	A medical student and/or observer being present at a sexual health care appointment without the patient's consent.

Human Right	Examples related to Sexuality and Reproduction	Examples of Violations
	You have the right to access any kind of sexual health service and information without spousal and/or parental/guardian permission.	A health care provider requiring parental/guardian consent in order to dispense contraception to someone under 16. A health care provider refusing to provide anonymous HIV testing and counseling to someone under 16.
	You have the right to confidentiality from teachers, social workers, and other professionals (within legal limits).	A teacher disclosing a student's sexual orientation and/or gender identity to other students.
	You have the right to not have intimate images shared publicly that were intended for private consumption.	The public distribution of naked selfies (intended for one person).
The enjoyment of the highest attainable standard of physical and mental health and social security	You have the right to access sexual and reproductive health services and health information that are evidence-based, culturally safe, accessible (affordable and physically and geographically accessible), available, and of good quality.	Not having access to abortion services (surgical and medical) in your community.
	You have the right to access the benefits from scientific progress, including the right to the newest medications and technological advances in medicine.	Being denied the newest medical abortion pill (Mifegymiso) approved and regulated by Health Canada. Not being able to access emergency contraception and/or having to talk to a pharmacist and explain why you are needing to access over the counter emergency contraception. Being denied medications used to prevent and treat STBBIs and HIV because of unaffordable cost.
	You have the right to refuse sexual health care services for any reason without having to explain why.	Being forced/coerced into a medical exam/procedure without consent (either before and/or during the procedure).

Human Right	Examples related to Sexuality and Reproduction	Examples of Violations
	You have the right to the most up-to-date, evidence-based, culturally safe, accurate, and comprehensive information regarding your sexual health.	Being taught inaccurate, false information regarding sexuality and sexual health at school.
	You have the right to receive a timely and effective referral for health care services that your health care provider(s) do not or will not provide.	A health care provider refusing to provide an abortion service or an appropriate referral to another provider.
	You have the right to social protections related to health insurance regardless of income or immigration status.	Not having access to a certain contraceptive method due to cost. An insurance company denying health care coverage on the basis of citizenship and/or refugee status.
	You have the right to pursue a safe and satisfying sex life (being able to decide, when, how, and what sexual activities you engage in) as long as the activities are consensual and there is no infringement on another person's rights.	Having a different legal age of consent for different sexual activities (i.e., in Canada, the age of consent for anal sex is 18 and for penis-vagina intercourse is 16).
Marry and found a family and enter into marriage with the free and full consent of the intending spouses and to equality in and at the dissolution of marriage	You have the right to start a family and/or enter into marriage with someone regardless of gender identity and sexual orientation.	Being refused the right to marry, start a family, and/or have children based on your sexual orientation and/or gender identity.
	You have the right to choose who, how, and when you engage in (and end) a relationship with someone. You have the right to consent or withdraw consent at any time within any kind of relationship you have.	Not being able to choose when, how, and with whom you get into a relationship. Being forced, coerced, and/or manipulated to stay in a relationship.
	You have the right to live in an environment in which diverse family forms are recognized and respected, including those not defined by marriage and/or blood.	Experiencing harassment and/or bullying because of your family structure.

Human Right	Examples related to Sexuality and Reproduction	Examples of Violations
To decide the number and spacing of one's children	You have the right to freely decide whether or not to have children, biological or adopted.	Being pressured or coerced into maintaining a pregnancy, giving birth, or becoming a parent against your will.
	You have the right to have control over and choice about your bodily autonomy.	Being refused access to contraception, abortion, or reproductive technologies because of legal, physical, economy, and/or political barriers.
	You have the right to family planning regardless of your sexual orientation and gender identity.	Being denied access to contraception, fertility clinics, and assisted reproductive technologies based on your sexual orientation and/or gender identity.
	You have the right to accurate, evidence-based information about all kinds of contraception and the right to refuse any kind of contraception for any reason.	A health care provider only offering to prescribe one kind of contraception.
Information and education	You have the right to receive information regarding sexuality, sexual health, reproductive health, and human rights, in line with your evolving capacities, so as to empower you to make decisions that are free, informed, and with your full consent.	Receiving information that degrades and/or makes a person's sexual orientation and/or gender identity invisible. Receiving information on abstinence as the only form of contraception.
	You have the right to receive information in and out of school, in community, and in health care settings.	Health care providers, educators, etc. giving inaccurate or stigmatizing information regarding sexual health and sexuality.
	You have the right to receive comprehensive sexuality education throughout every grade/level of schooling.	Being denied accurate, evidence-based sexuality education in elementary school.

Human Right	Examples related to Sexuality and Reproduction	Examples of Violations
	You have the right to ask questions about sexuality and receive up-to-date, accurate, evidence-based, and comprehensive information from health care providers and educators.	Being denied information about a range of sexual health options (e.g., contraceptive options or abortion services).
	You have the right to access sexual health care services and information without being degraded, humiliated, and/or shamed for asking questions.	An educator shaming a student for asking questions about sexuality and sexual health based on the belief and/or assumption that young people are not or should not be sexually active.
	You have the right to have a diversity of experiences reflected in your sexuality education curriculum.	A sexuality curriculum that ignores a student's age, sexual orientation, gender identity, gender expression, family formations, ability etc.
Freedom of opinion and expression	You have the right to individual opinions and expression of those opinions regarding sexuality, sexual/reproductive health, and gender as long as those expressions do not infringe on the human rights of others.	Legislation that forces an opinion about abortion onto others.
	You have the right to express your gender and sexuality, without fear of stigma and/or discrimination from others.	A school environment in which students cannot express their sexual orientation and/or gender for fear of stigma, degrading treatment, and/or abuse.
	You have the right to join associations and organize around issues related to sexuality, without fear of repression.	Being denied the right to form a club that focuses on youth sexuality.
	If your opinions differ from your health care provider regarding what is right for your body and your life, you have the right to advocate on behalf of yourself for the sexual health care that you need.	A health care provider refusing to provide information about abortion providers in the community because they believe abortion is wrong.

Human Right	Examples related to Sexuality and Reproduction	Examples of Violations
An effective remedy for violations of fundamental rights	You have the right to go through a thorough, fair, non-biased complaint process and take legal action if your sexual rights have been violated.	Being refused access to or deterred from accessing a complaints process, following a sexual rights violation. Being refused a fair, timely, and just investigation when reporting a sexual assault. A sexual violence and/or harassment complaint not being investigated and/or prosecuted.
Participation	You have the right to participate and be meaningfully engaged in decision-making that affects your life, regardless of age, race, immigration status, gender identity, sexual orientation, income, sex, pregnancy status, HIV status, religion, education, physical or mental abilities, or other reason.	Being denied the right to participate in political organizing, decision-making, and law making related to sexuality, sexual health, and sexual rights based on age, race, immigration status, gender identity, sexual orientation, income, sex, pregnancy status, HIV status, religion, education, physical or mental abilities, or other reason.

(For plain language versions of sexual rights and sexual rights specific to youth, see 2.2 resources).

Human Rights Principles

Human rights are informed by a set of fundamental principles. These principles include:

- Non-discrimination and equality
- Participation and empowerment
- Transparency and sustainability
- Accountability (including mechanisms for remedy and redress)

A human rights approach in the context of sexuality education centers these principles and works towards empowering students as **rights holders** with entitlement to all of the sexual and reproductive rights listed in table 2A. A human rights approach to sexuality education aligns with the principles and values guiding comprehensive sexuality education (for more information, see module 0.1).

Both the human rights approach and the comprehensive sexuality education approach emphasize the dignity and self-worth of the individual.

Comprehensive sexuality education empowers people to make decisions about their own bodies based on evidence while the human rights approach instills a sense of entitlement to the right to choose what is best for your own body; comprehensive sexuality education works to instill cultures of respect and equality while the human rights approach teaches students that they have the fundamental right to cultures of respect, equality, and dignity, free from discrimination.

Human Rights and Comprehensive Sexuality Education

Comprehensive Sexuality Education is in alignment with a human rights approach to education and at the same time, is a human right in and of itself.

Sexual rights are fundamental inalienable rights that individuals have on the basis of being human. Like all rights, they are interconnected; access to comprehensive sexuality education is a major factor in realizing the right to information and education, access to information and education also directly impacts how much choice and control we have regarding our sexuality. Similarly, without geographical and economic access to evidence-based confidential sexual health care that is free of discrimination, acting on information learned through comprehensive sexuality education becomes a challenge. The interconnected nature of human rights means that if someone has the right to sexual and reproductive health but does not have access to comprehensive sexuality education, their right to sexual and reproductive health is compromised.

These are some of the reasons why it is important to consider comprehensive sexuality education in relationship to human rights. Approaching sexuality education through a human rights lens allows us to see the ways that sexual rights are inextricably linked to sexual health. A rights-based approach to sexuality education encourages mutual respect, respect for diversity, and critical self-reflection as key components to building relationships with others (Equitas, 2008). It includes the teaching of human rights violations that create barriers to sexual health—the violation of the right to live free of violence, coercion, and discrimination being a major barrier to health. Taking a rights-based approach means addressing the structural barriers that people face when trying to incorporate information about sexuality and sexual health into their daily lives. Addressing these barriers is a first step in creating the motivation (in the IMB model) to take action to change (for more information on the IMB model, see module 0.4).

Human Rights Violations

In Canada, the general perception is that human rights violations happen outside of our borders in faraway countries. The reality, however, is quite different. Human rights violations are a large part of our past and our present. **Forced and coerced sterilization** is a human rights violation that is a part of Canada's history and continues to this day. Forced and coerced sterilization is a product of the eugenics movement, which linked wealth and other measures of social "success" to genetics. Eugenics sought to produce more people with characteristics that were seen as socially "desirable," while stopping characteristics that were seen as socially "undesirable" and an economic burden to the state. This means that the groups of people who were and continue to be among those targeted by forced and coerced sterilization include Indigenous, black and women of colour, people with disabilities (intellectual and physical), people living in poverty, and people with mental health struggles.

Some of the most atrocious human rights violations to happen at a national scale are both the means for and the products of colonialism. As a nation, Canada has and continues to violate the human rights of Indigenous peoples. These human rights violations come in the form of:

- Stolen lands, including unceded territory and violations of treaty rights.
- Stolen children, including the creation and maintenance of residential schools and the sixties scoop.
- Violence of all forms, including nutrition experiments and other forms of physical, emotional, spiritual, and sexual abuse in residential schools and forced/coerced sterilization of Indigenous women by the medical system.
- Sexual and gender-based violence that continues to manifest in great numbers on a national scale in the case of missing and murdered Indigenous women, girls, and trans people.
- Lack of access to safe housing, safe drinking water, and culturally-safe education on reserve communities.
- Poisoning of food and water systems from resource extraction and industrial activities.

YOU SHOULD KNOW

The residential school system was created and maintained by the Canadian government and various churches from the 1880s until 1996. The goal of the schools was to assimilate Indigenous children into Euro-Canadian Christian culture by separating them from their families and communities, forbidding them to speak their languages and practise their cultures. The school system was a place of institutionalized physical, sexual, verbal, and emotional violence and neglect carried out by white priests, nuns, and teachers on Indigenous children. It is now nationally recognized that the residential school system created intergenerational trauma that continues to be a root cause of negative health outcomes. Such outcomes include high suicide and self-harm rates among Indigenous youth, high instances of alcohol and drug use, high HIV rates, and high instances of sexual assault and sexual risk. Another institutional manifestation of colonialism that is a root cause of negative health outcomes is the sixties scoop. The sixties scoop was a cultural assimilation tactic that lasted for two decades. It involved the removal of Indigenous children in large numbers from their families and into white families far from their own communities. It was carried out by state child welfare agencies (Hanson, 2009; King and Lee, 2015).

All of these human rights abuses continue to manifest in different ways, significantly impacting Indigenous peoples' access to sexual and reproductive health and rights. Forced and coerced sterilization of Indigenous women continues to happen in Canada (National Post, 2015) and pollution related to resource extraction has caused various sexual and reproductive health concerns, including breast milk contaminated with PCBs (Hoover et al., 2012).

Recognizing that these human rights violations are a part of Canada's past and present is important in understanding that human rights violations happen at home and need to be considered when teaching sexuality education.

The following section focuses on non-consensual surgeries to illustrate how some human rights violations that occur in Canada are normalized based on discrimination against individuals with intersex traits. The section discusses intersex surgeries and female genital mutilation.

Both of these non-consensual surgeries violate the security of person, bodily integrity, and bodily autonomy; yet, one is normalized as part of "routine" medical procedures, while the other is stigmatized. Intersex surgeries performed on infants and female genital mutilation are both human rights violations that need to be addressed without stigmatizing and discriminating against entire populations.

Non-Consensual Surgeries

Non-consensual surgeries are human rights violations that continue to take place in Canada and are often normalized as part of routine medical practice. Forced and coerced sterilization of Indigenous and other marginalized women is one kind of non-consensual surgery that has and in some cases, continues to take place in Canada.

Surgery on infants with **intersex** traits is another non-consensual surgery that routinely takes place and is normalized as part of standard medical care. When a child is born with sex characteristics that do not fit strictly into the binary medical and social constructions of "male" or "female," the doctor and family will make a decision on how to surgically and/or hormonally alter the infant's body. After the first decision is made, it is common for people with intersex traits to undergo multiple invasive surgeries in childhood, adolescence, and into adulthood. These surgeries often cause trauma to the body and mind because they are physically invasive and because decisions made by the doctor and family in infancy may not reflect what the person themselves wants later in life. Intersex advocates identify these surgeries as human rights violations and call for the right to bodily integrity and self-determination through non-consensual surgeries and hormonal treatments (which are medically unnecessary) to be banned (OII, 2012; Free & Equal, 2015).

Female genital mutilation (also known as female genital cutting) is another kind of non-consensual surgery that ranges from removing all or part of the external female genitalia (including the clitoris, labia minor, and labia majora) to completely or partially closing the vaginal opening. It is an invasive surgery that has no health benefits and poses significant health risks. It is a practise that is performed globally with medical and non-medical intervention and in 2012, the UN General Assembly adopted a resolution to eliminate female genital mutilation (WHO, 2016). The reasons why it is practised are multiple and complex but the rationale is often based on social and cultural **gender norms** around modesty, cleanliness, and virginity that are attached to concepts of femininity and what it means to be a good woman, a good wife, and a good mother.

Although female genital mutilation is prohibited in Canada, social and cultural norms, assumptions, and expectations normalize non-consensual surgeries on intersex infants. This despite both kinds of procedures often being the same (e.g., the full or partial removal of the clitoris). Intersex advocates have made this comparison and pointed to the double standard about what is culturally acceptable and normalized by medicine in countries like Canada and the United States and what is seen as unacceptable.

Human Rights, Criminalization, and Canadian Law

There are a number of human rights violations that occur on a regular basis in Canada when individuals' sexual rights are not upheld (for more information, see table 2A). As this module illustrates, laws and policies impact whether or not human/sexual rights are upheld in a country. Currently in Canada, there are laws in place that criminalize people living with HIV and that criminalize sex workers. These laws contribute to human rights violations related to sexuality (i.e., sexual rights).

Currently under Canadian law, **sex work** and sex workers are criminalized by making it illegal to purchase, communicate, receive material benefit from, and advertise sexual services. From a human rights perspective, the 2014 law (The Protection of Communities and Exploited Persons Act) threatens sex workers right to health, to bodily autonomy, and to freedom from violence by creating conditions that force their work into unsafe and unprotected areas.

The **criminalization** of people living with **HIV** is another significant barrier to realizing sexual rights in Canada. Legislation requires that someone living with HIV must disclose their status to sexual partners before engaging in sexual activities that pose a "realistic possibility" of HIV transmission (CATIE, 2015). Failure to do so puts a person at risk for being charged under the criminal code. This has caused major concern in HIV/AIDS advocacy, public health, and legal communities because evidence suggests that it provides a disincentive for testing and could actually increase transmission rates (CATIE, 2015).

Both the criminalization of sex work and of people living with HIV exacerbate **stigma** and discrimination associated with sex work and HIV. This stigma and discrimination affects people's access to health services, violating people's right to health and leading to negative health outcomes. Criminalization also disproportionately impacts people who are **marginalized** due to immigration status, race, class, sexual orientation, and gender identity.

Educator Reflection Questions

- Was there anything about this module that surprised you? Why or why not?
- Was there anything that you read in this module that you did not agree with? Why or why not?
- If there was something that you did not agree with, what strategies will you put in place to discuss these topics in a way that allows for a diversity of opinions to be heard and discussed within your classroom? How will you actively foster respect, inclusion, equity, fairness, responsibility, and cooperation while leading activities and discussions on the topic of human rights?

2.3 SEXUAL RIGHTS

LEVEL 2 [3]

Big Ideas in Module 2.3
- All people are entitled to rights that span sexuality and sexual health.
- Sexual rights are human rights.
- Human rights violations happen everywhere, including Canada.

Learning Objectives
Students will:
- Consider the interconnected nature of human rights.
- Explore how sexual rights are integral to human rights.
- Develop a critical analysis of human rights in Canada and globally.

Cross-Curricular Connections
- Canadian Studies
- English
- Equity Studies
- Gender Studies
- History
- Law
- Politics
- Social Studies
- Sociology
- World Studies

Terminology
- Autonomy
- Contraception
- Discrimination
- Human rights
- Sexual rights
- Stigma

Materials
- Chalkboard or whiteboard
- Flip chart or large pieces of construction paper
- Chalk or markers
- Sticky notes
- **Educator Resource—Sexual Rights: Entitlement vs. Access**
- **Educator Answer Key—Sexual Rights: Entitlement vs. Access**

Background Information for Educators
Sexual rights are the application of human rights to sexuality and sexual health (2006a, updated 2010) and include the right to have full control over and freely decide upon all aspects of your own sexuality, reproduction, and gender identity, free from violence, discrimination, coercion, and harassment.

Sexual rights depend on all other **human rights**, which cannot be separated from one another. According to the World Health Organization (WHO), the purpose of sexual rights is to "protect all people's rights to fulfill and express their sexuality and enjoy sexual health, with due regard for the rights of others and within a framework of protection against discrimination" (2006a, updated 2010).

Student Readiness

Before students engage with this lesson, ensure that safer space guidelines and group norms have been established (and revisited) within your classroom (for more information on how to establish safer space guidelines within a classroom, see module 1.3). In order to effectively prepare for this activity, ensure students understand:

- What human rights are and why they are important (see module 2.2).
- That sexuality is not only something that exists in the private realm (i.e., does not only include sexual activity between partners).
- That sexuality and sexual health are experienced and influenced by individual and social factors.

Summary of Activities

Students will:

- Work on creating a mind map individually and as a large group.
- Explore the difference between entitlement and access to human/ sexual rights by either moving around the classroom or through an online (visual, but anonymous) questionnaire tool.
- Research a human rights violation that has (or still is) occurring in Canada and problem solve how they would address this issue as a human rights worker.

Activity 1 2 3

Instructions

1. Place "human rights" in the centre of your board or flip chart, circle it.
2. With your students, collectively brainstorm a definition for "human rights." If your students get stuck, provide them with the definition at the back of the book.
3. Give students 10 to 15 sticky notes each.
4. Ask your students to individually brainstorm different rights that humans are inherently entitled to because they are human. Students can write these on individual sticky notes and can choose to share as many (or as few) as they are comfortable.
5. On the board, write down some initial suggestions for categories and connect these with solid arrows to the circled human rights in the middle of the mind map. (For an example of category suggestions, see figure 2B).

6. Ask students to bring their sticky notes to the board and have them place their sticky notes in one of the categories. If they are unsure where a sticky note would best fit, tell them that they are welcome to create their own category.

7. Read out each sticky note and the category it was placed in. Ask students if there are other categories that the sticky note could be placed in.

8. Ask students to individually brainstorm a list of sexual rights they are inherently entitled to because they are human (for examples, see figure 2B). Students can write examples of sexual rights on their remaining sticky notes and can choose to share as many (or as few) as they are comfortable.

9. Invite students to come up to the board and place their sticky notes around the outside of the first round of sticky notes. Talk through each sticky note and ask students which sexual rights are connected to which human rights they have listed. Indicate the connections they make with dotted lines.

10. Group discussion: How are each of the sexual rights connected to human rights? Why is it important to consider sexual rights in the context of human rights?

QUICK TIP

For information that can be used to guide your class discussion, refer to table 2A.

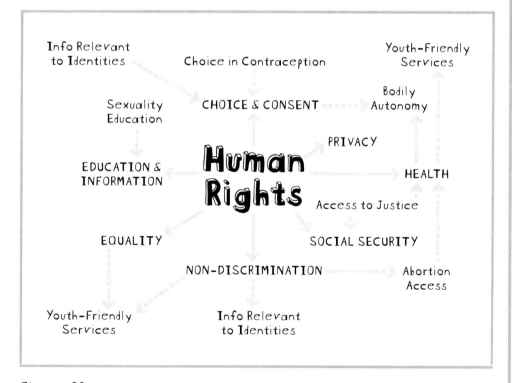

Figure 2B

Activity 2 [2] [3]

Instructions
Part 1: Creating Collaborative Working Definitions
1. Place the following words on large individual pieces of paper:
   - Autonomy
   - Contraception
   - Discrimination
   - Human rights
   - Sexual rights
   - Stigma
2. Place the sheets of paper throughout the classroom.
3. Ask students to make three columns in their notebooks and label the first column: Words that I do not know; the second column: Words I know; and the third column: Words I would like to know.
4. For the words the students know, ask them to write down elements of what they think the definition could be. Emphasize the fact that they do not have to have a full, polished/finished definition.
5. Explain that during intergovernmental proceedings at the United Nations, nation states, international government agencies, and non-governmental organizations work together to come up with working definitions on topics related to human rights. Part of this work involves bringing ideas to the table and being open to receiving feedback on ideas, being inspired to bring new ideas to the table, and challenging your own assumptions about what something means. This work also involves voting and deciding on definitions either by consensus (everyone agrees) or by majority rule.
6. Give each student a marker and ask them to take their notebooks and walk around the classroom. When they arrive at a word that they have a brainstormed rough definition for, ask them to share some of this definition by writing it down. Again, emphasize that the definition does not have to be polished, in fact it is better if the definition is a "working definition" or "in progress." Assure students that everyone is putting their best guess forward and that collectively, a definition will be created.
7. Once students have had a chance to walk around the classroom and share their ideas on paper, ask students to walk around the classroom a second time and read other students' ideas. Emphasize that it is important for students to also read papers that they did not contribute to. This is important because reading other people's ideas may spark a new idea for a student (even if they did not originally think that they had anything to contribute to that word/piece of paper). Encourage them to add new ideas to the pieces of paper/ working definitions.

8. Review the working definitions with the class. If there is any disagreement or contradictory statements on any piece of paper, discuss with the class and ask students to take a vote. You can decide based on the engagement and maturity of the class whether or not to come to a decision based on consensus or a majority rule vote.
9. Once the class has decided on the definition (either by consensus or majority rule), compare the class' definitions with those provided at the back of the book.

Part 2: Sexual Rights: Entitlement vs. Access
1. Begin by creating enough space so that students can move easily from one end of the room to the other.
2. Designate one side of the room as "yes," another side of the room as "no," and the middle of the room as "unsure."
3. Explain that between "yes" and "no" is a continuum of possibilities and that all students have to place themselves somewhere on the continuum after each question is read aloud.
4. Before beginning the activity, ask students:
   • What do you think the word "entitlement" means? You can draw their attention back to the first activity (human rights mind map) and ask them: What do you think entitlement means in the context of the human rights previously brainstormed? For instance, entitlement to the right to education.
   • What do you think the word 'access' means? You can draw their attention back to the first activity (human rights mind map) and ask them: What do you think access means in the context of the human rights previously brainstormed? For instance, access to the right to education.
   • What do you see as the differences and/or similarities between the meanings of these words? What are the implications in terms of human rights?

EDUCATOR ANSWER KEY
In the context of human rights, entitlement refers to inherent inalienable rights based on being human. Access is how attainable these human rights are in practise. It is important to name the human rights that young people are entitled to (so that young people know their rights and can advocate for these rights) as well as provide information on which rights are often difficult to access in practise.

5. Read each set of questions aloud from **Sexual Rights: Entitlement vs. Access**, pausing between statement sets to allow students to move around the room. *Each set of questions is numbered and includes A and B.*

6. After each round, one student from each area of the room will be given the option to speak about why they have placed themselves there.

7. After a student from each area of the room has had a chance to speak, you can use the **Educator Answer Key—Sexual Rights: Entitlement vs. Access** to help clarify what human rights young people are entitled to and how there can be discrepancies between what rights humans are entitled to and whether or not they can fully realize (or access) those rights.

8. Group discussion: How did this activity make you feel? Did you feel vulnerable or empowered (or neither) by moving around the room? Did the way you feel depend on the content of the question? How did it feel to speak about your choices? How did it feel to listen to other people? Were you surprised by any of the information read by the educator?

QUICK TIP

As the educator, you can give students a list of possibilities based on examples provided in table 2A.

Activity 3 [3]

Instructions

Part 1: Research

1. Place students in groups of three or four and explain that each group is made up of human rights advocates from a fictional non-governmental organization (NGO) working to end human rights violations in Canada and globally.

2. Each group must:
   - Research a human rights violation related to sexual rights, which has been and/or is currently practised in Canada.
   - Research a different human rights violation related to sexual rights, which has been and/or is currently practised in a country other than Canada.

3. For each violation, ask students:
   - Are there any similarities between the two violations?
   - What time period did these violations occur? Are they still happening?
   - Do you think that these violations are known worldwide? Why or why not?
   - Do you think that people all over the world consider this a violation? Why or why not?
   - What **social movements** have tried to address and work to change this human rights violation? Do you think that they have been successful? How can you tell?

Part 2

1. Choose one of the two human rights violations researched in the previous section that you want to focus on as human rights advocates in your fictional NGO
    *   Create a name and a vision statement for your group's fictional NGO.
    *   Optional: Create a visual logo for your group's fictional NGO.
2. Provide students with copies of *The Canadian Charter of Rights and Freedoms* and the *Universal Human Rights* and ask them to think about how these two documents could be used to advocate against the violation that their NGO is focused on addressing.
    *   Ask them to identify whether or not the issue they have chosen would fall under a section in the Charter, the Declaration of Human Rights, or both.
    *   Ask them to identify which section(s) their violation falls under.
    *   If they are having trouble figuring out where in the documents the issue fits, challenge students to come up with an argument (using evidence and logic) as to where it could fit and why.
3. Instruct students to imagine that their NGOs have been asked to present their case to Canada's Parliament and/or the United Nations. Ask each group to prepare their case as human rights advocates, ensuring that it is in line with their respective vision statements.

Wrap-Up

Summarize the module with the following points:
*   Human rights are interconnected; you cannot have one right without another.
*   Sexual rights are human rights.
*   Human rights violations happen everywhere, including Canada.

QUICK TIP

A vision statement should capture the long term goal(s) or "big picture" of what the NGO seeks to accomplish. A vision statement should be clear, concise (1–2 lines) and inspiring.

2.4 SEXUALITY, DISCRIMINATION, AND THE SOCIAL DETERMINANTS OF HEALTH

LEVEL 3

Big Ideas in Module 2.4

- Sexual health, like health more broadly, involves the whole person and is influenced by a combination of social/environmental factors and individual choices.
- Sexual health is only meaningfully realized when the root causes of negative sexual health outcomes are addressed. It is possible to address these root causes from a human rights perspective as well as from a social determinants of health perspective.
- Sexual health promotion must address individual health behaviours as well as systemic inequities and discrimination.

Learning Objectives

Students will:

- Understand a comprehensive concept of sexuality and sexual health.
- Understand the social determinants of sexual health.
- Discuss strategies for risk reduction and the promotion of personal and systemic health.

Cross-Curricular Connections

- Canadian Studies
- English
- Equity Studies
- Gender Studies
- History
- Human Geography
- Politics
- Social Studies
- Sociology
- World Studies

Terminology

- Ableism
- Aboriginal Status
- Cisgender
- Classism
- Colonialism
- Discrimination
- Food In/Security
- Harm Reduction
- Homophobia
- Incarcerated People
- Racism
- Sexism
- Sexual Health
- Sexuality
- Social Determinants of Health
- Stigma
- Transphobia

Materials

- Chalkboard or whiteboard
- Printed copies of **Case Studies: Social Determinants of Sexual Health**
- **Educator Answer Key—Case Studies: Social Determinants of Sexual Health**

Background Information for Educators

Sexuality is an integral part of being human. It is a complex set of personal, social, and spiritual experiences that go beyond sexual activity. In other words, sexuality is not just what our body does and what we do with our bodies, it is "experienced and expressed in thoughts, fantasies, desires, beliefs, attitudes, values, behaviours, practises, roles and relationships" (WHO, 2006a).

The World Health Organization defines **sexual health** as "a state of physical, emotional, mental and social well-being in relation to sexuality" (WHO, 2006a). Sexual health is not only the absence of disease or unwanted outcomes; it includes pleasure, sexual expression, and satisfying relationships and depends on access to sexual rights (i.e., freedom from violence and discrimination and autonomy over our bodies and our decisions).

Sexual health is only meaningfully realized when the root causes of negative sexual health outcomes are addressed. It is possible to address these root causes from a human rights perspective as well as from a **social determinants of health** perspective.

Like all aspects of health, sexual health is not only based on individual decisions and behaviours but also systemic and structural influences. Poverty, **racism, homophobia, transphobia, sexism, ableism**—to name a few examples—all affect a person's sexual health. These structural influences affect a person's sexual health through factors that include experiences of **stigma, discrimination**, and assumptions made in health care settings and by health care providers who prevent people affected by these forms of oppression from seeking care.

The legacy of **colonialism** in Canada affects the sexual health of Indigenous communities in particular ways, including legacies of abuse and violence from the state sanctioned residential school system and sixties scoop (for more information, see module 2.2); the gendered nature of violence affects the sexual health of women, trans people, and gender non-binary people by putting these populations at higher risk for sexual violence; and the lack of health care supports and **harm reduction** initiatives for **incarcerated people** contributes to their higher risk of HIV and other Sexually Transmitted and Blood-Borne Infections (STBBIs).

Just as sexual rights cannot be separated from other human rights, sexual health cannot be separated from other aspects of health (e.g., sexual health is compromised when mental health is compromised and vice-a-versa). This connection is clear for LGBTQ+ youth in North America. LGBTQ+ youth have higher rates of mental health struggles compared to their heterosexual, **cisgender** peers. With higher rates of mental health challenges come coping mechanisms such as substance use and "riskier" sexual activities that can put LGBTQ+ youth at higher risk of STBBIs and other negative sexual health outcomes. (For more information, see module 1.5, chapter 3, and module 10.3).

The following activities help students recognize the comprehensive nature of sexual health, its social influences, and possibilities for positive change for themselves and in the world.

Student Readiness

Before students engage with this lesson, ensure that safer space guidelines and group norms have been established (and revisited) within your classroom (for more information on how to establish safer space guidelines within a classroom, see module 1.3). In order to effectively prepare for this activity, ensure students understand:

- The definitions for discrimination and stigma. It is recommended that you use the definitions for the 2.4 terminology to discuss specific forms of systemic discrimination before beginning the activities.
- The definitions for sexual health and sexual rights. Ensure that students understand that sexual health cannot be fully realized without access to sexual rights.

Summary of Activities

Students will:

- Work on collectively creating a mind map that demonstrates the connection between individual and systemic/structural factors that determine health.
- Analyze sexual health scenarios and problem solve case studies.

Activity 1 3

Instructions

1. Explain to students that a person's health is affected by many things.
2. Write "Health" in the center of the board. Ask students for factors that affect health and include these as spokes coming out of the center.

EDUCATOR PROMPTS
- Think about aspects of where you live that could be health enhancing and health depleting.
- Think about the reasons why you live where you do.
- Think about the reasons why you eat what you do.
- How much choice do you have in where you live and what you eat? What factors hinder this choice?

The mind map that you co-create with your students should look something like figure 2C. Break larger ideas down and link similar ideas together.

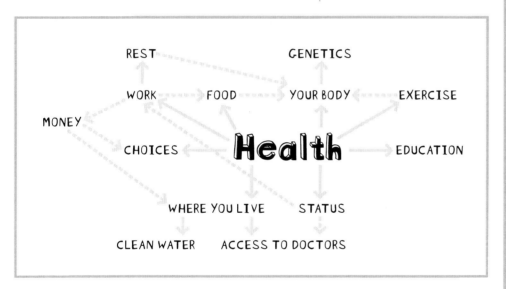

Figure 2C

3. Review the whole map you have created with students. Explain that this contains both individual determinants and some of the **social determinants of health.**
4. Explain that the following are some commonly recognized social determinants of health:
   - Income and income distribution
   - Education and job training
   - Employment/Unemployment and working conditions
   - **Food In/Security**
   - Housing
   - Geographic location (where you live)

QUICK TIP

When creating the mind map with your students, you can use solid lines to indicate the connections students make in the first brainstorm. After the first collective brainstorm, use the dotted lines to illustrate the connections between what students presented in the first brainstorm but had not necessarily thought of as connected. For instance, during the first brainstorm students might say: "Where you live affects your health." They might also say: "Your work and working conditions affect your health." As the facilitator, you can prompt them with a question like: "How might your work be connected to where you live?" You can then add in the word "money" and connect "money" with dotted lines to "where you live" and "work."

- Social inclusion/exclusion
- Social and community support and safety
- Access to technology and media
- Access to health services
- Discrimination based on:
  - **Aboriginal status** and/or Indigenous identity
  - Gender identity
  - Sexual orientation
  - Immigration status
  - Race
  - Ability/Disability

SEXUAL VIOLENCE IN CASE STUDIES
(for more information on trigger warnings, see modules 1.3 and 1.6)

Activity 2

Instructions

1. Explain that sexual health is an aspect of overall health and that the World Health Organization defines it as "a state of physical, emotional, mental and social well-being in relation to sexuality" (WHO, 2006a). Ask students to describe the qualities and characteristics of a "sexually healthy" person using this definition.

EDUCATOR ANSWER KEY

- Has accurate information about bodies and functions
- Is without disease/infection or is getting care for those diseases/infections or is actively reducing harms associated with those diseases/infections
- Expresses sexuality appropriately (meaning that bodily autonomy and the sexual decision-making of others is respected)
- Has satisfying relationships (emotionally, sexually, intimately, physically, romantically, and spiritually satisfying)
- Is free from violence and discrimination
- Makes own decisions about their body
- Has a positive self-concept

2. Print the **Case Studies** and cut into individual cases.
3. Divide students into small groups and distribute cases (one or more cases to each group, depending on size of class).
4. Ask groups to read case studies, discuss the questions attached to each case study, take notes, and share highlights of their discussions in the large group afterward.
5. Use the **Educator Answer Key—Case Studies** to guide the classroom discussion. For each case study, ask students which social determinants of health are relevant.

Wrap-up

Summarize the module with the following points:

- Sexual health is comprehensive and involves the whole person.
- Sexual health is affected by individual choices and behaviours as well as systemic factors.
- Promoting sexual health involves helping people make healthy choices as well as addressing systemic inequities.

2.5 EDUCATOR RESOURCE: SEXUALITY AND VALUES

Values and moral perspectives will inevitably come up in classroom discussions on sexuality. This can happen in one of two ways: as an opinion that is *implicit* or as an opinion that is *explicit*. It is impossible to avoid values in meaningful and educational conversations related to sexuality; they are a natural part of the discussion (for more information, see module 1.1).

So how do you navigate this sometimes sensitive territory? The first thing to keep in mind is that students will usually bring a diversity of moral perspectives and backgrounds with them to the classroom. This can be a good thing because, if it works out well, it will stimulate a lively discussion that encourages students to more closely examine their own values and to hopefully consider the points of view of others. It is not your job as an educator to decide what is morally correct or to settle debate like a judge in the courtroom. Your role in the classroom is to facilitate and guide discussion by asking questions like:

- How does that point of view stack up against the principles of **human rights**? (For more information, see modules 2.2 and 2.3).
- In this situation, what would be the fairest thing to do for everyone involved?
- In this situation, what would be the most equitable thing to do for everyone involved?
- If we agree that the way we treat each other people should be truthful and respectful, how would that apply here?
- Even if you disagree with someone else's point of view, how can you treat this person with dignity and respect while presenting a different point of view and/or considerations?
- That's one point of view. What are other perspectives you have heard on this issue?

The intent of these types of questions is to advance the discussion in a constructive way without necessarily determining its outcome. At the same time, it is important for you to address and challenge overt expressions of hate, **prejudice, discrimination,** or injustice (for more information, see module 1.5).

QUICK TIP

How do you tell the difference between expressions of hate, prejudice, and discrimination and someone expressing a point of view/opinion? This can be a fine line and is sometimes challenging to discern.

- One way to make the distinction is to consider both the impact and the intention behind an expression (for more information, see figure 1A in module 1.2). How have the comments of one person shifted the dynamics of the room? Were the words that were expressed full of hate and disrespect? Was fear used as a tactic to steer the conversation in a particular direction?
- Another way to make the distinction is to consider the different qualities of an opinion versus an expression of hate, prejudice, or discrimination. When someone states an opinion, they are doing so from an "I" place, taking ownership over and showing awareness about the fact that this is an opinion that comes from their values and experiences in the world. Expressions of hate, prejudice, and discrimination often generalize and stereotype a large group of people without awareness that these ideas come from somewhere and are not an unshakable "universal truth."

One way to help ensure that the sharing of opinions and ideas does not turn into expressions of hate, prejudice, and discrimination is to discuss and agree upon safer space guidelines before entering into any of the activities within *Beyond the Basics* (for more information on how to create and maintain safer space guidelines, to respond to discrimination, and to facilitate sensitive activities, see modules 1.3, 1.5, and 1.6).

Dealing with Conflicting Values

Because values and moral perspectives related to sexuality are so diverse across Canada, dealing with conflicting values is unavoidable.

Some students may have values that counter the rights of others. Remind students about *The Canadian Charter of Rights and Freedoms*, the *Universal Declaration of Human Rights*, and school policies on anti-harassment and codes of conduct (if applicable) as important standards to uphold.

Some students may have very specific beliefs about sexual activity and its appropriateness at their age, when unmarried, or outside of romantic partnerships. Point out that decisions about sexual activity are personal choices that can be guided by the values and norms that students have learned, whether from religion, their family, their peers, the media, their culture etc. Be sure to emphasize that everyone carries values and norms that come from a variety of sources, like family and culture. Everyone has (consciously and unconsciously) made decisions based on these values at one time or another and the same is true for decisions on sexuality. The most important idea to teach here is sexual consent and honouring mutual agreements (for more information, see chapter 8).

YOU SHOULD KNOW

Everyone comes from a culture with values that help guide decisions on sexuality and sexual activity. Often the dominant culture is perceived as being value neutral. In reality, this is not the case. Instead, these values become invisible and normalized as "common sense" or "logical" or "just the way things are." It is important that as an educator you work to actively challenge these assumptions by pointing out that everyone is a part of a culture that informs our values and how we make decisions around our sexuality. The next few modules in this chapter help students assess and make sense of their personal values and their relationship to family, cultural, and religious values.

Dealing with Discrimination and Intolerance

Sexuality education touches on and affects all aspects of life. It is therefore important to equally, directly, and firmly challenge all forms of oppression and discrimination, including (but not limited to) racism, homophobia, transphobia, sexism, classism, and ableism (for more information, see modules 1.2, 1.5, and 3.11). This is particularly important when considering the links between sexual health and mental health (for more information, see module 2.4). Given the high number of suicides among youth due to harassment, assault, and bullying—especially for LGBTQ+ students—this could mean life or death.

Dealing with Judgmental Comments

A student may make a comment, ask a question, or even use a word that is value-laden. Judgment and moral indignation are common responses to fear, ignorance, and the pressure to fit in. At the same time, making judgments is one way that we as humans discern when a situation is safe or unsafe and judgments help inform what our values are. The problem with being judgmental is not necessarily the judgment itself but how we choose to interact with and respond to our judgment. Will we act on our judgments in a way that threatens someone else's safety and disrespects their human rights? If our judgments result in bullying, harassment, and/or discrimination, someone's safety and human rights might be threatened.

Adolescence is a time where young people feel a lot of pressure to find their place in the world and also fit in with peer norms. This pressure can result in experimentation with boundaries, opinions, and judgments. They may be finding more power to act on their values, while also feeling powerless and vulnerable. Depending on the day, the topic, and the person, being "different" can feel threatening, empowering, and/or inspiring.

The most important message that educators can give (through role modelling and explicit responses) is that difference is common and expected. Help students appreciate and respect the diversity of opinion, experience, and aspirations while they articulate their own truths. Allow a diversity of truths and opinions to exist in your classroom and include empathy and curiosity as important tools for continuous learning. Being open-minded enough to understand opinions different from your own is key to refining (and at times evolving) your own worldview.

Educator Reflection Questions

- Think about some of the ways that your opinions on sexuality are different from your family. What strategies have you used to listen to opinions that differ from yours? Can you use any of these same strategies when facilitating activities that will bring up a difference in values and opinions between you and your students, as well as between the students themselves?
- Think about the strength of having a difference in opinion and how encountering different values and opinions has enriched your life and your learning. What has helped you experience these moments of enriched learning? What teaching methods can you use to ensure that a difference in opinion is an enriching experience for everyone in your classroom?
- Think about a time where you made a judgment about a situation and/or person and acted on that judgment. How did that action affect you? How did that action affect other people?
- Have you ever been in a situation where the difference between someone's opinion/belief and discrimination became blurred? How did you tell the difference and how did you approach the situation?

2.6 OPINIONS AND VALUES ABOUT SEXUALITY: MINE VS. PEERS AND FAMILY

LEVEL [1] [2] [3]

Big Ideas in Module 2.6
- Values and opinions related to sexuality are diverse even within families and peer groups.
- Forming your own opinions and values related to sexuality can be done with a combination of research and personal reflection.
- It is important to consider what your personal opinions and values are separate from peer pressure and/or family norms because this forms the basis for empowered decision-making.

Learning Objectives
Students will:
- Identify and explore their opinions related to different aspects of sexuality and relationships.
- Consider their own opinions as well as the opinions of their peers and family.
- Reflect on where their opinions align and diverge with peers and family.
- Reflect on how values are influenced by peers and family.

Cross-Curricular Connections
- English
- Equity Studies
- Family Studies
- Gender Studies
- Psychology
- Social Studies
- Sociology

Materials
- Chalkboard or whiteboard
- Printed copies of **Opinions and Values** (version for level 1, 2, or 3, as appropriate)

Background Information for Educators
Evidence-based facts, concepts, and resources are important components of sexuality education. They help students make informed decisions about their bodies, relationships, and experiences. With facts, concepts, and resources come opportunities to form and articulate

healthy opinions and values. Learning how to form and articulate well thought out opinions and values are the foundation to empowered decision-making.

Student Readiness

Before students engage with this lesson, ensure that safer space guidelines and group norms have been established (and revisited) within your classroom (for more information on how to establish safer space guidelines within a classroom, see module 1.3). In order to effectively prepare for this activity, ensure students understand that:

- It is impossible to avoid values in meaningful and educational conversations related to sexuality.
- Having different values from those around you is okay as long as the expression of those values is respectful and does not express hate or infringe on the rights of others.
- Ensure that they will be considering ways that their values might align or diverge from their peers and family and how they want to handle pressure to conform.

Summary of Activities

Students will:

- Work independently through a series of value statements related to sexuality.
- Have the option of discussing their personal reflections with the rest of the class.
- Have the option (level 3) of participating in a role play where they have a conversation with a friend or family member who has differing values from them.

Activity 1 ☐1☐ ☐2☐ ☐3☐

Instructions

Explain to students that every family is unique and that if they are having trouble with this statement, to think about the kinds of differences that can exist from one family to another. For instance, there are differences in family structures, family stories, and family cultures. The statement can also be read as: "It is okay for families to be different than mine." (For more information on family diversity, see module 4.8).

QUICK TIP

For level 1 students, it may be more accessible if you adapt the activity for an auditory learning style. In this adapted version, students' eyes are closed and the statements (and corresponding agree/disagree options) are read aloud by the educator. Students then have the option of quietly thinking through the statements and raising their hands anonymously when they feel called to do so.

For level 2 students, depending on the maturity and grade make-up of your class, you may want to start with the level 1 statement sets and then move onto the level 2 statement sets. If your class consists of only grade 8s, you may also consider using some of the level 3 statement sets depending on the maturity of students in your class.

Part 1—Reflection (Levels 1, 2, 3)

1. Distribute copies of **Opinions and Values** (the version for level 1, 2, or 3, as appropriate). Allow students to work independently and with privacy. Ask students to check off whether they agree with each statement and then guess how their friends and families would answer. Instruct students to pick their closest friend and one specific family member. Ask them to pick people whose values will likely be different.

2. After they have finished, ask students what they noticed about their own values. Which statements were the most difficult to answer?

3. Discuss: Do you tend to have the same values as your friends? Your families? What are the consequences (both positive and negative) of having similar values? Having different values?

4. Discuss: Have you noticed your values changing as you mature? Students can volunteer to give examples from the worksheet but it is not mandatory.

5. Discuss: What can you do if you feel pressured to have values different from your own? How can you know what you truly believe? Students can volunteer to give examples.

Part 2—Optional Role Play (Level 3)

1. Ask students to pair up and have each pair self-select who is "A" and who is "B."

2. Ask each student to choose a statement (from the level 2 or level 3 statement sets) that they want to explore in more depth. *It can be something that they find particularly relevant to their peer group or something that they find challenging to discuss with friends and/or family.*

3. Explain that for the first round, the pairs will role play the statement Student A selected. Student A can choose where on the spectrum of agreement or disagreement they want to be. Student A will work on crafting an argument for their selected position/opinion, keeping in mind that Student B is someone that they know and have a friendship or familial relationship with. Emphasize that it is just as important to construct a sound argument as it is to learn how to communicate information in a way that treats others with respect, dignity, fairness, and equity. The job of Student B in this round is to respond to Student A in a way that is realistic and respectful.

4. Explain that for the second round, the pairs will role play the statement Student B selected. Student B can choose where on the spectrum of agreement or disagreement they want to be. Student B will work on crafting an argument for their selected position/opinion, keeping in mind that student A is someone that they know and have a friendship or familial relationship with. Emphasize that it is just as important to construct a sound argument as it is to learn how to communicate information in a way that treats others with respect, dignity, fairness, and equity. The job of Student A in this round is to respond to Student B in a way that is realistic and respectful.

5. Once each pair has finished both rounds, bring the class back together to discuss:
   - How did that role play make you feel? Which round did you find more challenging and why?
   - What was the most challenging aspect of communicating your opinion? What was the most rewarding?
   - What was the most challenging aspect of listening to and responding to your partner's opinion? What was the most rewarding?
   - Do you feel more (or less) equipped to discuss your opinions and values with someone who might disagree with you? Do you feel more (or less) equipped to advocate for your opinions and values with someone who might disagree with you in a way that is respectful, fair, and even kind?

Wrap-up

Summarize the module with the following points:
- Sexual decision-making is influenced by our personal, family, peer, cultural, and/or religious values and norms.
- There is sometimes pressure to align your values with those of your peers and family.
- It is important to know your own values and opinions, and how they may change over time, so that you can make decisions that are right for you.

2.7 LET'S TALK ABOUT... TALKING ABOUT SEX!

LEVEL 1 2 3

Big Ideas in Module 2.7

- Part of developing comfort with a topic is learning how to accurately and clearly talk about it. With taboo subjects like sex and sexuality, this becomes incredibly important in order to avoid miscommunication and misunderstanding.
- Sexuality involves the whole person—emotional, physical, psychological, and spiritual. There are many ways to share sexual experience and expression with others. Sex is only one form of expression and the term itself does not have a universal meaning.
- There are multiple ways to consensually express sexuality and sexual feelings; one form of expression is not better or more valid than others.

Learning Objectives

Students will:

- Explore the concept of **euphemisms** and their use in sexual topics.
- Consider how the language we choose can limit understandings of sexuality.
- Broaden the concept of sexual experience beyond "having sex."

Cross-Curricular Connections

- English
- Equity Studies
- Gender Studies
- Psychology
- Social Studies
- Sociology

Terminology

- Euphemisms
- Sex negativity
- Sex positivity
- Sexuality
- Stigma

Materials

- Chalkboard, whiteboard, or flip chart
- Chalk or markers

Background Information for Educators

How we talk about a subject informs how we feel about it. The words we use (and the ones we avoid) can also shape our world and its possibilities. When it comes to sexuality, bodies, death, and other taboo subjects, we often resort to euphemisms. While they might allow us to broach the subject, euphemisms can bring about misunderstandings.

They also perpetuate taboos and **stigma**. Sexuality education that challenges and liberates students from stigma and **sex negativity** needs to look at euphemisms critically and replace euphemisms with informed, **sex positive** language.

Before facilitating these activities, take a moment to review the educator reflection questions in modules 1.1, 1.2, 2.1, 2.2, and 2.5. After reviewing these questions, begin to think about the euphemisms you use in your daily life when talking about taboo subjects (not limited to sexuality) and what the disadvantages and advantages are to using them. As an educator, this kind of preparation will help to develop your own critical analysis of euphemisms and deliver an effective lesson for your students.

Student Readiness

Before students engage with this lesson, ensure that safer space guidelines and group norms have been established (and revisited) within your classroom (for more information on how to establish safer space guidelines within a classroom, see module 1.3). In order to effectively prepare for this activity, ensure students understand:

- Why the words/language we use to communicate is important (for more information, see module 1.4).
- That miscommunication is common and happens in lots of different areas of life. Part of establishing healthy communication patterns around sexuality is recognizing when miscommunication is happening in order to clear up the misunderstanding and work towards less miscommunication in the future.
- That this module is about exploring why we use euphemisms and why they can cause harm when not clearly defined. This lesson is about exploring why we use euphemisms and why they can cause harm when not clearly defined.

Summary of Activities

Students will:

- Collectively brainstorm euphemisms for taboo subjects and explore why/how euphemisms are used and their advantages and disadvantages.
- Individually consider what terms like "doing it" and "having sex" mean to them and then collectively consider how these terms do not have static or universal definitions.
- In pairs, role play a scenario about friends miscommunicating.

QUICK TIP

This activity can be used with any age level. For levels 2 and 3, ask students about common dating terms. For level 1 (at your own discretion) you can replace the term "dating" with "private body parts" and/or "bodily functions."

QUICK TIP

Do not shy away from disagreement on definitions of terms. Use any disagreement as an opportunity to point out that there are multiple, sometimes contradictory definitions for terms that describe a very subjective experience like dating. Make connections to the ways that people use multiple, contradictory, and ever changing terms to talk about sexuality.

YOU SHOULD KNOW

While it is often assumed that "doing it" and "having sex" refer to frontal sexual intercourse (otherwise known as vaginal sex and coitus) between a person with a penis and a person with a vagina, "having sex" can take many different forms. This assumption can harm someone who does not have penis-vagina sex because it leads to misunderstandings about safer sex practises and STBBIs (i.e., which activities are "risky" and which are not) and it assumes that everyone is heterosexual and cisgender and only engages in hetero- and cis-normative sexual activities.

Activity 1 [1] [2] [3]

Instructions

1. Ask students for terms they commonly use to refer to "dating." Write them on the board.
2. Ask for definitions of each of the terms.
3. Ask students for terms referring to "dating" that might be outdated or old-fashioned (like "going steady" or "courting"). Write these on the board but off to the side. Bring to their attention that terms change all the time.
4. Ask students why they think that there is no single definition for terms about relationships and sexuality.

EDUCATOR ANSWER KEY

Relationships and sexuality are subjective experiences. The interpretations and definitions of each will vary person to person and throughout one's life.

5. Ask students for reasons why we use euphemisms for words connected to sexuality, death, private body parts, relationships, etc.

EDUCATOR ANSWER KEY

Anatomically correct terms may sound harsh, uncomfortable, embarrassing, overly scientific/medical, and/or unpleasant.

6. Discuss the benefits of euphemisms.

EDUCATOR ANSWER KEY
- Allows us to talk about something that is hard to talk about.
- Words can sound funny and be more fun to talk about when not actually speaking about them directly.
- Using euphemisms that are "in" may lead to an increased feeling of connection and belonging with others.
- Preserves some measure of privacy and vagueness that can act as a social protection.

7. Discuss the disadvantages of euphemisms and indirect communication. When might this become a problem? Prompt students with terms like "doing it" or "hooking up." What can go wrong with these euphemisms?

EDUCATOR ANSWER KEY
- Miscommunication
- Misunderstanding
- Possibility of non-consent to a relationship and/or sexual activity
- Getting hurt or feeling betrayed
- Does not change embarrassment and/or discomfort with subject
- Miscommunication can increase embarrassment and/or discomfort

8. Conclude this activity by noting how euphemisms can leave ideas too broad, unclear, and vague.

Activity 2 2 3

Instructions

1. Ask students to individually draw a chart with 2 columns and write "Having Sex" in the first column and "Doing It" in the second column (for an example, see figure 2D).
2. Ask students to individually reflect on what these terms mean to them and record their ideas in each column.

"Having Sex"	"Doing It"

Figure 2D

3. On the classroom board/flip chart create a similar chart with 2 columns and write "sexuality" in the first column and leave the second column blank for now.
4. Ask students to name aspects of sexuality and record them on the chart (for a refresher on what defines sexuality, see modules 0.1, 2.1, and 3.2).

EDUCATOR PROMPTS

- What defines sexuality?
- What are all the different components of sexuality?
- Humans can be sexual throughout their lifespan—what things shape our sexuality?
- What affects what we believe, desire, and feel comfortable with?

5. Write "consent-based sexual experiences" in the second column of the chart next to "sexuality." Ask students for examples of sexual experiences that are consent-based. What things do people who want to be sexual with each other do? How do they express their sexual feelings? Write these on the board/flip chart.

EDUCATOR ANSWER KEY

Make sure that you guide students towards thinking about more than just sexual activity. You can do this by relating the question back to some of their previous responses, making sure to touch on aspects of sexuality that go beyond the physical. For instance:

- People may express their sexual feelings through words.
- People may express their sexual feelings through their own body and/or connecting with other people's bodies.
- People may express their sexual feelings through sound.
- People may express their sexual feelings through the sharing of values within relationships.
- People may express their sexual feelings through thoughts, fantasies, and day dreaming.
- People may express their sexual feelings through touch (touching themselves and/or touching other people).
- People may express their sexual feelings in the form of poetry, music, a massage, holding hands, kissing, going on a romantic date, or having an intimate conversation.
- People may express their sexual feelings through different kinds of sexual activities such as masturbation (self-pleasure), mutual masturbation, oral sex, penis-vagina sex, anal sex, and digital penetration.

6. Review what is written on the board. Then ask students to review what they wrote on their own charts.

7. Explain that many of the ideas on the board/flip chart under the heading "consent-based sexual experiences" might be considered "doing it" or "having sex." Using 2 different symbols (such as + and ✶) ask students to indicate which of the ideas they recorded individually match up with the ideas on the board. (For an example, see figure 2E).
   - Every time a student sees an idea on the board that matches up with what they have under "having sex," they place a "+" beside that idea (on the board).
   - Every time a student sees an idea on the board that matches up with what they have under "doing it," they place a "✶" beside that idea (on the board).

Sexuality	Consent-Based Sexual Experiences
• Personal, social, mental, emotional, spiritual, and physical experiences • Expressed through attitudes, values, behaviours, practises, roles, relationships, beliefs, thoughts, fantasies, and desires • Experienced throughout the lifespan	• Sharing words, sounds, touch • Sharing thoughts and fantasies • Kissing • Massage • Holding hands • Going on a romantic date • Masturbation (self-pleasure) and mutual masturbation ++ • Oral sex ++ • Penis-vagina sex 　✗✗✗++++✗✗✗✗✗✗++++ • Anal sex +✗ • Digital penetration ++

Figure 2E

8. After everyone has had a chance to record their " + " and " ✗ " symbols on the board. Discuss with the class:
   - Where do you notice most of the " + " and " ✗ " symbols are located? Why do you think this is?
   - Did you notice places where " + " were clustered, but " ✗ " were not? Why do you think this is?
   - Do you notice anywhere where there could be discrepancies in the definitions and understandings of phrases like "having sex" and "doing it?" Why do you think that these discrepancies exist?
   - Can you see potential downsides and/or harms to using phrases that are not universally understood (like euphemisms)?

EDUCATOR ANSWER KEY

It is likely that most of the " + " and " ✶ " symbols are located beside "penis-vagina sex." Discuss the following points:

- "Having sex" and "doing it" are assumed to be universally understood as frontal intercourse involving a penis and a vagina. The reason for this is because of heterosexist assumptions about what constitutes sex (for more information, see module 3.3). In reality, the definition of sex and sexual experience varies widely between people and often shifts throughout a person's lifespan.

- Discrepancies exist in the definitions and meanings of "having sex" and "doing it" because people have different cultural, religious, social, and personal interpretations of these terms. For instance, someone who grew up in the Catholic faith may see penis-vagina intercourse as "having sex" because it is tied to social ideas of "losing virginity" but may not count anal intercourse, oral sex, and/or digital penetration as "having sex." Someone who identifies along the LGBTQ+ spectrum may not be engaging in "penis-vagina" sex but may be engaging in other types of sexual activities.

- The downsides and/or potential harms of using phrases that are not universally understood range from:
  - Misunderstandings between sexual partners
  - Miscommunication during sexual activities
  - Disappointment due to clarified assumptions and expectations around what "sex" means
  - Sexual assault (not receiving consent around particular sexual activities)
  - STBBI risk can be heightened if assumed that anal and/or oral sex does not "count" as sex and are therefore assumed not to pose a risk

QUICK TIP

The concept of virginity and "loosing your virginity" may come up in this activity. If it does come up, do not shy away from the topic as this is something that many young people are preoccupied with and likely receiving conflicting information about. "Losing your virginity" is a kind of heterosexist euphemism because it is using a word or a phrase to describe something that does not have a scientifically accurate and/or clear meaning. While it may not have a basis in science/biology, it does have meaning that is saturated with social, cultural, and gendered understandings. These social, cultural and gendered understandings are powerful and can cause anxieties (about what virginity is and is not) ranging from: What sexual activities do or do not count in terms of being classified a virgin or a non-virgin? If I have digital penetrative sex, anal, or oral sex, am I still a virgin? Will I actually lose something? If my hymen does not "break" or my "cherry does not pop" will I still be a virgin? Will there be blood and/or pain?

The pressures and consequences around "losing virginity" are different for people depending on the gender they are socialized in. For instance, people who are socialized as girls/women may worry about negative attention from "losing their virginity" whereas people who are socialized as boys/men may worry about negative attention from not "losing their virginity." The gendered stigma around "losing" or "not losing" your virginity is a reality for young people and the consequences of this stigma can be more or less severe depending on a young person's gender identity.

9. Discuss how people might be able to minimize misunderstandings around the meanings of "having sex" or "being sexual" or "being sexually active."

EDUCATOR ANSWER KEY

- Open discussion
- Asking
- Being specific in terms of language
- Talking with friends to become less self-conscious

10. Conclude this activity by noting how sometimes we limit our understanding with the words we use, such as equating "being together" or "dating" or "hooking up" with "having sex." Emphasize how varied sexual experience can be—with other people and with yourself.
11. If time allows, ask for other examples of how we might limit our ideas of being and living.

EDUCATOR ANSWER KEY

- Gender (how to be a girl/boy)
- Age (what is appropriate to do at your age)
- Fashion
- Life choices
- Various peer norms

Activity 3 [2] [3]

Instructions

1. Ask students to pair up with another student.
2. Ask each student in the pair to assign themselves as either Apple or Orange.
3. Divide the class up and ask that all Apples go to one side of the classroom and all Oranges go to the other side of the classroom.
4. Read the following scenario to the Apples.

Scenario

You were riding your bike alone late at night from a party that you don't want your parents finding out you were at, in a part of town that is unfamiliar. It is dark and past the time you said you'd be home. On your way home, you get a flat tire. You decide to ask a friend of yours who wasn't at the party, but who you know is good at fixing bikes, if they could help you figure out what to do. You know that your friend might be asleep but you call their cell phone anyway to ask them for help.

5. Instruct the Apple Student that in communicating their scenario to the Orange Student, they are not allowed to use the following words: bike, party, tire, flat.
6. Read the following scenario to the Oranges.

Scenario

Your friend at school is having trouble in science this year. You are really good at science and so your friend has been calling you a lot asking for help on homework assignments. There is a big year end project that's coming up and you're feeling stressed/anxious about completing your own project on time. You expect that your friend will probably call you to ask for help again and you are trying to figure out how to say no.

7. Instruct the Orange Student that in communicating their scenario to the Apple Student they are not allowed to use the following words: school, assignment, science, homework.
8. Once the Apples and Oranges have been given their scenario, ask students to return to their pairs and begin to act out the scenarios with the rules that they were given.
9. Allow the students to work through the scenarios for approximately 5 minutes. Use your judgment about when it is best to stop the role play (for more information on facilitating role play activities, see module 1.6).

10. In a large group, discuss:
    - How did the Apple students find the exercise? What was frustrating about not being able to use the words to describe what you needed/wanted to communicate? What assumptions did you make?
    - How did the Orange students find the exercise? What was frustrating about not being able to use the words to describe what you needed/wanted to communicate? What assumptions did you make?
    - Ask one of the Apples to read out their scenario and the words that they could not use.
    - Ask one of the Oranges to read out their scenario and the words that they could not use.
    - Ask students:
      - Now that you know what the other person was trying to communicate, how does it make you feel?
      - How do you think that kind of miscommunication could have been avoided?
      - How might "having sex" mean one thing to one person and something entirely different to someone else?
      - Do you think that there are consequences that come from miscommunications around sex and sexuality?

EDUCATOR ANSWER KEY

Allow students' experience of this activity to lead the discussion. Emphasize the following points as you bring the discussion back to how the use of unclear language around sex and sexuality can impact communication:

- Discrepancies exist in the definitions and meanings of "having sex" and "doing it" because people have different cultural, religious, social, and personal interpretations of these terms. For instance, someone who grew up in the Catholic faith may see penis-vagina sex as "having sex" because it is tied to social ideas of "losing virginity" but may not count anal sex, oral sex, and/or digital penetration as "having sex." Someone who identifies along the LGBTQ+ spectrum may not be engaging in "penis-vagina" sex but may be engaging in other types of sexual activities.
- Potential consequences to using phrases that are not universally understood range from:
  – Misunderstandings between sexual partners
  – Miscommunication during sexual activities
  – Disappointment due to clarified assumptions and expectations around what "sex" means
  – Sexual assault (not receiving consent around particular sexual activities)
  – STBBI risk can be heightened if assumed that anal and/or oral sex does not "count" as sex or pose a risk

Wrap-up

Summarize the module with the following points:

- We use euphemisms when other terms or concepts might sound harsh or be embarrassing.
- Sex and sexuality are defined broadly. "Having sex" has different meanings depending on the individual and the social/cultural context.
- Sexual euphemisms can contribute to misunderstanding and miscommunication. Direct and open communication can facilitate understanding, comfort, and connection.

2.8 SEXUALITY AND RELATIONSHIPS: LIVING YOUR VALUES

LEVEL 2 ☐ 3 ☒

Big Ideas in Module 2.8

- Values form the foundation of decision-making. Adolescence is a time of exploring and forming values and opinions that will guide the decisions you make related to sexuality, friendships, and relationships.
- Knowing your values is the first step in being able to live your values but it is not always easy to live up to your values. Courage and support can help.

Learning Objectives

Students will:

- Identify and articulate personal values about sexuality and relationships.
- Apply values to sexuality and relationship scenarios.
- Consider barriers to living up to personal values.
- Consider how to live up to personal values.

Cross-Curricular Connections

- English
- Equity Studies
- Family Studies
- Gender Studies
- Psychology
- Social Studies
- Sociology

Materials

- Flip chart, chalkboard, whiteboard, or interactive whiteboard
- Paper and markers
- Printed copies of **Values Scenarios** (version for level 2 or 3)
- **Educator Answer Key—Values Scenarios** (version for level 2 or 3)

Background Information for Educators

Learning to form opinions and to make decisions about sexuality and relationships is part of growing up. For adolescents, the media and peer norms can be particularly influential. For young people experiencing sexual and/or romantic relationships for the first time, decision-making can also be influenced by the highly emotional nature of such relationships.

Young people often have an intuitive sense of right or wrong. Articulating those senses and gut feelings can help clarify their values and enable them to better communicate their values, wants, and needs.

Student Readiness

Before students engage with this lesson, ensure that safer space guidelines and group norms have been established (and revisited) within your classroom (for more information on how to establish safer space guidelines within a classroom, see module 1.3). In order to effectively prepare for this activity, ensure students understand that:

- Values and opinions are influenced from a variety of places, including peer and family norms, as well as the media.
- It is important to clarify what your personal values are and how they relate to the values of your friends/peers and your family (for more information, see module 2.6).

Summary of Activity

Students will:

- Collectively brainstorm a list of common values that people live by.
- Walk around the room and quietly reflect on what values they consider most important.
- In small groups, work through scenarios about friendships, sexuality, and relationships and consider how values might play out in real life.

Activity 1 2 3

Instructions

1. As a class, generate a list of common values and principles that people live by. Give students a few examples to start with: respect, responsibility, honesty, equality, kindness, etc.
2. Write out each value (in large print) on a piece of paper and post the pieces of paper throughout the room.
3. Ask students to walk around the room, visit every value posted, and privately reflect on which ones they gravitate towards the most and which ones they gravitate towards the least.
4. Ask them to rank the values that they see from the most important to the least important (to them).
5. Without having to disclose their values, ask students to discuss the following question within the larger group: What is it about the values you chose that make them most important to you?
6. Distribute the **Values Scenarios** handout (the version for level 2 or 3, as appropriate).
7. Working in pairs or in small groups, have students complete the handout. Remind students to focus their answers on the scenario and not to talk about someone they know.

CYBER BULLYING, SELF-HARM, SEXUAL VIOLENCE AND COERCION. *(For more information on trigger warnings see modules 1.3 and 1.6).*

8. Reconvene as a class to discuss each scenario. *Because the scenarios contain sensitive and possibly triggering subject matter, carefully check-in with each group throughout the activity.*

9. As a class, ask students whether or not they saw similarities between the personal values each of the characters broke and their motivation for doing so. Based on the discussion, ask students to summarize some of the common reasons and circumstances that can lead people to violate their values (e.g., guilt, fear, shame, revenge, hurt, rejection, betrayal, anger). Then pose the question: What does it take to live up to our values?

EDUCATOR ANSWER KEY

- The courage to trust your instincts and take action that might go against your peer-group and social pressures to fit in.
- The courage to stand up for what you believe in and not always do what is easiest.
- Practise trusting your instincts, being courageous enough to "go against the grain" (be different).
- Knowing when and how to seek support from others.
- A willingness to make conscious decisions.
- Having access to role models and mentors who you can talk to if you are unsure about something and/or your instincts are different from your social context and peer norms.

10. Discuss: Why might we want to live up to our values? What good does that do?

EDUCATOR ANSWER KEY

- Feel empowered to take action and make decisions that feel intuitively good and make sense to you.
- Contribute to a positive self-concept and more confidence in your decisions.
- Become a role model within your peer group and contribute to changing potentially hurtful social norms.
- Discover and make new friends whose values align with yours.
- Become more authentic/true to yourself and receive support from your friends/community.

Wrap-up

Summarize the module with the following points:

- It is important to know your values.
- Your values apply to all aspects of life, including sexuality, friendships, and relationships.

CHAPTER 3

Sex, Gender, and Sexual Orientation

3.1 INTRODUCTION AND KEY TERMS

Educating students about gender identity, gender expression, and sexual orientation is a necessary and important component of comprehensive sexuality education. Comprehensive sexuality education acknowledges diverse identities related to sexuality and gender, while providing students with tools to critically analyze the ways that gender and sex are socially constructed. Gender and sex are both concepts that have been socially constructed as binary and static over time. Tools for critically examining gender norms and stereotypes, as well as binary understandings of gender and sex, are important because they can help affirm a student's lived experiences and identities, as well as provide opportunities for empowerment across all gender identities and expressions.

As educators, there is an opportunity to give students the tools to challenge **gender norms and stereotypes**, acknowledge the limitations of gender and sex as binary, and affirm and celebrate the diversity of gender identities, expressions, and sexual orientations. It should be noted that this approach to learning is something that needs to be integrated beyond sexuality education. Many of the activities found in *Beyond the Basics* and this chapter in particular can and should be taught in sociology, history, law, art, writing, and any of the social sciences, in addition to health. The Cross-Curricular Connections in each module highlight the courses that each module could apply to.

Giving students the opportunity to question gender norms and stereotypes is an important step towards rejecting assumptions and expectations related to gender and sexuality.

Gender norms are (mostly unwritten) rules, scripts, and roles prescribed by notions of masculinity and femininity that have been socially constructed and are reinforced by the dominant culture. Gender norms can limit people's ability to become fully confident and expressive human beings. An example of a gender norm is the **gender binary**. The gender binary refers to the system in which a society classifies all people into one of two categories (men and women), each with associated stereotypes and norms. Gender stereotypes are rigid beliefs about how men and women typically behave based on sexist prejudice. Gender norms and stereotypes are called out within this chapter as a building block for challenging assumptions about sexual orientation, gender identity, and gender expression.

Sexual orientation, gender identity, and gender expression can be sensitive (even controversial) topics. When facilitating sensitive topics, always keep in mind that they intimately relate to people's everyday realities and cannot be easily separated from the lived experiences of students in your classroom. It is recommended that you review chapter 1 and modules 2.1, 2.2, and 2.5 for information and tips on how to facilitate sensitive discussions with students.

Canada is a nation that has embraced democratic laws and enshrined many fundamental human rights within the *Charter of Rights and Freedoms*. To protect our human rights, the *Canadian Human Rights Act* prohibits discrimination based on sexual orientation. A bill has recently (spring 2017) been passed by the Federal government to add gender identity and gender expression to the list of prohibited grounds for discrimination. According to the *Canadian Guidelines for Sexual Health Education*,

> Inclusive and affirming supports are critical and should be provided for all youth and adults, regardless of their sexual orientation and gender identity. Providing sexual health education applicable to individual needs is one essential step in ensuring quality care and inclusive service (Public Health Agency of Canada, 2008, p. 9).

In general, Canada has seen a profound shift in attitudes and public policies related to gender and sexuality in recent decades. As a result, people with diverse gender identities, gender expressions, and sexual orientations are more likely than ever to lead healthy, happy, and fulfilling lives. Unfortunately, obstacles remain. LGBTQ+ youth as well as youth perceived to exist outside of masculine and feminine gender norms frequently face discrimination, prejudice, and violence (in all forms). Although many young people are resilient, the consequences can be devastating and tragic. Classroom sexuality education is a highly relevant and appropriate setting to address, and confront when necessary, issues of discrimination, prejudice, and violence based on gender identity, gender expression, and sexual orientation. (For more information on how to address discrimination, harassment, and bullying, see modules 1.5 and 3.11).

Gender and Sexuality: Key Terms and Definitions

YOU SHOULD KNOW

The LGBTQ+ acronym includes gender identities as well as identities related to sexual orientation. Fully spelled out the acronym contains: lesbian, gay, bisexual, transgender, and queer, with the plus indicating more identities such as asexual, intersex, pansexual, two spirit, and questioning. It is important to note that even though the LGBTQ+ acronym is used as a way to shorthand both queer and trans identities, sexual orientation and gender identity are two separate types of identities. The umbrella term "queer" does not include all identities within the LGBTQ+ acronym. People who identify as intersex, may not include themselves within the LGBTQ+ acronym.

The terms that are used to describe various aspects of gender and sexuality have evolved and will likely continue to shift over time. These are some of the current key terms and their definitions.

Gender refers to the ways that masculinity and femininity have been socially constructed and reinforced by the dominant culture through norms, scripts, and stereotypes. Gender is socially constructed as a binary (usually through classifications of woman or man), even though this is not the reality of how gender is experienced internally (gender identity) and expressed externally (gender expression).

Gender identity refers to an internal sense or awareness that all people have. For most, it can be described as a kind of "man-ness" or "woman-ness." But gender is not limited to two; it is not binary.

Gender expression is how a person publicly presents their gender. This can include behaviour and outward appearance such as how someone dresses, wears their hair, if they use make-up, their body language, and their voice.

For some people, their gender identity is consistent with their **assigned sex**. For some people, it is different. This means that some people who were assigned "male" or "female" by their doctor at birth express different gender identities later in life. Someone assigned male at birth may or may not later identify as a boy or a man, and someone assigned female at birth may or may not later identify as a girl or a woman. People whose gender identity and assigned sex are the same (e.g., someone who was assigned male at birth and identifies as a man) are called **cisgender** (cis is borrowed from chemistry, meaning same). People whose assigned sex and gender identity are different are called **transgender** (trans is borrowed from chemistry, meaning different). Transgender, like all gender identities, is internal and not something you can tell or determine in others.

Assigned sex the word assigned is used because doctors will usually determine a baby to be either male or female at birth. Doctors assign sex based on characteristics such as chromosomes and genitals. The ways that these sex characteristics can manifest in individuals' bodies is diverse and not as definite or binary as the categories of male and female suggest. Therefore, sex is not only assigned but the binary sex categories of male and female are socially constructed.

Intersex is an umbrella term used to describe people who have chromosomes, hormonal profiles, or genitals that do not typically fit into binary medical and social constructions of male and female. Biological sex, like gender, is not binary. Between 0.05% and 1.7% of people are born with intersex traits, although not everyone with intersex traits identifies as intersex (Free & Equal, 2015). It is the case that both historically and currently, intersex babies are operated on and/or assigned one of the two binary sexes at birth but these non-consensual medical interventions are being increasingly challenged. More and more advocates are now asking doctors and parents to recognize that the sex assignment of infants who present intersex characteristics (as with the gender assignment of any infant) is preliminary. This is an important development when it comes to our understanding of gender; because sex is not binary, we should be even more resistant to binary understandings of gender. (For more information on non-consensual medical interventions and human rights, see modules 2.2 and 2.3).

Trans and transgender are used as umbrella terms to describe people whose gender identity and assigned sex are different. They can be used for a range of identities and experiences; every community and individual may define trans differently. Trans is a term that someone chooses to describe their own identity. It is not something you can tell or determine in others. Some trans people choose to change their bodies (through hormones or surgical operations referred to as gender confirming surgeries) and some do not. A person does not need to pursue hormones and/or gender confirming surgeries to be transgender. Disclosure of a trans identity can bring many different social consequences, especially in schools, and should always be that individual's own decision. Same goes with disclosure of particular decisions people make in regards to transitioning, including gender confirming surgeries. These are personal decisions that no one should feel pressure to tell others about. What a person reveals about their own body and to whom is their choice, consistent with the right to privacy.

A word that was used in the past is transsexual. Transsexual is not an umbrella term and it is often considered derogatory. It is important not to use the word transsexual unless someone who identifies as transsexual has clearly and specifically asked you to.

Two spirit (or 2 spirit) is a term used by some Indigenous people to self-identify. It is an Indigenous specific term that can only be used by Indigenous people to identify themselves. While the term itself is Anishinaabe based, it has been taken up by different Indigenous nations to describe complex experiences and identities as well as cultural roles and responsibilities. Two spirit can sometimes refer to sexual orientation and at other times to gender identity, depending on the individual and/or their particular nation. It can also describe roles and responsibilities specific to different Indigenous nations that may or may not be tied to sexual orientation and/or gender identity. Like any other term that people use to self-identify, do not assume that just because someone is Indigenous and identifies as LGBTQ+, that they will use the term two spirit to identify themselves. (For more information, see 3.1 resources).

Gender creative and gender independent are terms often used to describe children who do not conform to binary constructions of gender. Children who are gender creative or gender independent may or may not grow up to identify as transgender.

Pronoun Use and Check-ins

Gender pronoun use is an important way to acknowledge and respect a person's identity. Use the pronoun(s) that a student identifies as theirs. If you forget, apologize and privately ask the student which pronoun(s) they use. A person's pronoun might be creatively constructed and may not fit into Standard English (for example, using they/them for a single person). Gender is fluid and non-binary. Part of accepting this fluidity is recognizing that your students' gender pronouns may change month to month, week to week and even day to day. While it is important to recognize and respect this fluidity, keep in mind that "change" has also been used against LGBTQ+ people to rationalize conversion therapy and accuse bisexual people of not being able to make up their mind. Conversion therapy was created on the premise of being able to change a person's sexual orientation and more specifically, "cure people of homosexuality." Although it is not widely practiced anymore, there are people who still falsely believe that being part of the LGBTQ+ community is something that should be and can be "cured." This misappropriation of change perpetuates biphobia, homophobia and transphobia.

Either at the beginning of the year (if you are a classroom teacher) or at the beginning of your lesson (if you are a community based educator) explain what a pronoun is and ask students to consider which they use. As students state their pronouns, consider writing them down on an attendance sheet to keep track. If you are a classroom teacher, consider regular pronoun check-ins. Do not assume that if a student uses a pronoun one day, that it will be the same the next. A fun way to ensure that you are using the correct pronouns and to encourage students to challenge their assumptions around the pronouns people use is to create pronoun buttons for all students to wear (and possibly change) every day. When doing pronoun check-ins, be sure to ask students to identify the exact pronouns they use (e.g., she/her and/or he/him and/or they/them or other pronouns that they have created or that other trans or gender non-binary people have created). It is common for people newly introduced to pronoun check-ins to indicate "I use female pronouns." Be clear with your students that this is not a sufficient identifier because it assumes that there are specific pronouns attached to assigned sex, when this is not the case. Pronouns refer to gender identity, not assigned sex. For instance, while someone may have been assigned female at birth, they might identify as a trans man and use the pronoun he/him.

What to do if you forget someone's pronoun and/or use the wrong pronoun?
Pause. Apologize. (Try not to over apologize). Ask what pronoun(s) the person uses. Communicate the steps you will take to avoid making the same mistake again. Finally, self-reflect and recognize that everyone makes mistakes and that making mistakes is part of being human. It is about how you respond to mistakes that matter! (For more information on how to practice allyship and how to apologize, see 1.7 resources).

Sexual orientation refers to a person's emotional, romantic, and/or physical, and/or sexual attraction to others. While sexual orientation can refer to all of these elements of attraction and human sexuality, **romantic orientation** more specifically describes the ways that people can experience romantic and emotional attractions. These may be separate from or connected to sexual and/or physical attraction. Sexual orientation and romantic orientation are not necessarily distinct identities; they are interrelated. Both are complex and attraction can manifest differently for different people. Categories are commonly used to understand our attractions, though are by no means inclusive of the vast variety of expressions that make up human sexuality.

Language about sexuality evolves constantly and deserves our continued attention and learning. Words and expressions may help us make sense of identities that people choose or may not choose. It is important to respect the "label" a person self-identifies with (if any).

Part of this respect means not assuming the term(s) that a person uses to describe their identities. Some common terms at the time of writing include: **heterosexual** or **straight** (attracted to a different gender), **lesbian** (a woman attracted to other women) and **gay** (a man attracted to other men, but can be used for all same-gender attraction). The term homosexual, which has a history of being used clinically, is outdated and carries a lot of social stigma—for this reason, it should be avoided. A person who is attracted to more than one gender may identify as **bisexual** and/or **pansexual**. People express their sexuality in a variety of ways and may prefer not to use any term or label to describe their attraction(s). Some people prefer to identify as **queer**, instead of or in addition to these other terms.

YOU SHOULD KNOW

Queer was historically used as a derogatory term for people who either were or were perceived to be LGBTQ+. In recent years, it has been reclaimed by some people within the LGBTQ+ community as a way of self-identifying and as a political statement against the oppression to which they have been subjected. With any kind of reclaimed language, it is important to use caution when using the word and this is especially the case if you are not part of the LGBTQ+ community. Refrain from using the word to describe someone else's identity, unless they have used the term "queer" to identify themselves.

Some Indigenous people use the term **two spirit**. People who are uncertain about and/or exploring their sexual orientation sometimes refer to themselves as **questioning**. Some people do not experience sexual attraction and they may identify as **asexual**. (For more information about these terms, see modules 3.3, 3.9, and 3.10).

Educator Reflection Questions

- Have you ever expressed yourself and/or been interested in things that you felt or were told you should not be because of your assigned sex and the gender you have been socialized into?
  - How were you made to feel about this? What were the reactions from those around you?
  - How did you respond to reactions from others and did their reactions influence any decision-making around your interests and/or how to express yourself?
  - How did it feel to be true to what you wanted and/or felt inside?
- Has there been any time in your life that you have felt limited and/or hampered by gender stereotypes?
  - How did this make you feel?
  - What did you do to challenge these assumptions and stereotypes directed at you?
- Everyone has a sexual orientation. Have you ever had to think about your sexual orientation? Have you ever had to "come out" about your sexual orientation?
  - If not, why do you think this is?
  - If so, how did the process of coming out feel? What kinds of supports (both inside and outside of school) do you wish were in place?

- Everyone has a gender identity. Have you ever had to think about your gender identity? Have you ever had to "come out" about your gender identity?
  - If not, why do you think this is?
  - If so, how did the process of coming out feel? What kinds of supports (both inside and outside of school) do you wish were in place?
- Think about the ways you have watched language around sexuality and gender change throughout your life. Now ask yourself:
  - Why is it important to stay informed about appropriate language use related to sexuality and gender broadly?
  - How can I stay informed and remain respectful and inclusive when discussing and teaching topics related to sexuality and gender?

Big Ideas in Chapter 3

- Gender and sex are both concepts that have been socially constructed as binary and static over time. Tools for critically examining gender norms and stereotypes, as well as binary understandings of gender and sex, are important because they can help affirm people's lived experiences and identities as well as provide opportunities to empower people of all gender identities and expressions.
- Human rights include freedom of expression of gender and sexuality as well as freedom from discrimination based on sexual orientation, gender identity, and gender expression.
- Gender identity and gender expression are distinct from sexual and romantic orientations.
- Gender identity is an internal sense of gender and cannot be assumed by the way a person looks. Gender expression is the way that gender is outwardly expressed. Gender identity cannot be assumed and/or inferred from gender expression.
- Sexual and romantic orientations are about attraction and the multiple ways that attraction can manifest (i.e., emotional, physical, intellectual, romantic, sexual, and spiritual).

3.2 SEXUALITY: IT'S MORE THAN WHAT A BODY DOES!

LEVEL 2

MEMORIES OF SEXUAL ASSAULT, HOMOPHOBIA, & TRANSPHOBIA
(for more information on trigger warnings, see modules 1.3 and 1.6)

Big Ideas in Module 3.2

- Sexuality is about more than sexual activity and bodily function; it is a complex set of personal, social, and spiritual experiences, roles, and relationships with others.
- Sexuality exists and changes throughout the lifespan.
- Having a comprehensive understanding of sexuality helps young people develop their sense of selves and promotes individual agency and responsibility.

Learning Objectives

Students will:

- Define what is meant by "sexuality."
- Identify the different facets of sexuality outside of sexual activity.

Cross-Curricular Connections

- English
- Equity Studies
- Family Studies
- Gender Studies
- Psychology
- Social Studies
- Sociology

Terminology

- Gender
- Gender expression
- Gender identity
- Gender norms
- Romantic orientation
- Sexual orientation
- Sexuality

Materials

- Chalkboard or whiteboard
- Individual papers

Background Information for Educators

Sexuality is a broad concept, it is more than sexual activity or what our body does and what we do with our bodies. It refers to a person's sexual interest in and attraction to others as well as the capacity to have erotic experiences and responses. Sexuality can be experienced and expressed in thoughts, fantasies, desires, and beliefs about sex and sexuality, attitudes towards sex and sexuality, our values, how we behave, what we do, and the roles (like gender roles) and relationships we have with others (WHO, 2006a).

Having a comprehensive understanding of sexuality beyond the narrow focus of sexual activity promotes agency and responsibility in shaping sexuality as an important part of health and life in general.

Student Readiness

Before students engage with this lesson, ensure that safer space guidelines and group norms have been established (and revisited) within your classroom (for more information on how to establish safer space guidelines within a classroom, see module 1.3). In order to effectively prepare for this activity, ensure students understand that:

- Sexuality is a big part of being human. Review the definition of **sexuality** with students as it appears in the definitions.
- Sexuality includes **gender identities, gender expressions, gender norms, sexual orientations, romantic orientations**, eroticism (what we find exciting, pleasing, etc.), pleasure, intimacy with others, and reproduction. Review definitions of terminology with students.
- The following activity may bring up uncomfortable or difficult memories or feelings. Identify who students can talk with if they need support during the lesson (guidance counsellors, teaching assistants, school social workers) or after the lesson (a counsellor, you, other supports in their lives). Place relevant phone numbers and websites from the National Support Services resource on the board. (For more information on trigger warnings and how to deal with disclosures, see modules 1.3 and 1.6).

Summary of Activities

Students will:

- Individually reflect on various aspects of sexuality.
- Individually generate themes from personal reflections.
- Collectively create a mind map based on themes.

Activity 1 2

Instructions

1. On the board, list what can influence a person's sexuality. Encourage students to add to the list. Give students permission to go as deeply as comfortable and remind them there is no requirement to share any personal stories or experiences.
2. Have students close their eyes, put their heads down, or soften their gaze. Give the following questions one by one and ask students to think about them privately, in their minds. All of the questions refer to families and/or environments in which they have been raised:
   - What words, if any, did you use for genitals when you were little?

- How did people show their affection?
- What were the values about nudity? Is it ok to be naked? With whom?
- Was there talk about being straight, gay, or otherwise? What messages about sexual orientation were given explicitly (was it presented as good or bad or neutral)? What messages were implied?
- Were there any differences in who does what according to their assigned sex or gender identity? What about freedom, responsibility, or expectations?
- What did you see in the news or in television shows that helped you understand sex and sexuality?

3. Ask students to open their eyes and/or raise their heads. Ask students to identify some of the themes that surfaced from their reflections and to write them down on a piece of paper. Clarify that by "themes" you mean the general topic areas (e.g., from the reflection that "my family is Catholic," the themes "Family" and "Religion/ Faith" can be identified). Assure students that their list of themes is confidential and they can choose what (not) to share.

4. Write the word "sexuality" on the board and draw a circle around it. Draw spokes radiating from this circle. Ask for themes that students identified and place appropriately on the spokes, moving from general to specific. (See figure 3A for an example).

EDUCATOR PROMPTS
- Gender identity
- Sexual orientation
- Values
- Religion
- Culture
- Age
- Ability
- Experience (including sexual trauma)
- Reproductive health
- Self-esteem
- Body shape and size
- Social skills
- How you see yourself
- How others see you
- Mental health
- Feelings
- Families

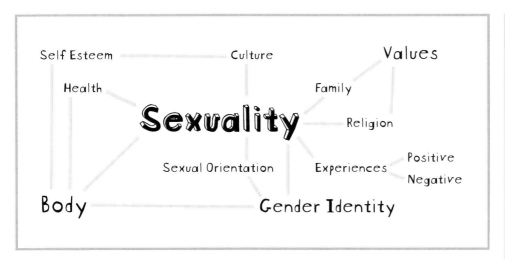

Figure 3A

5. Based on the collective mind map, discuss with students:
   a) What impact does it have if we reduce sexuality to only sexual activity?
   b) What can influence how we understand sexuality?
   c) Based on our broad understanding of sexuality, where do personal choice and responsibility come into play?
   d) What aspects of sexuality change over time?

EDUCATOR ANSWER KEY

a)

- It does not address the relationships we are a part of and how we relate to others.
- It does not address issues of power imbalances, of interpersonal or sexual violence.
- It does not make room to talk about what influences how we think about sex.
- Sexual activity may not always reflect who you are attracted to or how you identify.
- Sexual expression does not necessarily mean you are choosing to have sexual relations with a partner. Either alone or with a partner, there are many ways to explore and express sexual drives and desire.
- Whether people are currently sexually active or not, understanding our sexual preferences and desires and how our own body and heart work are keys to sexual and relationship satisfaction.

CONT'D NEXT PAGE

EDUCATOR ANSWER KEY CONT'D

b)
- How we are raised
- The messages we get through the media, television, movies, our friends, etc.
- Our faith or our family's faith
- Our own experiences (positive or negative)
- Our values
- Who we are in relationships with
- Our sexuality education

c)
- How we engage with the information we get—are we exercising critical thinking? Are we questioning our assumptions about sexuality?
- If or when we seek information if we are unsure of something
- How we talk about sexuality with our friends (and either challenge or perpetuate some stereotypes, use slurs or not, etc.)
- How we relate to others, in friendships or romantic relationships
- If we seek consent from others, if we respect boundaries

- Bystander intervention (e.g., the responsibility that bystanders witnessing sexual assault, harassment, bullying, and discrimination have to intervene and stop a situation from escalating)
- In our communication with others
- How we interrogate what we know or the messages we have received or continue to receive around sexuality

d)
All of them can
(Some other possible answers to explore with students)
- Gender identity (e.g., transitioning or feeling affirmed in their gender)
- Sexual orientation (e.g., coming to terms with who they are attracted to, may or may not be fluid throughout their lives)
- Who we are attracted to and/or who we want to be in relationships with
- Bodies (as we grow older, as we change, if someone becomes disabled, if we are sick or not, etc.)
- Relationships
- Family structures
- How we interpret our experiences as we develop critical thinking skills, get more information, gather more experience, etc.

Wrap-Up

Summarize the module with the following points:

- Sexuality is not just about sexual activity; it encompasses many different aspects of life across the lifespan.
- All aspects of sexuality change over time.
- Everyone has responsibilities and agency when exploring the various aspects of sexuality.

3.3 SEXUAL AND ROMANTIC ORIENTATIONS: IDENTITIES AND TERMINOLOGIES

LEVEL 2 [3]

Big Ideas in Module 3.3

- Everyone has a sexual orientation and a romantic orientation.
- There are many different words used to describe the sexual and romantic orientations that exist. These words change over time and the possibilities of how people might self-identify are infinite.
- Sexuality is complex and attraction can manifest very differently from person to person. Categories are commonly used to understand our attractions, though are by no means inclusive of the vast variety of expressions that make up human sexuality.

Learning Objectives

Students will:

- Explore different terminology used to describe sexual and romantic orientations.
- Explore the concept of "self-identifying."
- Critically consider why terms might or might not be useful.

Materials

- Chalkboard, whiteboard, or large sheet of paper
- Printed copies of **Sexual and Romantic Orientation Terminology**
- Printed copies of **Sexual and Romantic Orientation Definitions**
- **Educator Answer Key—Sex, Gender and Sexual Orientation Key Terms and Definitions**
- Scissors

Cross-Curricular Connections

- English
- Equity Studies
- Family Studies
- Gender Studies
- Psychology
- Social Studies
- Sociology

Terminology

- Aromantic
- Asexual or Ace
- Bicurious
- Biphobia
- Bisexual or Bi
- Closeted
- Coming out
- Demiromantic
- Demisexual
- Gay
- Gender identity
- Gray-asexual
- Gray-romantic
- Heterosexism
- Heterosexual
- Homophobia
- Homosexual
- Lesbian
- LGBTQ+

- Monoromantic
- Monosexism: Outing (someone)
- Monosexual
- Pansexual
- Polyamorous
- Polyromantic
- Polysexual
- Queer
- Queer platonic or QP
- Questioning
- Romantic orientation
- Sexual expression
- Sexual orientation
- Sexuality
- Two spirit

Background Information for Educators

Sexual and romantic orientations are a part of sexuality. **Sexual orientation** refers to a person's emotional, romantic, physical, and/or sexual attraction to others. While sexual orientation can refer to all of these elements of attraction and human sexuality, **romantic orientation** more specifically describes the ways that people can experience romantic and emotional attractions. These may be separate from, or connected to, sexual and/or physical attraction. Sexual orientation and romantic orientation are not necessarily distinct identities; they are interrelated. While one person may experience sexual, romantic, emotional, and physical attraction as one kind of attraction, another person may experience sexual attraction as distinct from romantic attraction. For instance, someone may identify as **bisexual** and as **aromantic**. This means that they could fall in love and/or be sexually attracted to multiple genders but that they do not experience romantic attraction to any gender.

Sexual expression is different from sexual orientation and romantic orientation because it does not refer to an identity. Sexual expression refers to the variety of ways that someone's sexuality can be expressed, including emotional, romantic, physical, and spiritual dimensions of sexual expression. It also encompasses the ways that people's sexuality may not fit into clear labels. For instance, someone who identifies as heterosexual might prefer to express their sexuality in ways that could be considered **queer**. Sexual expression encompasses everything from the kinds of sexual activities that people like to participate in, to the ways that romantic attraction is (or is not) expressed.

Labels are generalizations that exist on a continuum of needs, desires, interests, and attractions that may not explain or represent everyone who identifies with the particular label. They are often used to broadly categorize types of attraction. For example, when someone is generally attracted to people of a different gender, they may identify themselves as straight or heterosexual; when someone is generally attracted to people of the same gender, they may identify themselves as gay or lesbian. Regardless of what you might observe of others' behaviours, it is important to pay attention to how people identify themselves and to be respectful of these identities. For example, some people who identify as heterosexual may engage in sexual subcultures (e.g., BDSM) and because of this identify, as queer. Part of being respectful is learning when and how it is appropriate to use labels and language that someone else has identified with. This learning involves staying current and knowing the history of language, especially if it is reclaimed (for more information, see module 1.4). It also involves reflection on your own identities and considering whether or not you are able to use language that is specific to a particular community.

YOU SHOULD KNOW

Queer is reclaimed language that is used as an umbrella term for many sexual orientations. Some people also identify with the term to refer to a romantic orientation outside of normative definitions of romantic attraction (i.e., someone who identifies as heterosexual and aromantic, might identify as queer).

Even though **gender identity** is distinct from sexual orientation (for more information, see modules 3.1, 3.8, 3.9, and 3.10), terms used to describe gender identity and sexual orientation can often be lumped together. Some terms in this module (like **coming out**) can refer to both. Terms (or labels) are also constantly changing and being added to; the terminology and definitions provided in *Beyond the Basics* are not an exhaustive list. Your students are likely to have some of the most current information, although it may not always be accurate. If you do not know or have not heard of a term that a student is using, give

YOU SHOULD KNOW

"Coming out" is a figure of speech often used to describe a person's disclosure of their sexual orientation and/or gender identity. It is commonly misunderstood as a one-time event but is actually a lifelong and sometimes daily process. Heterosexual and cisgender people rarely have to go through the process of coming out because their sexual orientation and/or gender identity is generally assumed to be the norm.

your student the benefit of the doubt and then do your research. Come back to the student and/or the class with your research. (For ideas of where to find up-to-date information, see the chapter 3 resources and the Online Hub).

Finally, people's sexual and romantic orientations may (or may not) change or be fluid throughout their lives. Fluidity in terms of sexual and romantic orientations occurs from within (it cannot be imposed), with sexual and romantic identity possibly changing and/or expanding over time. That sexual and romantic orientation is not always static might be challenging for students to understand. One way to present the idea of fluidity is to say that while we can be born into our sexual orientation, we can still show variations in desire, wants, needs, or identity over our lifetime. The amount of variation can be different from person to person. While some people may find it very empowering to view their sexual orientation as something that they were born with, others find it more empowering to view their sexual orientation as a choice. There is no one right answer. It is important not to assume how someone views their sexual orientation. (For more information on the fluidity and exploration of sexual orientation and romantic orientation see the **Sexuality Galaxy** in module 3.9).

Student Readiness

Before students engage with this lesson, ensure that safer space guidelines and group norms have been established (and revisited) within your classroom (for more information on how to establish safer space guidelines within a classroom, see module 1.3). In order to effectively prepare for this activity, ensure students understand:

- That **sexuality** is not just what our body does. Review the definition of sexuality with students.
- That one component of sexuality is **sexual orientation** and **romantic orientation**.
- The definition of sexual orientation.
- The definition of romantic orientation.
- That gender identity and expression are distinct from sexual and romantic orientations.
- That people choose labels and identities to describe their sexual and romantic orientations for a wide variety of reasons. These labels and identities cannot be imposed from the outside. When it comes to sexual and romantic orientations, there are different terms that can help us build a wider understanding of the terms people may feel best suit, fit, capture, sum up, or empower them.

QUICK TIP

If any terms come up that you are concerned might be derogatory and/or reclaimed language, refer to modules 1.1 and 1.4. To find out more about words used within LGBTQ+ cultures in Canada, refer to 3.3 resources and the Online Hub.

Summary of Activities

Students will:

- Individually, or as a group, pair important terms related to sexual and romantic orientations with definitions.
- Discuss responses with the larger group.

Activity 1 2 3

Instructions

1. Split students up into smaller groups (between 2 to 4).
2. Print and cut up the definitions contained on the handout **Sexual and Romantic Orientation Definitions** (print enough so that there's one set for each group).
3. Have a large sheet of paper or a board ready with all the terms lined up (without definitions). (The terms can be found in the **Educator Answer Key—Sex, Gender and Sexual Orientation Key Terms and Definitions**).
4. Students are given the **Sexual and Romantic Orientation Definitions** as a pile of cut-out definitions they need to assign to each term.
5. Working in their smaller groups, have students discuss terms and definitions and pair up definitions with the appropriate terms. (Bonus points for anyone who can identify whether the term refers to a romantic orientation, a sexual orientation, both or neither). *If students want to work individually, print copies of the Sexual and Romantic Orientation Definitions for each student and place all of the terms on a large sheet of paper or board. Referencing the terms on the board, students write the terms directly on their handout next to the appropriate definitions. Answers can be taken-up and discussed as an entire class.*
6. Have students report back on the pairings. Discuss if there was any confusion between some of the definitions.
7. Ask students if they have any important terms that they feel were missing from the activity and would like to add. Explain that this list of terms is not an exhaustive list and that appropriate language changes over time. Provide students with the list of resources from this module and explain that these websites will help keep their information up-to-date as well as offer more information about sexual and romantic orientations. (For the most up-to-date information about terminology, visit the Online Hub).

Wrap-Up

Summarize the module with the following points:

- Everyone has a sexual orientation and romantic orientation.
- Sexual and romantic orientations can be fluid and change throughout the lifespan.
- Terms (labels) used to describe identity are constantly changing; stay up-to-date and respect the terms that people use to identify themselves.

3.4 EDUCATOR RESOURCE: GENDER NORMS AND GENDER STEREOTYPES

The difference between norms and stereotypes can be confusing but it is important to understand how the terms overlap and impact people differently. The following modules (3.4, 3.5, 3.6, 3.7, and 3.8) focus on norms and stereotypes because they have particular consequences for developing healthy sexualities and improving sexual health outcomes.

Challenging gender norms and thinking critically about the kinds of stereotypes we uphold is integral to ensuring that people of all genders develop the communication and negotiation skills to develop pleasurable, and healthy sexualities that reflect who they are, what they desire, and how they develop respect and intimacy with partners (sexual, romantic, or otherwise).

Gender Norms: Masculinities and Femininities

Gender norms are a set of expectations, rules, and scripts that are culturally specific and inform what is considered "normal" within a culture. While gender norms vary across cultures and nations around the world (even within what is commonly referred to as the "Western world"), they are commonly grouped into norms around masculinity and femininity. Often in the Western world, femininity and feminine norms are rigidly applied to people perceived as women/girls and masculinity and masculine norms to people perceived as men/boys.

Gender norms like these can be harmful to people of all gender identities and expressions. Emotional and social caretaking is a quality labelled as feminine and applied to those perceived to be women/girls. A girl or woman may feel pressure to be an emotional caretaker to friends and/or family even if this is not a part of her personality. The pressure to conform can create resentment and uncertainty around needs and boundaries related to caretaking. Similarly, a boy or man who is expected to be aggressive, uncaring, and non-communicative about his feelings (based on gender norms of masculinity) may be forced to hide and/or feel ashamed about having qualities associated with femininity.

While both can have negative consequences for boys/men and girls/women, when a girl or woman demonstrates masculine characteristics (for instance a girl/woman who is seen as "tough"), she is more likely to be accepted by society at large than a boy/man who displays feminine characteristics (for instance, a boy/man who is seen as a "sissy"). This de-valuing of feminine characteristics is what leads to **sexism**,

YOU SHOULD KNOW

This is a general analysis of systemic oppression (sexism particularly) that uses an individual example. In general, anyone who deviates from gender norms is viewed or treated negatively compared to those who fit into gender norms. There are different consequences for deviating from gender norms depending on a number of intersecting factors, including assigned sex, race, ability, and class. You may have examples in your life where you witnessed and/or experienced consequences of deviating from gender norms that changed depending on context and which norms were deviated.

---

transmisogyny, and **femmephobia**. Gender norms also have significant impacts for people who do not conform to the gender binary of man/woman and/or who identify as **trans/transgender**. The rigidity of these norms is part of what leads to transphobia. That someone could transgress, flow, and/or move between these norms is seen as wrong. This is part of what leads to hate, fear, **prejudice, discrimination**, and **oppression**.

Gender Stereotypes

A **stereotype** is a belief or assumption about the characteristics of different groups or types of people. It is a generalization about a large and diverse group of people. A **gender stereotype** is a rigid belief about how men/boys and women/girls, or entire groups of people, typically behave or should behave. Sometimes people use gender stereotypes (and stereotypes in general) as a way to make sense of something that they do not understand but stereotypes are limiting and cause harm across all gender identities. The harm and the severity of impact might look different across gender identities (and other social locations/life experiences) but is harmful nonetheless.

Stereotypes are packed full of assumptions that can lead to misunderstanding, prejudice, and discrimination (for more information, see module 1.1). Modules 3.5 and 3.6 will help students become aware of how stereotypes shape perceptions of themselves and others and how these stereotypes can influence interpersonal relationships. Critical awareness is an important step in resisting such stereotypes and in developing mutual respect among peers, partners, teachers, family etc.

Gender stereotypes are influenced by gender norms and assume that an entire gender grouping is or will do X (e.g., girls cannot play sports and only like shopping). But unlike norms, stereotypes are not expectations of what is normal, they are thought to be facts and treated as such. Where gender norms form the basis of gender discrimination, gender stereotypes are discriminatory (Monda, n.d.).

Educator Reflection Questions

- In what ways have you fit into gender norms? Has this changed throughout your life?
  - Think about times that you have fit into gender norms. How did you feel?
- In what ways have you not fit into gender norms? Has this changed throughout your life?
  - Think about times that you have not fit into gender norms. How did you feel?
- Have you ever thought about masculinity and/or femininity before? If so, have you thought about these concepts in relationship to yourself or others? Have you seen or experienced the ways each can be limiting? Why or why not?
- Can you think of any other social and cultural norms that are present in your life? How do these affect you?
- Have you been subject to any kind of stereotyping? How did this make you feel?
- Have you noticed the ways that gender stereotypes affect you? Have these stereotypes been positive or negative?
  - How did the positive stereotypes make you feel? How did the negative stereotypes make you feel?
  - Were there similarities and/or differences in these feelings?
- Have you ever rejected and/or challenged gender norms and/or stereotypes in your life? Have you done so outwardly and/or inwardly?
  - What did this look like? How did it feel to reject and/or challenge stereotypes? Were there consequences to this?
  - Can you think of people in your life that have rejected gender norms and/or challenged gender stereotypes? What were the consequences that these folks experienced? How so?

3.5 GENDER NORMS: MASCULINITIES AND FEMININITIES

LEVEL 2 **3**

Big Ideas in Module 3.5

- Rigid ideas and norms about masculinity and femininity limit everyone's ability to be fully themselves.
- Masculinity and femininity are fluid and are not necessarily attached to gender identities.
- Some people may conform to gender norms some of the time but gender norms do not capture everyone's experience all of the time.

Learning Objectives

Students will:
- Develop a critical understanding of gender norms.
- Develop strategies for challenging gender norms.

Cross-Curricular Connections
- English
- Equity Studies
- Family Studies
- Gender Studies
- Psychology
- Social Studies
- Sociology

Terminology
- Gender
- Gender binary
- Gender expression
- Gender identity
- Gender norms
- Gender stereotypes

Materials
- Paper
- Writing utensils
- 3 buckets (or boxes)
- Large printout or drawing of figure 3B

Background Information for Educators

Gender norms can limit the ability to become fully confident and expressive human beings. They refer to the mostly unwritten rules, scripts, and roles prescribed by societal notions of masculinity and femininity, including the notion of a **gender binary**, that have been socially constructed and are reinforced by the dominant culture.

While there is variation from culture to culture and nation to nation throughout the world and even within what is commonly referred to as "the Western world," gender norms can be commonly grouped into norms around masculinity and femininity. In the Western world, femininity and feminine characteristics are often rigidly applied to those perceived to be girls/women; whereas, masculinity and masculine characteristics are often rigidly applied to boys/men.

We see this play out in everyday contexts. When boys are more strongly encouraged to play sports, girls increasingly sit out in gym class. When boys are told they are not as studious as girls, they are more likely to place less effort into their schoolwork. As young people develop, this can intensify and deeply affect self-confidence and self-worth and skew a person's overall sense of self. Boys may suppress their abilities to express themselves emotionally or compromise their nurturing qualities or ability to ask for support because these characteristics are considered feminine and therefore not appropriate for boys. Girls may suppress their abilities to advocate for themselves or set firm boundaries because these characteristics are considered masculine and therefore not appropriate for girls.

Gender norms can negatively impact relationships in general and sexual and reproductive health in particular. A young woman who has expectations of herself as sexually passive may put herself at risk for unintended pregnancy or sexually transmitted infection if she feels out of place asking her partner to use a condom. A young man may feel that he should continuously pressure his partner to have sex because that is how he believes a "real man" should act, even if his partner has repeatedly refused. Failing to question or challenge these gender norms can lead to serious consequences, in the cases above, increased risk of unintended pregnancy, sexually transmitted infection, sexual assault, and intimate partner violence. (For more information, see modules 7.5, 7.7, 8.2, 8.3, 8.4, 9.4, and 10.4).

Student Readiness

Before students engage with this lesson, ensure that safer space guidelines and group norms have been established (and revisited) within your classroom (for more information on how to establish safer space guidelines within a classroom, see module 1.3). In order to effectively prepare for this activity, ensure students understand:

- That gender norms are particular to time, place, and culture; they are always changing.
- The differences and overlaps between the terms **gender, gender identity, gender expression, gender norms,** and **gender stereotypes.** (For more information, see modules 3.1 and 3.4).
- A working definition of what a gender norm is.

Summary of Activities

Students will:

- Individually and anonymously brainstorm ideas about masculinity and femininity and decide which box masculine characteristics go into and which box feminine characteristics go into.
- Collectively come to an agreement about where to place masculine and feminine characteristics on a diagram.
- Collectively discuss any disagreements and critically engage with why disagreement might exist based on discussion prompts.
- Collectively challenge gender norms.

Activity 1 2 3

Instructions

1. Provide two buckets (or boxes—a container in which you can place the pieces of paper) and label one bucket: FEMININE and the other: MASCULINE.
2. Ask students to write down examples of what femininity and masculinity mean to them. Ask them to write down as many examples as they can think of on separate pieces of paper. You can prompt them with questions like:
   - What does femininity/masculinity look like?
   - What does femininity/masculinity feel like?
   - An example of femininity/masculinity is _____.
3. When your students are done brainstorming, ask them to place the "masculine" characteristics in the MASCULINE bucket and the feminine characteristics in the FEMININE bucket.
4. Remove the labels from the buckets and pour all papers into a third bucket and mix. *Notice reactions from the students (we will revisit these reactions later).*
5. Place the drawing or large printout of figure 3B on the blackboard.

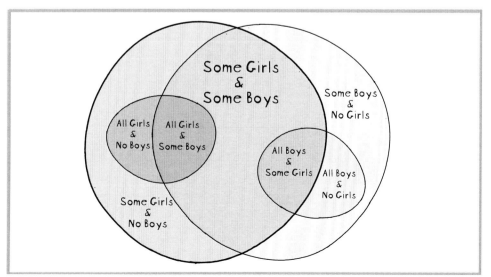

Figure 3B

6. Pull the papers from the third bucket one by one.
7. Read each statement out loud and ask your students to determine where on the diagram each characteristic belongs. If there is disagreement, discuss it. Ask students what they see in the world, what they feel is true, and what they can know for certain (very little—if any exception exists, you cannot put something into "all" or "none" areas. You can write these onto the map or attach the papers directly onto it with tape).
8. Struggles around placing characteristics into the "feminine" and "masculine" box will lead to the following discussion questions.

Discussion Questions/Prompts

a) Did you feel limited with the "masculine" and "feminine" buckets? What happened to characteristics we wanted to place in both?
b) What did you find challenging and/or surprising when trying to place the ideas about femininity and masculinity onto the BOY/GIRL image?
c) Why do you think norms exist if they are sometimes false or feel restrictive? How might gender norms affect what we do and what we think of ourselves, even when some of them ring true for us?
d) How did it feel when the two buckets were combined? What does it feel like when we challenge or take apart gender norms?
e) How can we challenge gender norms? *Prompt for things we can do ourselves and how we behave when other people challenge gender norms.*
f) Ask students to consider and share what gender norms they would like to challenge. Have they? If so, was it hard? If not, what are the hardest gender norms to challenge and why?

EDUCATOR ANSWER KEY

a) It is not necessary to restrict what we think of as feminine and what we think of as masculine, especially when the majority of people have a combination of both "feminine" and "masculine" characteristics.
b) Characteristics of "masculinity" did not necessarily fit onto the "BOY" areas of the circle and characteristics of "femininity" did not necessarily fit onto the "GIRL" areas of the circle.

c) Acknowledge that gender norms can limit all of us from being fully ourselves. Acknowledge that some gender norms of femininity and masculinity might feel true to us in some ways but can still be limiting as we have a diversity of identities, ways of expressing ourselves, and a diverse personality. We are also constantly changing as we age, as we move, and as our social communities and social cultures change and grow.

CONT'D NEXT PAGE

EDUCATOR ANSWER KEY CONT'D

d) Acknowledge that it might feel both empowering and scary to challenge and take apart gender norms. Even though we might want to fight against gender norms, sometimes it can feel unnatural, scary, or wrong to do so because it is what we are used to and likely have been told from a young age that we must adhere to.

e) Explore and embrace the ways that we have both masculine and feminine characteristics.

Try wearing clothing or doing an activity not often associated with your gender identity, see how it feels and notice whether or not you feel comfortable or self-conscious.

Start to ask questions about why characters are portrayed certain ways in television and movies. When you see young cisgender women, men, and transgender characters, ask yourself if this is an accurate portrayal of what it is like to be a young cisgender woman or a young cisgender man or a transgender person.

When we witness someone else challenging a gender norm, we can support them by affirming what they are doing and asking them about how we can support them further.

f) Really let these answers come from your students. If they are having trouble, you can further prompt with questions like:

Are there certain gender norms that are more strictly enforced than others?

Do you think that there are more consequences for boys/men if they challenge norms around masculinity, then if girls/women challenge norms around femininity? Why or why not?

If you feel comfortable enough to do so, this is a good opportunity to talk about how sexism and misogyny can sometimes make it harder for boys/men to challenge norms of masculinity and openly display feminine characteristics because femininity is generally less valued because of sexism and misogyny.

Wrap-up

Summarize the module with the following points:

- While gender norms fit *some* people's experiences of their gender, they do not fit for everyone all the time.
- Gender norms can limit all of us from being fully ourselves; gender norms limit everyone regardless of their gender identity.
- Recap the strategies students mentioned for challenging gender norms.

3.6 GENDER STEREOTYPES: HOW DO THEY AFFECT US?

LEVEL 2 [3]

The main activity in this module is suitable for Level 2. If you have a group of students that is in the Level 3 category and/or is a very mature Level 2, there is an optional warm-up and cool-down activity that will help make the entire module more relevant for older/mature students.

Big Ideas in Module 3.6

- Stereotypes reduce people into categories that are limiting and harmful.
- Even if a stereotype seems positive, the impact of the stereotype is still limiting and can cause harm.
- Gender stereotypes limit everyone's ability to be fully themselves.

Learning Objectives

Students will:
- Critically consider how gender stereotyping affects people of all gender identities.
- Make the links between different forms of stereotyping and strategize ways to avoid using stereotypes of all kinds.
- Learn how to challenge gender stereotypes.

Cross-Curricular Connections
- English
- Equity Studies
- Family Studies
- Gender Studies
- Psychology
- Social Studies
- Sociology

Terminology
- Gender norms
- Gender stereotypes
- Stereotypes

Materials
- Large open space to move around
- Paper
- Writing utensils

Background Information for Educators

A **stereotype** is a belief or assumption about the characteristics of different groups or types of people. A **gender stereotype** is a rigid belief about how men and women, or entire groups of people, typically behave or should behave based on their gender identity. Often, people use stereotypes because they sometimes make things simpler or easier to understand if unknown but stereotypes reduce people into categories that are limiting and harmful.

Students should become aware of how stereotypes shape their perceptions of themselves and of others. Doing so will help them navigate their assumptions and expectations when building interpersonal relationships. Ultimately, critical awareness and reflection are important steps in resisting stereotypes and in developing fair and mutually respectful relationships.

Student Readiness

Before students engage with this lesson, ensure that safer space guidelines and group norms have been established (and revisited) within your classroom (for more information on how to establish safer space guidelines within a classroom, see module 1.3). In order to effectively prepare for this activity, ensure students understand that:

- Gender norms and gender stereotypes are different concepts that work in concert to limit everyone's experience of who they are, who they could be, and how they experience gender. *Review the differences between gender norms and gender stereotypes using the terminology definitions.*
- Stereotyping is not limited to gender and affects many different kinds of social groupings.

Summary of Activities

Students will:

- Explore the differences and overlaps between gender norms and gender stereotypes by placing themselves around the room.
- Move around the room to experience the various effects and dynamics of stereotyping using fictional examples.
- Collectively discuss the ramifications of these effects and strategize to avoid stereotypes.
- Silently integrate and reflect on how stereotyping is personally experienced.

Optional: Warm-Up Activity 3

The optional warm-up activity will help give you a sense of where students' thinking is regarding gender norms and stereotypes; the optional cool-down activity gives you more of a sense of how students may be experiencing stereotypes and the impact that stereotypes have on them personally.

Warm-Up Activity 3

Instructions

1. Designate one side of the room as "gender stereotype," the other side as "gender norm," and the middle as "unsure."
2. Read the following statements one at a time. After each statement is read, instruct students to move to the place in the room that most accurately captures the statement. Reiterate that it is okay to be unsure and that these concepts are challenging to decipher.
3. Ensure students know that they do not have to share the reason why they chose where to place themselves unless they want to.
4. After each statement is read and everyone has moved to a spot in the room, you can ask students from each area to volunteer whether or not they want to share why they placed themselves there.

Statements

a) All boys/men like to play sports.
b) All girls/women like to wear dresses.
c) Showing affection is a strictly feminine quality and therefore, only girls/women should show affection.
d) Being tough and strong is a strictly masculine quality and therefore, only boys/men should be tough and strong.
e) All girls/women like to cook.
f) All boys/men like cars.
g) Being emotional and sensitive is a strictly feminine quality and therefore, only girls/women should be emotional and sensitive.
h) Engaging in physical labour is a strictly masculine quality and therefore, only boys/men should be engaged in physically laborious work.
i) Boys/men don't cry.
j) Girls/women don't fart.

QUICK TIP

Make sure students know that this is not an opportunity to debate. It is an opportunity to hear and discuss different perspectives and opinions and reasons why students have chosen the placement they have.

EDUCATOR ANSWER KEY

Ensure your students understand that there is value behind their reasoning for being in different locations in the room, even if they did not get the answer right. Reiterate that the differences between a gender norm and a gender stereotype are sometimes blurry and thinking through these differences is part of learning how to challenge gender norms and stereotypes. The differences can be succinctly described as: stereotypes are presented as fact, whereas norms are presented as expectations. Below are answers that specifically speak to the differences between gender norms and gender stereotypes.

a) **Stereotype:** because it is a statement that is presented as a fact about an entire social grouping of people. The gender norm that informs this stereotype is that liking to play sports is a masculine trait and therefore, all boys/men *should* like to play sports.

b) **Stereotype:** because it is a statement that is presented as a fact about an entire social grouping of people. The gender norm that informs this stereotype is that liking to wear dresses is a feminine trait and therefore, all girls/women *should* like to wear dresses.

c) **Norm:** because showing affection is applied to femininity as an expectation and then applied to girls/women.

d) **Norm:** because being tough and strong is applied to masculinity as an expectation and then applied to boys/men.

e) **Stereotype:** because it is a statement that is presented as a fact about an entire social grouping of people. The gender norm that informs this stereotype is that liking to cook is a feminine trait and therefore, all girls/women should like to cook.

f) **Stereotype:** because it is a statement that is presented as a fact about an entire social grouping of people. The gender norm that informs this stereotype is that liking cars (and other machines that move fast) is a masculine trait and therefore, all boys/men should like cars.

g) **Norm:** because being emotional and sensitive is applied to femininity as an expectation and then applied to girls/women.

h) **Norm:** because engaging in physical labour is applied to masculinity as an expectation and then applied to boys/men.

i) **Stereotype:** because it is a statement that is presented as a fact about an entire social grouping of people. The gender norm that informs this stereotype is that being emotionally stoic is a masculine trait and therefore, all boys/men do not (or should not) cry.

j) **Stereotype:** because it is a statement that is presented as a fact about an entire social grouping of people. The gender norm that informs this stereotype is that being dainty, delicate, and/or "proper" is a feminine trait and therefore, all girls/women do not (or should not) fart.

Activity 1 2

Instructions

As you move through the instructions and begin the activity, ask students to pay attention to how they are feeling and what they are thinking. They will be encouraged to share these reflections after.

1. Clear the room so students have space to move around.
2. Establish two opposite sides of the room or two corners and identify them as different "planets."
3. From the list below pick 4 to 6 pairs of words. Pick some from each level (A and B) to use during the activity.

Level A	Level B
Tall planet/Short planet	Green planet/Purple planet
Blue planet/Pink planet	Square planet/Round planet
Dog planet/Cat planet	Selfish planet/Greedy planet
Summer planet/Winter planet	Boring planet/Annoying planet
Ice planet/Fire planet	XYZ planet/ABC planet
Sporty planet/Artsy planet	Intellectual planet/Emotional planet

4. Read a pair of planets to your students, designating one side of the room as one planet and the opposite side as the other planet. Ask them to choose a planet out of the two—the one that describes them best—and move to that part of the room. *Level A categories may be easy to pick from. Level B categories are meant to cause some conflict and to be harder to choose from. Expect students to struggle when they choose. Encourage them to notice and remember what this struggle feels like and continue with the activity. These feelings will be important in the discussion after.*
5. Once students have divided themselves, announce to each side of the room and say: "I pronounce you the people of the ____ planet. You are all the same."
6. Ask students from one planet to describe in a few words what the people on the other planet are like and vice-versa. It can be silly. For example, "people from the tall planet can easily reach things and bump their heads all the time" and "people from the short planet have to talk louder to get heard and they are always more comfortable in airplane seats."
7. Then move to the next pair of words. Designate which side of the room is which planet and get students to rearrange according to the new planets. Continue down the list until you have moved through the ones you want to, or you see the students' attention begin to wane.

8. Ask students to gather (seated or standing) and discuss what kinds of feelings the activity brought up for them. Ask students to consider different parts of the experience, including: choosing a planet, hearing the pronouncement, being seen as part of the group, being called something that did not feel true, etc. Notice sentiments like, "why should I have to choose?" Explore this within the game and then ask them to reflect on where they might have seen or experienced this in real life.

EDUCATOR ANSWER KEY

- Feelings of belonging—it can be nice to belong to a group.
- Feelings of non-belonging—it can feel very lonely and disorientating when you are placed in a group of people who are understood as the same; you might feel different from them even if you seem to belong.
- Feelings of anger, frustration, being misunderstood, being unseen, being misrepresented (from having to choose between two things while feeling like neither describe you or feeling like both describe you and you do not want to be just one thing or feeling like this one thing is more important than everything else about you).
- Feelings of self-consciousness, being aware of whether you are in the "right place" or not. (If during the game you noticed students telling each other/their friends where to go, point this out. Ask students how it felt to be directed by others or to see people they know do something that does not seem true to who they are).

- Feelings of boredom, irritation, "it's a waste of time." Some of the pairs (especially level B pairs) may feel random. Students may say when hearing these planets: "Why are you making me do this?" Use this as an opportunity to point out that when people are made to choose things that are not meaningful, it can feel pointless, meaningless, and diminishing. Again, ask students to reflect on why you might have chosen seemingly meaningless categories. *Hint: the arbitrary categories, assumptions, and reductions that stereotyping both creates and reinforces can often seem meaningless to people being stereotyped because these categories do not accurately reflect their personalities and experiences.*

9. After having debriefed some initial feelings and reflections with your students, tell them that this game is called: Planet Stereotypes. Include a basic definition of stereotypes (a belief or assumption about the characteristics of different groups or types of people) to allow them to connect with the theme of the activity. Ask students to connect the activity to stereotyping in general and then gender stereotyping in particular. Ask them to reflect on and then share with the group some of their feelings and experiences during the activity

to how gender stereotypes affect people every day in the world. Given their reactions to the activity, you should be able to move into a conversation around why stereotyping in general is problematic and why gender stereotyping, specifically, is problematic.

EDUCATOR ANSWER KEY
Drawing on the conversation and answer key above...

- *Stereotyping* does not take the whole person into account and can cause people at the receiving end of the stereotype to feel lonely and out of place when placed in a group of people who are understood as the same. *Gender stereotyping* can cause people who identify as boys/men to feel stuck in gender norms of masculinity and girls/women to feel bound to gender norms of femininity even if their personality does not belong in these rigid categories.

- *Stereotyping* can lead to the assumption that one characteristic or identity defines the entirety of your being. This can lead to the person on the receiving end of the stereotype feeling angry, frustrated, misunderstood, invisible, or misrepresented. *Gender stereotyping* reinforces the gender binary of having to be either a boy/man or a girl/woman and being either masculine or feminine. Having only two choices to choose from can be very limiting if you feel like neither describes you or elements of both describe you more accurately.

- *Stereotypes* create a rigid set of categories around belonging and reduce people to one dimensional beings. *Gender stereotyping* is one example of narrowly defined categories. Reducing people's gender identities to two binary sets of behaviours and expectations creates unnecessary challenges when trying to communicate wants, needs, and desires within both friendships and intimate relationships.

✚ Optional: Cool-Down Activity 3

Before you facilitate this activity, refer back to the safer space guidelines created by the class (for more information on how to create safer space guidelines, please refer to module 1.3). Because this activity asks more personal and potentially sensitive questions, it is recommended that you read through module 1.6. Make sure students know that although everyone must be a part of the circle, they can decide whether or not they want to participate in each question. For instance, students who strongly relate to one of the statements can choose whether or not they want to disclose this by choosing not to step into the circle. In this way, students have more control over what and how much they share.

Cool-Down Activity 3

Instructions

1. Ask students to create a large circle so that everyone fits and has a place within it.

2. Pick and choose from the following statements. Read them one at a time. After each statement is read, instruct students to move into the circle if they feel that the statement resonates with them. Let them know that moving into the circle is completely optional and that they can choose how much or how little they want to move in. For instance, if a statement really resonates with someone, they may want to move all the way to the center of the circle. If a student feels slightly compelled by one of the statements, they may choose just to place one foot into the circle. If the statement does not resonate at all, then the student can stay where they are. Ask students to consider each statement carefully and move (or not) in silence to a place inside the circle that feels comfortable for them.

3. After each statement is read and everyone has moved (or not) to a spot in the circle that feels appropriate and authentic for them, ask students to quietly look around and silently consider who else has moved or not moved into the circle.

Statements

Step inside the circle if…

- You have ever experienced being stereotyped because of belonging (or perceived as belonging) to a social group.
- You are from a family that has been stereotyped because of belonging (or perceived as belonging) to a social group.
- You have felt harmed by a stereotype.
- You have felt limited by a stereotype.
- You have felt gender stereotypes do not reflect who you are (i.e., "all girls are X" or "all boys are Y)."
- You have experienced harm caused by gender stereotypes in friendships, family relationships, and/or intimate relationships.

4. End the activity by asking students what we can do to limit the damage stereotypes can cause. How can we avoid stereotyping people?

EDUCATOR ANSWER KEY

We can limit the damage stereotypes cause by becoming aware of when we use stereotypes to both think about (internally) and refer to (externally) groups of people. We can work to become aware of why we do this by asking ourselves questions like: Do I actually believe this about this entire group of people? Why or why not? Am I grouping these people together because I do not know anyone from this group and it makes it easier to think of them based on stereotypes I have heard? Am I grouping these people together because and I am afraid of them and I am looking for a way to make them less scary by grouping them into a simplified category? Am I grouping these people together because it feels like the easiest, most convenient thing to do? Becoming aware of how and why we stereotype groups of people can help to avoid stereotyping in the future and limit the damage stereotypes can cause.

Wrap-up

Summarize the module with the following points:

- Stereotypes manifest around religion, race, gender, sexual orientation, class, body types, ability, culture, and all kinds of ways in which we try to group people together.
- While we often place people into groups to better understand the social realities around us, stereotyping is problematic and can be hurtful, harmful, and/or frustrating.
- Stereotyping:
  - Limits us from being fully ourselves.
  - Makes us self-conscious and anxious about being the right thing and/or acting a certain way.
  - Makes us feel like we should try to belong in a group that does not necessarily feel like us, leaving a feeling of exclusion and inadequacy.
  - Makes us feel like a single story or detail about us erases everything else from who we are.
  - Makes us feel a lack of agency (or powerlessness) when we are assigned to a group instead of being given a chance to choose and select the group ourselves.
  - Keeps us from feeling fully known or seen, prevents us from knowing other people too.
  - Illustrates also that sometimes it is really nice to feel like we belong somewhere and sometimes stereotypes make it easier to organize people into groups.

3.7 GENDER NORMS AND STEREOTYPES: IDENTIFYING THEM IN THE MEDIA

LEVEL 2

Big Ideas in Module 3.7

- Gender norms and gender stereotypes work together to maintain gender expectations (including the gender binary), which limit everyone's ability to be fully themselves.
- Both traditional media and social media perpetuate harmful gender stereotypes. Learning how to analyze gender norms and stereotypes in the media is an important skill for building self-confidence and media literacy skills.
- The differences between gender norms and gender stereotypes can be succinctly described as: stereotypes are presented as fact, norms are presented as expectations.

Learning Objectives

Students will:

- Deepen their understanding of the concepts of gender stereotypes, gender norms, and the gender binary.
- Critically examine and reflect on how these concepts affect their everyday lives.
- Become aware of and critically evaluate common gender stereotypes in the media that they consume.

Cross-Curricular Connections	Terminology	Materials
- Art (visual, digital) - Communication Studies - English - Equity Studies - Family Studies - Gender Studies - Media Studies - Psychology - Social Studies - Sociology	- Gender binary - Gender norms - Gender stereotypes - Prejudice - Stereotypes	- Regular or interactive whiteboard - Magazines or access to online photo-sharing sites and social media platforms (like Tumblr or Instagram)

Background Information for Educators

A **stereotype** is a belief or assumption about the characteristics of different groups or types of people applied and generalized to a large, diverse group of people. This assumption or belief is often based on a combination of **prejudice** and social conditioning. A gender stereotype is a rigid belief about the personal characteristics or attributes of women or men as well as how men and women typically behave based on sexist prejudice.

The sets of "rules," expectations, and ideas that tell us how men and women *should* behave are referred to as **gender norms**. Gender norms and **gender stereotypes** help to maintain a **gender binary**. The term gender binary describes the system in which a society classifies all people into one of two categories (men/women), each with associated stereotypes and norms.

People learn gender stereotypes and norms from a variety of sources, including family, community, peers, and culture. Families are one of the key places where gender stereotypes and norms are perpetuated (or broken). Another very direct, blatant, and potentially harmful inculcation of gender stereotypes and norms occurs through traditional and social media. Becoming aware of how gender stereotypes and norms are perpetuated in the media helps student identify, manage, and resist their influence.

Student Readiness

Before students engage with this lesson, ensure that safer space guidelines and group norms have been established (and revisited) within your classroom (for more information on how to establish safer space guidelines within a classroom, see module 1.3). In order to effectively prepare for this activity, ensure students understand that:

- Gender norms and gender stereotypes are different concepts that work in concert to limit everyone's experience of who they are, who they could be, and how they experience their own gender identity.
- Review the differences between gender norms and stereotypes using the definitions.
- Stereotyping is not limited to gender; it affects many different kinds of social groupings.
- People learn stereotypes and norms from a variety of sources, including media, family, community, peers, and culture.
- Stereotypes and norms can be challenged and broken.

Summary of Activities

Students will:

- Collectively brainstorm how gender stereotypes and norms are depicted or challenged in images they find in the media (online or in magazines).
- Work in small groups to find images online and in print that both depict and challenge gender norms and gender stereotypes.
- Work in small groups to strategize how to gain more control over the media's influence on their ideas of gender.
- Discuss findings as a class with the option of turning what students have learned into a social media communications platform.

Activity 1 2

Instructions

Students can be asked in advance to provide images that they find in magazines and newspapers or online photo sharing sites and social media platforms that either depict or defy gender stereotypes and/or norms. Make available images that challenge gender stereotypes and norms in case few of those are provided by students. If you are having trouble finding images that challenge gender stereotypes and/or norms, refer to 3.7 resources. Pool all images together and redistribute them for the activity.

1. Write the words "gender stereotype" and "gender norms" on the board and ask students to define what they mean.
2. Ask students why gender stereotypes and gender norms are problematic.

EDUCATOR ANSWER KEY
- They limit our full human potential (who we can imagine ourselves being or what we can imagine ourselves doing).
- They tell us a single story about ourselves or other people, erasing all other important details of who we are and what our lives are about.
- They group people into categories that are limiting, not truthful or accurate
- They lead to misunderstanding, discrimination, and unfair treatment, especially when we do not fit into neat categories.

3. Share with the class this statement: "All gender stereotypes and norms limit people; there is no such thing as a positive stereotype or norm." Ask students what they think it means and discuss.

EDUCATOR ANSWER KEY

Explain that even when the content of the stereotype or norm seems positive (e.g., men should be masculine and therefore all men are strong, women should be feminine and therefore all women are refined), they are still limiting and reductive (e.g., men are limited from their right to be vulnerable, women from being rugged).

4. Ask students to give examples of seemingly positive stereotypes and norms then brainstorm as a group how they are in fact limiting.

EDUCATOR ANSWER KEY

- *Men are chivalrous:* It scripts how people are supposed to act when dating (e.g., guys open the door, women are reserved, men pay, etc.). It puts limits on when men are supposed/expected to be kind and respectful (i.e., with women they are interested in romantically/sexually, instead of with everyone, which would benefit their relationships overall). It signals that men are the ones who "help," never the ones who are being "helped" which can make it tougher to ask for help when men need it or make it seem like women are unable to take care of themselves.

- *Women are really good cooks:* It limits what women or men should be interested in getting good at. It signals that cooking is the domain of women. It signals who should be taking care of making food in social situations. It might make a woman who hates cooking, or is bad at it, feel inadequate, lesser, etc.

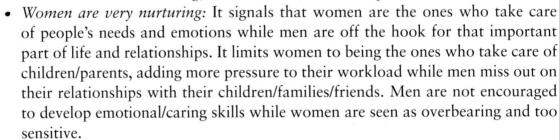

- *Women are very nurturing:* It signals that women are the ones who take care of people's needs and emotions while men are off the hook for that important part of life and relationships. It limits women to being the ones who take care of children/parents, adding more pressure to their workload while men miss out on their relationships with their children/families/friends. Men are not encouraged to develop emotional/caring skills while women are seen as overbearing and too sensitive.

- *Men are very good at technical jobs/tasks:* It discourages women from developing this set of skills. Men who are not good or not interested in these particular fields might feel incompetent. This limits what are considered valid interests/talents for men/women.

5. Divide the students into small groups and give each group access to various images of people (through magazines or online photo-sharing sites). Their task is to select examples that either depict or challenge gender stereotypes and norms.

6. Have each group report to the class on the images they have found. As each group reports, ask the class:
   a) Does the stereotype or norm depicted challenge or reflect your reality?
   b) What can you deduce about the people in the ads?
   c) Are there contradictions in the images or other ways of reading the same image?
   d) What is missing from the series of images or particular pictures? Does it capture every way to be "a woman" or "a man"?
   e) What about people who may not identify with these gender categories? Or for whom this does not fit into their idea of how they identify? How much variety do we see in the majority of the media we consume?
7. Share this statement with students: "Studies show that the more we are exposed to an image, the more it affects what we find acceptable and desirable." Reflect on this as a class and how it may relate to gender stereotypes and norms in the media. Ask the class for strategies to gain more control over what influences their own ideas of how people should look, think, and behave.

EDUCATOR ANSWER KEY

Encourage students to take the lead on answering how to gain more control as they will likely have very insightful answers that will be challenging to predict. Letting students take the lead on sharing their strategies goes a long way in providing opportunities for empowerment. If your students are having trouble coming up with their own strategies, you can provide some of the examples below:

- Find ways of filtering your own media consumption. You can do this by asking yourself: What kind of images, social media accounts, television shows, movies, magazine articles, and blog posts make me feel happy and good about myself? What media makes me feel unhappy, sad, less than and generally not good about myself?
- Create your own blog, Tumblr, Facebook group, or other social media page that challenges and critiques images that do not make you feel good about yourself.
- Unfollow people, organizations, companies, and other social media accounts that do not make you feel good.
- Start conversations with your friends about what you can do as a group to gain more control over the images and media that you consume.

8. ✦ Optional: Have each group turn what they have worked on and learned from this activity into a social media communications platform with the express messaging/goal of challenging gender norms and gender stereotypes. This part of the activity can be done through a social media platform appropriate to the message (e.g., a Tumblr account, a blog, a vlog, an Instagram account, a podcast, or a YouTube video) and can be presented back to the class at a later date.

Wrap-up

Summarize the module with the following points:
- Gender norms and stereotypes are, in part, perpetuated through the media that we consume: television, movies, music, magazines, the internet, social media, advertising.
- We can try to keep a perspective on what we see around us with the knowledge that mass media is often trying to sell us something (whether it be products or a certain image, or both).
- Gender norms, gender stereotypes, and the gender binary limit how we are able to imagine ourselves and others, instead of depicting the variety of ways we can be and want to be seen.

3.8 GENDER: IDENTITY, EXPRESSION, NORMS, AND STEREOTYPES

LEVEL 2 [3]

Big Ideas in Module 3.8

- Gender is socially constructed (as opposed to biologically fixed). It is socially constructed as a binary (only two options i.e., woman/man), even though in reality people's gender identities and gender expressions are much more fluid and complex.
- Everyone has a gender identity and gender expression; you cannot tell someone else's gender identity based on their gender expression.
- Gender norms are unfair, restrictive, and harmful to all of us, even when some of them make sense to us and reflect our experiences.

Learning Objectives

Students will:
- Understand how everyone is limited by gender norms and the gender binary.
- Understand that everyone transgresses gender norms and the gender binary to some degree.
- Understand that the ways that a person relates to and experiences gender is fluid and will change throughout their life.

Cross-Curricular Connections
- English
- Equity Studies
- Family Studies
- Gender Studies
- Psychology
- Social Studies
- Sociology

Terminology
- Coming out
- Equity
- Gender
- Gender binary
- Gender expression
- Gender identity
- Gender norms
- Marginalized
- Sexual orientation
- Social justice
- Stereotypes

Materials
- Open space large enough for all students to stand in a circle
- A copy of the **Educator Resource— Prepared Statements Related to Gender** printed, cut into strips, and put into a bucket
- 3 to 4 identical pieces of blank paper for each student
- An empty bucket or hat to hold the pieces of paper, once crumpled

Background Information for Educators

It is common to notice things that you perceive as different. "Different" is identified and understood as separate from things that are defined as "normal" by the dominant culture. When someone moves outside of what is considered "normal," we generally notice and give that transgression a name, whereas those who stay within what is considered "normal" do not get labeled. For example, when people identify as gay, they typically go through a **coming out** experience. Coming out means communicating to yourself and others your **sexual orientation** and/or **gender identity**. It is commonly misunderstood as a one-time event but is actually a lifelong and sometimes daily process. Heterosexual and cisgender people rarely have to go through the process of coming out because their sexuality and gender identity are generally assumed to be the norm.

The truth is, everyone has a gender identity and everyone has a sexual orientation—and both of these can develop and change. The conversation around **gender** and sexual identity, consequently, should include everyone. Naming what is dominant and what is **marginalized** is important. It allows students to start thinking about power imbalances and how to shift them. This is the basis of positive social change and the move towards **social justice** and **equity**.

Another important reason to open a conversation around gender identity, **gender expression**, and sexual orientation with your students is to create better self-awareness. Self-awareness allows students to start thinking about their place in the world and fosters their empathy for others.

Through this lesson and the corresponding activities, keep in mind that there is a diversity of experiences and identities in every classroom that is not always apparent. When facilitating these exercises, always keep this in mind and respect the diversity that is known and unknown.

The activities in this module encourage all students to think about the various ways that they transgress **gender norms** and **stereotypes** (consciously or unconsciously) leading to an increased understanding about how limited the **gender binary** is to everyone. The activities also help students uncover the ways in which we all have a gender identity and a gender expression through the creation of a gender profile.

YOU SHOULD KNOW

Avoid using the term normal to describe a trait or a behavior. Instead, use expressions like "more common" or "less common" as they are sufficiently descriptive without defining or reinforcing norms.

While we are referring to the gender binary of woman/man, it is important to be aware that the terms cisgender and transgender are not the only kinds of gender identities that are possible. This is important to avoid reproducing another kind of gender binary (i.e., cisgender and transgender as being the only two options).

Student Readiness

Before students engage with this lesson, ensure that safer space guidelines and group norms have been established (and revisited) within your classroom (for more information on how to establish safer space guidelines within a classroom, see module 1.3). In order to effectively prepare for this activity, ensure students understand:

- That everyone is assigned a sex at birth and that assigned sex is different from gender identity (for more information, see module 3.1).
- That gender identity is different from sexual orientation.
- What "coming out" refers to and why if everyone has a gender identity and sexual orientation, it is only people with marginalized identities and orientations that have to "come out."

Summary of Activities

Students will:

- As a large group, reflect on prepared statements about gender and silently use their bodies to step into a circle to establish "common ground."
- Individually and anonymously share ways in which they break gender norms to demonstrate the limitations of the gender binary and to normalize its transgression.

Activity 1—BASIC 1 2

The basic instructions are meant for all students in Levels 2 and 3; the advanced instructions can be facilitated at the discretion of the educator, based on the group dynamic, group cohesion, and the trust that the students have with each other and the educator. The advanced version allows students to take more risks.

Instructions

1. Read the following statements as students stand in a circle. If a statement is true for a student, ask them to step into the circle. If it is not true, ask them to remain in the outer circle. Ask students to do this exercise in silence and to pay attention to their feelings and thoughts throughout.

Statements

- I think there are specific rules for being a boy or a girl.
- I think that the rules for women and men are changing over time. For example, things are different now than in the 1950s.
- I think there are lots of similarities between boys and girls.
- I am an exception to at least one gender stereotype and/or norm.

EDUCATOR PROMPTS

- Explain what a stereotype and norm are using module 3.4 and/or the terminology definitions.
- Prompt students to think of these exceptions to gender stereotypes and norms and let them know that there will be an opportunity to share these anonymously (in Activity 2, instruction 1).

Statements Cont'd

- I have been told that I'm not feminine enough or masculine enough.
- I would feel comfortable wearing a dress.
- I would feel comfortable cutting my hair very short.
- I would feel comfortable wearing one or more earrings.
- I would feel comfortable wearing a pink sweater.
- I would feel comfortable crying in front of my friends at a sad movie.
- I would feel comfortable hugging my friends who are the same gender as me.
- I love to play sports (or a sport).
- I am a caring person.
- I like to build things.
- I am really competitive when I play games.
- I am an introvert. (Definition, if needed: introverts tend to be reserved and often take pleasure in solitary activities.)
- I have been made fun of for being "girly."
- I have been called "tomboy" before.
- I have heard of people who change their gender identity.
- I have been told to "man up".
- My gender identity is important to me.

2. Ask students how the exercise felt for them and what they noticed.

Activity 1—ADVANCED 2 3

The key to the advanced version of Activity 1 is for students to come up with and then share statements that are true for them (self-disclosure) and to see who else these statements are true for. It is a way to establish common ground. It is important that this self-disclosure is clearly stated as a ground rule of the exercise. Otherwise, "outing" or unwanted disclosures become a real risk. (For more information on establishing safer spaces and facilitating sensitive activities, see modules 1.3 and 1.6). Even with clear ground rules, outing remains a risk in this exercise. It might be worth reminding the group that offering their statement and stepping into the circle is up to them and what they want to and feel ready to share. The person offering the statement takes the first risk, establishing some safety for others to follow. If you feel comfortable and it feels appropriate, you can choose to go first by modifying one of the prepared statements that you feel is true for you (or coming up with your own).

Instructions
1. Have students stand in a circle.
2. Ask a volunteer to step into the circle and share a statement about gender that is true for them. *You can read them examples from the educator resource* **Prepared Statements Related to Gender** *to help students think of their own statement.*
3. Ask students for whom the statement is also true to join the first student by stepping into the circle. Remind students to silently acknowledge their peers standing with them in the circle. Ask them to notice their thoughts and feelings.
4. Allow other students to take turns sharing statements. Encourage the group towards deeper sharing by adding in some of the prepared statements. *If a student does not want to share a statement, ask them to pick one of the* **Prepared Statements Related to Gender** *out of a hat.*
5. Ask students how the exercise felt for them and what they noticed.

EDUCATOR ANSWER KEY (FOR BOTH THE BASIC AND ADVANCED VERSIONS OF ACTIVITY 1)

- There is a diversity of experience—not everyone had the same answers.
- The differences in answers is a kind of gender profile. If we asked 300 questions, the profiles would be even more unique. These gender profiles are unique and individual and we bring whatever label to ours we want to bring.
- These labels can be thought of as our gender identity. No one besides you knows what your gender identity is. Gender identity is not something that can be figured out/identified by someone else. Gender identity is internal. Gender expression however, is the outward expression of gender and can include body language, expressions used, physical dress/attire, the make-up you choose or do not choose to wear, etc. Gender expression and gender identity can change and be fluid throughout a person's life.

Activity 2

Instructions

1. Have students write down a typical "boy" and "girl" stereotype and norm about masculinity and femininity that they break and/or challenge onto anonymous slips of paper. For anonymity, instruct everyone to write something or draw something, crumple the paper, and put it into a bucket (without their name). *Recall what students came up with in Activity 1 and invite them to add more.*

 At another time or during the next class, read these aloud or compile and display them creatively. *If you cannot think of any, you can use and/or modify ones from the **Prepared Statements Related to Gender**.* For anonymity, take everyone's hand written responses and compile in your own writing, or on your computer. *Ensure that no one sees the handwriting on the papers, and destroy them afterwards. Add to the list yourself if there are too few responses.*

2. Remove/exclude papers that would identify a student specifically.
3. Engage students in a discussion using the following prompts:
   a) What is your reaction hearing these? Were you surprised? Were they expected?
   b) Why are there strict rules/norms around gender if most of us break and/or challenge them?
   c) What are the consequences for breaking gender norms, expectations and stereotypes?

EDUCATOR ANSWER KEY

Give students time and space to think through the prompts. It is okay if they are having trouble answering; wrestling with these questions is an important part in the process of developing critical thinking skills. There is no one right answer to these prompts, instead there are multiple possibilities. Some suggestions of possible answers include:

b)
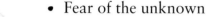
- Fear of the unknown
- Interpretations of religious conventions and rules that have been embedded into culture
- A societal and cultural preference for ridged structure and rules

c)
- The consequences might depend on family culture, school culture and peer culture. *Give students room to take the lead on this answer and help them draw out the conclusion that rules around gender are unfair, restrictive and oppressive to us all.*

Wrap-Up

Summarize the module with the following points:
- Everyone has a gender identity.
- The gender binary of "woman/man" is socially constructed and does not accurately reflect the diversity of gender identities and expressions or the fact that gender identity can change and be fluid throughout a person's life.
- Everyone transgresses gender norms and the gender binary to some degree.
- We have created very strict rules about gender but these rules do not capture the real complexity of gender or the complexity of how people relate to gender.
- You cannot know someone else's gender identity unless a person discloses it to you. Disclosing gender is a personal choice.

3.9 GENDER GALAXY

LEVEL [1] 2 [3]

Big Ideas in Module 3.9

- Assigned sex, gender identity, gender expression, and sexual orientation are all distinct concepts and aspects of a person's identity and experience in the world. Understanding the difference between these labels can better equip students to understand their own experiences and empathize with their peers.
- The sex a person is assigned at birth does not determine their gender identity.
- Although both sex and gender are constructed as binary (being only two i.e., female/male and woman/man) there are many more possibilities for each.

Learning Objectives

Students will:

- Distinguish between assigned sex, gender identity, gender expression, and sexual orientation.
- Learn to respect other people's identity and choices.
- Understand what is gained and lost by the gender binary.

Cross-Curricular Connections

- Art (visual, digital)
- English
- Equity Studies
- Family Studies
- Gender Studies
- Media Studies
- Psychology
- Social Studies
- Sociology

Terminology

- Agender
- Androgynous or Androgyne
- Aromantic
- Asexual or Ace
- Assigned sex
- Bicurious
- Biphobia
- Bisexual or Bi
- Cisgender
- Cissexism
- Closeted
- Coming out
- Demiromantic
- Demisexual
- Femmephobia
- Gay
- Gender
- Gender binary
- Gender creative and gender independent
- Gender expression
- Gender fluid
- Gender identity
- Gender non-binary and gender queer
- Gray-asexual
- Gray-romantic
- Heterosexism
- Heterosexual
- Homophobia
- Homosexual
- Intersex
- Lesbian
- LGBTQ+
- Monoromantic
- Monosexism
- Monosexual
- Neutrois
- Outing (someone)
- Pansexual
- Polyamorous
- Polyromantic
- Polysexual
- Queer
- Queer platonic or QP

- Questioning
- Romantic orientation
- Sexual expression
- Sexual orientation
- Sexuality
- Third/3rd gender
- Trans
- Trans-feminine
- Trans-masculine
- Transgender
- Transmisogyny
- Transphobia
- Two spirit

Materials
- A projection or printed copies of the **Gender Galaxy**
- A projection or printed copies of the **Sexuality Galaxy**
- **Educator Resource—Gender and Sexuality Galaxy Definitions**
- A way for each student to individually view the interactive image such as computers, tablets, or smartphones, *if you do not have access to the technology for each student to view the image, print copies of all of the above mentioned materials*
- Images of celebrities (from magazines or online)
- Paper and drawing utensils (pencil crayons, markers, crayons) or technology/software for digital drawing/painting

Background Information for Educators

The term **assigned sex** is used instead of just "sex" because doctors will usually determine a baby to be either male or female at birth. Doctors assign sex based on characteristics such as chromosomes and genitals. The ways that these sex characteristics can manifest in individuals' bodies is diverse and not as definite or binary as the categories of male and female suggest. Therefore, sex is not only assigned but the binary sex categories of male and female are also socially constructed.

Intersex is an umbrella term used to describe people who have chromosomes, hormonal profiles, or genitals that do not typically fit into binary medical and social constructions of male and female. Biological sex, like gender, is not binary. Between 0.05% and 1.7% of people are born with intersex traits, although not everyone with intersex traits identifies as intersex (Free & Equal, 2015). It is the case that both historically and currently, intersex babies are operated on and/or assigned one of the two binary sexes at birth but these non-consensual medical interventions are being increasingly challenged. More and more advocates are asking doctors and parents to recognize that the sex assignment of infants who present intersex characteristics (as with the gender assignment of any infant) is preliminary. This is an important development when it comes to our understanding of gender. Because sex is not binary, we should be even more resistant to binary understandings of gender. (For more information on non-consensual medical interventions and human rights, see modules 2.2 and 2.3).

Gender refers to the ways that masculinity and femininity have been socially constructed and reinforced by the dominant culture through norms, scripts, and stereotypes. Gender is socially constructed as a binary (usually through classifications of woman or man), even though this is not the reality of how gender is experienced internally (gender identity) and expressed externally (gender expression). **Gender identity** refers to an internal sense or awareness that all people have. For most, it can be described as a kind of "man-ness" or "woman-ness." But gender is not limited to two; it is not binary. **Gender expression** is how a person publicly presents their gender. This can include behaviour and outward appearance such as how someone dresses, wears their hair, if they use make-up, their body language, and their voice.

Students are often taught a binary gender and sex model that presents a masculine gender and a feminine gender in opposition to one another and aligned with a male sex assignment and a female sex assignment. In the following activities, the **Gender Galaxy** offers a model full of infinite gender possibilities and options to discover and explore. It challenges conventional binaries (e.g., the **gender binary**) so that students can reflect on the multiplicity of gender identities and expressions that exist in the world.

The **Sexuality Galaxy** is a companion to the **Gender Galaxy** that allows students to explore and discover a range of possibilities related to sexual and romantic orientations. **Sexual orientation** refers to a person's emotional, romantic, physical and/or sexual attraction to others. While sexual orientation can refer to all of these elements of attraction and human sexuality, **romantic orientation** more specifically describes the ways that people can experience romantic and emotional attractions. These may be separate from or connected to sexual and/or physical attraction. Sexual orientation and romantic orientation are not necessarily distinct identities; they are interrelated. Both are complex and attraction can manifest very differently for different people. Categories are commonly used to understand our attractions, though are by no means inclusive of the vast variety of expressions that make up human sexuality.

See the 3.9 resources, as well as modules 3.1, 3.3, 3.4 for more terms and ideas that you may encounter. It is also recommended that you read chapter 1 before facilitating these activities in order to check-in with your own values and assumptions, to create a safer space for learning, and to learn about appropriate ways to respond to discrimination, harassment, and bullying.

YOU SHOULD KNOW

Terminology changes over time as does what is appropriate and respectful. Your students are likely to have some of the most current information, although it may not always be accurate. If you do not know or have not heard a term that a student is using, give your student the benefit of doubt and then do your research. Come back to the student and/or the class with your research. (To help keep your information current, see the chapter 3 resources and the Online Hub).

Student Readiness

Before students engage with this lesson, ensure that safer space guidelines and group norms have been established (and revisited) within your classroom (for more information on how to establish safer space guidelines within a classroom, see module 1.3). In order to effectively prepare for this activity, ensure students understand:

- That everyone is assigned a sex at birth and that assigned sex is different from gender identity. (For more information, see module 3.1)
- That gender identity is different from sexual orientation.
- The terms gender, gender binary, and gender norms and how all of these are related (for more information, see modules 3.5 and 3.8).

Summary of Activities

Students will:

- Individually narrate their own story of self-exploration and discovery through the many planets and space phenomena contained within the **Gender Galaxy** and the **Sexuality Galaxy**.
- Collectively interpret the gender expressions of celebrities using mixed-media.

Activity 1 [1] [2] [3]

The instructions for Activity 1 are for the **Gender Galaxy** but the same instructions can be applied to the **Sexuality Galaxy**. The definitions for both galaxies can be found in the **Educator Resource—Gender and Sexuality Galaxy Definitions**. It is important to explore both galaxies with your students so they can begin to understand the differences and overlaps between gender identity, gender expression, assigned sex, sexual orientation, and romantic orientation.

Instructions

1. Project or print the image of the **Gender Galaxy**.
2. Ask your students for their immediate reactions to the image. Tell them to write down (or draw) and then optionally share with the group what they think of this image and what it means to them.
3. Go through the terms and images included in the **Gender Galaxy** with your students. *If using the online version, make sure you use each hyper link to explore the various solar systems, neighbouring galaxies, and other space phenomenon!*
4. Ask: How does this image allow for an understanding of gender and sex that is not binary?
5. Explain that the image is meant to be self-exploratory and limitless. Each student can explore and narrate their own experience of assigned sex, gender identity, gender expression, sexual and romantic orientations. *The **Gender Galaxy** offers limitless combinations of masculine and feminine: notice how the two are not necessarily opposed to one another, but instead exist within a universe of possibility. You can be very much of both genders, or very little. One does not take away or add to another. For many of your students, this will be a completely new idea. Take time to ask (and listen to) questions.*
6. If you have the technology for each student to view the **Gender Galaxy** individually, allow them to access the link. If you do not have this technology, provide handouts of each galaxy and the definitions.
7. Ask your students to imagine themselves as existing within the **Gender Galaxy** and give them time to explore how they relate to the different planets, solar systems, asteroid belts, and neighbouring galaxies.
8. Ask them to imagine themselves as a space traveller (like the rocket/space bot within the image) and, using the writing prompts, ask them to begin to write or draw their own story of planetary and space exploration. Make clear that they can use the images to

QUICK TIP

For level 1 and 2 students you can re-word this question as: How does this image make you feel? Does it help expand how you see yourself in your own universe?

facilitate their learning and self-discovery about gender and sexuality. Emphasize that there is no one story; there are an infinite number of stories that could be created individually and will be created by the diversity of experience within your classroom.

Writing Prompts:
a) If gender were a galaxy and I was a space traveller, I would...
b) Self-exploration of my gender identity looks like...
c) Self-exploration of my gender identity feels like...
d) Self-exploration of my gender expression looks like...
e) Self-exploration of my gender expression feels like...
f) When I was little my gender galaxy looked like...
g) When I grow up, my gender galaxy may look like...
h) When I was little my gender galaxy felt like...
i) When I grow up, my gender galaxy may feel like...
j) If gender were a galaxy...

9.   Optional: Invite your students to share their story with the class as a drawing, in writing, or orally. If the **Gender Galaxy** image provided does not speak directly to students' experiences, invite them to draw their own **Gender Galaxy**. As students share their stories, be mindful of reactions within the room and assumptions that you may make and cultivate sensitivity to any disclosure taking place. (For more information, see chapter 1).

EDUCATOR ANSWER KEY

Although there are no clear answers to this activity, there are key messages that you can emphasize:
- Everyone has a unique story when it comes to exploring gender, gender identity, and gender expression.
- All stories and experiences exploring gender, gender identity, and gender expression are valid.
- Gender identity and expression are fluid and ever evolving/changing.
- Gender is something we have a choice around expressing.
- Respecting multiple gender expressions means avoiding assumptions about what gender expression says about a person's gender identity. Gender identity is internal and not something that you can tell about a person based on their appearance.

Activity 2 3

Only gender expression should be discussed in this activity. Remind students that we cannot tell a person's sex, gender identity, or sexual orientation by looking at them. Even if we know a celebrity's dating history, we cannot know the whole story or their sexual orientation for sure. Gender expression however offers some agency in how individuals present their gender and can be interpreted by someone else. This is the only category that should be discussed in this activity and the diversity of interpretations between students should be emphasized.

QUICK TIP

Try to include a mixture of transgender and cisgender celebrities. While cisgender celebrities may be easy to find and may provide obvious examples of hyper-masculine or hyper-feminine gender expression, trans celebrities such as Laverne Cox, Caitlyn Jenner, and Chaz Bono may also express their gender in hyper-feminine or hyper masculine ways. Even though you are including a mix of trans- and cis- gender people, be sure that you are only discussing gender expression. Make sure to also provide a mix of contemporary and older examples of celebrities. Contemporary examples may include: Jaden Smith, Amandla Stenberg, Miley Cyrus, Angel Haze, Ruby Rose, Lady Gaga, and Brittney Griner. Older examples may include: David Bowie, Prince, Michael Jackson, and Annie Lennox. Including contemporary and older examples highlights how gender expression is something that has existed in different forms throughout time.

Instructions

1. Present students with images and/or short video clips of celebrities representing a wide range of gender expressions. *Choose celebrities that all or most of them will know.*
2. Divide your class into small groups and have them discuss where the celebrities' gender expression might be located within the **Gender Galaxy.**
3. Come back together as a class and discuss: What kinds of discussions did you have as a group? What questions came up during your group discussion? Were there any disagreements within your group about where a celebrity's gender expression might exist within the **Gender Galaxy?** If so, why do you think you had these disagreements?

EDUCATOR ANSWER KEY

When debriefing the exercise, reinforce that there is no correct answer to where the celebrities' gender expressions might exist in the Gender Galaxy. The lesson in this exercise is to note that gender expression is interpretive, subjective, and changing. We all express our gender somehow, both consciously and unconsciously. Some are very playful in their gender expressions, some like to mix things up, some like to really play up their femininity or masculinity, some like to present outside of the binary, some feel very comfortable in more traditional presentations of their gender. Some grow up loving to wear dresses, or the color blue, or overalls, or glittery heels, but may not feel the same later in life. Gender expressions are unique puzzles for all of us with pieces that can move and change throughout our lives.

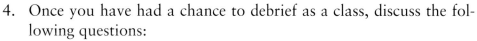

4. Once you have had a chance to debrief as a class, discuss the following questions:
   a) Why do you think we have strict rules and norms for interpreting or understanding gender?
   b) What do we gain from having two gender categories?
   c) What do we lose from simplifying gender into two categories?
   d) What happens when we break or do not fit into these limited gender categories? How does it feel? What does it matter?

EDUCATOR ANSWER KEY

Give students time and space to think through the questions. It is okay if they are having trouble answering; wrestling with these ideas is an important part in the process of developing critical thinking skills. There is no one right answer to these questions, there are multiple possibilities. Some suggestions of possible answers include:

a)
- Fear of the unknown
- Interpretations of religious conventions and rules that have been embedded into culture
- A societal and cultural preference for ridged structure and rules

b)
- Simplicity
- Convenience
- Convention

CONT'D NEXT PAGE

EDUCATOR ANSWER KEY CONT'D

c)
- Freedom
- Imagination
- Diversity
- Everyone loses out/everyone is limited when gender is simplified into two distinct binary categories.

d)
- Sometimes there are social consequences due to discrimination, stigma, and prejudice.
- This can be extremely harmful to individuals and society at large.
- Everyone has a gender expression. Most of the time, there are ways that we do not neatly fit into gender boxes. There are also times in our life where we challenge gender norms and break gender rules and stereotypes.

Wrap-Up

Summarize the module with the following points:
- It is important to have respect for all people.
- While we assume things like gender are natural and obvious, there is nothing straightforward or simple about it.
- Gender has different expressions across culture (e.g., Scottish men wearing kilts) and time (e.g., 18th century fashion for European men of a certain standing included wigs, make-up, and heels), and varies from person to person.
- Strict gender norms limit everyone's exploration of their gender identity and gender expression.

3.10 ASSIGNED SEX, GENDER IDENTITY, GENDER EXPRESSION, AND SEXUAL ORIENTATION: THE WORDS WE USE

LEVEL 2

Big Ideas in Module 3.10

- Assigned sex, gender identity, gender expression, and sexual orientation are all distinct concepts and aspects of a person's identity and experience in the world. Distinguishing between these categories can better equip students to understand their own experiences and empathize with their peers.
- There are many different words used to describe gender identity, gender expression, and sexual and romantic orientation. These words change over time and the possibilities of how people might self-identify are infinite.
- Everyone has the right to self-identify. It is important to never make assumptions about someone's identity and to listen carefully to how people identify themselves. (For more information on language use, see module 1.4).
- Gender and sexuality are complex but some people use categories to capture complex, intersecting identities. These categories are by no means inclusive of the vast variety of experiences and expressions that make up human sexuality and gender.

Learning Objectives

Students will:
- Distinguish between assigned sex, gender identity, gender expression, and sexual orientation.
- Learn appropriate and respectful terminology used to describe assigned sex, gender identity, and sexual orientation.

Cross-Curricular Connections
- English
- Equity Studies
- Family Studies
- Gender Studies
- Psychology
- Social Studies
- Sociology

Terminology
- Androgynous
- Asexual
- Assigned sex
- Bisexual
- Boy
- Cisgender
- Effeminate
- Female
- Gay
- Gender
- Gender expression
- Gender fluid
- Gender identity
- Gender queer
- Girl
- Heterosexual/ Straight
- Homosexual
- Intersex

- Lesbian
- Male
- Man
- Pansexual
- Queer

- Questioning
- Romantic orientation
- Sexual orientation

- Tomboy
- Transgender
- Two spirit
- Woman

Materials

- Chalkboard, flip chart, or whiteboard
- Chalk or markers
- Individual pieces of paper with the terms used in this lesson printed largely (for terms, see instructions)
- **Educator Resource—Sex, Gender, and Sexual Orientation Key Terms and Definitions**

YOU SHOULD KNOW

Terminology changes over time as does what is appropriate and respectful. Your students are likely to have some of the most current information, although it may not always be accurate. If you do not know or have not heard a term that a student is using, give your student the benefit of the doubt and then do your research. Come back to the student and/or the class with your research. (To help keep your information current, see the resource sections within chapter 3 and the Online Hub).

Background Information for Educators

The following activity helps students distinguish the difference between assigned sex, gender, gender identity, gender expression, and sexual orientation and builds awareness around the words we use in reference to these concepts. The following explains some of these terms in more depth.

The term **assigned sex** is used instead of just "sex" because doctors will usually determine a baby to be either male or female at birth. Doctors assign sex based on characteristics such as chromosomes and genitals. The ways that these sex characteristics can manifest in individuals' bodies is diverse and not as definite or binary as the categories of male and female suggest. Therefore, sex is not only assigned but the binary sex categories of male and female are socially constructed.

While this module defines what terms mean and provides some guidance about the context of language and what language is appropriate to use (and when), it cannot capture the infinite possibilities and changes over time. For instance, there are some people who might fit into the category of transgender but they may not self-identify as transgender, instead they might identify as a man or a woman. If you are unsure how someone identifies, do not make assumptions and listen carefully to how they describe themselves.

Intersex is an umbrella term used to describe people who have chromosomes, hormonal profiles, or genitals that do not typically fit into binary medical and social constructions of male and female. Biological sex, like gender, is not binary. Between 0.05% and 1.7% of people are born with intersex traits, although not everyone with intersex traits identifies as intersex (Free & Equal, 2015). It is the case that both historically and currently, intersex babies are operated on and/or assigned one of the two binary sexes at birth but these non-consensual medical interventions are being increasingly challenged. More and more advocates are asking doctors and parents to recognize that the sex assignment of infants who present intersex characteristics (as with the gender assignment of any infant) is preliminary. This is an important development when it comes to our understanding of gender. Because sex is not binary, we should be even more resistant to binary understandings of gender. (For more information on non-consensual medical interventions and human rights, see modules 2.2 and 2.3).

Gender refers to the ways that masculinity and femininity have been socially constructed and reinforced by the dominant culture through norms, scripts, and stereotypes. Gender is socially constructed as a binary (usually through classifications of woman or man), even though this is not the reality of how gender is experienced internally (gender identity) and expressed externally (gender expression). **Gender identity** refers to an internal sense or awareness that all people have. For most, it can be described as a kind of "man-ness" or "woman-ness." But gender is not limited to two; it is not binary. **Gender expression** is how a person publicly presents their gender. This can include behaviour and outward appearance such as how someone dresses, wears their hair, if they use make-up, their body language, and their voice.

Sexual orientation refers to a person's emotional, romantic, physical and/or sexual attraction to others. While sexual orientation can refer to all of these elements of attraction and human sexuality, **romantic orientation** more specifically describes the ways that people can experience romantic and emotional attractions. These may be separate from or connected to sexual and/or physical attraction. Sexual orientation and romantic orientation are not necessarily distinct identities; they are interrelated. Both are complex and attraction can manifest very differently for different people. Categories are commonly used to understand our attractions, though are by no means inclusive of the vast variety of expressions that make up human sexuality.

While this module does not contain or explore the infinite possibilities discussed in module 3.9, it does discuss the appropriateness of some common terms that people use to identify themselves. This is particularly important because terms used to describe gender identity and sexual orientation can often be lumped together, even though gender identity is distinct from sexual orientation. (For more information, see modules 3.1, 3.3, 3.8, and 3.9).

Before facilitating these activities, it is also recommended that you read chapter 1 in order to check in with your own values and assumptions, to create a safer space for learning, and to learn appropriate ways to respond to discrimination, harassment, and bullying.

Student Readiness

Before students engage with this lesson, ensure that safer space guidelines and group norms have been established (and revisited) within your classroom (for more information on how to establish safer space guidelines within a classroom, see module 1.3). In order to effectively prepare for this activity, ensure students understand that:

- Sex and gender are not binary, there are many more possibilities for each.
- Everyone is assigned a sex at birth and that assigned sex is different from gender identity. (For more information, see module 3.1)
- Gender identity is different from sexual orientation.

Summary of Activities

Students will:

- Collectively define the key terms: assigned sex, gender identity, gender expression, and sexual orientation.
- Individually place words related to key terms into appropriate categories and discuss placement as a class.

Activity 1

Instructions

1. Remind students of the power of language and words that have been hurtful (for more information, see module 1.4). *Maintain an awareness of the dynamics in the classroom as you move through the activity. While students can and will giggle at new ideas, ensure that no teasing, taunting, or making fun happens (for more information on how to create safer learning spaces, facilitate sensitive activities, and respond to discrimination, see modules 1.3, 1.5, and 1.6).*

YOU SHOULD KNOW

Language is powerful and the way we use it is important. Language can (intentionally and unintentionally) communicate our assumptions, values, biases, and judgments. Just as language is powerful, it is also political. Reclaimed language is one example of very political and highly charged language. Reclaimed language is language that has been used at some point to hurt, shame, discredit, and/or discriminate against a group of people and has since been reclaimed as a political act of resistance and defiance. It is important to note that while reclaimed language may be used in a positive, empowering way by some groups of people, it does not mean that it is widely accepted in every circumstance. It is important to use caution and care. This is true whether or not you are a part of the community or an outsider to the community that has reclaimed the language as a political act of resistance. This is because there is usually a diversity of opinions within the community about when it is and is not appropriate to use. Reclaimed language can still be very hurtful to some within the community and as an educator it is important to err on the side of caution and not use reclaimed language if you are uncertain. Likely, you can find another, less charged word to describe the same thing.

2. Discuss the various terms you will be exploring: assigned sex, gender identity, gender expression, and sexual orientation.
3. Divide the board into 4 columns with Assigned Sex, Gender Identity, Gender Expression, and Sexual Orientation at the top of each column. Be sure to leave space for additional rows underneath.
4. Ask your students:
    *   When we use the term **assigned sex**, what are we talking about?
    *   When we use the term **gender identity**, what are we talking about?
    *   When we use the term **gender expression**, what are we talking about?
    *   When we use the term **sexual orientation**, what are we talking about?

5. Pass around pieces of paper with the terms below printed largely enough to read from the board (one word on each piece of paper). *If there are more students than words, you can group students together and ask them to pick a term from a pile at the front of the class.*

ANDROGYNOUS	GENDER QUEER	MALE
ASEXUAL	GIRL	MAN
BISEXUAL	HETEROSEXUAL/ STRAIGHT	NAIL POLISH
BODY HAIR		PANSEXUAL
BOY	HIGH-PITCHED VOICES	QUEER
CISGENDER		QUESTIONING
DRESSES	HOCKEY JERSEY	SUIT AND TIE
EFFEMINATE	HOMOSEXUAL	TOMBOY
FEMALE	INTERSEX	TRANSGENDER
GAY	LESBIAN	TWO SPIRIT
GENDER FLUID	LIPSTICK	WOMAN

The objective is not to provide an exhaustive list of all the terms and identities that might fit under these categories; it is an opportunity for students to work out the differences between these broad terms by exploring where they fit. The activity is less about the terms themselves and more about distinguishing the differences between categories. (For a more comprehensive list, see 3.10 resources).

6. Ask each student (or group of students) to share their understanding of the term they have. *Ask for input from other students if you notice that the initial answer needs expanding.*

7. After you have briefly discussed the meaning as a class, ask the student(s) to place it on the board in the column they think it corresponds to. (For an example and answers, see **Educator Answer Key—Table 3A**).

8. Move through all the words and their corresponding categories. *Mistakes in this exercise are rich learning opportunities. These categories might be new to your students. When a word is placed in the wrong category, take the opportunity to explain why it is different from their initial or previous idea, move it, and re-establish the definitions you explored at the beginning.*

9. Once all of the words are placed in their columns, circle the words that are not always appropriate or respectful to use.

10. On the board, write in big letters "Appropriateness depends on..." and include a list of all the circled words and discuss what determines the meaning and power of words. What determines when and where certain words are appropriate and useful, and other times hurtful. Does it depend on who uses it and how (e.g., "queer")? Explore this with your students and include a brief summary beside each word. (For more information on appropriate language usage, see modules 1.4, 3.1, and 3.3).

EDUCATOR ANSWER KEY

Appropriateness depends on...

Effeminate: usually used to describe someone who identifies as a boy/man and who expresses a more feminine gender. This term has been used to hurt in the past but some people have reclaimed the word as a way of identifying their gender expression. Like all reclaimed language, it is important that you use caution with this word.

Homosexual: a clinical term for people who are attracted to the same gender. Some people find this term offensive because it was historically used to describe queerness as a disease that could be cured. This word is rarely used by people within the LGBTQ+ community. When used by someone outside of the LGBTQ+ community, it can be interpreted by those in the community as derogatory and offensive.

Queer and genderqueer: Queer was historically used as a derogatory term for people who either were or were perceived to be LGBTQ+. In recent years, it has been reclaimed by some people within the LGBTQ+ community as a way of self-identifying

CONT'D NEXT PAGE

EDUCATOR ANSWER KEY CONT'D

and as a political statement against the oppression to which they have been subjected. With any kind of reclaimed language, it is important to use caution when using the word and this is especially the case if you are not part of the LGBTQ+ community. Refrain from using the word to describe someone else's identity, unless they have used the term to identify themselves.

Tomboy: usually used to describe someone who identifies as a girl/woman and who expresses a more masculine gender. This term has been used to hurt in the past but some people have reclaimed the word as a way of identifying their gender expression. Like all reclaimed language, it is important that you use caution with this word.

Two spirit (or 2 spirit): is a term used by some Indigenous people to self-identify. It is an Indigenous specific term that can only be used by Indigenous people to identify themselves. While the term itself is Anishinaabe based, it has been taken up by different Indigenous nations to describe complex experiences and identities as well as cultural roles and responsibilities. Like any other term that people use to self-identify, do not assume that just because someone is Indigenous and identifies as LGBTQ+, that they will use the term two spirit to identify themselves.

Wrap-Up

Summarize the module with the following points:
- Assigned sex, gender identity, gender expression, and sexual orientation are all distinct concepts.
- Labels can be useful and empowering by describing experiences and identities.
- The appropriateness of language depends on time, place, and who is using the word.
- Learning about and keeping current on the language that is appropriate, accurate, and non-offensive is important for cultivating respectful, accountable, and allied relationships.

3.11 HARASSMENT AND BULLYING

LEVEL ☐1 ☐2 ☐3

Big Ideas in Module 3.11

- Harassment and bullying are unacceptable behaviours that affect many students inside and outside of the classroom.
- Harassment and bullying are often motivated by larger systems of oppression, such as homophobia, transphobia, and sexism.
- Students who are (or are perceived to be) LGBTQ+ and/or do not conform to gender norms experience bullying and harassment at disproportionally higher rates.

Learning Objectives

Students will:
- Learn to identify bullying and harassment.
- Understand the impact on the person experiencing bullying/harassment, the perpetrators, the bystanders, and the greater environment (school, team, etc.).
- Strategize around dealing with and intervening in bullying and harassment at school.

Cross-Curricular Connections
- Art (visual, digital, photography)
- Communication Studies
- English
- Equity Studies
- Family Studies
- Gender Studies
- Media Studies
- Psychology
- Social Studies
- Sociology

Terminology
- Ableism
- Bullying
- Classism
- Cyberbullying
- Harassment
- Homophobia
- Oppression
- Racism
- Sexism
- Transphobia

Materials
- Flip charts or large pieces of paper
- A way to display the school's anti-harassment and anti-bullying policies (photocopies, online link, or interactive white board)
- Sticky notes (8 to 12 per student) and pens
- Wall space and/or flip charts for posting sticky notes onto
- Access to a computer/projector and/or interactive whiteboard
- Markers, paint, crayons, and/or pencil crayons
- Art paper

Background Information for Educators

Students of all ages have at least some understanding of **bullying**. Some have participated in bullying directly and some have been bullied. They generally know it is not okay but they may not understand the full impact of sustained bullying over time. (For information on how to appropriately challenge bullying and **harassment** as an educator, see module 1.5).

Statistics show a disproportionately high number of suicides among LGBTQ+ youth. While this could be based on a number of factors, their experience is exacerbated by relentless and sometimes unbearable bullying. Schools have a responsibility to help young people understand the impact of their behaviour on others (in positive and negative ways) and to prevent bullying (including **cyberbullying**), harassment, and their consequences.

Bullying and harassment are often motivated by larger systems of **oppression** such as **homophobia, transphobia, sexism, racism, ableism,** and **classism.** All forms of bullying and harassment need to be addressed with students—the abuse of power is common across all forms. (For more information on systems of power, oppression, bullying, and harassment, see modules 1.2, 1.5, and 2.4).

For specific techniques on dealing with homophobia and transphobia, check out *How to Handle Harassment in the Hallways in Three Minutes* (Toronto District School Board). For information on crisis lines and other support services for youth, see the National Support Services resources.

Student Readiness

Before students engage with this lesson, ensure that safer space guidelines and group norms have been established (and revisited) within your classroom (for more information on how to establish safer space guidelines within a classroom, see module 1.3). In order to effectively prepare for this activity, ensure students understand that:

- This module is not about assigning blame. It is about learning how to most effectively challenge and intervene when bullying and harassment happens.
- Most people have been affected by bullying and/or harassment at some point in their life (as a bystander, a perpetrator, someone who has experienced bullying/harassment, or all three at different points).

- Bullying and harassment can take many different forms but some of the most common forms of bullying and harassment occur because either someone is (or is perceived to be) LGBTQ+ and/or challenges gender norms.

Summary of Activities
Students will:
- Individually reflect on harassment and/or bullying incidents witnessed at school.
- Collectively analyze the range of experiences that perpetrators, people who have experienced bullying, and bystanders go through, the dynamics between them, and the variety of possible responses and interventions.
- Create an anti-bullying campaign in small groups.

Activity 1
For level 1 students, especially those in grades 1 to 4, this activity can be adapted to encourage reflections through art. Instruction 3 is an opportunity for students to personally reflect on a bullying or harassment incident through drawing and/or painting. Instructions 4 and 5 are an opportunity for students to walk around the room with their individual drawing and paint/draw their thoughts/feelings under the various headings.

Instructions
1. Ask students to define harassment and bullying. After they have had a chance to answer, you can provide the standard definitions below to make sure everyone is clear. *Emphasize that harassment and bullying can be based on many different things, including religion, age, sexual orientation, gender identity, gender expression, race, culture, body size, abilities, etc.*
   - Harassment: can be intentional and/or unintentional but is always biased and targeted towards an individual who belongs to (or is perceived to belong to) a particular social group or environment. It can include any pattern of behaviour that creates an intimidating, demeaning, or hostile environment. This can be verbal, physical, and/or emotional.
   - Bullying: early definitions defined bullying as a pattern of negative behaviour being carried out repeatedly by individuals against other individuals. More recently however, bullying is being thought of as representing larger systems of oppression that are manifested in repeated actions by an individual (or groups of individuals) who are exercising power against another individual (or groups of individuals) (Meyer, 2014).

{TW}

BULLYING AND HARASSMENT
(for more information on trigger warnings, see modules 1.3, 1.5, and 1.6)

2. Ask students if anyone knows the school/school board's policy on harassment. Regardless of the answer, share it with them. Ask why they think the policy exists and why it is useful for them to know.

3. Ask students to privately think of an incident that happened at school that would fit the definition of harassment or bullying that you have just discussed. Ask them to think of a specific incident that they have witnessed or been a part of. Invite them to identify what part they played (person who experienced bullying, perpetrator, or bystander), keeping in mind the taboo around identifying as a perpetrator. Remind them to reflect as honestly as possible, and assure them that these stories will not be shared during the exercise. (For more information on how to facilitate sensitive activities, see module 1.6).

4. Post the following questions around the room as large, legible titles. They can be on flip charts or the wall—anywhere with enough space to post sticky notes underneath.
   - How did the person who experienced bullying feel? What impact did it have?
   - How did the person who experienced bullying respond? How else could they respond?
   - How did bystanders respond? How else could they respond?
   - Why did the perpetrator do it? What were their intentions?

5. With that one incident in mind, give each student 8 to 12 sticky notes. Ask students to write 2 to 3 answers (one per sticky note) in response to the question headings. Encourage them not to disclose the details of the incident (e.g., names and places) while still answering the questions.

6. Ask students to post each sticky note under the appropriate heading.

YOU SHOULD KNOW

The reason for not revealing specific details is to respect privacy and to encourage honest reflection. The point of this exercise is to create understanding and empathy, not judgment about who is right/wrong with regards to a particular incident.

---

7. Tell students to walk around the room and quietly read all of the answers under each heading.

8. As a group, ask students to identify any commonalities or trends in the responses. *Use the **Educator Answer Key** to discuss differences and similarities between incidents and what we can understand from them.*

EDUCATOR ANSWER KEY

	Person who experienced bullying		Bystanders and witnesses	Perpetrator
	feelings and impact	responses and options	responses and options	motivations and intention
Answers to include *Try to illustrate these points using the answers from sticky notes*	• Harassment and bullying are defined by their *impact* and not *intention*. • The harm done to someone can be severe, whether intended or not. • People who experience bullying are not the only people impacted; it affects the entire school environment.	• There are multiple options in the moment and afterward. • Everyone deserves to feel safe and respected in school.	• It can be difficult to intervene but bystanders are in a very powerful position to change a bullying scenario. • There are multiple options available, including giving support to bystanders. • They may feel scared to stop the situation in the moment but they can support the person bullied afterward and/or tell an authority figure who may not face the same kind of threats.	• Sometimes motivated by a lack of information, understanding, or empathy. • Sometimes motivated by pain and feelings of exclusion. • Sometimes they do not realize they are hurting others.

CONT'D NEXT PAGE

EDUCATOR ANSWER KEY CONT'D

	Person who experienced bullying		Bystanders and witnesses	Perpetrator
	feelings and impact	responses and options	responses and options	motivations and intention
Additional information	• Harassment and bullying can be physical, verbal, emotional, online etc. • If behaviour that is meant to be funny actually hurts, tell the person that it hurts and explain why.	• People who experience bullying stay silent sometimes for reasons including fear of reprisal, believing that they are to blame, feelings of shame and embarrassment, not knowing who to tell, not feeling safe to tell, not trusting adults or authority figures at school etc.	• Distribute and discuss: *How to Handle Harassment in the Hallways in Three Minutes* (See 3.11 resources). • We can make intervening easier by accepting, encouraging and normalizing peer-intervention. • We can become more courageous in intervening in bullying incidents by acting as role models to other students.	• Anyone can be a perpetrator. Being a perpetrator does not necessarily mean that you are a bad person, only that you may have exhibited inappropriate behaviour. • The positive actions you take after the inappropriate behaviour(s) can help to mend the situation with the people impacted. • Pay attention to how people react to your behaviour (including emotional, verbal, physical, and online behaviour) and apologize promptly. • It is still bullying even if that is not the intention. • Bullying is about the impact. Even if the intention was to be funny, or to get closer to someone through teasing them, if the impact is hurtful, this needs to be addressed and taken seriously (see figure 1A).

Activity 2 2 [3]

Instructions

1. Ask students to define harassment, bullying, and cyberbullying. After they have had a chance to respond, you can provide these standard definitions to make sure everyone is clear:

   - Harassment: can be intentional and/or unintentional but is always biased and targeted towards an individual who belongs to (or is perceived to belong to) a particular social group or environment. It can include any pattern of behaviour that creates an intimidating, demeaning, or hostile environment. This can be verbal, physical, and/or emotional.

   - Bullying: early definitions defined bullying as a pattern of negative behaviour being carried out repeatedly by individuals against other individuals. More recently however, bullying is being thought of as representing larger systems of oppression that are manifested in repeated actions by an individual (or groups of individuals) who are exercising power against another individual (or groups of individuals) (Meyer, 2014).

   - Cyberbullying: refers to bullying that happens online. Cyberbullying can originate online and still affect someone in all areas of life. It often seeps into (and/or is amplified by) a student's life at school.

2. Show students the following videos (see 3.11 resources):

   - It Gets Better Canada (2010)
   - Cyberbullying Virus (2013)—"Reach Out" An Anti-Bullying Campaign (2012)
   - Stand Up for Your Friends (2014)

3. Divide the class into groups of 3 to 5 students and ask them to discuss the following questions:

   - What is your first reaction to each of these videos?
   - What messages were these videos trying to send?
   - Do you think that they were effective at communicating their messages?
   - What could they have done to better communicate their messages?

4. Ask each group to brainstorm ideas for an anti-bullying campaign. Explain that they can create a general campaign or choose a specific topic to focus on (e.g., cyberbullying, sexual harassment, homophobic or transphobic bullying, etc.).

5. Ask each group to take their brainstorming ideas and turn them into an anti-bullying campaign using the media of their choice. *This can be done as a homework assignment.*

Wrap-up

Summarize the module with the following points:

- Bullying and harassment negatively affect the entire school environment.
- When it happens, bullying and harassment need to be stopped immediately and work needs to be done to create a culture that does not tolerate it.
- There are people to support you, if you are harassed or bullied outside of school or online. *Identify support people within your school for students.*
- Bystanders are in a powerful position to intervene and stop bullying and harassment when it happens.
- Anyone could potentially harass or bully, this is especially true for people who have experienced harassment or bullying themselves.
- Realizing that you may be bullying or harassment someone is the first step in ending the behaviour. *Ensure that you are not sending students to people within the school who have been known to shame and punish students who have made a mistake and express a desire to change their behaviour.*

3.12 THE MASKS WE WEAR: DISCLOSURES, RESILIENCE, AND THE CREATIVITY OF SURVIVAL

LEVEL 3

Big Ideas in Module 3.12

- Students who identify as LGBTQ+ are often pressured to "come out" but choosing not to come out can be a survival tactic.
- Resilience is about finding creative ways to survive; sometimes making the decision not to disclose information about yourself is a creative survival strategy.
- We sometimes make strategic assessments about what to disclose and when. This means that at one point or another, we may choose to hide parts of ourselves, big and small. Learning how to recognize this as strategic and resilient instead of cowardly is an important part of building self-esteem.

Learning Objectives

Students will:

- Understand the concept of disclosing personal information, including sexual orientation, gender identity, and other issues (for more information, see module 1.6).
- Understand that privacy and concealment are options and useful survival strategies when there is a lack of safety and support.
- Consider ways to make disclosure safer for each other and as a school.

Cross-Curricular Connections

- Art (visual, digital)
- English
- Equity Studies
- Family Studies
- Gender Studies
- Psychology
- Social Studies
- Sociology

Terminology

- Coming out
- LGBTQ+
- Marginalization
- Resilience

Materials

- Chalk or whiteboard
- Situation cards

Background Information for Educators

For adolescents especially, different experiences can be difficult to share with peers and community. The fear of rejection, social isolation, homelessness, violence, and uncertainty can be enough to keep otherwise important parts of the self hidden.

There can sometimes be significant pressure on **LGBTQ+** students to "come out," especially when portrayed as a necessary next step in their actualization and/or coming of age.

The reality, however, is that **coming out** may not be appropriate for every student. It is important to recognize that to "stay in the closet" or choose to maintain privacy is a survival tactic and an act of **resilience** and creativity (for more on youth resilience, see module 1.7). This also applies to other experiences of **marginalization** (like trauma and war, poverty, mental health, and/or addiction issues at home, migration histories, violence, etc.).

Aside from actively making the school safer for all diversity to express itself, a supportive community should make room for survival strategies like these.

YOU SHOULD KNOW

"Coming out" is a figure of speech often used to describe a person's disclosure of their sexual orientation and/or gender identity. It is commonly misunderstood as a one-time event but is actually a lifelong and sometimes daily process. Heterosexual and cisgender people rarely have to go through the process of coming out because their sexual orientation and/or gender identity is generally assumed to be the norm.

Student Readiness

Before students engage with this lesson, ensure that safer space guidelines and group norms have been established (and revisited) within your classroom (for more information on how to establish safer space guidelines within a classroom, see module 1.3). In order to effectively prepare for this activity, ensure students understand that:

- While everyone has a gender identity and sexual orientation, "coming out" is something that heterosexual, cisgender people do not have to do because the default expectation or assumption is always heterosexual and cisgender.

- Outing someone is not okay. People can choose whether or not to come out and whatever decision is made is an act of courage.
- The first person someone needs to come out to is themselves. Once someone has come out to themselves then that person can decide who, where, and when to come out.
- Coming out is never a one-time event.

Summary of Activities

Students will:
- In small groups, discuss the concept of disclosing difficult personal experiences.
- Either individually or as an entire class, reflect on the advantages and disadvantages of disclosure, the types of information that may require conscious disclosure, the reasons why disclosure can be difficult, and ways to best receive and support someone's disclosure.

Activity 1 3

(For more information on how to facilitate sensitive activities and approach the topic of disclosure, see module 1.6).

Instructions
1. Introduce the topic by defining "coming out." Ask students to brainstorm a collective definition.
2. Discuss why "coming out" can be difficult to do and reasons why someone might want to wear a "mask." Ask students why certain things (like being LGBTQ+) require a coming out process.

EDUCATOR ANSWER KEY

Reasons why someone might want to wear a "mask":
- Fear of consequences (both perceived and material) of revealing certain stigmatized aspects of your identity and experience (such as revealing mental health and/or addiction struggles, coming out as LGBTQ+, revealing that you/your family lives in poverty, HIV status, etc.).
- A desire to maintain privacy.
- Not feeling ready to disclose.

Reasons why certain things require coming out:
- Assumptions of normativity (when things that are common are taken to be normal). Because of normativity, straight people do not have to "come out" as straight and cisgender people do not have to "come out" as cisgender.

3. Put students into groups of 3 to 5 and ask them to brainstorm other things that are difficult to share with peers. Encourage them to think of different realms of life.

EDUCATOR PROMPTS

Try to give examples and prompt for less charged, or less stigmatized, aspects of life. Then, move into talking about the more challenging, more stigmatized subject areas.

Start with prompts such as:
- Personality traits (people may not want to reveal personality traits like sarcasm or pessimism or large egos when they are first getting to know someone)
- Food preferences and dietary restrictions
- Allergies
- Preferences for hot and/or cold environments

Then move into prompts such as:
- Medical conditions/diagnoses
- Family structures
- Sexual orientation
- Gender identity
- Mental health status
- Immigration status
- Ethnic, cultural, and linguistic identities

4. Optional: If art-making is an option, allow students to create masks (from paper cut-outs, papier-mâché, clay, etc.) to represent various ways we disguise or conceal our truths. Carry out the rest of the discussions using the masks as conversation starters.
5. Within the small groups, ask students to identify the commonalities between things that are difficult to disclose.

EDUCATOR ANSWER KEY
- They are things that can be hidden
- They carry some kind of cultural taboo
- They are/can be shaming
- They are/can be embarrassing
- They are things that are devalued
- There are social and/or material consequences
- They are uncommon or experienced only by a few people
- They are things we fear we are alone in experiencing

6. As a class, ask students to report back on their list of things that are hard to disclose and the commonalities between them. *To create a safer space, make sure that students know that they do not need to provide specific details about what has been difficult to disclose in their life. Instead, they can share general topic areas in broad strokes that either do or do not apply to their lives (e.g., dietary restrictions, personality traits, family structures, cultural backgrounds, sexual orientation, gender identity etc.).*

7. As a class, ask students to brainstorm the advantages and disadvantages of disclosing difficult truths and/or removing their masks. *This can also be a personal, reflective writing exercise.*

EDUCATOR ANSWER KEY

Benefits:
- Finding commonalities and developing new bonds/friendships with people who have similar experiences
- Building community
- Being a role model for peers
- Being a support person/safe person for other people to talk to who have had similar experiences
- Letting go of the fear of others finding out
- Opportunities to change the system that has contributed to you feeling like you had to hide a part of yourself

CONT'D NEXT PAGE

EDUCATOR ANSWER KEY CONT'D

Disadvantages:

- Social, emotional and/or physical/material consequences
- Being fearful
- Having parts of your life challenged and disrupted
- Being the "go to" person on a certain issue/experience can be emotionally draining
- The expectation that you are there to educate others on your life/identity/ experiences
- Being fearful that if the "wrong" people found out, your life would be turned upside down

8. Ask students to put themselves into "someone else's shoes" who has something to disclose and answer the following questions. *This is meant to build empathy among students. Prompt for respectful, positive, healthy, constructive, and empathetic ways of responding to people who feel vulnerable and fear being marginalized, stigmatized, shamed, and/or embarrassed.*

- How would they like to be received?
- What would make the disclosure safer and easier?
- What kinds of support would they need from a friend?
- What could make the school environment safer?

9. Optional: If you know your class well and there is already trust established between classmates, this part of the activity can be turned into a variation on the improve drama game *freeze* where each question above is a scene. As a class, choose the type of disclosure you want to explore and who the characters are (e.g., coming out as queer or trans to a family member, telling someone you trust about addiction in your family, telling someone you just met about your mental health challenges, disclosing to a friend that you were sexually assaulted, etc.). Start the first scene (How would you like to be received?) with two students, one playing the role of the person disclosing and the other playing the role of the person receiving the information. This first scene is about telling and receiving the disclosure. Encourage other students in the class to call "freeze!" if the person receiving the disclosure starts to react negatively. Once the actors hear the word "freeze!," they must stop talking and moving. The student who called "freeze!" walks up to the frozen scene and chooses which character to replace in the scene by gently tapping the top of their shoulder. Their task is then to change the scene in a way that would make the disclosure safer and easier (What would make the disclosure safer and easier?). This can continue until the last scene (What could make the school environment safer?). In the last scene, students do not have to

replace a character but they can call "freeze!" and join in the scene, creating a different dynamic and opening up more possibilities of support and safety.

Role playing sensitive subject matter with students is a delicate balance of rich learning through "placing yourself in someone else's shoes" and at the same time, requires a keen understanding of the social dynamics and personalities of your students. (For more information and tips about how to facilitate role play effectively and safely, see module 1.6).

Wrap-Up

Summarize the module with the following points:

- Coming out and disclosures of all kinds take courage and a level of safety. Disclosure always depends on person, place, and timing. There is no right or wrong answer for whether or not to disclose something. It involves careful consideration of multiple competing (sometimes contradictory) factors.
- There are many ways to support someone disclosing a difficult truth. These include: emotional support, material support, systems navigation, advocating on behalf of the person, and helping to find/ connect with community.
- We all wear masks to greater or lesser degrees depending on time, place, and many other factors. Choosing not to disclose a part of ourselves is a viable survival strategy that draws on resilience and creativity.
- Encourage students to think of other ways that they are creative and resilient in their everyday lives.

YOU SHOULD KNOW

Systems navigation refers to both helping someone to find the resources they need and to navigate the systems that those resources exist in. For instance, if a student discloses being sexually assaulted, you could help that student figure out the systems that they have access to for pursuing recourse and the next steps, even if those next steps are simply meeting with a counsellor.

CHAPTER 4

PUBERTY, BODIES, AND SEXUAL AND REPRODUCTIVE HEALTH

4.1 INTRODUCTION AND TIMING OF CLASSES

Puberty is a major transition in young people's lives. It is marked by significant physical, emotional, mental, and social changes. It is important to provide accurate, accessible, and inclusive information to students so that they can navigate their experiences and the questions they have, while feeling as supported and empowered as possible.

By the time students begin sexuality education in school (e.g., human health, growth and development/puberty classes), they will likely have already received a number of competing messages about sexuality; many may have seen explicitly sexual images—either deliberately or unintentionally—on the internet, social media, or through friends and siblings.

Human sexuality exists throughout the lifespan. Some students may have had sexual experiences before puberty. It is important to keep in mind that these can consist of consensual exploration as well as non-consensual abuse (for more information on consent and sexual violence, see chapter 8). For most adolescents, puberty is coupled with newly formed romantic and sexual desires. This can be exciting and confusing. Young people may also feel additional pressure to belong and be accepted. This is why it is especially important for educators to help students develop emotional, communication, and social skills. (For more information, see modules 4.6, 5.5, 5.6, and chapter 7).

Puberty classes create an opportunity to provide the building blocks for positive attitudes about bodies, diversity, sexuality, sexual health, and relationships. This chapter covers a wide breadth of information beyond the biology of puberty, for all ages and grade levels.

Timing of Classes

To be most effective, puberty and sexuality education needs to be timely and developmentally appropriate. On average, puberty begins between the ages of 8 and 13. Many of the physical, emotional, and social changes that make up the experience of puberty are profound and potentially anxiety provoking for young people. It is therefore important that children start learning about the physiological changes associated with puberty before experiencing it themselves. For this reason, many of the modules in chapter 4 are aimed at levels 1 and 2.

All-gender or gender-segregated classes?

All-gender classes can normalize changes during puberty, destigmatize sexual health, and demystify differences between people. There is no information that a child should not have because of their assigned sex or gender identity. Effective sexuality education emphasizes similarities among students and promotes empathy and respect.

At the same time, many students are more comfortable with asking questions related to puberty and sexual health in gender-segregated environments. If you are teaching in gender-segregated classes, ensure that all students learn the same information about each other in order to promote empathy, respect, and communication skills. It is also crucial to strategize ways to include transgender, gender diverse, and intersex students in meaningful ways that do not further marginalize them and their experiences; transgender, intersex, and gender diverse students often become excluded and silenced through such segregation.

Involving families and the wider community

You may want to organize a meeting with parents and guardians to explain what students will be learning in the sexuality education program. *Beyond the Basics* also provides a sample letter to parents/guardians (see 4.1 resources). This can help promote understanding

QUICK TIP

If you have the option of all-gender classes, conduct an anonymous poll with students to find out what kind of class arrangement they prefer when discussing topics related to puberty. This has the potential to help empower young people/students by showing them that their feedback and needs are valued.

If you are required to provide gender segregated classrooms, anonymously ask your students which gender grouping they would feel the most comfortable in.

and communication in other realms of a student's life and offer parents and guardians resources and support in this learning process.

Before you begin

Before you begin, we recommend that you work through the educator reflection questions below and review chapter 1. In particular, modules 1.1, 1.2, 1.3, 1.4, 1.5, and 1.6.

Educator Reflection Questions

- If you were taught puberty in school, do you remember what you were taught and which grade you were in? Do you remember what was missing and what questions you had that were left unanswered? Do you think that the puberty education you received was relevant to your life experience? Why or why not?
- What do you wish you had learned before, during, and after you started puberty?
- What do you think is the goal of teaching students about puberty? Do you think that this goal unintentionally leaves anyone out? If so, how could you modify the way you approach the modules to ensure inclusion and equity?

Big Ideas in Chapter 4

- It is okay to learn and be curious about sexuality and sexual health.
- People have the right to bodily autonomy and integrity, including the control over their sexuality, their bodies, and their decisions.
- There are many different ways of expressing sexuality and a diversity of sexual experiences.
- When a student faces a challenge or has a concern, help is available.
- Bodies are diverse in the ways they look, the ways they function, and the ways they respond.
- Difference and diversity are everywhere, including in family structures and family histories.
- There is a diversity of reproductive options available to humans and therefore, people come to be born in a diversity of ways.

4.2 EDUCATOR RESOURCE: PUBERTY, BODIES, AND SEXUAL HEALTH

Puberty is a time of massive physical, emotional, and social change. On average, the age of puberty onset ranges from 8 to 13 years. It is important to keep in mind that everyone's body is different and that timelines for the onset of puberty range, as well as the length of time that puberty occurs. There is a range of evidence that indicate slightly different information about the average age of puberty onset, as well as puberty timelines. Part of the reason for this is that the age and timeline of puberty is different depending on genetics, and many social and environmental factors. (For more information on the social determinants of health, see module 2.4).

This module provides general information about puberty, bodies, and sexual health, including the biology of menstruation, the biology of sperm production, and practices that encourage self-care and curiosity in getting to know our own bodies and bodily processes.

Bodies and Language

People have diverse bodies and a diversity of ways that bodies function and respond to stimuli. Sexuality education is often taught in a way that further marginalizes students who already experience marginalization based on identities and bodies that do not fit into dominant ideas about what is considered "normal." For instance, people with disabilities are often left out of sexuality education. They are left out in terms of curriculum content and because they may not attend gym class (which is the place where sexuality education most often occurs).

People with disabilities may be left out of sexuality education content because they are often stereotyped as non-sexual and therefore not in need of knowledge on sexuality education. This is a prevalent myth that is being challenged by disability activists and by disability rights movements. As an educator, it is important that you challenge any assumptions you have about what disability looks like, stereotypes of who people with disabilities are, and beliefs you have about disability in relationship to sexuality so that you can speak to the realities and needs of all your students (for more information, see modules 4.7 and 5.4). One of the ways to bring perspectives on disability and sexuality into the classroom is highlighting the voices of people with disabilities who are activists working to challenge the myths and stereotypes that exist surrounding disability and sex (for more information, see 4.7 and 5.4 resources).

Bodies, Gender Identity, Assigned Sex, and Language

The lessons in this chapter are not separated by **assigned sex** (commonly categorized as female and male) or **gender identity**. This was an intentional choice for three main reasons:

1. For some people, gender identity matches with assigned sex and for some people it does not.
2. Separating information into "male" and "female" categories does not recognize people who identify as **intersex** (and/or have bodies that have been labelled as having intersex traits).
3. Regardless of the anatomy that people have, it is helpful to have information about the ways other people's bodies work.

(For more information on language use, gender identity, and assigned sex, see modules 1.4, 3.1, 3.8, 3.9, and 3.10).

As an educator, you need to be equipped to discuss anatomy and biological changes that are commonly experienced in bodies during puberty. When speaking about biological, bodily functions, it is important not to attach or assume a gender identity. It is equally important for you to recognize that people who identify as intersex (and/or have bodies that have been labelled as having intersex traits) may not fit into some of the **Sexual and Reproductive Anatomy Diagrams** in 4.9 handouts and other bodily changes described. Having this awareness is important because you do not know who is in your class, what their composition of hormones and chromosomes are, and you cannot make assumptions about what people's bodies look or feel like.

In *Beyond the Basics*, the terminology we often use to talk about bodily processes is very specific and dependent on the anatomy involved. For instance, in the following modules we use the language "people with vaginas," "people with uteruses," and "people with penises." Using this terminology and being as specific as possible recognizes that people's gender identity may not align with their reproductive organs, external genitalia, and/or other sex characteristics, such as hormonal and chromosomal profiles. It also recognizes that external genitalia can look very different person to person and that a person's anatomy can change over their lifetime.

YOU SHOULD KNOW

A person's anatomy might change for a variety of reasons. These reasons can include surgeries due to health concerns such as a hysterectomy (removal of the uterus), a mastectomy (removal of a breast), or a prostatectomy (removal of the prostate gland). **Gender confirming surgeries** can also change a person's anatomy. Using accurate language when discussing bodies is important because a person might identify as a woman, have a vagina and a vulva but no uterus. Because a person without a uterus will not experience menstruation, it is important to be specific and say "person with a uterus" when discussing menstruation.

Puberty

When discussing **puberty** and bodies with anatomically correct and specific language, students might have questions about which body parts they have. In order to navigate this effectively, educators can begin classes about puberty with a definition and examples of **assigned sex** (**female, intersex,** and **male**), being sure to indicate the differences between assigned sex and **gender identity**. It is also important to include the 4.9 handout **Sexual and Reproductive Anatomy Diagrams** in all discussions about puberty and bodies to help give students visual context for the information they will be learning.

People with a uterus and an ovary might experience...

Hormones
- Hormones released by the **pituitary gland** stimulate **ovulation**.

Ovulation
- The release of an **egg** (**ovum**) from the ovary.
- Usually one egg is released once a month (but sometimes more than one is released).
- When the egg is released, it travels through the **fallopian tubes** to the uterus.
- Usually, people cannot feel ovulation.
- If the egg is not fertilized (by **sperm**), it dissolves.

Menstruation (commonly known as a "period")
- Menstruation usually starts between 12 and 13 years of age but can start as early as 8/9 or as late as 15/16.
- Menstruation happens when **hormones** from the ovaries send a signal to the uterus to grow a lining (**endometrium**).

- The lining of the uterus contains nutrients that help the fertilized egg grow.
- Approximately every month this lining is shed (menstruation) unless **fertilization** takes place.

YOU SHOULD KNOW

Pregnancy starts with the fertilization of an egg by sperm, creating an embryo. Usually fertilization happens in the fallopian tube and the embryo travels into the uterus and implants in the lining of the uterus. Sometimes however, the fertilized egg implants in the fallopian tube. This is called ectopic pregnancy, which is very dangerous for the person who is pregnant, and treatment is mandatory.

- Once the lining has been shed, another one starts to grow (this happens on approximately a monthly basis).
- Menstruation typically happens approximately once a month, although this can fluctuate to greater or lesser degrees throughout the life cycle.
- On average, menstruation can last for 2 to 7 days and menstrual cycles can be anywhere from 21 to 45 days but for adolescents, it is common for menstruation to be shorter and menstrual cycles to be longer (UpToDate, 2017).
- It is important to get to know how long your menstruation lasts, how many days your menstrual cycle is, and what your flow looks like (e.g., is it heavy some days and light others? Do you experience clotting?) *There are many "period apps" that currently exist. These help people track their menstrual cycles (including tracking how long your average cycle is and what symptoms you experience month to month) and may appeal to your students.*
- Getting to know what is normal for your own body can help determine if you are pregnant and can help in building a sexual health profile. Building a sexual health profile involves getting curious about your body and getting to know what is "normal" for your body so that you can more easily/quickly assess when something is unusual or may require a visit to your health care provider.
- Menstruation is not a sickness/disease and it is important for you as an educator to normalize it as one of many bodily processes that starts during puberty.

- While menstruating, you can continue to participate in daily activities. Sometimes menstruation can cause cramping in the lower abdomen, backaches, headaches, nausea, and feelings of lethargy. Some ways to cope with these possible symptoms include: taking a warm bath, mild exercise, or placing a heating pad on the abdomen and/or back.

- People who menstruate may want to develop self-care habits that involve taking a warm shower or bath to alleviate cramping and to wash any dried menstrual blood from **external genitals**, anus, and/or pubic hair areas.

- People who menstruate have a diversity of ways of catching the menstrual blood, which is on average 30 ml per cycle (UpToDate, 2017). There is no "right" or "wrong" way of catching menstrual blood and some of the ways that people choose include:

  – **Drugstore brand pads or sanitary napkins** (thrown out after each use). There are a variety of different pad brands, sizes, and styles suited for different kinds of flow. Scented pads should be avoided as they can cause skin irritation. No matter what brand or style of pad you choose to use, change pads frequently (every 3 to 4 hours) and dispose of in the garbage.

  – **Reusable cloth pads** (can be washed and reused after each use). Reusable cloth pads are a more expensive up-front investment but they can save money over the long term and can be bought at most health food stores.

  – **Tampons** (thrown out after each use). Tampons can be used while swimming and come in a variety of brands, styles, and sizes to match your flow and preferences for vaginal insertion (i.e., you can insert using either cardboard or plastic applicators, or using your finger). All tampons have a string that is securely attached and is used for removal from the vagina. Tampons are held in place by the vagina and cannot fall out or get lost once inserted. It is important that your students know that if they choose to use tampons, they know which is most appropriate to their menstrual flow; that they need to change it regularly; and that it should only be inserted if/when they see menstrual blood (i.e., not worn preemptively). These practices are important in order to avoid Toxic Shock Syndrome (TSS). TSS is a rare but serious bacterial infection that has been linked to tampon use.

– **Menstrual cups** (washed and reused after each use). Menstrual cups can be used while swimming. There are a couple of different brands and styles of menstrual cups. They take some practise to get used to inserting but they may be left in for longer periods of time than tampons. If students are interested in this option, direct them to the 4.2 resources on puberty.

People with testicles and a penis might experience...

Hormones

- Hormones released by the **pituitary gland** stimulate sperm production in the testicles.

Fluid

- Fluid produced by accessory glands, including the **prostate gland** and **seminal vesicles,** keep sperm alive (**semen**).

Erections

- Erections happen when the penis fills up with blood and becomes longer and/or harder (often the penis sticks out from the body when an erection occurs).
- Penises come in many shapes and sizes, some are **circumcised,** some are not; one is never better than the other. Penises can look different while erect and while flaccid.

YOU SHOULD KNOW

Circumcision of penises is a personal choice that parents make. While there is evidence of health benefits (e.g., UTI prevention), it is not a medically necessary procedure (CPS, 2015; AAP, 2012). There is also no difference in sensation or performance. This is just one way penises look different from person to person. It is a common practice in Canada and performed by medical professionals usually within the first 10 days of a baby with a penis being born. Circumcision involves the removal of the foreskin (or prepuce) so that the glans (or head) of the penis is exposed. If someone with a penis has not been circumcised, their foreskin will separate from their glans slowly, over time. Once this happens, people with uncircumcised penises should clean themselves by pulling back the foreskin (so that the glans is exposed) and wash underneath with mild soap and water.

- Erections are sometimes referred to as "boners" or "getting hard," or "having a hard-on."

- Erections can happen for a variety of reasons and while they often happen in response to sexual thoughts, they sometimes happen at random times and for purely physiological reasons.
- Getting erections at inconvenient and potentially awkward times can lead to feelings of embarrassment and fear. Ensure that students know that this is something that is common for people with penises to experience, especially during puberty.
- Having an erection does not mean that ejaculation must follow. Erections will subside on their own.

YOU SHOULD KNOW

It is a common myth that people with penises have to ejaculate if they have an erection and the way that this may play out in social situations that young people encounter is through gender norms and expectations of sexual activity. For instance, people with penises who identify as boys/men may use the fact that they have an erection to pressure and coerce someone else into sexual activity by saying that they need to ejaculate or else they will get painful "blue balls" (**epididymal hypertension**). While someone with a penis and testicles may indeed experience an aching sensation from blood being built up and retained in the genitals, this is not an excuse to pressure/coerce someone else into sexual activity. One very effective and appropriate way to deal with any pain associated with "blue balls" is to find a private space and time to masturbate/self-pleasure.

Ejaculation
- The release of semen from an erected penis.
- One ejaculation contains millions of sperm.
- Ejaculation often occurs when there is stimulation of the penis but it can also happen without stimulation, especially at night (see nocturnal emissions).

Nocturnal emissions
- Nocturnal emissions are often referred to as "wet dreams."
- It is ejaculation that occurs while sleeping and is not necessarily in response to any kind of physical stimulation.
- It sometimes happens as part of a sexual dream but is not necessarily connected to sexual thoughts and can simply be a physiological release while sleeping.
- Experiencing nocturnal emissions can lead to feelings of embarrassment and fear. Ensure that students know that this is something that is common for people with penises to experience during puberty and into adulthood.

- Some people with penises do not have nocturnal emissions and others have them very often. As an educator, it is important to normalize all of these experiences as each person's body and bodily functions are different.

Sexual Health

Sexual and reproductive health is introduced in this chapter as it relates to puberty and bodies in broad strokes. (For information on Sexually Transmitted and Blood Borne Infections, see chapter 10). *Beyond the Basics* recognizes sexual health as a broad concept that encompasses the social, emotional, and mental aspects of health alongside the physiological and reproductive aspects. In this chapter, there is an emphasis on getting to know your own unique body as a way to regularly practise self-care and put sexual health knowledge into practise (by building on the knowledge that you have of your own body). You will find detailed information and background on puberty and sexual health as you move through the next couple of modules (particularly 4.3 and 4.4).

People with breasts may want to consider...

Breasts are glandular organs located on the chest with the potential to secrete milk. While *Beyond the Basics* often uses the language of "breast(s)," in order to reduce any shame/stigma attached to the word, it is also important to be aware of how only using the word "breast" might unintentionally alienate transgender and/or gender non-binary students. The term "chest tissue" can be used in addition to "breast(s)" because this kind of language recognizes that transgender men, trans-masculine people, and/or gender non-binary people who want (but have not yet had) gender confirming top-surgery (removal of breasts and construction of nipples) may feel negatively towards their breasts.

- Breast/chest tissue grows during puberty and nipples and **areola** become larger in size and can become darker in colour.
- **Nipples** are sensitive to pleasure and pain.
- It is common for two breasts to grow at differing speeds and differing sizes.
- It is common for breasts to enlarge and be sore/tender in the week/days leading up to menstruation.
- It is common for breast tissue to feel different at different points of the menstrual cycle.

- Breast tissue can feel lumpy at certain times in the cycle. Getting to know the feeling of these lumps and taking note of when in your cycle they appear is helpful in getting to know what is normal for your body. Knowing what is normal for your body helps you to discern when or if there is a symptom or lump that is out of the ordinary.
- If an unusual lump in your breast tissue is found, consult a health care provider as soon as possible.

People with a cervix may want to consider...

- Researching the Human Papilloma Virus vaccines that exist and asking your health provider for more information (for more information on HPV, see modules 10.2 and 10.3).
- Asking a health care provider about what the current guidelines are for Pap smears and screening for HPV and cervical cancer.

People with testicles may want to consider...

- That testicles are extremely sensitive sex-glands that exist outside of the body (external genitals) and are housed in a sac of skin and tissue called the **scrotum.** Because testicles are so sensitive, they are sometimes a source of pleasure and sometimes a source of pain.
- That testicles start producing sperm and the testosterone hormone at puberty.
- That one testicle often hangs lower than the other and can grow faster than the other during puberty.
- Knowing what is normal for your body. This helps to discern when or if there is a symptom or feeling that is out of the ordinary.

Sexual health issues that affect people with any genitalia and anatomy...

Tinea Cruris
- Commonly known as "jock itch," Tinea Cruris affects people in places where there is a lot of sweat.
- It is a skin rash that presents as an itchy, red irritation.
- It affects the crural fold (in the groin area) from sweat that accumulates within folds of skin and skin rubbing together, causing the irritation.
- It is more often present in people with penises and testicles due to there being more skin folds that easily rub together; however, Tinea Cruris can also be present in people with **vulvas.**

Urinary Tract Infections (UTI)

People with vaginas are more likely to experience a UTI because they have shorter urethras. For those who have vaginal, penetrative, sexual intercourse with people with a penis, urinating after sexual intercourse can help prevent UTIs. People with vaginas must also develop a practice of always wiping their vulva and anus front to back to help prevent UTIs. Using spermicide can also increase your risk of a UTI.

- A UTI is a bacterial infection of the urinary tract, making it painful and challenging to urinate (and feeling like you have to urinate at all times).
- It is easily treated with antibiotics.
- It is important to go to a health care provider soon after suspecting you have a UTI; if a UTI is left without treatment, the infection can travel up to other organs (like the kidneys), causing severe pain and other possible complications.
- UTIs most often occur in people with vaginas because the **urethra** is shorter; bacteria can more easily travel up through the urinary tract.

Yeast Infections

- Yeast infections occur when there is an imbalance in the **Ph balance** of your genitals.
- They most often occur in people who have vaginas but people with penises can get them too. Regardless of your anatomy and the kinds of sexual activity you are engaging in, yeast infections can be passed on through genital contact.

Educator Reflection Questions

- How did you first learn about puberty? What (if anything) would you have changed about that first learning experience?
- How comfortable or uncomfortable are you using anatomically correct language to describe puberty, body parts, and bodily functions?
  - What words do you most commonly use? Do these words change depending on your audience? If so, why do they change?
  - What kinds of information, motivation, resources, and/or support will it take to ensure that you are able to comfortably and confidently use the anatomically correct names when discussing puberty?
- What were the norms and your family culture around naming (or not naming) body parts and bodily functions? For instance, did you openly talk about bodily functions (like urination and defecating)? What kinds of words were you taught to use to name your body parts?

- What were the norms and your family culture around talking about puberty?
- Can you think of three specific examples of how sexuality education leaves out people with disabilities? What assumptions are inherent when people with disabilities are left out of sexuality education? Where did you learn these assumptions and what are three strategies for unlearning them?
- Can you think of three examples of the ways that you might assign a gender to body parts (either intentionally or unintentionally)?
  - Now, using these three examples, can you think about ways to reframe your language and remove any assumptions or reference to gender?
  - Can you think of words you regularly use that already do this? For instance, maybe you already use the term "partner" or "spouse."

4.3 PUBERTY AND SEXUAL HEALTH

LEVEL [1] [2]

All-gender classes can normalize changes during puberty and demystify differences between people. At the same time, many students are more comfortable with asking puberty questions in gender-segregated environments. If you are opting for segregated classes, ensure that all students learn the same information and be conscious not to exclude or silence trans and gender non-normative students (for more information, see modules 4.1 and 4.2).

Big Ideas in Module 4.3

- Puberty is a time of physical, emotional, and social changes; these changes can feel exciting, scary, overwhelming, and/or empowering.
- Having accurate information about puberty and sexuality can help students navigate the changes associated with puberty.
- It is important for students to start to get to know what is "normal" for their own unique bodies.

Learning Objectives

Students will:

- Identify and explore their opinions related to different aspects of sexuality and relationships.
- Consider their own opinions as well as the opinions of their peers and family.
- Reflect on where their opinions align and diverge with peers and family.
- Reflect on how values are influenced by peers and family.

Cross-Curricular Connections

- Biology
- Gender Studies
- Psychology
- Social Studies
- Sociology

Terminology

- Androgens
- Cervical mucus
- Cervix
- Clitoris
- Erogenous zones
- Foreskin
- Glans
- Hormones
- Hypothalamus
- Labia
- Labia majora
- Labia minora
- Menstruation
- Orgasm
- Penis
- Pituitary gland
- Pre-Menstrual Syndrome (PMS)
- Scrotum
- Semen
- Sperm

- Testicles (testes)
- Uterus
- Vagina
- Vulva

Materials

- Chalkboard or whiteboard
- Sticky notes
- Question box or envelope

Background Information for Educators

Puberty is a period of massive change. By the time you are facilitating these lessons, many of your students may have already experienced many changes. Puberty classes can bolster their adaptive abilities and resilience to these changes by providing them with an idea of what to expect, by validating their feelings and experiences, by developing their skills to encounter uncertainties and negotiate relationships, and by helping them make informed choices.

Lack of information on sexuality and sexual health, as well as misinformation, can have serious negative consequences: fear and embarrassment; isolation and shame; risk and harm from sexual experiences; and participation in gender scripts that limit the kinds of emotional, romantic, physical, and sexual relationships that are possible (for more information on gender norms and stereotypes, see modules 3.4, 3.5, 3.6, and 3.7).

It is important to stress to students that although puberty is a time of significant bodily, social, and emotional changes, they should get to know what is "normal" for their unique bodies. Students can learn this through observing or touching their own bodies and taking note of the changes over time.

Student Readiness

Before students engage with this lesson, ensure that safer space guidelines and group norms have been established (and revisited) within your classroom (for more information on how to establish safer space guidelines, see module 1.3). In order to effectively prepare for this activity, ensure students understand that:

- Puberty is a very normal part of human development.
- Everyone experiences puberty differently and on differing timelines; there is no one way to experience puberty since every person and every body are unique.

- Assigned sex and gender identity are different. Review the definitions of each with your students before beginning this module. (For more information on assigned sex and gender identity, see module 3.1).
- Having questions about puberty and sexuality is very normal and asking questions is encouraged!

Summary of Activities

Students will:

- Collectively establish community agreements and safer space guidelines, emotional expectations, appropriate language, a definition of puberty, and critically examine sources of information.
- Work in small groups to identify common experiences of puberty (regardless of anatomy).
- Individually and anonymously write down questions related to puberty and sexuality. *Questions will be discussed in the following class.*

Activity 1

Instructions
Part 1

1. Explore the feelings students may have about discussing sexuality and puberty by drawing faces with different expressions on them (e.g., happy, sad, confused). Ask: What feelings might people have when discussing sexuality and puberty? *Be sure to validate every feeling mentioned, add ones not mentioned, affirm that often feelings can be contradictory, and remind students that whatever they feel is okay.*

2. For students in level 2, hand out 5 to 8 sticky notes. Write on the board "talking about puberty feels like…" and ask students to write down the first thoughts that come to mind on their sticky notes. Students may choose which sticky notes they want to place on the board.

QUICK TIP
If you do not feel comfortable drawing each kind of emotion, look online for common emojis to express various emotions and print each one big enough so that students can see them from the board.

EDUCATOR ANSWER KEY
- Happy to learn
- Relieved to be informed
- Embarrassed
- Nervous
- Self-conscious
- Bored
- Confused
- Intrigued
- Worried about the future
- Excited to grow
- Dreading change

Part 2

1. Establish ground rules. Use suggested ones below and/or co-create and add to them with the class:
   - Whatever you are feeling is okay, e.g., feeling embarrassed, confused, bored are all okay.
   - Choose how you react to your feelings, e.g., giggling is okay to ease discomfort and nervousness. Laughing at others is not okay. Taking deep breaths is okay. Disrupting the class or leaving the room are not okay. *This is a great opportunity to introduce the practice of trigger warnings and to differentiate between leaving the classroom as a disruption and leaving the classroom to take care of yourself.*
   - Exercise discretion and privacy. Do not share anything personal about your friends or someone in your family that they would prefer to keep private.
   - Be kind, considerate, and respectful. Do not make fun of other people's questions, e.g., laughing at, pointing, teasing, whispering about someone else.
   - Be curious! Your questions are welcome!

Part 3

- Draw 4 columns as you explain that there are different categories of words for different contexts. At the top of each column write:
  - Baby words
  - Scientific words
  - Polite words
  - Slang
- Ask students for the "Baby words" for urination. Then do the same for the next 3 columns. Below are some examples of other words that you can use with your class to explore all 4 columns. Use your own discretion based on how well you know your classroom, their maturity, and what other examples are being brought forward by your class:
  - "pee pee," "urinate," "go to the washroom," and "take a piss."
  - "poo poo," "defecate," "go to the washroom," and "do a number 2."
  - "bum," "buttocks," "behind," and "butt."
  - "boobie," "breast," "bust," and "boob."
  - "wee wee," "penis," and "dick/cock/prick."
  - "wee wee," "vulva," "vagina," and "pussy/vag/va-jay-jay."
- Explain the implications of each of the columns: Not everyone uses the same baby words; some polite words are not clear/accurate and in certain contexts, someone saying they had to "go and take a piss" might be shocking. Explain that the most appropriate words for discussing puberty are scientific words: they are clear, accurate, and specific. Let students know that they will be learning the scientific words for body parts, biological processes of puberty, and bodily functions.
- Ask students to suggest words that might be part of the common definition of puberty and write them on the board. Then create a definition together based on the suggested words. Explain that the changes are physical (bodies) as well as emotional (feelings), mental (mind), and social (how we relate to each other).

EDUCATOR ANSWER KEY—WORDS THAT MIGHT BE PART OF A COMMON DEFINITION OF PUBERTY

- Changes
- Body
- Hormones
- Developmental stages
- Child/teen/pre-teen
- Becoming an adult

EDUCATOR ANSWER KEY—CREATE A DEFINITION TOGETHER

Puberty is the change from child/teen/pre-teen to adult. It includes changes that are physical, emotional, mental, and social.

Part 4

1. Draw a circle on the board with spokes. Put the words "puberty" and "sexuality" in the circle.
2. Ask: Where have you heard about puberty and sexuality? Where do you get your information?
3. Write each word at the end of a spoke (for an example, see figure 4A).
4. Ask students to evaluate the trustworthiness of the different sources and share how they came to their conclusions. If they know of some good sources/books, they can bring them in for fellow students to take a look. Summarize the best sources for students to get accurate information, i.e., doctors, nurses and other health care providers, schools, books, and some online sources (for examples of books and online sources with accurate, youth-friendly information, see the 4.3 resources).
5. Discuss the images that they may see that are intended for adults, as that may come up as a source of information, be viewed by accident, or be sought after. Discuss that some of these images may be confusing and/or disturbing, e.g., seeing sexual activities they do not understand or seeing violent sexual activities.

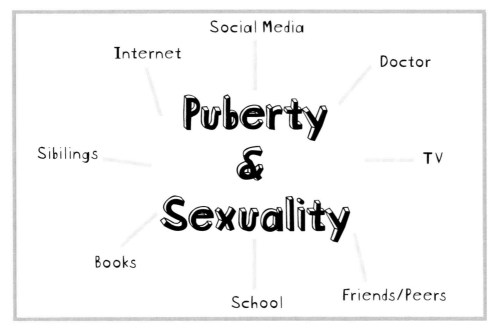

Figure 4A

Activity 2 [1] [2]

Instructions

1. Introduce the activity using the following points:
   - Puberty involves changes in body, mind, emotion, and connection to others. The changes that are easiest to notice are in the physical body.
   - Most people start to experience these changes between 8 to 13 years of age but for others, it can start at a younger or older age. Every body is different and everybody experiences puberty differently, at different ages, and for different lengths of time.
   - Puberty starts when the **hypothalamus** and **pituitary gland** release **hormones** and the rest of the body responds.
2. Organize the class into groups and ask each group to list at least 3 changes to expect during puberty, regardless of assigned sex or gender identity.
3. Take one example from each group to compile a list on the board. These broad terms emphasize commonalities between people and help students feel included. The final list should include:
   - Body shape change (e.g., muscle growth, shoulders broadening, hips widening)
   - Height growth
   - Weight gain
   - Body hair growth (e.g., pubic hair, underarm hair, hair on other parts of the body)

- Voice change
- Increased perspiration and body odour
- Pimples and acne
- Genital growth
- Signs of fertility (e.g., production of eggs and sperm)
- Intensified emotions (e.g., mood swings)
- Intensified attractions, sexual thoughts, and feelings
- Changes in sense of self

4. Based on student interested and comprehensive and changes listed on the board, engage students in a conversation with additional points from the following information.

Shape changes and increased height

- Growth happens gradually and in spurts. Between toddlerhood and puberty, growth tends to be gradual. At puberty, there are often growth spurts that can include "growing pains."
- In general, people assigned female at birth tend to experience growth spurts earlier than people assigned male.
- Estrogen and testosterone are the main hormonal triggers for pubertal growth. People assigned male at birth make more testosterone and some estrogen. People assigned female at birth make more estrogen and some testosterone.
- Estrogen widens the lower body, stimulates breast growth, and generally makes bodies "curvier." Testosterone thickens skin, widens the upper body, and stimulates hair and muscle growth. Because everyone's hormonal combination and proportion is different, we all grow in these ways to different degrees (e.g., some people assigned male at birth experience temporary breast development because of the estrogen in their bodies).
- As body size increases, feet, arms, legs, and hands can begin to grow before the rest of the body. This may cause a period of feeling clumsy.
- Stretch marks or little scars can form on the skin from rapid growth.
- How shape and height changes is determined by genetics as well as social and environmental factors. Food high in nutrients, healthy sleep patterns (young people need approximately 9 hours of sleep per night), and physical activity are important for growth and development.

Weight changes

- Weight gain is very common during puberty.
- We are bombarded with images from the media about weight and beauty that shape our cultural understandings of healthy, "normal," and beautiful bodies. Healthy bodies come in all shapes and sizes (for more information, see chapter 5).
- It is important to learn and practise self-acceptance and to create positive spaces. Fat-shaming and other kinds of body shaming are systemic injustices (for more information, see chapter 5).

Body hair growth

- During puberty, new hair grows in the pubic area (around the **vulva** and the **penis**) and under the armpits. Facial, back, chest, and buttocks hair also usually thickens.
- Some people have a lot of body hair, some people have very little.
- Trimming or removing hair is a cultural and social practice often driven by the media and the cultural and social norms of the time. There is no health reason to remove (or not to remove) hair. Engage students in a discussion about the freedom and right not to adhere to gender norms, e.g., girls *should* shave their legs and boys *should* never shave their legs. (For more information on gender norms, see modules 3.4, 3.5, and 3.7).

Voice change

- **Androgens** are a group of hormones (the primary and most well-known being testosterone) that cause the voice box (larynx) to grow. The more testosterone there is, the more the voice deepens. If this happens quickly, the voice might "crack" or "squeak."
- On average, adult pitch is reached at 15 years of age, although the voice may not fully settle until the early twenties.

Perspiration and body odour

- During puberty, the sweat glands develop, leading to an increase in perspiration (sweat).
- Increased sweat (and oil) make it more likely for bacteria to grow on the skin, especially under the armpits. This can lead to strong body odour that many people find unpleasant. To avoid body odour, you can use deodorant or antiperspirants. Deodorants are made to address the smell of sweat by killing the bacteria that grows on skin. Antiperspirants stop sweat entirely by blocking sweat glands with aluminum. (For more information on the differences between antiperspirant and deodorant, see the 4.3 resources).

- Good hygiene is important. Wash feet, hands, groin, and armpits regularly and change/wash clothes often. Soap and water is all that is needed to wash the body. Do not use products like douches. They can harm the body, increase susceptibility to sexually transmitted infections, and disrupt the body's natural PH balance.

YOU SHOULD KNOW

Douches are often marketed to people with vaginas as a way of "cleaning" the vagina and preventing vaginal odours. They sometimes contain just water or water and vinegar; douches sold in drugstores usually contain fragrances and antiseptics. Doctors and gynecological associations strongly recommend against vaginal douching because it has been linked to increased susceptibility to infections, adverse pregnancy outcomes, pelvic inflammatory disease, and cervical cancer (Cottrell, 2010). The vagina is a self-cleaning organ. While it is good hygiene practice to clean the surface and folds of the vulva with mild soap and water on a regular basis, cleaning the vagina is unnecessary. Vaginal odour is natural/normal. If you have a vagina, it is a good idea to get to know your vaginal odour so that you begin to understand what is normal for your body and your body's hormonal cycles.

Pimples and acne

- Acne is so common that it is considered a "normal" part of puberty. The skin produces a waxy substance (called sebum) that may clog pores and lead to acne.
- Acne is a condition of the skin that shows up as different types of bumps. These bumps can be blackheads, whiteheads, pimples, or cysts.
- Ways to keep the skin healthy include: eating healthy food, sleeping well, and washing the face with mild soap. It is important to know that adhering to all of these practices does not necessarily mean that you will not get pimples or acne. Pimples and acne depend on a number of factors, some of which cannot be controlled without a health care provider.
- If acne affects self-image, you may want to consult a health care provider to discuss options.

Genital growth
(For anatomy diagrams, see 4.9 resources)

- During puberty, the colour of the genitals darkens and they increase in size. The **labia minora** and (to a lesser degree) the **labia majora** become bigger. The **clitoris** also grows. **Testicles** inside the **scrotum** start growing and producing hormones and **sperm**. The scrotum hangs lower and becomes darker in colour. The penis grows larger after the testicles have increased in size.
- The tip and opening of a penis' **foreskin** becomes wider, progressively allowing itself to be pulled back toward the shaft of the penis and behind the **glans**.

Signs of fertility
(For anatomy diagrams, see 4.9 resources)

- To be fertile is to have the capacity to reproduce.
- Signs of fertility for people with **vaginas** and people with **uteruses** is the increase of vaginal discharge (**cervical mucus**), which looks like a sticky or egg white like matter and the beginning of **menstruation**. *Vaginal discharge is a common part of puberty and bodily function that may happen up to a year before first period/menstruation. Explain to your students that getting to know what their vaginal discharge typically looks like can help to know their own body and what is normal for them. Knowing what is normal for their body can help determine "abnormal" vaginal discharge. Advise students to consult a health care professional if they experience vaginal discharge that is out of the ordinary for their body.*
- Signs of fertility for people with penises include the first ejaculation of **semen** from the penis. One of the ways that ejaculation of semen from the penis can occur during puberty is in **nocturnal emissions** or "wet dreams." Wet dreams can happen all on their own, not connected to sexual dreams or thoughts. Some people get them, some people do not. Their frequency tends to be highest during puberty but they can also continue into adulthood, often with less frequency.

Intensified emotions

- Mood swings are common throughout puberty and are in part caused by surges of hormones. Mood swings are when people feel really happy one minute and then really angry or even sad the next. Mood swings may come and go, as they often fluctuate with hormones.

QUICK TIP

Ensure that all your students (regardless of gender identity) know what menstruation is. You can talk about menstruation in a non-gendered and accurate way by referring to "people with uteruses." (For a more comprehensive definition of menstruation, see the language key and module 4.2).

- **Pre-Menstrual Syndrome (PMS)** is one way that intensified emotions can manifest for people who experience menstruation. Not everyone who experiences menstruation experiences PMS. People experience PMS to greater or lesser degrees and through a variety of symptoms such as: mood swings, greater emotional sensitivity, increased water retention (bloating), tenderness in breast/chest tissue, diarrhea, headaches, and acne. PMS usually happens before menstruation and does not always look or feel the same month to month.

Changes in sense of self

- During puberty, young people have to deal with rapid physical changes and this can leave some feeling self-conscious. Other people's reaction to the young person can also change (e.g., if someone suddenly looks older and is treated as such).
- Because puberty can start at different times for different people, some people find it difficult to cope with early physical changes or with waiting for them to happen.
- Social changes during puberty can include: seeking more independence and responsibility; developing a new identity as part of becoming an adult; developing a stronger individual set of values and morals and points of view (what is "right" and "wrong") as the capacity to think abstractly grows; and changing relationships/ friendships and who people want to spend time with. These changes are influenced by peer/social groups, cultural background, and family expectations.
- Peer pressure increases around this time, coupled with a strong desire to fit in.
- If a student is having a rough time navigating the complex emotions that come with puberty and they need to talk to someone, encourage them to talk to someone they can trust. If they cannot identify someone they can trust, you can provide these toll-free, national crisis counselling lines, specifically for young people. (For more phone numbers and websites, see **National Support Services** in the resources section).
  - Klinic Crisis Line: 1-888-322-3019
  - Kids Help Phone: 1-800-668-6868

Intensified attractions, sexual thoughts, and feelings

- As puberty sets in, students may feel intensified romantic and sexual attraction. Attraction may be towards celebrities or people they know; towards people of various gender identities and gender expressions, characteristics, and age. It may also become more exciting to think about being in a relationship with other people. (For more information, see modules 2.8, 3.3, 3.8, 3.9, 4.6, and chapter 7).
- People may start having more direct and stronger sexual feelings and fantasies.
- **Masturbation** is a common way to physically explore your own body and sexuality. People of any assigned sex and gender identity can masturbate (or self-pleasure). Not everyone masturbates but most people do. It is not an unhealthy behaviour, despite myths that say so.
- People masturbate differently; there is no "right" way. The densest distribution of nerves in the body are in the **clitoris** and in the penis. At the same time, **erogenous zones** are all over the body. Each person finds different things pleasurable.
- Masturbation sometimes leads to **orgasm**, which is a strong, pleasurable feeling in the genitals and throughout the body. It may (or may not) happen alongside ejaculation from the penis or vulva. Similarly, ejaculation from the penis or vulva may (or may not) happen alongside an orgasm.

YOU SHOULD KNOW

There is disagreement within scientific communities about what is commonly called "female ejaculate fluid" is made of and where it comes from. A recent study found that female ejaculate is produced in the Skene Glands, which produces prostatic fluids that empty into the urethra. Some people who were assigned female at birth are born with Skene Glands and some are not. The Skene glands are surrounded by tissue, which includes clitoral tissue (Crew, 2015; All Things Vagina, 2016).

Activity 3 [1] [2]

Instructions

1. Explain the following process to students for writing down questions:
- Everyone gets a piece of paper. Write down questions about puberty or sexuality that you have. If you have no question, write a sentence about your favourite sport, meal, or pastime.
- Work on your own and do not write your name—the questions are anonymous.

- Use scientific words if you know them. If you do not know the scientific word, use the word that you know and then indicate on your question that you would like to know the accurate, scientific word.
- Fold your paper once and I will come to collect them. Questions will be answered during the next class. *Some educators prefer to keep a box for questions on their desk so that students can place questions anonymously in the box on an on-going basis.*

2. Arrange for a follow-up session where student questions are answered.

Educator Tips and Tools

- If you do not know the answer to a question being asked, acknowledge your gap in knowledge, do the required research, and then follow up with your students. This is a good way to practise and role model humility. It also helps to build trust with your students by showing them that you took their questions/concerns seriously enough to conduct outside research and bring that research back to them. If you are doing research outside of *Beyond the Basics* and are looking for reliable sources of information, see the resources section or visit the Online Hub.
- Practise validation. Acknowledge the curiosity behind the question.
- Get clarification. If it is a straight forward question, answer it. If there can be multiple interpretations, discern what is really being asked. If possible, give the answer to more than one interpretation of the question.
- Be empathetic by showing your appreciation of the curiosity, confusion, or concern underlying the question, and normalize those feelings.
- Be informative. Answer the question with facts, tendencies, and possibilities.
- Talk about values. Outline the responsibilities and ethics relevant to the question. Encourage students to know their own values, the values of their families, as well as cultural and faith teachings.

Wrap-up

Summarize the module with the following points:
- Puberty involves physical, mental, emotional, and social changes.
- Everyone begins and ends puberty at different times during their adolescence. They also grow at different speeds and in different ways.
- There are reliable, accurate sources for puberty and sexuality information, such as the information contained in this book; there are also less reliable and inaccurate sources.
- As you talk more about puberty, bodies, sexual health, and sexuality, it will feel more and more comfortable.

4.4 SEXUAL HEALTH: BODIES, SEXUALITY, AND SEXUAL RESPONSE

LEVEL 3

Big Ideas in Module 4.4

- Bodies and the ways sexuality is expressed are diverse, so are the ways that people engage in sexual activities and experience sexual response.
- The ways bodies respond to sexual activities are diverse and responses can change from day to day, moment to moment. There are an infinite number of possibilities and combinations of response and no one way is "right."
- People (often unknowingly) hold a variety of assumptions and myths about sexuality and bodies. Discerning between myths and facts is an important part of learning how to make informed decisions.
- Consent and pleasure are integral to sexuality and ensuring positive sexual experiences.

Learning Objectives

Students will:

- Explore myths and facts about human bodies, sexuality, and sexual health.
- Develop a broad understanding of sex in relationship to diverse bodies, sexualities, and sexual response.
- Critically analyze the non-linear model and the linear model used to describe human sexual response.

Cross-Curricular Connections

- Biology
- Gender Studies
- Psychology
- Social Studies
- Sociology

Terminology

- Intersex
- Puberty
- Sexual Health
- Sexual Response
- Sexuality
- Transgender

Materials

- Printed copies of **Sexuality Statement Sets**
- Optional: **Educator Answer Key— Sexuality Statement Sets**
- Printed copies of **Models for Human Response**
- **Educator Answer Key—Models for Human Response**

Background Information for Educators
(For more information about sexual health, see module 4.2)
Just as it is important to give adolescents the correct information about sexuality, it is important to help them develop critical thinking and questioning skills when it comes to sex, bodies, **sexuality**, and **sexual health**.

If you have the option, *Beyond the Basics* recommends that you have all-gender classes. All-gender classes can normalize changes during **puberty**, destigmatize sexual health, and demystify differences between people. There is no information that a child should not have because of their assigned sex or gender identity. Effective sexuality education emphasizes similarities among students and promotes empathy and respect.

If you are opting for segregated classes, ensure that all students learn the same information about each other in order to promote empathy, respect, and open communication. It is crucial that if you have gender-segregated classrooms, you strategize ways to include transgender, gender diverse and intersex individuals in meaningful ways that do not further marginalize them and their experiences; **transgender, intersex**, and gender diverse students often become excluded and silenced through gender segregation. If you are providing gender-segregated classes, anonymously ask your students which gender grouping they would feel the most comfortable in.

Bodies are diverse and the ways that people engage in and respond to sexual activities are just as diverse. The definitions of sexuality and sexual health are both broad and encompassing of many different facets of being human, including the psychological, emotional, and social elements of sexuality and sexual health (for more information, see modules 0.1 and 2.5); there are a variety of components that contribute to a person's sexuality and to sexual health. Similarly, the kinds of sexual activities a person might choose to engage in and their sexual responses are diverse and ever changing and evolving.

The circular and linear models about the human **sexual response** are included in this lesson. Just as it is important to discern between fact and myth, it is important to critically engage with models for human function and behaviour; there is no right or wrong model for human sexual response and human sexual response does not always fall into these two models.

QUICK TIP
If you have the option of all-gender classes, conduct an anonymous poll of students to find out what kind of class arrangement they prefer when discussing topics related to sexual health. This has the potential of helping to empower students by showing them that you will take their feedback into consideration and act appropriately on their requests and give everyone an opportunity to state their needs.

Not only are bodies diverse but the ways bodies respond are diverse and responses can change from day to day, moment to moment. There are an infinite number of possibilities and combinations of response and no one way is "right." While the linear model of sexual response from Masters and Johnson is much more popular than the non-linear model proposed by Basson, both models hold truth and apply to human reality. The existence of these two models (and many more) remind students that human beings are diverse in their bodies, responses, and experiences.

Student Readiness

Before students engage with this lesson, ensure that safer space guidelines and group norms have been established (and revisited) within your classroom (for more information on how to establish safer space guidelines within a classroom, see module 1.3). In order to effectively prepare for this activity, ensure students understand that:
- Myths about sexuality are everywhere and that some common myths will get challenged in this module.
- Although we are discussing two different models of sexual response, sexual response is as diverse as people are unique.
- Although this module analyzes two types of human sexual response, it does so in general terms. Ensure that students understand that this module is not an opportunity to talk about the individual sexual responses of others.

Summary of Activities

Students will:
- work in small groups to decipher between myths and facts about sexuality.
- work in small groups to critically analyze two leading models about human sexual response.

Activity 1 ③

Familiarize yourself with the information contained in 4.2 and the **Educator Answer Key—Sexuality Statement Sets** before facilitating this activity.

Instructions
1. Introduce the lesson by drawing on the following points:
   - People often carry a number of myths about bodies and sexuality and may hold on to particular myths depending on their social group, family, and media they consume.

- It is important to discern between myths and facts about bodies and sexuality because it is part of being able to make informed decisions about sex and sexual health.
- Identify places, websites, hotlines, and people that students can go to for more information (for ideas, see the 4.4 resources).

2. This activity is modeled after the common game *Two Truths and a Lie*. Each set of 3 statements will contain 2 statements that are true and 1 that is false. Print and cut out the **Sexuality Statement Sets**. Have small groups of 2 to 5 students work on one or multiple sets of statements. Depending on your students and the amount of time, you can have multiple groups working on the same statement sets or only one group working on each set.

3. Debrief the statements as a class. *You can give students the Educator Answer Key as a handout, if you see fit.*

Activity 2 [3]

Instructions

1. Give students the handout **Models for Human Sexual Response.**

2. In small groups or pairs, ask students to answer the questions on the handout. Debrief as a class using the **Educator Answer Key— Models for Human Sexual Response.**

3. Summarize the exercise by reiterating:
   - Different people have different responses. The same person may respond differently at different times.
   - You can have sexual pleasure and satisfaction without orgasm.
   - Sexual desire and arousal are significantly affected by relationship dynamics, intimacy, and the perceived and actual risk involved in exploring sex and sexuality.
   - Sexual arousal *does not* equal consent (for more information on consent, see chapter 8).

Wrap-up

Summarize the module with the following points:

- There is a lot of information about bodies, sexuality, and sexual health. It is important to discern between facts and myths and to engage with information critically.
- Learning and unlearning are lifelong processes.
- Reiterate where students can get accurate sexual health information and support.

4.5 UNDERSTANDING TOUCH: RESPECTFUL TOUCH, PLEASURABLE TOUCH, AND ABUSIVE TOUCH

LEVEL 2

Big Ideas in Module 4.5

- Abusive touch often happens in everyday contexts from people that are known to survivors. It is important to talk about all forms of touch in order to decipher between respectful, pleasurable, and abusive touch.
- Abusive touch is about power differences and boundary violations.
- Touching yourself sexually for pleasure (masturbating) is a common and safe practice. While masturbation is private touch, it is not a secret.
- All touch can be talked about. Secret touches are not okay (CWHN, 2014).
- Touch that is inappropriate might feel good, bad, or confusing. Intention, outcome, and context all matter when distinguishing inappropriate and appropriate forms of touch.

SEXUAL ABUSE
(For more information on trigger warnings, see modules 1.3 and 1.6)

Learning Objectives

Students will:

- Discern between appropriate and inappropriate touching by considering intention, impact, and context.
- Debunk myths about masturbation and consider their own choices.
- Consider the dynamics of sexual abuse using a story, understand the tricks that "tricky people" use when perpetrating abuse, and consider who the trusted adults are in their own lives.

Cross-Curricular Connections

- Equity Studies
- Gender Studies
- Psychology
- Social Studies
- Sociology

Terminology

- Survivor

Materials

- Printed copies of **Touch is Complicated!**
- **Educator Resource—Touch is Complicated!**
- Printed copies of **What can I do?**
- Printed copies of **Jordan's Story**
- Chalkboard or whiteboard

Background Information for Educators

This module discusses different kinds of touch. The benefit of teaching about disrespectful or inappropriate touch, self-pleasurable touch, and abusive touch together is that it helps build a general and comprehensive wisdom about bodies and boundaries. Singling out abuse as a separate, sexual topic obscures the fact that it often happens in everyday settings and as a result of power differences and boundary violations. The right to bodily autonomy and the removal of shame from sexual experience cut across all of these topics related to touch.

Sexual violence affects people of all ages and backgrounds. Proceed with the understanding that any student may be a survivor and/or witness of sexual violence and that discussions on this topic can be upsetting, overwhelming, or triggering. Acknowledge this at the beginning of every session and allow students to discretely take space if they need. Do your best to keep discussions focused, open, and respectful to everyone. (For more information, see module 1.6).

Child sexual abuse happens when someone uses power over a child to involve the child in any sexual act. In the majority of cases, children and youth know their offender. Often, they are family members, people in the community, and/or in a care taking role for the child. The offender may be an adult or another young person. Sexual abuse can happen once or can continue for years.

Sexual abuse hurts children in different ways. Because of power difference, **survivors** find it extremely difficult to stop the abuse on their own or disclose their abuse. Abuse can happen with physical and psychological coercion, threats and lies, and self-blame and shame on the part of the survivor.

YOU SHOULD KNOW

The term survivor is used to describe survivors of sexual violence. It is a way to recognize that people who have experienced sexual violence are not passive victims, they are active survivors working to survive and thrive.

Abuse prevention education equips students with the ability to discern abuse and affirms their right to disclose. The sooner a child discloses, the sooner their recovery can begin. Survivors need different kinds of support: individual counselling, family counselling, medical help, legal and court support, as well as more immediate basic needs. (For a list of crisis lines, see **National Support Services** in the resources section).

Trauma that is not attended to can spur lasting effects, resulting in anxiety, depression, social isolation, and sexual and relationship issues. Many survivors cope with the pain using mechanisms like self-harm, substance use, and chaotic sexual behaviours. The effects of trauma that are not attended to can also last through generations. This is often referred to as intergenerational trauma and has become a part of the conversation around traumatic events throughout history that effect large populations of people, such as residential schools, colonialism, the holocaust, and other cultural genocides. The ways that intergenerational trauma affects individuals is diverse.

In Canada, professionals and educators who suspect child abuse have a responsibility to report it to the local child protection agency. Educators should also refer to their school board policies.

Student Readiness

Before students engage with this lesson, ensure that safer space guidelines and group norms have been established (and revisited) within your classroom (for more information on how to establish safer space guidelines, see module 1.3). In order to effectively prepare for this activity, ensure students understand that:

- This module addresses all forms of touch.
- Sexual abuse is discussed in one of the activities.
- In this module, the term survivor refers to people who have survived sexual abuse.
- All human beings have the right to bodily autonomy and to be free from experiencing abuse, violence, and coercion.
- Experiencing abusive touch is not your fault.
- There are supports available to students who are survivors. *Ensure that you have identified these supports ahead of time. Before starting the activities, inform students what these supports are and where they can find them.*

Summary of Activities

Students will:

- Work in small groups (or individually) and discuss a scenario about different types of touch and answer questions to discern between appropriate and inappropriate touch by considering intention, impact, and context.

- Collectively brainstorm possible reasons why people masturbate.
- Individually read (or listen to) a story about abuse and receive a handout that will help them identify who they can disclose abuse to if needed.

Activity 1 3

Instructions
1. Explain that this class is about different kinds of touch. Distribute **Touch is Complicated!** to students in small groups of 3 to 4. Ask students to discuss the scenarios, answer the questions, and report back. *The scenarios can also be worked through individually and then discussed as a large group.*
2. As a class, have each group share highlights from their discussion. *To save time, you can have different groups talk about different scenarios. The* **Educator Resource—Touch is Complicated!** *can help prompt discussion.*
3. Discuss as a class:
   - What makes any touch okay or not okay?

EDUCATOR ANSWER KEY
- Both intention and outcome matter. If the intention was positive and healthy but the outcome was negative, we need to strategize about how to notice and communicate with the other person. If the intention and the outcome were negative unhealthy experiences, we need to strategize next steps and identify people we can disclose to.
- Introduce the distinction between private touch and secret touch. **Private touch** happens when everyone involved is able to control that touch in a space where they feel safe, comfortable, and have privacy. E.g., masturbation (or self-pleasure) is something that should be done privately. **Secret touch** happens when someone else is asking, manipulating, coercing, and/or forcing you to keep the touch secret. Secrets are based in shame, privacy is not.

- Sometimes the intention of a touch is good but the experience is not. How do we find out if a touch has the outcome we want? How can you know if a touch is wanted or not?

EDUCATOR ANSWER KEY

- Ask
- Observe
- Check in
- Communicate
- Notice context

- Touch is not just good or bad; it is contextual. What are times when a handshake might be bad? When might a slap on the back be good?

EDUCATOR ANSWER KEY

- Touch is bad if forced, if it is against someone's faith practices, or if it's mean-spirited.
- Touch is good if understood and consented to, like in a sport or game (e.g., tag) or to help someone who is choking.

4. Reinforce the idea that whether touch is appropriate or not depends on context, meaning, and the impact it has. Drawing on some of the scenario examples, highlight that sometimes touch can be inappropriate but not abusive. Reinforce that your body is your own and no one has the right to cross your boundaries, touch you in a way that you do not want to be touched, hurt you, or harm you.

Activity 2 3

Instructions

1. Explain that another kind of touch that is related to the idea that your body is your own is self-pleasure. Explain that self-pleasure is also known as **masturbation**. It means touching yourself sexually and sensually to feel good.
2. Explain that there is a lot of misinformation about masturbation. Clarify that:
   - People of any gender identity or sex can masturbate.
   - It is your choice whether you want to. Some people do, and some do not.
   - Sometimes masturbation leads to orgasm, a strong pleasurable sensation in the body.

- There are myths that portray masturbation as unhealthy. These are untrue and in fact, masturbation is safe from STBBIs and pregnancies.
- People who masturbate do it for many different reasons.

YOU SHOULD KNOW

The ways that people masturbate are varied. For instance, while some people may masturbate using their hands, other people may prefer to masturbate using sex toys. For many people it is a combination of both methods. If sex toys are shared, they need to be cleaned according to the manufactures' instructions in order to prevent STBBIs.

3. Given that masturbation is pleasurable, private, and safe from STIs and pregnancies, ask the class to brainstorm reasons that people may masturbate. Use the list below as a guide:

TO FEEL PLEASURE	TO GET TO KNOW YOUR BODY	TO RELEASE SEXUAL URGES
TO RELAX	TO GO TO SLEEP	IN LIEU OF HAVING PARTNER SEX
TO EASE MENSTRUAL CRAMPS	TO EASE PHYSICAL PAIN	TO BOOST ENERGY
TO PROCRASTINATE	CURIOSITY	TO BOOST YOUR MOOD
FOR COMFORT	TO CONNECT WITH YOURSELF	TO ENJOY A FANTASY

4. Conclude this activity by reminding students: Whether someone masturbates is up to them. Many families, cultures, and faiths have specific values about masturbation. It is important to get to know and understand your values.

SEXUAL ABUSE
(For more information
on trigger warnings, see
modules 1.3 and 1.6)

Activity 3 [3]

Instructions

1. Remind students about appropriate touch and sexual touch and that they will be learning about inappropriate sexual touching. Tell students that they will hear/read a fictional story about a young person who has a bad experience with inappropriate sexual touching.
2. Hand out printed copies of **Jordan's Story** to students. Read as a class or individually.
3. Discuss as a class:
   - Is Jordan a boy or a girl?

EDUCATOR PROMPTS

Jordan could either identify as a boy or a girl, or any other gender identity. Reiterate here that sexual abuse can happen to a person of any gender identity.

- What kinds of touch can sexual abuse involve?

EDUCATOR PROMPTS

- Like we learned in Activity 1, no kind of touch is inherently good or bad.
- Sexual abuse may involve touch that feels good, bad, and/or confusing.
- The way to identify inappropriate or abusive touch is that it is secret. Ask: When did the uncle ask Jordan to keep it a secret?

- Some myths portray abusers as scary people lurking in dark alleys but this is not always true. Most often, sexual abusers are people we trust. In the same way that touch is not clearly "good" or "bad," people are not "good" or "bad." It is important to recognize "tricky people" who do things to manipulate and abuse young people. What do you think were the tricks that Jordan's uncle used?

EDUCATOR ANSWER KEY
- Gained Jordan's trust by giving special privileges (like calling him "Casey" when no one was around).
- Isolated Jordan to play "private" games.
- Made Jordan feel "special" and portrayed the abuse as their special secret.
- Lied and said that he was teaching Jordan about love.
- Blackmailed Jordan into "protecting" him by not disclosing.
- Made Jordan feel guilty for wanting to stop.

4. Affirm that:
   - It is never a survivor's fault that abuse happens.
   - Abuse is not a secret that the survivor has to keep.
   - Follow gut feelings and instincts: if it feels wrong, you are probably right.
   - It is important that survivors tell someone until the abuse stops.
5. Distribute **What Can I do?** to students and have them privately consider who the adults they trust might be.

Wrap-up
Summarize the module with the following points:
- It might have been a challenging class, as these topics are challenging with lots of potential emotions and tensions floating around the room.
- Touch that is inappropriate might feel good, bad, and/or confusing. Intention, outcome, and context all matter when distinguishing inappropriate and appropriate forms of touch.
- All touch can be talked about. Secret touches are not okay (CWHN, 2014).

YOU SHOULD KNOW
Private touch happens when everyone involved is able to control that touch in a space where they feel safe, comfortable, and have privacy. E.g., masturbation (or self-pleasure) is something that should be done privately. Secret touch happens when someone else is asking, manipulating, coercing, and/or forcing you to keep the touch secret. Secrets are based in shame, privacy is not.

- Touching yourself sexually (masturbating) is a common and safe practice. Decide whether or not to masturbate according to your values and be open to this decision changing throughout your life. While masturbation is private touch, it is not a secret. This is an important distinction to make with your students.
- Tell someone you trust if you experience inappropriate or abusive touch and know that no matter what, it is not your fault.

4.6 RELATIONSHIPS: DEALING WITH CRUSHES AND EMOTIONAL PAIN

LEVEL 2 [3]

Big Ideas in Module 4.6

- Developing emotional and social skills for navigating attraction, relationships (of all kinds), and emotional pain are important for mental health and well-being throughout the lifespan.
- Direct and assertive communication is valuable in all relationships.
- The appropriateness of disclosing if/when you have a crush depends not only on your intentions but also on the impact. (For more information on intention vs. impact, see figure 1A in module 1.2).

Learning Objectives

Students will:

- Consider appropriate ways to address crushes and attraction.
- Consider emotional pain we feel within relationships (of all kinds) and ways to deal with them.
- Consider how to support others and how to receive the support we need in dealing with emotional pain.

Cross-Curricular Connections

- Gender Studies
- Psychology
- Social Studies
- Sociology

Materials

- A room that students can move around in
- Printed signs marked "Appropriate" and "Inappropriate"
- Chalkboard or whiteboard
- Blank paper and a pen for each student

Background Information for Educators

Romantic and sexual relationships often begin in adolescence. Coupled with uncertainty, intense feelings, and the social risks that they involve, these relationships can cause significant stress and anxiety for young people and additional anxieties and stressors for students with diverse sexual/romantic orientations and gender identities/expressions (for more information, see chapter 3).

Discussing relationship norms and useful skills with students while normalizing struggles specific to attractions and romantic/sexual relationships can help.

Relationships of all kind require skills that we gain through experience (trial and error) and formal education. These social and emotional skills are important for good mental health, well-being and better life outcomes. They are also useful across relationships: temporary or life-long, intimate or distant, chosen or circumstantial.

Adolescents are often corrected for "wrong" behaviour that they exhibit to deal with emotional pain. This lesson refocuses the discussion away from being "good" and towards ways to deal with emotional pain that match students' personal experience, skills, and circumstances.

You may want to supplement this lesson with more activities on healthy relationships and friendships found in modules 7.2, 7.3, 7.4, 7.5, 7.6, and 7.7.

Student Readiness

Before students engage with this lesson, ensure that safer space guidelines and group norms have been established (and revisited) within your classroom (for more information on how to establish safer space guidelines, see module 1.3). In order to effectively prepare for this activity, ensure students understand that:

- This module will discuss crushes and feelings of attraction. It is okay to have crushes and it is okay not to have crushes.
- Instead of prescribing a "one size fits all" approach, this module will help students identify skills that they already have for dealing with emotional pain.

Summary of activities

Students will:

- Individually reflect on a story (read aloud by educator) and physically move around the room to explore the line between appropriate and inappropriate behaviour.
- Collectively discuss what makes the behaviour appropriate or inappropriate and brainstorm appropriate options.
- Individually reflect on the various ways that they deal with emotional pain and place these into categories.
- Collectively brainstorm what supports are available and what support could look like when dealing with emotional pain.

Activity 1 2 **3**

Instructions
1. Ask the class:
   • What is a "crush"? What are other words we have for being attracted to someone?

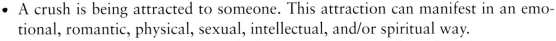

EDUCATOR ANSWER KEY
   • A crush is being attracted to someone. This attraction can manifest in an emotional, romantic, physical, sexual, intellectual, and/or spiritual way.
   • Students will likely come up with the most current words to describe attraction and you can prompt for common phrases, such as: liking someone, crushing out, swooning, smitten, etc.

   • How do you know if you might have a crush?

EDUCATOR ANSWER KEY
   • Think and daydream about them often
   • Are very aware of where they are in a room
   • Talking about them a lot
   • Changing your life with your crush in mind (e.g., picked up new interests)
   • Noticing things that remind you of them
   • Teasing
   • Flirting
   • Feeling nervous or self-conscious
   • Ignoring them

   • Who can people have crushes on?

EDUCATOR ANSWER KEY
Anyone. Attraction can surprise us.

2. Explain that it is okay to have crushes and it is okay not to have crushes. Explain that there are many options when you have a crush.

3. Designate two opposing walls in the classroom as "Appropriate" and "Inappropriate." Read each of the following 3 stories to students. As you read each story, ask students to place themselves along the continuum, based on whether they think the actions taken are appropriate or not, okay or not okay. Pause between lines to give time for students to move as stories escalate. Remind students that there are no wrong opinions and encourage them to be honest. You can prompt students to move by asking, "Is that okay?" after each line of the story.

Activity 1 Stories

Essa & Finn

Essa likes Finn. Essa doesn't tell Finn. It's been 2 years.

Essa's friends all know about the crush. They all talk and joke about it. It's Essa's favourite topic.

Essa asks a friend to talk to Finn, to see if Finn has a crush on anyone. Finn says, "I don't know, why?"

Essa constantly looks at Finn's social media posts and downloads copies of Finn's pictures.

Essa sends Finn a message on social media through an anonymous account: "I like you but you have no idea who I am."

After a week with no response, Essa sends Finn a second message through the anonymous account: "You're a heartbreaker. Why won't you notice me!!!!!"

Essa feels frustrated and wants Finn's attention. Essa forbids all of their friends from ever "liking" anything that Finn posts.

Lex & Coe

Lex likes Coe. Lex goes up to Coe in the library and asks if they can sit together. Coe says, "sure."

Lex and Coe end up sitting in the library together every Tuesday; they have the same spare period. One day, Lex brings Coe a small box of chocolates. Coe says, "Thanks!"

On Valentine's Day, Lex gives Coe a hand-drawn card. Coe says, "Thanks! You're such a good artist!"

Lex looks down and says to Coe, "Hey, um, I have a crush on you. And I'm wondering if you'd be interested in going out with me sometime?"

Coe is uncomfortable, and says, "No, actually, I'm not, like, into you like that. Sorry Lex."

Mel & Naz
Mel likes Naz. Mel asks to walk Naz home. Naz says, "Sure." They walk home together.

The next day, Mel says, "Nice outfit, Naz!" Naz says, "Oh thanks!"

Two days later, Mel says, "Great body, Naz! I like how tight your sweater is!" Naz laughs uncomfortably.

After a week, Mel lines up behind Naz when they are leaving class and stands so close that they are touching but Naz doesn't notice.

Later that day during gym class, Mel bumps up against Naz on purpose and touches Naz's bum. "Oops. Sorry! Accident!" says Mel. "Uh, it's Ok," says Naz.

4. Regroup and discuss:
   • What makes something okay or not, appropriate or not?

EDUCATOR ANSWER KEY
   • The impact on the other person.
   • Respecting privacy.
   • Respecting other people's boundaries, bodies, and autonomy.

   • What does it feel like to tell someone directly that you have a crush on them?

EDUCATOR ANSWER KEY
- Nervous
- Scared of rejection
- Fear of humiliation
- Unsure
- Exciting
- Brave

- Even though it can be scary, what are the benefits to being direct about your feelings?

EDUCATOR ANSWER KEY
- It might be better to know than not know
- Better chance to start a relationship well
- Can move on if you get rejected
- There is no shame in being attracted to someone
- Uncertainty can be hard to deal with

- What are some ways to be assertive if you want to tell your crush? Brainstorm as a class.

YOU SHOULD KNOW

There is an important distinction between being assertive and being aggressive. Gender norms around masculinity and femininity teach girls/women not to be assertive; when they are, it is often mislabelled as aggressive and stigmatized. Assertion in men/boys on the other hand is commonly celebrated. It is important for people of all gender identities to understand the differences between being aggressive and being assertive as this will help to increase communication and appropriate boundary setting within relationships.

EDUCATOR ANSWER KEY

- Make the distinction between being assertive and being aggressive with your students. Ask them what they think the difference is and clarify any relationship myths and gender norms that come up.
- Directly telling your crush how you feel and what kind of relationship you are looking for.
- Ask your crush out on a date. Make sure to clarify your feelings for them and what "going on a date" means to you.

Activity 2 2 3

Instructions

1. Explain: When we are connected to someone—be they family, friends, partners, teammates, neighbours, anyone—there is a chance that we can feel hurt by them emotionally. It is the nature of being connected. If someone is purposely trying to hurt us emotionally, that is abuse. Often, there is unintentional but inevitable emotional pain. *When introducing this activity, prompt students to consider the lesson in module 4.5 about intention, impact, and the context surrounding the emotional pain, in order to distinguish between emotional abuse and emotional pain.*

2. Ask: What are different kinds of unintentional emotional pain that you have seen in the world around you?

EDUCATOR ANSWER KEY

- Being rejected by your crush (hurt and rejection)
- Being disappointed that you are not allowed to go to a certain party (disappointment)
- Not being picked for a team (disappointment)
- Your friends have something you want (jealousy)
- Family breakup (sadness, grief)
- Missing a faraway loved one (longing)
- Being yelled at by a loved one (hurt)
- Struggling with school work (frustration)
- Disliking aspects of your life or body (resentment)

3. No one likes emotional pain. What are some ways to deal with it? Prompt students to think of short and long term coping mechanisms, both "good" and "bad" ones, creative and conventional ones. Help them see broadly how many of our behaviours are based on coping with pain.

EDUCATOR ANSWER KEY
- Get friend support
- Express your feelings
- Cry
- Accept it
- Acknowledge your pain
- Know that everyone gets rejected sometimes
- Know that relationships are about compatibility not merit
- Get angry
- Seek revenge
- Put the other person down
- Take it very personally
- Try to hurt someone else
- Distractions and addictions like social media, video games, drugs, and alcohol

4. Ask each student to draw 4 quadrants on a piece of paper (see figure 4.1) and fill in each quadrant with ways of dealing with unintentional emotional pain. They can draw from the list generated by the class and add others that they want to keep more private. Ask students to keep their answers private.

Ways to deal that are easy and immediate for me	Ways to deal that have negative consequences (on other people, on my health, on relationships, on my priorities)
Ways to deal that I have used and are successful	Ways to deal that I want to use more often

Figure 4.1

5. Ask students to review their papers and discuss as a class:
   - Looking at the lower right quadrant "Ways to deal that I want to use more often," what are some things that our friends and families can do to support you in doing these? How can they make it easier for you?
   - How might you know how to best support someone else who is experiencing emotional pain?

EDUCATOR ANSWER KEY

Support looks very different from person to person. You may not know exactly how to best support someone else through their emotional pain; it is important that you ask them directly how they would like to be supported. If the other person does not know what they need, ask them how you can best support them to build the coping skills that they would like to use more often.

Wrap-up

Summarize the module with the following points:
- Crushes are feelings of attraction towards another person. It is okay to have them and it is okay not to.
- If you have crushes, you can do nothing or you can choose to let them know.
- Direct and assertive communication is valuable in all relationships, including when talking to your crush. Whether it is appropriate to disclose your crush depends on both your intentions and the impact. (For more information on intention vs. impact, see figure 1A in module 1.2).
- Many behaviours that we do that are hurtful to us or to others are done when we are in emotional pain. We all need ways to cope with pain. Know that you have options.

4.7 SEXUALITY AND DISABILITY

LEVEL 2 [3]

Big Ideas in Module 4.7

- Every body is unique and everybody has the right to have a healthy, fulfilling, and pleasurable sexuality, dating-life, and sex-life.
- Stereotypes are harmful to everyone. People with disabilities are often stereotyped in relationship to sexuality, which limits opportunities for learning and communication.
- Learning how to communicate in relationships is an essential component of experiencing satisfying and pleasurable emotional, romantic, and sexual connections, regardless of your abilities.

Learning Objectives

Students will:

- Challenge assumptions, myths, and **stereotypes** about people with disabilities in relationship to sex and sexuality.
- Appreciate the diversity of sensations within the body and learn how to communicate about these.
- Learn how to communicate about likes and dislikes related to the body.

Cross-Curricular Connections

- Equity Studies
- Gender Studies
- Psychology
- Social Studies
- Sociology

Terminology

- Ableism
- Stereotypes

Materials

- Paper and writing utensils for students
- Optional: Computer and projector or Smart Board
- **Educator Resource—Body Scan Script**
- Printed copies of **Robyn's Story**

Background Information for Educators

People with disabilities exist everywhere. Disability is a spectrum of experiences that may or may not change throughout the lifespan (for more information, see module 5.4). People with disabilities are often thought of as non-sexual (e.g., not interested in sex, not worthy of sexual intimacy, and/or virginal) or as sexually deviant (e.g., hypersexual and/or fetishized). This module aims to dispel myths and stereotypes about people with disabilities. Dispelling these myths is a first step in helping students challenge their own assumptions and bias about people with disabilities. This builds a foundation for students with a diversity of abilities to challenge **ableism**.

YOU SHOULD KNOW

Ableism is a systemic form of oppression of people with disabilities, including the presumption that living with an able body is expected, normal, and fixed in time/space. Like all forms of systemic oppression, it can be unknowingly upheld by anyone, including people within the social grouping itself (i.e., internalized ableism, internalized homophobia, internalized transphobia, internalized racism, etc.).

This module builds specific communication skills for people with and without disabilities. It can be challenging for all people (regardless of ability) to get to know what does and does not feel good in their bodies. It can be equally challenging to effectively and assertively communicate what feels good and what does not (for more information on assertive communication, see module 7.5). Communication is an essential part of pleasurable sex and becomes particularly important for people with disabilities. People with disabilities (particularly physical disabilities) may have chronic pain, muscle spasms, and/or limited sensation in different parts of the body (and these can all shift and change day to day, moment to moment).

Student Readiness

Before students engage with this lesson, ensure that safer space guidelines and group norms have been established (and revisited) within your classroom (for more information on how to establish safer space guidelines, see module 1.3). In order to effectively prepare for this activity, ensure students understand that:

- This module is not just for people with disabilities—it is for everyone.
- People with disabilities exist everywhere and disability is sometimes visible and sometimes invisible—do not make assumptions about who has and who does not have disabilities.

Summary of Activities

Students will:

- Be led through a relaxation/guided imagery exercise and individually reflect on the experience of being in their own body.

- Work in small groups to communicate their experiences of the guided imagery exercise.
- Watch videos by disability activists and as a large group discuss how the videos challenged assumptions about disability and sexuality.
- Work in small groups to answer questions from a story about a young person navigating a dating relationship.

Activity 1 2 3

Instructions

1. Ask students to make their way into a position they are comfortable staying in for approximately 5 to 10 minutes. *Students can sit on a chair, place their heads on their desk, or find a comfortable, clean spot on the floor to sit or lie down.*
2. Ask students to take a minute to settle into this position and let them know that they will be here for approximately 5 to 10 minutes.
3. Read aloud the **Educator Resource—Body Scan Script**. *Modify as necessary to suit your style of teaching and your classroom.*
4. Once students have come back into and are more present in the space, instruct them to take their writing materials and write down the 3 bodily sensations or feelings that stood out the most to them.
5. Divide students up into groups of 2 or 3. Ask them to describe the 3 things they noticed to their partner(s).
6. As a class discuss:
   - What was challenging about the exercise?
   - What was comfortable and/or uncomfortable and why?

EDUCATOR ANSWER KEY

Allow students' experience of the exercise to lead the discussion. Facilitate the discussion with the following points in mind:

- Knowing how your body is feeling from moment to moment is something that can be uncomfortable and challenging but strategies that can help include doing exercises like guided imagery where you close the eyes and listen to the breath. Knowing what is happening for you in your own body is the first step in learning how to communicate your needs to someone else. Communication of needs is important in any relationship.
- Communicating to someone else about what is happening for you in your body can be challenging, scary, and awkward. Validate that these feelings are common and that the only way to learn how to communicate about what is happening in your body is to practise.

Activity 2 [3]

Instructions

1. Introduce the activity by discussing sex and disability using the Educator Background Information and the following questions:

2. If you have access to a projector or a Smart Board, choose from the following videos to play for your class (if you have time, show 2 and/or all 3):
   - (This video contains strong language) (Sex)abled: Disability Uncensored
   - Laci Green's Sex+ YouTube channel
   - (This video contains strong language) Jules' Tools for Change: Kaleigh Trace and Hot, Wet, & Shaking

3. Discuss reactions from the videos using the following questions:
   - Did anything about these videos surprise you? If so, what surprised you and why do you think that you were surprised?
   - What challenged your assumptions about people with disabilities, about sex, and about sexuality?
   - Have your assumptions changed after watching these videos, why or why not?
   - What stereotypes do these videos break? What stereotypes do these (if any) reinforce?
   - Do watching these videos change what you think about sex and sexuality?

YOU SHOULD KNOW

People with disabilities may have very different answers than people without disabilities. For people with disabilities they may have to navigate and challenge these stereotypes every day and therefore some of this information may not come as a surprise. For some people without disabilities this information could be surprising. If this comes up in the discussion, try not to make assumptions about what people's experiences are in relationship to disability and do not shy away from this difference. Instead, notice it and without singling out individual students (and if it feels appropriate) ask the class if they think that people with disabilities might have different reactions to these videos, in comparison to people without disabilities.

EDUCATOR PROMPTS

Allow students' experience of watching the videos to lead the discussion. If you are looking for ways to take the conversation deeper, you can ask them:

- Where do we learn stereotypes about people with disabilities?
- How can we unlearn these stereotypes?
- Why might these stereotypes be harmful?
- What is the benefit (to everyone) of challenging stereotypes?

EDUCATOR ANSWER KEY

Allow students' experience of watching the videos to lead the discussion. Keep the following points in mind while facilitating the discussion:

- Stereotypes are not based on fact, instead they are a product of prejudice, unchallenged assumptions and social conditioning.
- Challenging stereotypes may at first feel uncomfortable but perpetuating stereotypes limits everyone's sense of themselves and the world around them.

Activity 3 2 3

Instructions

1. Either read aloud or hand out copies of **Robyn's Story** to the entire class.
2. Ask students to individually reflect on Robyn's story.
3. Divide students up into groups of 4 or 5 and ask them to talk through the questions from **Robyn's Story** and be prepared to present their answers to the class.

Wrap-Up

Summarize the module with the following points:

- Every body is unique and everybody has the right to have a healthy, fulfilling and pleasurable sexuality and dating-life and sex-life.
- People with disabilities have sexualities, even though they are often assumed to be and portrayed as pure, virginal, sexless, undesirable, and/or sexually deviant. They are often left out of conversations about sexuality and sex-ed because of these assumptions.
- It is challenging for everyone to communicate their wants and needs when it comes to bodies and yet, this skill is essential for increasing pleasure and satisfaction in sexual relationships.

4.8 FAMILIES AND DIVERSITY

One way to make your classroom a more inclusive space for a diversity of families is having books available about a variety of family structures. The 4.8 resources offer many examples of children's books that address themes such as divorce, adoption, LGBTQ+ families, single-parent families, surrogacy, death of a parent, parented by grandparents and/or other family members, etc.

LEVEL 1 2

Big Ideas in Module 4.8
- There is no one definition of family. Families come in a diversity of forms and every family form is experienced differently.
- It is important to recognize and celebrate this diversity as it increases all students' sense of belonging.

Learning Objectives
Students will:
- Understand the concept of diversity.
- Identify similarities and differences between students in the context of diversity.
- Identify different kinds of families and develop respect for them.

Cross-Curricular Connections
- Art (Visual, Photography, Digital)
- English
- Equity Studies
- Gender Studies
- Psychology
- Social Studies
- Sociology

Terminology
- Diversity
- Family

Materials
- **Educator Resource—Questions for Similarities and Differences**
- Chalkboard or whiteboard
- Room to arrange students in two concentric circles
- Blank paper
- Pencil crayons, markers, and crayons

Background Information for Educators

There are many kinds of families and families are always changing. Students in a class come from very different family stories, even if the structure of their families are similar. It is important to instill an awareness of diversity in family histories and structures as well as respect and appreciation for differences and similarities.

Family members become part of families in different ways. It is important that educators and school communities acknowledge the origins of all students and the compositions of their families. When we assure young people that differences between people are positive, natural, and to be expected, they will be better equipped to encounter differences all around, as well as within themselves, with compassion and acceptance.

Student Readiness

Before students engage with this lesson, ensure that safer space guidelines and group norms have been established (and revisited) within your classroom (for more information on how to establish safer space guidelines, see module 1.3). In order to effectively prepare for this activity, ensure students understand that:

- There is not one kind of "normal" family structure.
- Families that look similar in terms of structure can be experienced differently.
- Differences between people and families are positive and to be expected.

Summary of Activities

Students will:

- Answer a series of questions with different partners, changing partners as each new question is asked.
- Collectively and in small groups brainstorm what makes a family.
- Individually create their own children's story about their own family structure.

Activity 1 1 2

Instructions
Part 1
1. Write the word **Diversity** on the board. Ask for definitions and guesses.
2. Offer the following definition, which is one of many: Diversity is the state of having many different forms, possibilities, types, ideas, etc. For instance, a box of crayons with 30 different colours is diverse in colour. A box of 30 crayons that are all red is not diverse.

3. Evenly arrange students in two concentric circles so that there is an inner circle and one outer one, each with the same number of students. Students in each circle should be facing each other and looking at one person (their partner in the activity).

4. Read a question from **Educator Resource—Questions for Similarities and Differences** and get each student to tell their partner their answer. After both students have answered, have the inner circle rotate clockwise so that everyone has a new partner. Read the next question. Continue until all questions have been answered, or as time allows.

5. Ask students:
   - What was it like to find out your answer was the same as someone else's?
   - What was it like to find out your answer was different?
   - In what ways are people made to feel bad about being different? What does it feel like when that happens?
   - Why do you think that people say that "difference and diversity enrich us"? How does that work?

EDUCATOR PROMPTS
Let students lead these answers but if they are really quiet or getting stuck, here are some questions you can ask to help prompt them:
   - Did you feel excitement, belonging, relief, happy, and/or nothing?
   - Did you feel annoyed, anxious, scared, embarrassed, and/or nothing?
   - Have you ever felt left out of something because you were different from the rest of the group? How so and how does it feel to be different?
   - If everyone liked the same things or had the same experiences or personalities all of the time, do you think that this might get boring? How so?

6. Ask students to list what they have observed as the ways that people are diverse. Explain that everyone who makes up the complete picture is part of its diversity, not only the people who are less common i.e., if a student offers "being gay" as an answer to being diverse, the assumption is that being heterosexual/straight is "normal" and being gay is the remarkable difference. Reframe this so that the diversity is in "sexual orientation" so that everyone is part of the diversity, including the most common, popular, or dominant group.

7. Explain that to appreciate and respect diversity, we have to:
   - Recognize difference (not ignore it).
   - Recognize the common, popular, dominant way of people without giving more value to it.
   - Appreciate everything and everyone as part of the complete picture of diversity.
8. To wrap up this activity, ask students: If I had asked you those questions 2 years ago, how many answers would have been different? How about in 5 years from now? Do you think any of your answers will change? Explain that many of our similarities and differences change over time based on where we are and who we are among.

Part 2
1. Discuss:
   - What makes a family a family?

EDUCATOR ANSWER KEY

- Love
- Choice to be a family (i.e., chosen family)
- Support
- Sometimes blood/genetic relationships (but sometimes not)
- Connection
- Community
- Culture and tradition

- What are the ways that families are diverse?

EDUCATOR ANSWER KEY

- Size
- Who is a part of it
- Whether there are kids or not
- How the family came to be a family
- How people are related
- How the family changes over time
- Family structures

2. Widen students' responses so that their definitions capture all kinds of families.

EDUCATOR ANSWER KEY

Examples of kinds of families include: chosen families, biological families, adoptive families, families with queer parents, families with trans parents, step families, polyamorous families, families that share co-parenting relationships/arrangements with multiple people, foster families, extended families, immediate families, interracial families, biracial families, mixed-race families, families with a diversity of abilities/disabilities, single-parent families, childless families, divorced families.

You can offer this definition of **family** to summarize the students' responses: Any combination of two or more individuals bound together over time by ties of mutual consent, choice, birth, adoption, or placement.

3. Instruct students to work within groups of 2 or 3. Ask half the groups to brainstorm for "different kinds of families" and the other half of the groups to brainstorm "different ways to make a family." Some of their answers might overlap. *For students on the younger side of level 1 (grades 1 to 4), ask them to draw their answers to this question.*

4. Reconvene as a large group and compile a list on the board.

EDUCATOR ANSWER KEY

Examples of Different kinds of families	Examples of Different ways to make a family
<ul><li>Chosen families</li><li>Biological families</li><li>Adoptive families</li><li>Families with parents who identify on the LGBTQ+ spectrum</li><li>Step families/Blended families</li><li>Polyamorous families</li><li>Families that share co-parenting relationships/arrangements with multiple people</li><li>Foster families</li><li>Extended families</li><li>Immediate families</li><li>Interracial, biracial, and mixed-race families</li><li>Families with a diversity of abilities/disabilities</li><li>Single-parent families</li><li>Childless families</li><li>Divorced families</li><li>Multi-generational families</li><li>Non-nuclear families</li><li>Nuclear families</li></ul>	<ul><li>Adoption</li><li>Foster care</li><li>Step-families</li><li>Family friends becoming family (chosen family)</li><li>Co-parenting arrangements between multiple people</li><li>Marriage</li><li>Two or more adults of any gender identity and sex</li><li>One adult with a child or with children</li><li>Assistive reproductive technologies</li><li>Sperm donors</li><li>Egg donors</li><li>Surrogate parents</li><li>Penis-vagina sexual intercourse</li></ul>

5. Affirm that diversity is part of families' stories. Affirm that we all have different stories.
6. Refer back to Part 1 of the activity and what students said about what it felt like to be similar and to be different from others. Ask students: What does it mean to accept someone's differences when it comes to families?

EDUCATOR ANSWER KEY

- Not assuming that everyone has the same family story and/or structure as you (even if on the surface they seem similar).
- Cultivating respect and acceptance for diversity and difference.
- If you are curious about someone's family, asking yourself why you are curious and then asking yourself if it is appropriate and respectful to ask the questions that you want to ask.
- Recognizing that everyone has similarities and differences when it comes to families.
- Not assigning higher or lower values to different kinds of families based on structure, composition, or story of how they came to be.

Activity 2

For students on the younger side of level 1 (grades 1 to 4), break this activity up into 2 parts. Part 1: Have students "show and tell" by either reading their story aloud to the class or choose a couple of stories (that highlight a diversity of families) and read them aloud over several classes. Part 2: Have students create their own children's story.

Instructions

1. Ahead of class, ask students to bring in their favourite children's story about families.
2. Ask the class:
   - Why did you choose to bring in this story?
   - What is your favourite part about the story?
   - Does the children's story you brought in reflect your own family in some way?
3. Make sure students have something to write with and ask them to individually reflect on the following questions. *Encourage them to write and/or draw their responses and assure them that these are meant to be a rough brainstorm.*
   - What could you do to make the story more reflective of your family structure? What elements would you add? What elements would you take away?
   - What makes this story compelling to you and could you think of ways to increase the compelling aspects?
   - If given the opportunity to change, add, or improve the story in any way, what would you include?

4. Give students 10 to 20 sheets of blank paper and different colouring utensils. Explain that they are going to create their own children's story using their rough brainstorm notes. Their story should have visuals and words. They can choose to draw or use another kind of artistic medium such as painting, digital art, and/or photography.

5. Once their stories are finished, give them the option of reading their finished stories to the class.

Wrap-up

Summarize the module with the following points:

- All of us are made up of qualities, stories, and experiences that are similar to some people and different from some people.
- It is important to recognize differences and similarities without assigning a higher or lower value to them.
- There are infinite ways to make and/or define "family."
- Different kinds of families make the world and our classroom community a richer place.

4.9 HUMAN REPRODUCTIVE OPTIONS

LEVEL 1 2

Big Ideas in Module 4.9

- Humans are mammals; learning about mammalian reproduction helps teach the basic biology of human reproduction.
- In human reproduction, the large gamete (egg) and small gamete (sperm) must combine and implant. This process is called fertilization and conception.
- There are a variety of reproductive options that humans have to make fertilization, conception, and pregnancy possible.

Learning Objectives

Students will:

- Learn about basic mammalian reproduction.
- Learn about human reproductive options.

Cross-Curricular Connections

- Biology
- Social Studies
- Sociology

Terminology

- Cervix
- Chromosomes
- Conception
- DNA (deoxyribonucleic acid)
- Egg
- Embryo
- Endometrium
- Epididymis
- Fallopian tubes (oviducts)
- Fertilization
- Gamete
- Gestation
- Ovaries
- Pregnancy
- Semen
- Seminal fluid
- Sperm
- Testicles (testes)
- Uterus
- Vas deferens

Materials

- Chalkboard, whiteboard, or Smart Board
- Printed copies of **Mammalian Card Deck**
- Printed copies of **Sexual and Reproductive Anatomy**
- Printed copies of **Human Reproductive Options Chart**

Background Information for Educators

The story of pregnancy and birth is nothing short of miraculous even though approximately 370,000 babies are born every day in the world. The miraculous part has to do with the science: from 2 cells, approximately 3.72 trillion cells eventually make up the human body.

Learning about **fertilization, conception,** and **pregnancy** helps students understand how humans reproduce so that they feel agency over their choice about when and/or whether they want to reproduce.

Removing this conversation from puberty (module 4.3) allows us to de-emphasize the idea that the purpose of puberty is to become reproductive. Many post-pubertal people are not able to reproduce and many of those who can choose not to. The ability to reproduce is only one aspect of puberty.

Removing this conversation from discussions of family formation and structure (module 4.8) allows us to affirm that:
- Some families consist of children; some do not.
- Some families with children have children through reproductive technologies; some through adoption; some through previous relationships (blended/step families); some through foster placements; and some through penis-vagina sexual intercourse.

Student Readiness

Before students engage with this lesson, ensure that safer space guidelines and group norms have been established (and revisited) within your classroom (for more information on how to establish safer space guidelines, see module 1.3). In order to effectively prepare for this activity, ensure students understand that:
- This module talks about how mammalian babies are made from a scientific perspective.
- Humans are mammals and have options available to them to assist with reproduction that other mammals do not have.

Summary of Activities

Students will:
- Learn the basics of mammalian reproduction.
- Compete with each other in small groups to see who can accurately remember (and reconstruct) the story of mammalian reproduction the fastest.

- Learn about reproductive technologies that humans have access to and work in small groups to plan a lesson/teach their peers about one of the human reproductive technologies.

Summary of Activities

Activity 1 outlines basic requirements for mammalian reproduction. Activity 2 outlines options that human beings have for reproduction.

Activity 1 [1] [2]

For younger lever 1 students (grades 1 to 4), you can modify this activity by spending more time on instructions 1 to 4 and asking them to draw or paint the story of mammalian reproduction instead of going through instructions 5 to 7.

Instructions
1. Ask students for the characteristics of mammals.

EDUCATOR ANSWER KEY
- Warm blooded
- Give birth to live young (not eggs)
- Sexual reproduction
- Hair, fur, feathers, or scales

2. Ask students to name mammals they know (e.g., cat, bear, lion, whale, platypus, humans, etc.).
3. Explain that all mammals make their young the same way. Each baby mammal is made from:
   - 1 small **gamete** with genetic information (**chromosomes**) and lots of mobility, and
   - 1 big **gamete** with genetic information (**chromosomes**) and less mobility.
4. Tell the basic story of mammalian reproduction:
   - Small gamete (sperm) and large gamete (egg) meet. That is called **fertilization.**
   - The 2 cells become 1 and implant themselves in the uterus. That is called **conception.**
   - The cells then start to divide inside the uterus, eventually creating millions of cells. After a period of time, a baby mammal is made. This period is called **gestation.**

- Every species takes a different amount of time for the gestation to finish. For instance, kittens and puppies take about 2 months to grow. Elephants on the other hand take almost 2 years to grow. Humans have a 9 month gestational period.
- The baby mammal is born alive (not as an egg that needs to be hatched).

5. Split your class up into 4 groups. Print and hand out the **Mammalian Card Deck** to each group with images faced down.

6. Explain: Now that you have heard the basic story of mammalian reproduction, place the cards (depicting basic mammalian reproduction) in order as fast as you can. The first group to finish and to have the correct story order wins.

7. Have the winning group explain the story to the class using their cards.

Activity 2 ☐1☐ ☐2☐

For younger level 1 students (grades 1 to 4), modify this activity by talking about different human reproductive options through children's stories. Break up the activity into four different lessons and take the time needed to explain each method and answer questions using the **Human Reproductive Options Chart** and the **Sexual and Reproductive Anatomy** diagrams. As you go through each method, read the recommended story aloud to explain how everyone has a different story about how they were made because of the diversity of human reproductive options.

Instructions

1. Compare and contrast these details about the egg (large gamete) and sperm (small gamete) in humans:

Egg	Sperm
• Large in size	• Small in size
• Contains genetic information	• Contains genetic information
• Moves slowly	• Moves quickly
• 1 or 2 are made over a month	• Millions are made every day

2. Provide printed copies of **Sexual and Reproductive Anatomy**. Allow students some time to study them.

3. Explain that humans have multiple ways of reproducing because of reproductive technologies. Project the **Human Reproductive Options** chart and the **Sexual and Reproductive Anatomy** diagrams onto a screen.

4. Ask students to study the chart and diagrams. Split the class into 4 groups and assign each group a different method.

5. In their groups, students must plan a 2 to 5 minute lesson for the rest of the class. They can use the anatomy diagrams provided or they can think of another way to present/explain their method, including art, movement, drama, and/or tableaux.

Activity 3

Instructions

1. Discuss: What are the commonalities that we all have as human beings in the world? *Emphasize that we have commonalities despite belonging to different communities or groups or being "made" differently.*

QUICK TIP

You can encourage your students to get creative by giving bonus points for presentations that include art (visuals, photography, music, drama, etc.) while demonstrating the scientific accuracy of each method.

EDUCATOR ANSWER KEY

Challenge students to find basic common denominators true for all humans, inclusive of differences of upbringing, culture, religion, race, gender, sex, dis/abilities, class, experience, and aspirations. Some possible answers include:

- We all have **DNA**
- We are all made from 2 gametes (1 large and 1 small)
- We all have bodies
- We all have need love and caring
- We all need nourishment
- We all produce waste
- We all breathe oxygen
- We all circulate blood

Wrap-up

Summarize the module with the following points:

- Humans are mammals and reproduce like other mammals.
- Humans have developed technologies that assist reproduction. These continue to advance and add to the different ways that all of us come to be.
- There is vast diversity among humans, including how we each came to be.

CHAPTER 5

Self-Concept, Body Image, Self-Acceptance, and Peer Support

5.1 INTRODUCTION

Because sexuality encompasses the physical, mental, emotional, social, and spiritual aspects of a person, comprehensive sexuality education speaks to the entire person's sense of health and well-being. The modules in this chapter cover topics focused on developing emotional, mental, and social well-being while dealing with the growing pressures young people face in relationship to "perfection," whether that be the "perfect" body, grades, or online profile. The modules not only offer building blocks for creating a positive sense of self and self-care strategies, they provide opportunities for students to practise integrating empathy into their lives and peer groups. While this chapter covers a wide range of issues related to bodies and **body image**, eating disorders (or disordered eating) are not included.

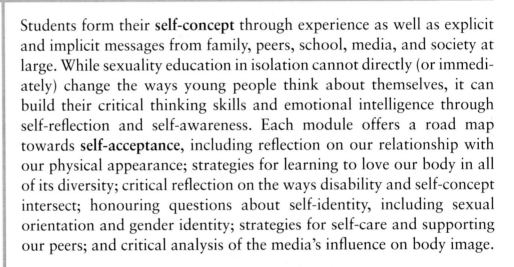

YOU SHOULD KNOW

Eating disorders are a mental illness that is caused by a mixture of biological, social, and cultural factors. Eating disorders are intentionally left out of *Beyond the Basics* because research shows that educating about eating disorders directly does not decrease their prevalence amongst adolescents. It is recommended that educators teach other skills proven effective at preventing and minimizing harm caused from disordered eating. These skills include assertive communication and decision-making (modules 7.4 and 7.5), healthy relationships (modules 7.2, 7.3, and 7.7), media literacy (module 5.7 and chapter 6), self-care (module 5.5), and challenging harassment and bullying (modules 1.5, 3.11, and 8.5). (For more information about eating disorders, see 5.1 resources. For crisis lines, see National Support Services in the resources section.).

Students form their **self-concept** through experience as well as explicit and implicit messages from family, peers, school, media, and society at large. While sexuality education in isolation cannot directly (or immediately) change the ways young people think about themselves, it can build their critical thinking skills and emotional intelligence through self-reflection and self-awareness. Each module offers a road map towards **self-acceptance**, including reflection on our relationship with our physical appearance; strategies for learning to love our body in all of its diversity; critical reflection on the ways disability and self-concept intersect; honouring questions about self-identity, including sexual orientation and gender identity; strategies for self-care and supporting our peers; and critical analysis of the media's influence on body image.

Educator Reflection Questions

Self-acceptance can be challenging to learn at any age. When you are an adolescent it can be even harder. Think back to when you were your students' age:

- Did you struggle with self-acceptance and developing a healthy self-concept?
- What were the influences that most affected your self-concept (either positively or negatively)? How do you think that these influences have changed (or stayed the same) over time and how do you think that this might impact your students?

What about now?
- Have you ever noticed yourself passing judgments on your own body, or on the bodies of others? If so, what strategies could you use to help limit those judgments of yourself and others?
- Have standards of perfection and unattainable beauty ideals had an influence on your self-concept and/or body image?
- What does "body positivity" mean to you?

Big Ideas in Chapter 5
- Self-concept is influenced by a variety of sources, including media (traditional and new media), family, peers, school, and societal norms.
- While social media can contribute to the pressure adolescents feel in terms of presenting a perfect image to the world, social media is also a place where adolescents may feel empowered to control their image and represent their own life experiences in the world.
- Young people can develop tools for critical analysis, empathy, and self-care to help them filter out negative messaging about their bodies and move towards greater self-acceptance.
- All bodies are worthy of love, acceptance, celebration, and positive representation.

5.2 LEARNING TO BE BODY POSITIVE

LEVEL ☐1☐ ☐2☐ ☐3☐

Big Ideas in Module 5.2

- Being body positive means celebrating all bodies and recognizing that all bodies are worthy of love, acceptance, and positive representation.
- Body size does not represent health status.
- Young people experience a huge amount of pressure to conform and fit into beauty standards that are unrealistic. Part of developing resilience in the face of these pressures is learning self-care strategies.

Learning Objectives

Students will:
- Develop a critical analysis of health and body size.
- Explore the phenomenon of comparing self to others.
- Discern between helpful and unhelpful comparisons.
- Explore how they care for and appreciate themselves.

Cross-Curricular Connections

- English
- Equity Studies
- Gender Studies
- Media Studies
- Psychology
- Social Studies
- Sociology

Terminology

- Self-care
- Self-concept

Materials

- Chalkboard, whiteboard, or flip chart paper
- Paper
- Sticky notes
- Writing and drawing utensils
- Printed copies of **The Pros and Cons of Comparison**
- Printed copies of **I Treat Myself Well**
- **Educator Answer Key—The Pros and Cons of Comparison**

Background Information for Educators

All bodies are worthy of love, acceptance, and positive representation. Body positivity is the celebration of diverse bodies: big, small, short, tall, bodies of colour, bodies of varying abilities, queer, trans and intersex bodies, etc. It maintains that all bodies are beautiful and challenges the idea that there are "good" and "bad" bodies or that skinny bodies are healthy and large bodies are unhealthy.

With young people, there is tremendous pressure to conform to certain ideals of beauty and appearance. Some people spend an inordinate amount of time and energy trying to achieve the "perfect" body at the expense of their health. It is also common for young people to compare their bodies with models, actors, and their peers. While comparison can be helpful in some aspects of one's life, comparison related to body weight, height, and development can lead to behaviours that compromise health. Being able to discern between when comparison is healthy and when comparison in unhealthy is an important part of **self-care** and a step towards self-acceptance.

Self-care tools are vital to resist the enormous pressure of unrealistic beauty standards. Caring for and appreciating our bodies allows us to more readily move through hardship, ask for support from others, and ultimately develop a positive body image and healthy **self-concept**.

Student Readiness

Before students engage with this lesson, ensure that safer space guidelines and group norms have been established (and revisited) within your classroom (for more information on how to establish safer space guidelines, see module 1.3). In order to effectively prepare for this activity, ensure students understand that:

- Most people experience pressure to conform to societal norms and unrealistic beauty standards at some point in their life; different bodies experience these pressures very differently.
- During this lesson, it is unacceptable to make comments about the physical characteristics of people in the classroom or use identifying qualities.
- The purpose of this lesson is not to discuss the specifics of nutrition. The purpose is to critically analyze the ways that health is portrayed in relationship to body size.

Summary of Activities

Students will:

- Individually reflect on what healthy and unhealthy mean to them.
- Collectively de-bunk myths on body size and health status.
- Working in small groups, discern between helpful and unhelpful comparisons they may make about themselves against others.
- Individually reflect (through drawing or writing) on ways that they already practise self-care and appreciation.

Activity 1 [1] [2] [3]

Part 1

For Level 1, especially grades 1 to 4, students can draw their answers either directly on the board (or flip chart) or on separate pieces of paper that can be posted under the appropriate headings.

Instructions

1. On the board, write "Healthy" on one side and "Unhealthy" on the other.

2. Hand out 6 to 8 sticky notes for each student and ask students to write the first couple of associated words that come to mind when they think of the word healthy. Then ask them to do the same for the word unhealthy. Prompt with questions like:
   - What do each of these words look like?
   - What do each of these words feel like?
   - What do each of these words taste like?
   - What do each of these words smell like?
   - What do each of these words sound like?

3. Ask students to place their sticky notes under "Healthy" or "Unhealthy." If they are unsure of where their sticky notes should go, or if their sticky notes could go in either of the word categories, ask them to place them somewhere on the spectrum between "Healthy "and "Unhealthy."

4. Ask students to pick out one of their sticky notes and share a reflection with the class based on the questions below. *Sharing is optional but try to get a least 5 students to share their reflections from different points on the spectrum.*
   - Why did you place this sticky note here?
   - What information influenced your decision? Was it intuitive or did you remember reading something or hearing something somewhere?
   - Consider the different ways that you can evaluate information and information sources to determine what is healthy and what is unhealthy. How do you know which information sources are reliable and which are not?

EDUCATOR PROMPTS

The last question is challenging for anyone to answer because there is no right or wrong answer but especially challenging for Level 1 students. If you or your students (at any level) are stuck on how to answer the question, ask them to think through the following questions/prompts. This will give them an opportunity to develop the critical thinking skills that are important in learning how to assess the accuracy of information.

- Who will stand to benefit from you believing this information? *If anyone stands to benefit from you believing this information (especially monetarily) it may be a less reliable source (e.g., companies intending to make profit on diet drugs and diet programs).*
- If you believe the information, are you more likely to spend money on things that you do not need? *If you are more likely to spend money based on this information, take a closer look at the information source (and/or get a second opinion) in order to understand whether or not you actually need the items.*
- What is the science behind the information? How much agreement or disagreement is there within scientific communities? *Sometimes there is widespread agreement within the scientific community about what is unhealthy (e.g., smoking cigarettes). But sometimes there is widespread disagreement (e.g., what constitutes obesity and whether or not being plus size is healthy or unhealthy).*

5. After students have shared their reflections, ask the class:
   - Consider all of the sticky notes on the "Healthy" side of the spectrum, can skinny people be all of these things? How about plus size people? Why or Why not?
   - Consider all of the sticky notes on the "Unhealthy" side of the spectrum, can skinny people be all of these things? How about plus size people? Why or why not?

EDUCATOR ANSWER KEY

The take away from this activity is that there is no easy "black or white" answer to what makes someone healthy and what makes someone unhealthy. Each person has a unique health profile that includes (but is not limited to) genetic, social, psychological, emotional, economic, political, and environmental factors. You cannot tell how healthy or unhealthy someone is by looking at their outward physical appearance. Skinny people can be unhealthy, just as plus size people can be healthy.

6. Ask students to consider where we get our information about which body size is unhealthy and/or healthy. How factual is this information? What are some strategies for evaluating the evidence? *(For educator prompts, see question 4).*

✛ Optional: Part 2 follow-up activity 2 3

1. Show your students the following videos (see 5.2 resources):
   • Marie Southard Ospina and Bustle Magazine: *What is the Body Positive Movement?* 2 3
   • Sex Positive with Laci Green: *Fat Shame* 2 3
   • It Gets Fatter Project: *Health and Fatness* 3

2. As a class, discuss:
   • Reactions to the video(s)
   • Did anything surprise you about the videos?
   • What moments felt comfortable and uncomfortable and why?
   • Moving forward, what is one thing you could do to change the way you think, talk, and communicate about body size and health?

Activity 2 1 2 3

Instructions

1. Remind students that:
   • During this lesson, it is unacceptable to make comments about the physical characteristics of people in the classroom or use identifying qualities.
   • Everyone goes through moments of feeling self-conscious and/or dissatisfied with the way they look.
   • They need to be gentle with themselves and their peers. One way to do this if they feel self-conscious during the discussion is to close their eyes and take deep breaths.

2. Divide the class into small groups. Ask each group to fill in **The Pros and Cons of Comparison**. *The Educator Answer Key is from the students' perspective. It may be helpful for you to fill out a copy for yourself before facilitating the group discussion with your students.*

3. As a class, ask each group to report back with their answers and discuss:
   • How do you discern between helpful comparisons and unhelpful ones?
   • How do you discern between realistic and unrealistic comparisons?

Activity 3 [1] [2] [3]

Instructions

1. Working individually, ask students to complete the student handout **I Treat Myself Well**. Encourage students to draw their answers as much as possible. *This allows more ambiguity in their answers and connects to a different part of the cognitive process.*

2. Give options to students to share one or two things from their completed handout with the class.

3. Explain that one of the key components of developing a positive body image is to learn how to treat yourself well. Ask the class: Why do you think this is the case?

EDUCATOR ANSWER KEY

Sometimes we are the hardest on ourselves. Learning how to cultivate self-compassion and self-love will help boost confidence in who we are. Learning self-compassion and self-love helps us learn that we deserve compassion and love from others. We can be our own worst critic, our "flaws" are subjective. Learning how to soothe ourselves is a helpful strategy for beginning to understand self-care. While it may be extremely challenging for anyone to learn how to treat themselves well and put these strategies into practise, it is even more challenging when you are grappling with strong messages from outside sources (like media, peers, and family) that influence the way you develop perceptions about what is (or is not) a "flaw" and what is (or is not) "beautiful."

Wrap-up

Summarize the module with the following points:

- Body size does not indicate health status.
- As bodies change during puberty and adolescence, many people feel self-conscious and/or dissatisfied with the way they look.
- Being conscious of helpful/realistic and unhelpful/unrealistic comparisons develops wisdom and resilience.
- Caring for ourselves is an important part of body positivity.

5.3 DEVELOPING A HEALTHY SELF-CONCEPT

LEVEL 2 [3]

Big Ideas in Module 5.3

- Self-concept is influenced by internal and external factors as well as individual and systemic factors (including systemic discrimination).
- Self-concept is based on belief, perception, and evaluation of reality. While there are many parts of our realities that cannot be changed, our perception is something that we can influence.
- Developing a healthy self-concept is about developing an accurate and compassionate perception, not necessarily a positive one.

Learning Objectives

Students will:

- Learn what the term self-concept means and how it is related to body image and self-esteem.
- Apply the concept of "perspective" by turning problems into open-ended questions.
- Consider what they would need in order to accept and show more of themselves.

Cross-Curricular Connections

- Art (visual)
- Equity Studies
- Gender Studies
- Psychology
- Social Studies
- Sociology

Terminology

- Self-concept
- Systemic Discrimination

Materials

- Long pieces of paper
- Writing and drawing utensils
- Paint
- Glue
- Old magazines
- Chalkboard or whiteboard
- Printed copies of **Self-Concept**
- Printed copies of **Mask**
- ✛ Optional: Materials for paper mâché mask making

Background Information for Educators

Self-concept is influenced by individual factors (personality traits, self-efficacy, what you have been taught by family, etc.) and systemic factors, including **systemic discrimination** (i.e., classism, ableism, racism, homophobia, transphobia, and sexism). Self-concept is also about perception and not necessarily an individual's entire reality. Developing a healthy self-concept is not necessarily about having a positive perception but having an accurate and compassionate one that allows for growth and change.

The way youth perceive themselves is influenced by their personality, families, communities, culture, as well as experiences of poverty, racism, sexism, homophobia, and so on (for more on discrimination, see modules 1.2, 1.5, and 2.4). Sexual risk, substance dependence, social isolation, and violence can all contribute to (and result from) an unhealthy self-concept.

Helping adolescents accept the reality of their selves and circumstances, as well as understand the potential for change, are important parts of healthy self-concept development.

Student Readiness

Before students engage with this lesson, ensure that safer space guidelines and group norms have been established (and revisited) within your classroom (for more information on how to establish safer space guidelines, see module 1.3). In order to effectively prepare for this activity, ensure students understand that:

- Developing a healthy self-concept is not about always having "a positive outlook" and it is not about being "perfect."
- During the course of their lives, most people experience some form of self-consciousness, self-doubt, and/or negative feelings about themselves. This module helps to identify ways to navigate these feelings through compassion and empathy.

Summary of Activities

Students will:

- Individually reflect on self-concept in relationship to the body and use art as a tool to discover what influences self-concept.
- Collectively, or working in small groups, turn problems and dead-ends into open-ended questions.
- Individually reflect on qualities about themselves that they show or hide from others through mask making.

Activity 1 2 3
Instructions

1. Explain: Self-concept refers to the ways that we think about ourselves based on belief, perception, and evaluation. Self-concept includes self-esteem, self-worth, and self-image. Self-concept is influenced by families, peers, communities, media, and cultures. Self-concept is also influenced by experiences of stigma and discrimination.

2. Give each student the handout **Self-Concept** and ask them to fill out each of the four quadrants. Challenge them to provide at least three written answers in each quadrant. Assure them that they will not have to share this writing.

3. Give each student a big piece of paper (make it long enough so that they can lie on it and draw an outline of their bodies).

4. Once each student has their own piece of paper, ask them to pair up. Each student in the pair will help draw the other persons outline on the piece of paper.

5. Individually, have students reflect on what they wrote on the **Self-Concept** handout and use the outlines/maps of their bodies to visually depict what they wrote in the four quadrants on their body maps.

EDUCATOR PROMPTS

Prompt students by asking them the following questions: How does what happens outside of you influence how you feel about yourself internally. Where would you place each quadrant on your body map? Considering how one quadrant impacts the other, where would you place these quadrants in relationship to your body? What stories do you tell yourself, where do these stories come from, and how do these stories influence how you see and value yourself?

6. Allow for lots of time to creatively explore this activity. When you think that students are ready to debrief the exercise, ask the entire group:
    *   How did this activity feel? Did it make you feel more of less comfortable in your body?
    *   Did this activity give you any new perspectives about how you see yourself?
    *   Did this activity provide any insight about how your experiences in the world have influenced the way you think about yourself?

7.  Optional: Students present their body maps to the class, explaining some of the elements of their art and how it relates to their self-concept.

Activity 2 2 3

Instructions

1. Explain: There are some things we easily appreciate about ourselves (e.g., abilities, values, personality, accomplishments, appearance, etc.) and some things we do not. "Perspective" is how we see (or understand) situations. Even with factors we cannot change, by changing our perspective, we can change how we experience something.

EDUCATOR ANSWER KEY
- Glass half empty/full
- Optical illusions
- Rainy days (can be seen as frustrating if they interfere with plans but are good for gardens, crops, etc.)
- Electric power failures (can interfere with plans but can be an opportunity to bond with family/friends without the distraction of technology)

2. Ask the class for examples that illustrate how changing our perspective can change how we experience something.

3. Bring the class together or divide students into groups of five to eight. Explain: This is a game where one person makes a random, imagined suggestion starting with the words: "Let's…" The following words can be anything (e.g., let's bake a cake, let's climb a mountain, let's write a poem, etc.). In response, the rest of the group must voice reasons why we cannot (e.g., we do not have flour to bake a cake, there is no mountain nearby, we have no pens to write, etc.). Go through this with students until they get the hang of it and make note of each idea and reasons against it.

EDUCATOR ANSWER KEY

Students will come up with countless things to do and reasons why not. Here are some examples:

Bake a cake	Climb a mountain	Write a poem
No flour	No mountain	No pen
Allergic to cake	No boots	Can't rhyme
Don't know how	Too tired	Dislike poetry

4. Change the rules. Have students rephrase their reasons as questions starting with "How might we…" For example, "No flour" becomes "How might we get flour?" "No mountain nearby" becomes "How might we get to a mountain far away?" "No pens" becomes "How might we get some pens?" Go through the old ideas and a few new ones in this new format.

EDUCATOR ANSWER KEY

Students will come up with countless questions. Here are some examples:

Bake a cake	Climb a mountain	Write a poem
How might we get flour?	How might we simulate or practise climbing a mountain?	How might we acquire a pen?
How might we change the ingredients to make it safe to eat?	How might we acquire boots?	How might we learn to rhyme?
How might we learn how to bake a cake?	How might we put strategies in place so that we are less tired?	How might we express ourselves differently?

5. Discuss what the difference is between stating a problem and framing a "How might we..." question. What does the first way of speaking believe? What does the second?

EDUCATOR ANSWER KEY

The first way of speaking believes that there is no solution. The second way of speaking believes that there is a solution that can be found.

6. Give the following examples (or other examples you come up with) to the class and ask students to apply the concept of shifting perspectives with "How might I..." questions for each. *If you are coming up with your own examples, probe for a perspective that offers acceptance, not only change.*

In this exercise, you are not asking students to come up with answers about how to feel less selfconscious or less jealous, you are asking for examples to reframe the examples into questions as a way to prompt students to think through shifting perspective by asking questions.

Feeling self-conscious that you have acne

EDUCATOR ANSWER KEY

There are an infinite number of possibilities, here are some examples.
- How might I feel less self-conscious about having acne?
- How might I focus on aspects of myself I feel confident about?
- How might I spend more time on aspects of my life I am grateful for?

Being benched on a sports team

EDUCATOR ANSWER KEY

There are an infinite number of possibilities, here are some examples.
- How might I feel less angry about being benched on a sports team?
- How might I learn from my mistakes?
- How might I become a better player by watching others?
- How might I be grateful for being on this sports team?

Being jealous of someone else's new clothes

EDUCATOR ANSWER KEY

There are an infinite number of possibilities, here are some examples.
- How might I feel less self-conscious about my own clothes?
- How might I creatively make my clothes feel new, even if they are not?
- How might I feel less jealous of someone else's new clothes?

Getting a terrible report card

EDUCATOR ANSWER KEY

There are an infinite number of possibilities, here are some examples.
- How might I use this to help motivate me next term/semester?
- How might I find compassion for myself despite getting a terrible report card?

Activity 3 2 3

This activity is instructed as a 2-dimensional mask making activity. If you would like to make it a 3-dimensional mask making activity, the same activity could be done with paper mâché masks.

Instructions

1. Give each student a copy of the **Mask** handout or the option of drawing their own mask. You can cut out the mask or keep it on the rectangular sheet. Make sure that there is space on both the front and back of the mask to write or draw for the next part. *For a more fun, more diversified blank canvas, print masks on different colours of paper.*

2. On the front/outside of the mask, ask students to write or draw the qualities, values, and personalities that they show to the world. Encourage them to include how different people perceive and appreciate them.

3. On the back/inside of the mask, ask students to write or draw the qualities, values, and personalities that they do not show to the world. Encourage them to include things that no one knows or that only a few people know.

4. Allow students to keep their words and drawings private and invite those who want to, to share some of the things they have included on their mask.

5. Ask students the following questions:
   - What determines what a person shows and what they do not? *Invite students to think about individual factors as well as systemic factors.*
   - What might it feel like if your outside is totally different from your inside?
   - What do you think it would be like to feel comfortable showing everything about yourself?
   - What do you need in order to show some of your hidden parts?

EDUCATOR ANSWER KEY

Allow students to lead this discussion. If they are having trouble coming up with answers, here some prompts you could offer:

What determines what a person shows and what they do not?
- Feeling embarrassed, ashamed, or self-conscious
- Experiences of racism, ableism, homophobia, transphobia, and/or classism
- Being taught that certain qualities, characteristics, personality traits, or aspects are either "good" or "bad"

What might it feel like if your outside is totally different from your inside?
- You might feel inauthentic or fake
- You might always feel guarded, protective, or private
- You might feel uncomfortable and not confident to speak-up on issues that matter to you
- You might not be able to form meaningful and satisfying friendships

What do you think it would be like to feel comfortable showing everything about yourself?
- You might feel relieved
- You might feel more confident

What do you need in order to show some of your hidden parts?
- What makes you feel comfortable in a new situation?
- Think about people who you feel comfortable showing the hidden parts of you to, why are you able to show these parts of yourself to them and not other people?
- Are there any supports that you need in order to show some of the hidden parts of yourself?

Wrap-up

Summarize the module with the following points:

- There are many things we can change and many things we cannot. Our perspective is one of the things we can.
- Asking "How might we…" or "How might I…" allows us to get into a proactive, creative mindset.
- We all have "masks" that we wear. Fear, shame, and a lack of safety (from individual and systemic factors) often stop us from showing our true selves. (For more information, see module 3.12).
- Having our inside and outside selves match can bring a sense of peace, freedom, confidence, and community. Self-acceptance is a big part of starting to show more of your hidden parts.

5.4 DISABILITY SPECTRUMS AND SELF-CONCEPT

LEVEL 2 3

Big Ideas in Module 5.4

- Disability exists everywhere and on a spectrum of experience that is visible and invisible and can change throughout a person's life.
- Discrimination and stigma are part of the external factors that people with disabilities must navigate when developing self-concept.
- Everyone experiences inconsistencies between how they are perceived by others and how they perceive themselves. Reflecting on these differences helps to challenge our assumptions about other people and develop empathy for those whose life experiences may be different.

Learning Objectives

Students will:

- Challenge assumptions, myths, and stereotypes about people with disabilities.
- Appreciate the diversity of experiences of disability.
- Reflect on how they experience themselves within the world and how the world experiences them.

Cross-Curricular Connections

- Art (visual)
- English
- Equity Studies
- Gender Studies
- Psychology
- Social Studies
- Sociology

Terminology

- Discrimination
- Infantilized
- Self-concept
- Stigma

Materials

- Paper and writing utensils for students
- Large pieces of construction paper
- Art supplies (markers, crayons, paint, old magazines, etc.)

Background Information for Educators

People with disabilities exist everywhere. Disability can be visible and/or invisible to an outside observer. It can manifest physically, mentally, intellectually, or emotionally. Disability exists on a spectrum and can include chronic illness, chronic pain, and mental illness. Having and/or living with or without a disability can change throughout the lifespan. Disability is not fixed in time or space and as people's bodies change with age, living with a disability becomes more and more common. Nevertheless, it is common for people living with a disability to experience **stigma** and **discrimination**.

Sometimes discrimination can exist in a physical form (e.g., restaurants having stairs instead of a ramp to get inside) and sometimes discrimination can exist in the form of verbal harassment and bullying (e.g., calling someone a "retard," stupid, or crazy). Sometimes stigma and discrimination are masked in comments that may be well-intentioned or even considered positive but are actually harmful. These subtler forms of discrimination are ones that assume disability is always a tragedy and that people with disabilities should be pitied and **infantilized**.

This module considers disability as a spectrum and looks at the ways it intersects with self-concept. In doing so, students are encouraged to critically reflect on the ways that they see and/or experience people with disabilities. They are also encouraged to reflect on how the ways they imagine themselves to be might differ from who the world imagines them to be and how these intersect to create and challenge their self-concept.

Student Readiness

Before students engage with this lesson, ensure that safer space guidelines and group norms have been established (and revisited) within your classroom (for more information on how to establish safer space guidelines, see module 1.3). In order to effectively prepare for this activity, ensure students understand that:
- This module is for people with and without disabilities.
- You can never tell whether or not someone has a disability by looking at them.
- Most people experience some kind of pressure to conform to societal norms and unrealistic beauty standards but different bodies experience these pressures very differently.
- People with disabilities are not one homogenous (all the same) group and there is a huge diversity of experiences of disability.
- This module deals with the topic of bodies, **self-concept**, and discrimination.

Summary of Activities

Students will:

- Individually narrate their stories as a first and then third person narrator using writing prompts.
- Individually express their stories through art.
- Collectively watch a video and discuss the portrayal of people with disabilities.

Activity 1 2 3

Instructions

Part 1: Third Person Storytelling

1. Optional grounding exercise: Ask students to close their eyes and imagine that they are in the middle of a square in the middle of a busy city. There are people walking all around them. As people walk by, they are looking at you. Pick one person as they walk by and imagine what it is like to be them, looking at you.

2. Ask students: what does it feel like to be in this space, looking at yourself from the outside?

3. Ask them to slowly open their eyes. Explain that this is a stream of conscious writing exercise, where they will be given a writing prompt and should write whatever comes to their mind. They should write in the third person but do not need to worry about spelling or grammar. The objective is to keep writing until the 5 to 10 minutes is up.

4. Provide them with one of the following writing prompts (or give your students a choice between them).
    - They had a look of...
    - There was something about them...
    - They seemed like...
    - In this light, they looked like...

5. Discuss: How did it feel to write in the third person, from the perspective of an observer? What did you notice? What did you like about the experience? What did you dislike?

Part 2: First person storytelling

1. Optional: Ask students to close their eyes and think about a physical place that brings them joy and comfort, this can be a place they go to all the time, have been to just once or twice, or maybe have never been to at all. Ask them to picture themselves there right now and ask: What does it feel like to be in this space? Is it easeful and comforting? Do you feel like you can be yourself here? What does being yourself mean?

2. Ask them to slowly open their eyes. Explain that this is a stream of conscious writing exercise, where they will be given a writing prompt and should write whatever comes to their mind. They should write in the third person but do not need to worry about spelling or grammar. The objective is to keep writing until the 5 to 10 minutes is up.

3. Provide them with one of the following writing prompts (or give your students a choice between them).
   - I am the narrator of my own story…
   - I feel my best when…
   - I see myself as…
   - When I look in the mirror, I see…
   - I come from a long line of…
   - Inside the boundaries of my skin…
   - My body feels good when…

4. Discuss: How did it feel to write from the perspective of the first person? What did you notice? What did you like about the experience? What did you dislike? How did this feel in comparison with writing about yourself in the third person?

Optional: Part 3: Narration through art

1. Ask students to re-read each of their stories and quietly reflect on their experiences from the first person and third person perspectives. In their reflections, ask students to consider:
   - Were there any places in your two stories that overlapped? How does this overlap feel?
   - Were there any places in your two stories with differences? How do these differences feel?
   - If you were to imagine story 1 being a circle and story 2 being another circle, where would these circles be in relation to one other? (e.g., wide apart, close, touching, overlapping, etc.).
   - Draw the ways that these circles would or would not overlap.

2. Using the art materials provided, visually express what elements of these stories overlap and which do not.

3. Optional: Ask students to present their art to the class.

Part 4: Inspiration Porn

Inspiration porn is a term disability activists use to describe societal expectations/assumptions of them that do not reflect their experiences or realities. Well-intentioned or not, these expectations are usually pity or infantilize people with disabilities. Inspiration porn assumes that the lives of people with disabilities are void of anything meaningful or worth living for and assumes that everyday tasks like waking up in the morning are heroic acts for them. These types of outsider expectations (from people who do not have a disability) prevent people with disabilities from describing, naming, and claiming the many different and nuanced ways they experience life. (For more information, see Stella Young's Ted Talk in 5.4 resources).

Instructions
1. Play the Ted Talk by Stella Young *I'm not your inspiration, thank you very much* for your students (for the link, see 5.4 resources).
2. Ask them the following questions:
   - What did you think of Stella Young's talk?
   - Have you ever heard of the term "inspiration porn"?
   - Have you ever seen a video or read a story that could be classified as "inspiration porn"?
   - Was there anything that surprised you?
   - Was there anything that challenged your ideas about people with disabilities?

Wrap-Up

Summarize the module with the following points:
- Disability is visible and invisible. It exists everywhere and is a spectrum of experience.
- People with disabilities experience overt and subtle forms of discrimination. Subtle forms of discrimination can seem positive on the outside but may limit and/or negatively impact a person's self-concept.
- Self-concept is influenced by internal and external factors (the ways that you see yourself and the ways that society sees and treats you).
- Being able to tell your own life story can be an empowering experience.

5.5 SELF-CARE STRATEGIES

LEVEL ☐1 ☐2 ☐3

Big Ideas in Module 5.5

- Self-care is the act or practise of taking care of oneself in ways that are *loving, gentle,* and *supportive.*
- Developing self-care strategies is one way to help build a healthy self-concept and put body positivity into practise.
- Self-care looks differently for everybody. Distinguishing between what actually works for you and what you think should work for you are important for establishing self-care strategies.

Learning Objectives

Students will:

- Learn how self-care relates to appreciating and loving oneself.
- Explore self-care strategies unique to each of their needs.

Cross-Curricular Connections	Terminology	Materials
• Art (visual) • English • Gender Studies • Psychology • Social Studies • Sociology	• Self-care	• Chalkboard or whiteboard • Writing paper and pens/pencils • Construction paper • Markers, pencil crayons, and/or paint • Old magazines

Background Information for Educators

Self-care is a way of putting body positivity and a healthy self-concept into practise; it reinforces these somewhat abstract ideas into tangible practises. Figuring out how to care for yourself (what works well for you and what does not) can be more challenging than it seems. Part of this challenge is sifting though what other people say *should* feel supportive/affirming and what *actually* feels supportive and affirming for you.

Self-care needs are diverse and strategies are not one-size fits all. What may be helpful and work for one person, may not be helpful or work for another. This is important to talk about with your students because it helps them move away from doing something because they think they "should" and instead doing something because it actually helps them practise self-care.

Other modules (5.2 and 5.3) in this is chapter provide an introduction to the links between self-care, self-concept, and body positivity and begin to get students thinking about what their self-care needs are. This module builds on self-concept and body positivity by providing activities that help your students identify what they appreciate and love about themselves and then move into identifying how to take care of what they love and appreciate.

Student Readiness

Before students engage with this lesson, ensure that safer space guidelines and group norms have been established (and revisited) within your classroom (for more information on how to establish safer space guidelines, see module 1.3). In order to effectively prepare for this activity, ensure students understand that:
- There are no right or wrong answers when it comes to self-care.
- Learning how to take care of ourselves can be a lifelong process.
- Self-care strategies might change throughout a person's life.

Summary of Activities

Students will:
- Individually write letters to themselves to reflect on what they appreciate and love about themselves.
- Individually create posters representing how they take care of different aspects of themselves.

Activity 1

Instructions
1. Write the word "love" on the board and ask students what they think of when they hear this word. Write their answers on the board.
2. Write the word "care" on the board and ask students what they think of when they hear this word. Write their answers on the board.

EDUCATOR PROMPTS

- What do these words feel like?
- What do these words look like?
- What do these words smell like?

3. Ask your students to consider all of the words on the board and quietly think about how they relate (or do not relate) to how they feel about themselves. Explain that this is a reflection exercise and they will not have to share their thoughts.

4. Ask students to take their reflections and write their thoughts in the form of a letter to themselves. Emphasize that this is a personal reflective exercise and they will not have to share their writing.

5. After students have finished their letters, debrief the exercise by asking open-ended questions like:
   - What surprised you about the activity?
   - What did you find challenging about the activity?
   - What did you find empowering about the activity?

6. Wrap up the activity by explaining that learning to love and appreciate different aspects of yourself is one part of learning how to care for yourself.

Activity 2 [1] [3]

Instructions

1. Explain: Self-care is the act of caring for yourself beyond physical survival needs. It is unique to everyone and part of self-care is figuring out what feels like an affirming and supportive practise to you. Part of your self-care might include reading every night for at least 30 minutes before bed, writing in a journal on a weekly basis, playing soccer every Tuesday and Thursday evening, or maybe it is learning how to play the drums. Whatever your self-care strategies are, they are usually something that does not depend on someone else and is a way of loving, supporting, affirming, and caring for the whole of who you are.

2. Write the following two questions on the board and ask students to reflect on them:
   - What aspects of yourself could you care for?
   - Are there different self-care strategies you need for each part of yourself? What are they?

3. Compile their answers on the board under each question and group their answers into the following 3 to 4 categories:
   - Body
   - Mind
   - Heart
   - Optional: Spirit

4. Give each student 3 (or 4 if you are including Spirit) pieces of construction paper and ask them to label each with the categories.

5. Explain that their task is to think of a way that they could (or already do) care for one of these aspects of themselves and represent it in poster form. They can draw, paint, collage and/or write words on their self-care posters. Emphasize that the point is not to encourage other people to adopt your self-care strategy. It is about creating a poster that you feel affirmed by, one you might want to hang on your wall as a reminder of what self-care strategies work for you.

6. ✚ Optional: Have students choose one of their posters to present to the class.

Wrap-Up

Summarize the module with the following points:

- Learning how to practise self-care starts with being able to identify what we love and appreciate about ourselves.
- Self-care needs are diverse. It may take some exploring to figure out what self-care strategies work for you.

5.6 OFFERING PEER SUPPORT

LEVEL 2 [3]

Big Ideas in Module 5.6

- A safe and supportive environment is key to developing self-acceptance and a healthy self-concept.
- One part of a safe and supportive environment is peer support. Teaching students about peer support involves critical thinking and emotional skills such as compassion and empathy.
- While support is often portrayed as helping someone "stay positive," acknowledging difficult feelings is essential; it helps to deepen interpersonal connections.

Learning Objectives

Students will:

- Practise empathy with peers.
- Create affirmative messages beyond "staying positive."

Cross-Curricular Connections

- Art (visual)
- English
- Gender Studies
- Psychology
- Social Studies
- Sociology

Materials

- Printed copies of **Empathy Lab**
- **Educator Resource—Empathy Lab**
- Optional: Art supplies
- Optional: Small slips of paper and coloured pens
- Optional: Small containers, plastic toy dispenser "eggs," small boxes, or small colourful envelopes

Background Information for Educators

Self-acceptance and a healthy self-concept can be bolstered by a supportive and safe social environment. Having a safe and supportive social environment includes personal, emotional, and physical supports as well as community and structural supports that challenge racism, transphobia, homophobia, sexism, ableism, and classism. Other modules in *Beyond the Basics* have addressed ways that you can contribute to building safe and supportive classroom and school communities that challenge systemic discrimination, prejudice, bias, bullying, and harassment (see chapter 1 and modules 2.1, 2.4, 2.5, and 3.11). It is important to teach students the critical thinking skills to challenge discrimination, harassment, and bullying as well as teach emotional skills (like empathy and compassion) to young people so that they can support each other in helpful ways.

Popular culture often confuses "cheering up" and "staying positive" with support. While these are sometimes useful, true connection between people cannot sidestep difficult emotions. Not allowing yourself to be vulnerable is not strength; youth need all of their experiences and feelings to be acknowledged by adult allies and their peers. Navigating difficult experiences together is key to deepening interpersonal connections.

Student Readiness

Before students engage with this lesson, ensure that safer space guidelines and group norms have been established (and revisited) within your classroom (for more information on how to establish safer space guidelines, see module 1.3). In order to effectively prepare for this activity, ensure students understand that:

- While the concept of "staying positive" or "cheering someone up" may work for certain people at certain times, it is important to offer peer support that emphasizes empathy, compassion, and affirmation.
- It is okay and normal to feel the range of human emotions. Being strong does not mean that you do not ever feel vulnerable. In fact, strength and deepened human connection often comes from learning how to accept vulnerable feelings and being supported in that vulnerability.

Summary of Activities

Students will:
- Work through scenarios in small groups to practise empathy.
- Individually and anonymously create affirmative messages (using words and art) for peers that acknowledge other students' realities and affirm their worth.

Activity 1 ☐ 3

Instructions

1. Ask students: What are the ways you can support someone else?

EDUCATOR ANSWER KEY

There are many possible answers to this question. Here are a few:

- Listen
- Try to be non-judgmental
- Ask if they want support
- Ask how they would feel supported
- Empathize (understand their reality, feel "with" instead of "for" them)
- Accompany them in seeking help, information, and resources
- Keep confidentiality

YOU SHOULD KNOW

In modules 4.5 and 7.7, students are taught that being asked to keep secrets by "tricky" people can be a sign of an abusive relationship. In that case, the "tricky" people often have some kind of power over the person asked to keep their secret; secrets become less about privacy and more about blackmail. Confidentiality is not about blackmail. It is about keeping something private because it is not yours to share. But confidentiality also has limits. Sometimes these limits are mandated by law as in the case of professionals (like educators and social workers) required to disclose if they suspect someone under 16 is in an abusive/dangerous situation and/or if there is a risk of self-harm and/or suicide.

2. Place students in small groups and give each group one or two scenarios from **Empathy Lab**.
3. Explain: This exercise creates a "laboratory" for empathy. It is not what you would do in real life but a set of skills you need for offering support.
4. Ask students to read the scenario(s) they are given, discuss, and record their answers.
5. As a class, debrief each scenario. Use the Educator Resource as a guide.

6. Discuss:
   - Why is it not always obvious what someone is feeling?
   - People need different things even if they are feeling something similar. How can we find out what they need?

EDUCATOR ANSWER KEY

- We each wear masks that can hide and distort what we are actually feeling. We also interpret other peoples' feelings based on what we know to be true about ourselves but people are unique and complex.
- The best way to find out what someone needs is to ask. Do not make an assumption about what someone needs based on what you would need.

Activity 2 2 3

Instructions
1. Ask students to think of affirmative messages the characters in Activity 1 scenarios might benefit from hearing. Explain that affirmative messages do not have to be "positive." They can affirm how the person is feeling, including feeling left out, sad, misunderstood, and so on. Have students share their suggestions for affirmative messages and help them work on improving their messages.

EDUCATOR ANSWER KEY

Encourage them to think of specific messages that would either:
- Acknowledge someone's reality (what they are feeling, needing, experiencing)
- Remind someone of their worth and value in times of doubt
- Affirm someone's right to be exactly who they are

For example:
- Tan: I know you might be missing your grandfather. I'm sorry he passed away.
- Tay: What's happening with the photo is wrong. I promise not to look or pass on the photo if I ever come across it. I'm on your side.
- Teagan: Your scooter *is* fun and so are you. I like your sense of humour and how generous you are to people.
- Arooj: I know you might be feeling lonely in this school. I just want you to know that I think you're cool.
- Marley: I wanted to say that I know you're a good person.

2. Once students understand how affirmative messaging works, ask them to think of other general examples that apply to all students in the class or school. Make sure that students stay general in their messages. Ask them to write down and or/visually express through art 2 to 5 affirmative messages. Urge them to consider the common struggles that adolescents their age tend to have. Advise them to steer clear of platitudes like, "You're awesome!" You can choose to display these around the classroom with your students' permission, wrap up the activity, or move to instruction 3.

3. ✦ Optional: Have students anonymously write their affirmations onto small slips of paper and hide them around the class or school over the next few days or weeks. They can fold the papers creatively, make them artful, and/or use small receptacles or envelopes. The point is for them to be anonymous and general for other students to find and read.

Wrap-up

Summarize the module with the following points:

- We all struggle, even though we all have different ways of expressing those struggles and we all deserve support from others.
- Supporting someone else means paying attention to how they are feeling, what they are needing, and asking them how best to help.
- Someone's actions may not always obviously reflect what is happening for them underneath their outward action and/or appearance. The only way we know what is going on for someone and how or why they are struggling is if we ask them.
- We can affirm someone else by acknowledging their reality and reminding them of their worth.

5.7 BODY IMAGE, SELF-REPRESENTATION, AND THE MEDIA

LEVEL 2 3

Big Ideas in Module 5.7

- Normative beauty standards set unrealistic expectations of bodies and physical appearance that place enormous pressure on adolescents.
- Both traditional and new media reinforce the idea that the image adolescents' present to the world must be perfect, which increases insecurities and shame when they do not measure up.
- While new forms of media (i.e., social media) can contribute to the pressure that adolescents feel in terms of presenting a perfect image to the world, social media is also a place where adolescents may feel empowered to control their image and represent their own life experiences in the world.

Learning Objectives

Students will:

- Understand the concept of body image.
- Discuss what influences self-image.
- Critically consider who is and who is not represented in traditional and new media.
- Critically consider self-representation using social media.

Cross-Curricular Connections

- Art (visual, photography, digital)
- English
- Equity Studies
- Gender Studies
- Media Studies
- Psychology
- Social Studies
- Sociology

Terminology

- Ableism
- Ageism
- Classism
- Fatphobia
- Gender expression
- Gender normativity
- Homophobia
- Normative
- Racism
- Sexism
- Transphobia

Materials

- Chalkboard, whiteboard, or Smart Board
- Printed copies of **Body Image Definitions**
- Printed copies of **Curated Photo Series**
- Access to social media photo sharing platforms (e.g., Instagram, Snapchat, Tumblr, Flickr, etc.)
- Access to online and print magazines, advertisements, and newspapers (access to a printer if taking images from online editions of traditional media sources)

Background Information for Educators

Adolescents are under increased pressure to look a certain way. Traditional media (like print magazines and advertisements) contribute to this pressure by representing a single "**normative**" beauty standard. New media, such as social media and photo sharing platforms can be an empowering alternative for self-representation.

Most young people are both conscious of and dependent on these technologies for image building and their "personal brand." Many adolescents will talk about how fake social media images can be while at the same time being deeply invested in them. In a world where many things feel out of their control, being able to represent themselves can be empowering and a cause for endless stress/anxiety.

Because adolescents are undergoing rapid physical changes and are increasingly aware of their sexuality, they are already naturally self-conscious. Insecurity and shame can have serious negative impacts, including feeling out of control. When an adolescent feels out of control, or needs to maintain control, they may resort to coping mechanisms like disordered eating, substance use, and digital media dependence.

It is important to frame adolescent use of social media realistically. These media are entertainment, tools for connection and community, as well as self-image explorations. The objective of this lesson plan is not to dissuade or promote social media use. It is to increase students' awareness of their media use and their self-image and to develop critical thinking skills in the consumption of various media (including new and traditional media).

Student Readiness

Before students engage with this lesson, ensure that safer space guidelines and group norms have been established (and revisited) within your classroom (for more information on how to establish safer space guidelines, see module 1.3). In order to effectively prepare for this activity, ensure students understand that:

- Most people experience pressure to conform to societal norms and unrealistic beauty standards at some point in their life but different bodies experience these pressures very differently.
- Social media is not inherently bad or good. It is about how you use and interact with social media that makes it either a positive or a negative experience.

- The purpose of this module is not to dissuade or promote social media. The purpose is to explore ways of critically examining how social media is consumed and to develop strategies for using social media as a tool for empowerment and connection.

Summary of Activities

Students will:
- Collectively brainstorm contributing factors to positive and negative body image.
- Individually create 2 series of photo/image collages taken from traditional media sources (such as print magazines, newspapers, and/or advertisements).
- Work in small groups to curate a series of social media photos and consider how self-representation shows, distorts, and hides reality.

Activity 1 2 3

Instructions

1. As a class, create a definition for the term "body image." *Use the educator prompts if your students are stuck.*

EDUCATOR PROMPTS

Ask the class:
- You likely hear the term "body image" often. What immediately comes to mind when you hear this word?
- If you were trying to explain "body image" to someone who is younger, what would you say?

---

2. Distribute the **Body Image Definitions** handout. Discuss the differences between the class' definition and the one on the handout.
3. Using the handout as a reference, ask the class to name influences that contribute to positive and negative body image. Prompt them for individual, cultural, and systemic influences. Note them on the board in a chart like the example in table 5.1.

Table 5.1

BODY IMAGE

Positive Influences	Negative Influences
<ul><li>Eating well</li><li>Having good friends</li><li>Being active</li><li>Having fun using your body</li><li>Feeling strong</li><li>Sincere compliments</li><li>Matching current ideals of attractiveness*</li><li>Learning about Body Positivity(see module 5.2)</li></ul>	<ul><li>Being criticized for how you look (both directly and indirectly)</li><li>Feeling lazy</li><li>Discrimination (e.g., fatphobia, racism, sexism, homophobia, transphobia, gender normativity, classism, ableism, ageism)</li><li>Not matching current ideals of attractiveness*</li><li>Feeling isolated or lonely</li><li>Sudden changes to abilities or function (e.g., injury, pain)</li><li>Being overly focused on external image</li><li>Consuming media that show lots of "perfect" bodies or body-shaming messages</li><li>Dieting</li></ul>

*Ideals of attractiveness change with time and place

4. If not already discussed, ask the class how they think **fatphobia, racism, sexism, homophobia, transphobia, gender normativity, ableism, classism,** and **ageism** negatively influence body image.

EDUCATOR ANSWER KEY

They determine ideals of attractiveness and desirability that are skewed and unrealistic. They also ask everyone to fit into a very narrow beauty standard and contribute to feelings of loneliness and isolation.

5. Discuss: How does being conscious of systemic and cultural influences on body image benefit us?

EDUCATOR ANSWER KEY
- Less likely to blame ourselves for everything.
- Provides opportunities to engage with culture and media more wisely.
- Might feel empowered and inspired to challenge normative beauty standards.
- Might be able to make more informed decisions about how we relate to ourselves and each other.
- Might change our perception of what is beautiful.

Activity 2 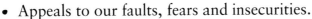 2 3

Instructions
Part 1
1. Tell students: In one study, 52% of all teens said they felt pressure from the media to change their body image.
2. As a class, discuss the statistic with the following questions:
   - What are the ways that media "pressures" us to do anything?

EDUCATOR ANSWER KEY
- Appeals to our faults, fears and insecurities.
- Creates desires and the "need" to consume their product.

- How does it affect advertisers or companies if people have negative body image? How about it people have positive body image?

EDUCATOR ANSWER KEY
Negative body image:
- More likely to use products to improve ourselves/our appearance if we feel like we are lacking.
- More likely to buy things to feel better (the adrenaline rush of shopping).

Positive body image:
- Less likely to spend money on the companies and products that are being advertised.
- More likely to pursue activities that make you feel better from the inside out (e.g., making art, playing music, playing sports, etc.).

Homework

3. Ask students to find images from traditional media sources such as advertisements, magazines, and newspapers (online or print). They can also take pictures of billboards that they see (and print these if they have access to a printer).

4. Have students create a collage with the images and answer the following questions:
   - What kinds of bodies were easy to find?
   - What kinds of skin colours and tones were easy to find?
   - What kind of hair was easy to find?
   - What ages were easy to find?
   - What kind of gender expressions were easy to find?
   - What kind of lives were represented?
   - What kinds of relationships and ways of loving were represented?

EDUCATOR ANSWER KEY

- Skinny bodies, able-bodied bodies, very fit/muscularly toned bodies, cis-gender bodies
- White and fair skin tones, smooth skin (without wrinkles, blemishes, acne, or exyema)
- Shiny hair, hair without kinks or afros, straightened hair
- Younger people
- Normative gender expressions (expressions that fit into easily identifiable feminine and masculine categories and often attached to cisgender bodies)
- Affluent lives, lives free of struggle and hardship
- Monogamous, straight/heterosexual relationships and love

5. Have students find or write/draw images of representations either not easy to find or missing altogether and create a second collage with these images. For those missing, ask students to make note of why they think that is.

6. Have students bring both collages into class and prepare to discuss the following:
   - Who was easier to find representations of? Who was challenging to find representations of? Remind students of the list of questions they answered after creating the first collage. What elements of these people fit into the representations that were easiest to find?

EDUCATOR PROMPTS

- If you were able to find images of "plus-size" models, were you able to find plus-size models of colour?
- If you found images of people subverting gender norms around gender expression, were they white, rich, skinny, and otherwise stereotypically beautiful (e.g., Ruby Rose and Miley Cyrus)?

- Why do you think that it was easier to find lots of representations of one kind of person and not others?

EDUCATOR ANSWER KEY

The advertising world and fashion/beauty companies make money off of playing into people's insecurities and creating (and maintaining) fear around certain aspects of bodies and outward characteristics and appearances. Systemic discrimination and prejudice both fuel and compound many of the fears and insecurities that beauty/fashion companies and advertisers play into.

Part 2
Instructions
1. Divide the class into small groups.
2. Ask each group to select an electronic photo sharing platform (e.g., Tumblr, Instagram, Snapchat, Facebook, etc.) and a hashtag that shows self-taken photos (e.g., #selfie). Ask the group to curate a series of 10 to 15 compelling images from that hashtag.
3. Have each group answer questions about their images from the **Curated Photo Series** handout.
4. Have each group show their images to the class and present their report.
5. As a class, discuss the use of social media and digital technology and how they affect self-image. Be sure to touch on how they can be empowering and disempowering. Ask the class for strategies to manage the disempowering effects of photo sharing platforms.

Wrap-up

Summarize the module with the following points:

- Body image and self-image are about the relationship with ourselves and all of us struggle with them in different ways. They are affected by individual will and choice as well as cultural and systemic factors.
- Even if it does not seem obvious, media used to sell products is invested in the public having a negative self-image.
- Images in the media (traditional and new forms of media) are often carefully distorted. They present an inaccurate and unrealistic idea of reality.
- Ideals of attractiveness in popular media often perpetuate existing systemic injustices (i.e., about race, size, disability, class, gender normativity, skin tone, etc.).

CHAPTER **6**

Media Literacy and Sexuality

6.1 INTRODUCTION

Media has a powerful effect on all of its consumers. Young people need to develop the skills to distinguish between the ways sexuality and relationships are represented in the media and how they unfold in real life. It is important for young people to learn that most representations of sexuality, relationships, and bodies are unrealistic and that as consumers of media, young people have choices. Young people have choices in the kinds of media they consume and how often they consume it. Through media literacy skills within a **comprehensive sexuality education** approach, students learn how to apply a critical eye to challenge these messages rather than absorb them wholesale.

Every advertisement has a message beyond "buy this." Advertisements create ideals that represent a small percentage of reality in order to play on people's insecurities and increase sales. To sell products, the media also hypersexualizes objects and people, including images of children in advertisements targeted at adults. This **hypersexualization** is a product of and feeds into gender norms and stereotypes that disproportionately impact cisgender girls and women and transgender and gender non-conforming people. Without applying a critical eye, we normalize this kind of sexualization and the gendered impacts remain unchallenged and invisible.

Access to media has increased with advances in digital and communication technologies, making media highly accessible to produce and consume. This includes **pornography**. As access to mainstream pornography increases, young people are consuming this type of media at younger ages than ever before. A sensitive and nuanced treatment of the topic is necessary. Young people should not be shamed for watching pornography and the topic should not be ignored. While pornography can present an unrealistic and potentially harmful picture of human sexuality, accessible sexual images can also provide an opportunity for young people to safely explore their sexuality. Ensuring that young people have the skills to consume pornography with a mindful, critical eye is an important part of media literacy.

At the same time as hypersexualized media content and mainstream pornography are becoming widespread, sex and violence are increasingly being presented together in the media. Whether in online games, advertisements, videos, shareable images, or police crime dramas on television, young people are exposed to more and more graphic depictions of sexuality and violence, including **sexual violence** and coercive sex. Media that conflates sex and violence normalizes and trivializes the sexual violence that underpins **rape culture** (for more information, see chapter 8); equipping students with the skills to critically consider the media they consume is a necessary part of challenging rape culture and ending sexual violence.

A lot of popular media promotes limited ideas about gender, bodies, sexuality, and families. It is therefore important to ask: Who is missing from this depiction (which bodies, what kinds of sexualities, which races, etc.)? Who gets to represent who? For what purpose? And how does this depiction of reality affect how we think about ourselves and each other? At the same time, the media is one of the most powerful influencers of sexual and relationship scripts. It is important for young people to have the skills to challenge **gender norms** and **gender stereotypes**, build confidence in a diversity of bodies and experiences, and maximize conscious decision-making.

The advent of social media creates more platforms for young people to find connection and **empowerment** as well as disconnection and disempowerment. Every form of media and communication tool has the potential for both. For example, sexting might empower young people to express themselves sexually, sexting might also expose them to **bullying, cyberbullying,** and **harassment.** This chapter provides young people with opportunities to critically reflect on social media tools and consider their best use.

Comprehensive sexuality education needs to include media literacy skills to help young people critically analyze the media content they are consuming in order to assess who has created the media and for what purpose. Whose interests does it serve? Who does it empower? Who does it disempower? Which gender norms does this media challenge and which does it uphold? This chapter equips students with the ability to analyze and evaluate media representations, imagery, and messages in order to engage with any piece of media critically.

Educator Reflection Questions

- Do you feel represented in the media? Was there ever a time that you did not feel represented in the media? Why do you think this is?
- Which parts of your identity do you think the media speaks to, which do they leave behind? Do you think that most people in your family feel this way? Why or why not?
- Do you find social media to be an empowering or disempowering space for you? Why or why not?
- Have you ever felt nervous about a post or a picture that you have shared on social media? Why or why not?
- When you do not feel represented in the media, how does this make you feel? Think now about how many of your students may not feel represented in the media, how do you think that this affects how they see themselves and the ways that they interact with the world?
- Think back to when you were your students' age, how did the media affect your self-image, self-esteem, and shape your understanding of your own sexuality? How does this compare to now? If you think that there is a significant difference from when you were their age, why do you think that this difference exists? How do you think media literacy skills would have benefitted you at their age?
- To what extent do you think that the media has (and continues to) shape the ways that you envision relationships, gender stereotypes, and sexuality?

Big Ideas in Chapter 6

- Representations found in the media are often unrealistic but the effect on consumers might make you think otherwise. Media literacy helps young people analyze and evaluate media representations, imagery, and messages, helping to dilute the power that the media has over consumers.
- Social media and other new ways of communicating have the potential to be an empowering tool; however, the same tools have the power to be disempowering if used without critical thinking and reflection around potential consequences.
- All forms of media have become more accessible, widespread, sexualized, and violent.
- Like other forms of media, the easy availability of online, mainstream pornography presents young people with unrealistic bodies, distorted sexual scripts and responses, and sexually violent imagery at younger ages and in a more saturated way than ever before.
- Young people need the skills to evaluate the differences between fantasy and reality as they begin to explore their sexuality and relationships.
- A sensitive and nuanced treatment of the topic of pornography is necessary. Pornography is neither good nor bad—like other kinds of media, it exists on a spectrum of empowering and affirming to disempowering and harmful. Young people should not be shamed for watching pornography and the topic should not be ignored.

6.2 MEDIA REPRESENTATION AND BIAS

LEVEL 1 2 3

Big Ideas in Module 6.2

- Media, whether fictional (dramas, movies, etc.) or non-fictional (news, documentaries, etc.), is a subjective reflection of reality.
- While non-fictional media should provide a balance in perspectives, when this balance becomes skewed, it is considered media bias.
- It is especially important to understand non-fictional media as an outlet for reporting on events from perspectives that contain bias.
- Bias refers to the ways that perspective and subjectivity influence how an issue is presented. Bias in the media is not inherently wrong but bias can be harmful, especially if we cannot see or critically consider bias.
- Applying critical thinking to all media consumption means asking questions about which perspectives are represented and why.

Learning Objectives

Students will:

- Reflect on the types and functions of different kinds of media.
- Critically reflect on the illusions inherent in media representation, including the news.

Cross-Curricular Connections

- Art (drama)
- Communications Studies
- English
- Equity Studies
- Gender Studies
- Media Studies
- Politics
- Psychology
- Social Studies
- Sociology
- World Studies

Terminology

- Marginalization
- Representation

Materials

- Chalkboard or whiteboard
- Projection or printed copies of optical illusions from Optics4Kids website
- Optional: Whistle or bell

Background Information for Educators

Although media has become more widely available than ever through digital platforms, the media formats and channels that are most available to young people still vary depending on different factors. Class, age, geography, culture (including family culture), gender identity, sexual orientation, and social connections all shape their media consumption.

What is consistent is that media, in whatever form, is **representation**: even media that we think of as reflecting an objective reality, like the news, is a subjective representation of reality from a certain perspective. This perspective or subjectivity is also called **bias**. Sometimes the perspective or angle is obvious and central, like opinion editorials, other times it is subtler and can only be uncovered after asking questions like, what stories are not being told or whose voices are missing from this story?

Media bias in the news is different than "fake news." Bias is not inherently wrong or inherently untrue, it is a series of choices made in reporting what happened and why, which are based on the subjective perspectives that we as people all have. "Fake news" is when false facts and events are represented as truths in order to advance an agenda.

As consumers of media, it is important to develop critical thinking skills to see the difference between reality and representation and to uncover media bias that purports to be objective or unbiased. Developing critical thinking skills helps media consumers analyze: how intentionally media is constructed; how it can reflect some peoples' realities, while distorting that of others; who media is constructed for; whose voices, realities, and experiences media centers around; and whose voices experience **marginalization**.

Student Readiness

Before students engage with this lesson, ensure that safer space guidelines and group norms have been established (and revisited) within your classroom (for more information on how to establish safer space guidelines, see module 1.3). In order to effectively prepare for this activity, ensure students understand that:

- Media is not inherently good or bad. It is a tool that must be engaged with critically.
- Critically engaging with the media is a process of asking questions about what we consume.
- This module discusses representation, including representation of race, class, sexual orientation, and gender identity.

Summary of Activities

Students will:

- Move around the room and in pairs to identify traditional and new media sources.
- Use optical illusions to collectively discuss the illusions in the media.
- Individually research how a topical issue is represented in the news, paying attention to bias.
- In groups, create drama skits about the potential impact that bias in the media can have on local, national, and global events.

Activity 1

Instructions

1. Explain that today's lesson will be about media. Clear the classroom or move to an open space. Ask students to keep moving around the room. When you indicate (with a clap, a whistle, or a bell), have students stop and pair up with the person closest to them. In this pairing, ask them to name as many forms of media as they can.
2. After a couple of minutes, have students move around again. Give another indication (with a clap, a whistle, or a bell) and have students pair up again, with someone new. In this pairing, ask students to come up with as many answers to the question: What is the purpose of the media?
3. Ask students to return to their seats and share answers from both questions.

QUICK TIP

To make it more challenging, complete a couple of rounds and set a timer for 30 seconds for each round. This can make the activity feel more exciting as students are racing against the clock and both students in the pairing have to say as many examples of media as possible in 30 seconds.

EDUCATOR ANSWER KEY

Allow students' answers to guide the discussion. If they get stuck, some possible answers may include:

- Forms of media: newspapers, magazines, television, movies, video games, direct mail, billboards, posters, pamphlets, internet, blogs, online magazines, online newspapers, online community forums, social networks, social media, podcasts, web radio, online videos, vlogs, online photo sharing platforms, texting, etc.
- Purpose of the media: entertainment, advertising, marketing, promotion, fundraising, information sharing, event reporting, opinion creation/sharing, knowledge production, knowledge consumption, community building, story sharing, photo sharing, communication, etc.

4. Write the forms of media that students' share onto the board under two categories: "Traditional Media" and "New Media." The items under each may include:

Traditional Media	New Media
Newspapers, magazines	Internet, blogs, online magazines,
Television, movies	online newspapers, online community
Direct mail	forums
Billboards	Social networks, social media
	Podcasts, web radio
	Online videos, vlogs, short-form vlogs
	Photosharing platforms
	Texting

5. Discuss the difference between these media. Prompt with the following questions:
   - Do traditional media and new media have different purposes? Do these two categories of media have different target audiences? How do the purposes of each overlap?
   - Who has decision-making power over each kind of media? Who has control over the content? Who gets to create it? Who gets to censor it? Who gets to influence it?
   - Who receives the content? Is there any way that the receiver can influence or interact with the sender?
   - How are people held accountable for the content they create? What rules exist? How are these rules decided, governed, and enforced?

EDUCATOR ANSWER KEY

- Traditional media and new media often have overlapping purposes and overlapping target audiences. Key differences include: who gets to create and control content, channels for interaction between content creators and content consumers, and accountability mechanisms.
- Traditional media restricts the creation of knowledge and opinions to a small number of powerful people and companies with a lot of money, while new media makes a diversity of knowledge, experiences, and opinions more accessible to everyday consumers. New media has become a public accountability tool where people can document what is happening to them in real time, including everyday experiences of oppression and discrimination.

CONT'D NEXT PAGE

EDUCATOR ANSWER KEY CONT'D

- Traditional media is broadcast-based (where a few people send content to many people) and new media is more interactive and more in the user's/consumer's control. In new media, the users, consumers, and creators are one.
- Traditional media is governed by industry standards, bills of rights, journalism ethics and etiquette, and government policies. It is difficult to enforce these regulations with new media and its users/consumers.

Activity 2

Instructions

1. Choose 2 or 3 optical illusions from the Optics4Kids website (see 6.2 resources).
2. Project the images on a large screen and print out copies.
3. Ask students:
   - In the optical illusions, what is the difference between our perception and reality?
   - How do you think optical illusions work?
   - Are there optical illusions in the media? What about other kinds of illusions (where perception and reality are different)?
   - Images in the media are called "representation." What do you think representation is and how do you think representation is different from reality?

EDUCATOR ANSWER KEY
- Optical illusions highlight how much our perception shapes what we see as reality. When looking at optical illusions, our perception easily masks the reality of the image. Once we see the optical illusion for what it is, this allows us to clearly see the differences between our perception and reality.
- Optical illusions work by misleading the brain through the use of colour, shades, light, and patterns. As the brain is trying to process an image, the optical illusion deceives the visual brain pathways into perceiving things that may or may not be there (Optics4Kids, 2016).
- Optical illusions exist in the media in the form of airbrushing and photoshopping models, actors, and pop-stars. In general, illusions exist in the ways that perception is passed off as reality, when it is in fact just one way of seeing and representing reality. Representations of gender, sexuality, race, class, love, relationships, and connection are often illusions in media because there are a diversity of realities that get distilled into one way of perceiving these diverse experiences.

CONT'D NEXT PAGE

EDUCATOR ANSWER KEY CONT'D

- Representation in the media is a representation of reality based on perception. Representation is one way of perceiving reality. Representation involves distilling a diversity of experiences into one consumable image or story.

Activity 3 3

Instructions

1. Define **bias** as a class. Ask: What kinds of media can bias be found in? Why is it important to identify bias? Does bias in the media have an effect on the outcome of local, national, and/or global events? *Emphasize with students that bias is not inherently wrong but that it is important to know how to identify bias, especially in media that advertises itself as unbiased.*

EDUCATOR ANSWER KEY

Bias refers to the ways that perspective and subjectivity influence how an issue is presented. Media bias refers to the ways that perspective and subjectivity influence the reporting of events and issues, including what is and is not reported. Bias can be found in every type of media, including news. It is important to identify bias in order to limit the harm that bias can cause when passed off as objective truth. Bias in the media can have an impact on local, national, and international events, especially when bias passes as objective truth.

---

2. Choose a recent issue in the news that would be covered by traditional media outlets as well as discussed on new media sources.
3. As homework, ask students to find 2 to 4 instances of coverage of the same issue from different perspectives. Ask students to find 1 to 2 examples from traditional media and 1 to 2 from new media. When looking for different perspectives, ask students to consider:
   - What is the narrative or story that is being told?
   - Who are the key players in this news story?
   - Is there someone portrayed as the protagonist and someone as the antagonist? Is one key player portrayed in a more positive light than the other?
   - How do the words and images reinforce the story/narrative that is being told?

4. On a subsequent day, drawing on students' homework, collectively brainstorm all of the different ways that this current issue was reported. Ask: Do these reports contain bias? If so, what does this bias look like? *Emphasize that bias can be found in all media (traditional and social) and that sometimes it is more obvious than other times.*

5. Collectively, group the different reports into categories of bias and assign catchy news headlines to each grouping.

6. Ask students to consider how media bias affected their own perception of the issue. Ask: Do you think that bias has the power to affect the larger public perception and change the outcome of local, national, or global events?

7. Split the class into smaller groups and discreetly assign each group one of the headlines brainstormed by the class. Ask: What kind of outcomes (local, national, and/or global consequences) are possible based on this headline?

8. Each group chooses an outcome that they think could happen and creates and presents a drama skit based on this outcome.

9. After each group's presentation, the rest of the class must guess which representation/news headline the skit is based on.

10. After each group has gone, debrief the activity as a class. *Emphasize that this activity illustrated how common bias is in media and how much bias affects public perceptions of issues, in turn influencing the outcome of local, national, and global events.*

✦ Optional: Activity 4 3

Instructions

1. Choose an issue in the news. Choose an issue that is topical, has relevance in the lives of your students, and is widely reported on (across many mediums i.e., print, television, online, etc.).

2. As an entire class, brainstorm all of the different ways that this issue could be represented as a news story.

3. Split the class into two groups and ask each group to choose a representation of the issue and create a news story about it.

4. One at a time, each group acts out their news story.

5. The group that is acting has 2 minutes to act out the news story. The group watching must come up with a headline that captures the representation of the issue that the acting group is trying to convey.

6. After each group has gone, debrief the activity as a class. Ask:
   - Was it challenging to act out a particular representation of the issue?
   - Did it make it easier or harder to represent the issue when you could exaggerate the story?

- Does exaggeration help clarify or distort reality?
- Was it challenging to come up with a headline? Why or why not?
- Do you think that the headline chosen for your group captured the representation of the issue you were trying to convey? Why or why not?
- What was challenging about trying to convey your issue in a short amount of time? What did having very little time cause you to do with your news story?

7. Conclude this activity by affirming that representing a complex issue in a short amount of time is part of what news does. Media in general and news in particular are not pure reflections of reality, they are limited representations. Because reality is complex with many different voices, perspectives, and experiences, news does not always capture this complexity or nuance.

Wrap-up

Summarize the module with the following points:

- The media is made up of various forms (broadly categorized as "traditional" and "new") working to achieve different and sometimes overlapping goals. One form of media is not inherently better than the other and a critical eye should be applied to all types of media.
- Media are representations of reality, not actual reality. Distinguishing between the two is an important skill and useful for all kinds of media.
- Even media that presents itself as factual and objective, like news, operates from a certain perspective and contains bias. Because reality is complex with many different voices, perspectives, and experiences, news does not always capture this complexity or nuance.

6.3 MEDIA: REALITY, REPRESENTATION, AND INFLUENCE

LEVEL [1] [2] [3]

Big Ideas in Module 6.3

- People often consume media as if it were reality but media is not reality, it consists of constructed **representations** of a select number of realities.
- Media, like television and movies, often portray unrealistic lives, unrealistic bodies, and unrealistic stories about romance, friendships, and sexuality.
- When media is treated as reality, people often consciously or unconsciously compare themselves to representations of reality. Developing tools to critically assess the media we consume can help interrupt these habits of comparison.

Learning Objectives

Students will:

- Critically analyze the influence of consuming media.
- Develop media literacy skills to become informed media consumers.
- Critically consider the ways appearance, relationships, gender, race, class, ability, and sexual orientation are represented.

Cross-Curricular Connections

- Art (drama, creative writing)
- Communications Studies
- English
- Equity Studies
- Gender Studies
- Media Studies
- Psychology
- Social Studies
- Sociology

Terminology

- Representation
- Self-concept

Materials

- Printed copies of **Reality Check** (version for level 1 or level 2 and 3, as appropriate)
- ✚ Optional: **Educator Resource—Reality Check** (for level 1 version)
- Equipment for showing short clips of media and social media campaigns (i.e., computer, projector, screen, or Smart Board)
- Blank paper
- Writing and drawing utensils

Background Information for Educators

Media, like television shows, web series, and movies, are constructed representations of reality. Their purpose is primarily to entertain and to advertise. Even if they are called "reality shows," or they are meant to be educational or informational, representations are still constructed.

What young people see in the media can affect their sense of their own bodies, their identities, and their expectations of friendships and intimate relationships. Media has this effect in part because it is easy to compare ourselves to images portrayed in the media.

Being able to consume media with a critical awareness will allow students to notice the difference between representation and reality and take more control over their sense of self.

Student Readiness

Before students engage with this lesson, ensure that safer space guidelines and group norms have been established (and revisited) within your classroom (for more information on how to establish safer space guidelines, see module 1.3). In order to effectively prepare for this activity, ensure students understand that:

- Media is not inherently good or bad, it is a tool that must be engaged with critically.
- While this module critically examines popular television shows, the goal is not to stop watching the show but rather, to watch the show with more awareness.
- Critically engaging with media is a process of asking questions about the media we consume.

Summary of Activities

Students will:

- Individually complete a worksheet analyzing their favourite show/ movie, paying attention to how appearance, bodies, relationships, gender, race, class, ability, and sexual orientation are represented.
- Collectively reflect on the worksheets in relationship to media consumption and our sense of self.
- Individually create an outline for a television pilot that more accurately reflects students' realities.

Activity 1 [1] [2] [3]

Instructions

Part 1

1. Explain that there is a difference between representations of bodies, relationships, and sexuality in the media and the reality of these things. Explain that this is even the case in "reality" television shows and documentaries.

2. Ask students to individually write down a quick brainstorm of the components of a person's sexuality (gender, sexual orientation, desires, body image, self-concept, culture, values, spirituality, and sexual history, including sexual trauma).

3. Ask students to individually write down a quick brainstorm of what they consider to be a positive, healthy relationship (e.g., honest, respectful, consensual, good communication, equal treatment, based on trust, comfortable, intimate, etc.).

4. Ask students to give examples of their favourite television shows, web series, or movies.

5. Hand out **Reality Check** and have students complete it. For the level 1 worksheet, there is an accompanying **Educator Resource— Reality Check**. It is recommended that you refer to the educator prompts to assist students in completing the worksheet. Optional: Students working on the same show/movie can work in pairs.

6. Have students present their answers from the **Reality Check** worksheet.

7. Optional: If there is time, have them show a short 2-minute clip that typifies why it is their favourite show/movie.

8. Discuss as a class:
   - What is the effect of consuming media that seems to (but does not) reflect reality?
   - How does it affect our sense of selves when actors and models generally present unattainable standards of beauty?
   - How does it affect our expectations of relationships when television/movie relationships are often simplified and idealized?
   - How does it affect the ways we understand the many components of our sexuality?
   - What can we do as consumers of media? How can we consume media (including our favourite shows/movies) wisely?

QUICK TIP

For level 1 students (particularly grades 1 to 4), it is recommended that you focus on one component of a person's sexuality that is appropriate to the age and maturity of your students such as gender, self-concept, or values. Ask students to either draw and write, or just draw, their answers.

EDUCATOR ANSWER KEY

- This can lead to unrealistic and unhealthy comparisons, questioning why your life does not look like it does on television/movies or feeling isolated or abnormal. It can create aspirations that are not grounded in reality and lead to disappointment.
- This can leave you feeling less than desirable or less than beautiful and isolated or abnormal.
- Miscommunication is more likely to occur if we make assumptions about a relationship. We might feel hurt when we realize that no relationship is perfect and that happy endings do not always occur.
- We might feel like our sexuality must fit into a box and be uncomplicated. We might feel that one part of our sexuality is more important/valued than another.
- We can consume media more wisely by developing media literacy skills such as: critical awareness, limiting consumption, understanding the purpose of different kinds of media, understanding that media does not document reality (even in "reality" television shows), finding ways to not only become a consumer of media but also an influencer, and speaking out if something is offensive, unhealthy, or problematic.

Part 2
1. Remind students of the **Reality Check** worksheet and discussion from Part 1.
2. Ask: If you could create a television show that accurately reflected your reality, what would it look like? Have students write down their answer. Level 1 students (particularly grades 1 to 4), can either draw and write or just draw their answers.

EDUCATOR PROMPTS

Provide students with the following questions as a guide:
- Who would your lead character(s) be?
- What would your lead character(s) be struggling with and what would give them joy? What would their dream be? What would their friendships and relationships look like?
- Where would it be set?
- What would be the highlights of the plot?
- How would the story and the characters be represented?

3. From the answers to these questions, create an outline for a television show pilot. For level 1 students (particularly grades 1 to 4), it is recommended that instead of asking them to create an outline and screen play for a television show, you ask them to create a story with pictures and words (such as a children's book, graphic novel, and/or comic strip).

4. Optional: As a homework assignment, ask students to write a screen play for the pilot.

Activity 2 [2] [3]

Instructions

1. Give each student a blank piece of paper and ask them to fold their papers into thirds.

2. In the first third, students write "I feel passionate about…" In the second third, students write "it makes me mad when I see (or don't see)_____in the media." In the last third, students write "I could change this by…"

3. Ask students to either write or draw their answers to each statement in the blank space of each third.

4. Ask students to consider what they have written/drawn. Then ask: how could you use social media to most effectively influence media to change?

5. Homework: Using a social media platform of their choosing, have students take what they have written/drawn and use it to influence media by creating a social media campaign. If there are students in your class that are not allowed to use social media, or do not have access to social media, ask the class to create a campaign strategy and sample campaign material (e.g., a prepared social media tool kit and/or a poster).

6. Have each student present their campaign (or campaign strategy) to the class.

7. As a class, discuss:
   - How did it feel to speak back to the media and become a media influencer?
   - Do you think that there are ways that are more effective than others to influence the media? Why or why not?
   - As a media influencer, are there any potential harms to be aware of?

EDUCATOR ANSWER KEY

Let students lead this discussion as they have insights and perspectives that are relevant to the ways that their generation engages with the media. Throughout the discussion, it is important to emphasize that becoming a media influencer can feel empowering because with more people influencing media, more people are able to create diverse representations of reality. Creating diverse representations can positively impact people who consume and are influenced by media. While it is almost impossible not to consume, engage with, and be influenced by one form of media or another, there are ways to minimize any potentially harmful or negative effects. One of the ways to minimize harm is to find appropriate channels and platforms to influence media. While becoming a media influencer can reduce some potentially negative effects of consuming media, it is important for young people to be aware of their privacy online, especially when it comes to internet predators and/or internet trolls (for more information, see module 6.5).

Wrap-up

Summarize the module with the following points:

- Media, like television, movies, and web series, are constructions of certain realities. They represent reality but are not reality.
- Uncritically consuming media has a strong effect on how we see ourselves, our sexuality, what we expect of our friendships, relationships, romantic partnerships, and what we desire in our lives.
- Developing media literacy skills such as being able to consume all kinds of media with critical awareness is very important for developing confidence and a healthy self-concept.
- Becoming media influencers is one way of creating diverse representations of reality and reducing the potential harms of consuming media.

6.4 HYPERSEXUALIZATION AND OBJECTIFICATION IN ADVERTISING

LEVEL 2 [3]

Big Ideas in Module 6.4

- Advertising has an overt message and an underlying one. Both are part of a strategy to sell products, images, and lifestyles.
- Sexualizing products by objectifying people sells the product and a specific idea about sex, sexuality, and relationships based on gender norms.
- The hypersexualization of young people in advertising has negative consequences on the mental and sexual health of young people. These consequences are gendered.
- Applying critical thinking skills when consuming advertising and other types of media is important because it can prevent young people from internalizing media messages that promote limited experiences, bodies, and misleading expectations.

Learning Objectives

Students will:

- Become aware of hypersexualization within advertising (including of children).
- Discuss the potential effects of hypersexualization on consumers.
- Consider ways to minimize the harm caused by consuming hypersexualized advertising.

Cross-Curricular Connections

- Communications Studies
- English
- Equity Studies
- Gender Studies
- Media Studies
- Psychology
- Social Studies
- Sociology

Terminology

- Gender binary
- Gender norms
- Hypersexualization
- Infantilization
- Objectification
- Sexism

Materials

- Advertisements/media/images curated ahead of time from 6.4 resources
- Printed copies of **Underlying Messages**
- Printed copies of **The Child Objectification Test**
- Projector or Smart Board

Background Information for Educators

As the nature and uses of media change, the lines between entertainment, news, and advertising blur. Through targeted online advertisements, video sponsors, and cross-marketing tactics, we are exposed to thousands of advertisements each day (Lamoureux, 2012). Advertising companies spend at least 23 billion dollars in Canada per year. This money translates into sales of more than 200 billion dollars (CMA, 2007). Each advertisement in each medium is carefully crafted for maximum effect.

Sexualizing products by objectifying people is a popular method used in advertising. This is sometimes referred to as sexual objectification and **hypersexualization. Objectification** is the process of perceiving, representing, and/or treating someone as an object. Sexual objectification is the process of perceiving, representing, and/or treating a person like a sex object that serves another person's sexual pleasure (Heldman, 2012).

Objectification is a part of hypersexualization. Hypersexualization is differentiated from healthy explorations of sexuality based on a number of factors, including whether a person's inherent value is represented as entirely based on their sexuality, whether or not ideas of sexuality are inappropriately imposed from the outside, and whether or not a person is treated as a sexual object (APA, 2007).

YOU SHOULD KNOW

The term "hypersexualization" has sometimes been used to call for the increased criminalization of certain communities, including sex workers (for more information, see modules 2.2 and 2.3). This module applies a critical lens to encourage media literacy skills instead of contributing to the problematic and harmful narratives that use the language of "hypersexualization" to criminalize communities.

Many advertisements specifically portray children in hypersexualized ways. This trend portrays children imitating adult dress and behaviour in ways that also sexualize them. Girls are often depicted as sexy and sassy, while boys are often depicted as tough and reckless (for more information, see modules 3.4, 3.5, 3.6, 3.7, and 3.8). Along with the hypersexualization of girls, there is a concurrent **infantilization** of women in popular images, advertisements, and aesthetics.

Hypersexualization and sexual objectification profoundly affect young people and are related manifestations of **sexism, rape culture,** and **sexual violence.** (For more information, see chapter 8). Research links the hypersexualization of young people with three of the most common mental health problems among girls and women: low self-esteem, eating disorders/disordered eating, and depression (APA, 2007).

Objectification is gendered, meaning that it has consequences that are different depending on a person's gender identity. Sexism and sexual violence disproportionately affect cis- and trans- girls/women and anyone who does not conform to restrictive **gender norms** and the **gender binary.** Among girls and young women, objectification is correlated to decreased condom use, decreased sexual assertiveness, and increased shame around sexuality (APA, 2007). Among boys and young men, while the research is not as extensive, the effects of gendered objectification are linked to restrictive gender norms (for more information, see modules 3.4, 3.5, 3.6, 3.7, and 3.8). Boys/men are socialized to present themselves as invincible and infallible, which can lead to low levels of empathy and self-compassion. Their human need for connection, affection, and love may not have space to thrive when there are only a few allowable outlets for their pain, including aggression towards others.

In the current media landscape of highly gendered objectification and hypersexualization, students with critical awareness can maintain a higher level of autonomy and are more likely to make informed decisions about their media consumption, their sexuality, and their overall wellness.

Student Readiness

Before students engage with this lesson, ensure that safer space guidelines and group norms have been established (and revisited) within your classroom (for more information on how to establish safer space guidelines, see module 1.3). In order to effectively prepare for this activity, ensure students understand that:
- Advertising is not inherently good or bad, it is a tool that must be engaged with critically.

- Hypersexualization and objectification in advertising is different than young people feeling empowered by choosing to express their sexuality on their own terms.
- This module explores the advertising and media trends around the hypersexualization and objectification of children. The module does not talk directly about sexual violence but some of the classroom discussion could be triggering for students who have experienced some form of sexual objectification and/or violence.

Summary of Activities

Students will:

- Work in small groups to examine underlying messages in advertisements.
- Collectively evaluate advertisements for the sexual objectification of children and the impacts of objectification.
- Work in small groups to develop and creatively present media, communications, and/or marketing campaigns that challenge the hypersexualization and objectification of young people.

Activity 1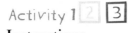

Instructions

1. Explain:
   - Advertising has a clear purpose: to find buyers for their products.
   - Advertisers attempt to associate products with sexual appeal and sexiness.
   - Sometimes the product sold is not clear in advertising. Sometimes it is the underlying message that is subconsciously driving consumer uptake.
2. Find an advertisement from 6.4 resources that has an overt product message and an underlying message. Show this to the students and model for them how to analyze the following questions:
   - What is this advertisement selling?
   - What are the underlying messages or values being sold?
3. Distribute **Underlying Messages.** Working in pairs or groups of 3, ask students to find 3 advertisements (images or videos) that match the following criteria and complete the worksheet:
   - Image 1—An advertisement showing a woman in a sexualized manner
   - Image 2—An advertisement depicting a man in a sexualized manner
   - Image 3—An advertisement depicting two people in a sexualized manner
4. Ask each group to present one of their three images, outlining the product(s) sold and the underlying messages and values.

POSSIBLE MENTIONS OF SEXUAL VIOLENCE

(for more information on trigger warnings, see modules 1.3 and 1.6)

5. Discuss as a class:
   - What effect do these images have on how people see themselves? Does this change depending on the gender identity of the person viewing/consuming these images?
   - What effect do these images have on what we expect from others in romantic and sexual relationships? Does this change depending on the gender identity of the person viewing/consuming these images?
   - How could these expectations create problematic habits and unhealthy behaviours? Does this change depending on the gender identity of the person viewing/consuming these images?

EDUCATOR ANSWER KEY

The following are generalized answers. Students may come up with better, more nuanced answers based on the specific advertisements they have chosen.

- Self-concept and confidence can be negatively affected. For instance, never feeling good enough; feeling that self-worth is directly correlated to the ways you look; that "sexiness" and attraction is very narrowly defined as being purely physical. Self-concept and confidence can be negatively affected regardless of your gender identity but the ways that girls/women are hypersexualized in advertising can have more negative consequences than that of boys/men. One of the reasons for this is because girls/women are often portrayed as the passive, vulnerable, sexual objects of boys/men.
- In sexual relationships, we might expect that engaging in sexual activities is always easy and always sexy and we might expect that consent to engage in sexual activities is assumed based on clothing choices. In romantic relationships, we might expect people who identify as men to be aggressive and people who identify as women to be passive.
- The expectations could lead to: a narrow view of sex and sexuality, increased sexual violence (assault/harassment/coercion), and relationships that are restricted by narrow definitions of gender. Due to the ways that girls/women are hypersexualized in advertising (i.e., passive sexual objects existing for men's pleasure) the impacts on girls/women are often more harmful than that of boys/men. For instance, research has shown that the hypersexualization of girls/women is correlated to decreased sexual assertiveness and decreased condom use (APA, 2007).

Activity 2 2 3

Before teaching this activity, curate images and advertisements of current children's products (e.g., toys, clothing, games, etc.) from the 6.4 resources.

Instructions

1. Explain: Children's products are increasingly sexualized and advertisements are using more sexualized images of children. *For the purposes of this activity, children is defined as anyone twelve years old and under.*
2. Define sexual **objectification.**
3. Show students the curated images and advertisements of current children's products.
4. Distribute copies of **The Child Objectification Test.** As a class, answer the questions of the test and connect them to the series of images and/or videos you have curated.
5. Discuss as a class:
   - How do you feel about these images? What surprised you about these images? Was there anything that made you feel uncomfortable? Was there anything that made you feel confused? Could you relate to any of these images, or do you feel reflected in any of these images? Why or why not?
   - Why do you think children's products are becoming more sexualized? And why do you think that children are becoming more sexually objectified in advertising (and other media) messages? What drives people to buy products? How do advertisers capitalize on imagery that sells? Do messages that sexualize children help to sell products? Does sex sell?
   - Does objectification affect different gender identities differently?
   - How can you minimize the negative effects of this kind of imagery?

EDUCATOR ANSWER KEY

The following are examples of possible answers. Students may come up with better, more nuanced answers based on the specific images chosen.

- Validate the feelings of your students. Ensure that they know it is okay to feel a range of feelings when viewing these kinds of images, including: confusion, anger, empowerment, jealousy, curiosity, desire to buy the product, disempowerment, and/or sadness.

- In general, sex has effectively been used to sell products, including products made for children. Sex also signifies adulthood. Sometimes children and young people feel like they want to grow up or experiment with aspects of adulthood. Being exposed to advertisements that show children and children's products in hyper-sexualized ways could be appealing to children/young people as it represents an aspect of adulthood.

- Sexual objectification is gendered; there are different messages for different genders contained in advertising, affecting gender identities differently. Advertising upholds restrictive gender norms and the gender binary (for more information, see modules 3.4, 3.5, 3.6, 3.7, and 3.8). Girls/women are portrayed as passive, weak, and as sex objects usually existing for the pleasure of boys/men, while boys/men are often portrayed as strong, confident, aggressive, and entitled to receive sex from girls/women. These patterns of gendered sexual objectification can have lasting consequences on both boys/men and girls/women but the effects on girls/women can be more harmful with negative impacts to mental health, physical health, self-esteem/body image, and sexual health (APA, 2007).

- Think about images that help you feel empowered and stir feelings of affirmation and self-love. Find examples of these images and place them somewhere that you will see often. You could also avoid buying products or supporting stores and brands that use hypersexualized images of children in their advertising. You could also apply critical thinking (that you are learning in this module/chapter) to advertisements that hypersexualize children.

Activity 3

Instructions

1. As a class, brainstorm: How could you use media, communication, and/or marketing technologies to challenge the hypersexualization of young people?
   - What kinds of media, communications, and/or marketing technologies could be used?
   - What kinds of messages would these forms of media/communication/marketing carry?

2. Divide students into small groups. Assign each group the homework of coming up with their own media, communications, and/or marketing campaign for challenging and/or learning to think critically about the hypersexualization of young people. In creating their campaign, ask students to consider the following questions:
   - How will your media, communications, and/or marketing campaign challenge the hypersexualization of young people?
   - What is the main issue within hypersexualization that you are aiming to challenge with your campaign?
   - What is the main message of your campaign?
   - Who is the target audience?
   - Why do you think that the medium you have chosen is the best way to present your campaign (e.g., print advertisement vs. a social media campaign?)

3. Have students present their media, communications, and/or marketing campaign to the class, addressing the above questions in their presentation.

Wrap-up

Summarize the module with the following points:
- Advertising uses various methods to encourage interest, develop desire, and promote consumption but sexual images immediately call attention to a product. In this way, sex can effectively sell products through promoting both an overt and an underlying message.
- The saturation of hypersexualized and objectifying images has been proven to affect the self-esteem, mental health, sexual health, and relationship expectations of young people in gendered ways; critical awareness can help to minimize these affects.

QUICK TIP

There are a range of campaigns students could create. Some examples include the creation of a print advertisement, a social media campaign, a video, a blog post, or a photo sharing platform. As long as their campaign uses some kind of communications, media, and/or marketing technology, the campaigns can be diverse in their mediums.

6.5 RESPONSIBLE USE OF SOCIAL AND DIGITAL MEDIA

LEVEL 2 [3]

Big Ideas in Module 6.5

- Social and digital media can be used to either empower or disempower and harm young people. Increasing the opportunities for **empowerment** means teaching online safety and responsible social media engagement.
- **Consent** is an important concept to examine when considering how to use social and digital media responsibly.
- There are serious legal and social consequences for using social and digital media for purposes such as **cyberbullying**, sexual **harassment**, and/or **cyberstalking**.

Learning Objectives

Students will:

- Become aware of the impact of social and digital media on themselves and their peers, including laws that prohibit the distribution of sexual images.
- Become familiar with the concept of consent (for more information, see chapter 8).
- Consider how creating an online safety plan is integral to ensure that empowering experiences on social media (such as self-representation and community building) do not turn into disempowering or harmful experiences.

Cross-Curricular Connections

- Art (visual, digital)
- Communications Studies
- English
- Equity Studies
- Gender Studies
- Law
- Media Studies
- Psychology
- Social Studies
- Sociology

Terminology

- Consent
- Cyberbullying
- Cyberstalking
- Discrimination
- Empowerment
- Harassment

Materials

- Printed copies of **Information Sharing**
- Printed copies of **Social and Digital Media Scenarios**
- **Educator Answer Key—Social and Digital Media Scenarios**
- Printed copies of **Social and Digital Media Safety Plan**
- Writing and drawing materials
- An assortment of stickers
- Paper
- ✛ Optional: Projector or Smart Board

Background Information for Educators

Digital and communications technologies, including cell phones, smart phones, the internet, and social media constitute a world of possibility for young people. These technologies are platforms for self expression, self-representation, learning and imagination, and tools for communication, connection, and/or community engagement.

These possibilities also come with risk and vulnerability. Abuse, violence, and **discrimination** can take a range of forms online, including cyberbullying, cyberstalking, sexual predation, harassment, and assault. Consent from all involved is something that needs to be obtained before posting any kind of images or photos that are not yours to post. (For more information on consent and sexual violence, see chapter 8). Harm can follow as a consequence of sharing private information, images, and photos (both consensually and non-consensually). It is therefore important to think through all of the possible consequences of sharing information, images, and photos, before they are shared/posted and to make a decision based on knowing all of the information and having consent from everyone who might be impacted. (For a list of crisis lines, see **National Support Services** in the resources section).

YOU SHOULD KNOW

With some exceptions, the circulation of naked, partially naked, and/or sexual or intimate images of people under 18 years of age is prosecutable by law. (For more information, see 6.5 resources).

In order to maximize the benefits of these platforms and minimize their risks, it is important for young people to use them ethically, to set limits, to recognize danger, and to get help and support when needed. It is important for educators to support students in navigating the sometimes uncertain terrain of maximizing social media platforms for empowerment while minimizing their risk.

Student Readiness

Before students engage with this lesson, ensure that safer space guidelines and group norms have been established (and revisited) within your classroom (for more information on how to establish safer space guidelines, see module 1.3). In order to effectively prepare for this activity, ensure students understand that:

- Social and digital media is not inherently good or bad, it is a tool that must be engaged with thoughtfully and critically.
- This module discusses consent, cyberbullying, and sexual violence.
- Creating online safety plans is a way of keeping yourself, your friends, and everyone at school safe.

Summary of Activities

Students will:

- Place stickers around the room indicating social and digital media habits and in small groups, discuss what is appropriate to share over social media and when.
- In pairs, work through a series of scenarios identifying problematic behaviours and creating action plans and prevention strategies.
- Choose a preferred social/digital media platform and individually create a series of posts that represent the empowering aspects of social media.
- Individually create a social/digital media safety plan.

Activity 1 2 3

Instructions

1. Place Sheets of paper around the room with the following headings:
   - I use a mobile device (phone, tablet, etc.)
   - I access social media using my mobile device
   - I have seen an embarrassing post and/or advertising
   - I have regretted a social media post that I made
   - I have been impacted by cyberbullying (either directly or indirectly experienced and/or contributed to)
2. Pass around an assortment of stickers. Ensure that each student gets at least 4.
3. Ask students to walk around the room, look at each heading, and place one of their stickers under the headings that apply to them.
4. Once everyone has placed their stickers around the room, ask students to walk around, noticing where stickers are clustered.
5. Place students into small groups of 3 to 4. Using the **Information Sharing** handout, have each group determine the circumstances under which it is appropriate and safe to share the following over social media:
   - Their screen name or handle
   - Their age
   - The name of their school
   - The name of their street
   - The names of their friends
   - Their phone number
   - A photo of their pet

- A video of themselves playing sports
- A photo of themselves in underwear
- A photo of a friend in their underwear

YOU SHOULD KNOW

There are no definite answers to most of these items; however, being cautious about what you post online and obtaining consent before posting information, images, and photos of others are two good general rules. The Educator Answer Key provides some general questions that can help structure students' assessment of what to post online and when. The only place where there are strict laws related to the posting/distribution of images is in regards to child pornography laws and the *Protecting Canadians from Online Crime Act*. Sharing a photo of themselves or a friend in their underwear, which involves partial nudity, needs to be considered within the legal context; any type of sexual image of a person under 18 is considered child pornography and illegal in Canada. Even consensual "sexting" between youth under 18 could be considered illegal, depending on the images involved. (For more information, see 6.5 resources).

6. Make sure that students note where there was agreement, disagreement, and/or debate. Ask them to consider:
   - Why was there disagreement (if any) and how did it get resolved (if at all)?
   - Were there any items where there was no disagreement or debate? Why do you think this was the case?
   - Are there any guidelines to assess what is appropriate and safe, when would you apply these?
7. Come back together as a large class and have one person from each group present their answers. Highlight the differences and similarities between the boundaries that each group sets for each item.

EDUCATOR ANSWER KEY

There are no definite or right answers to most of this activity (except for the last two items where child pornography laws and consent must be taken into consideration); however, there are some general guidelines that can help your students think through their answers. Conclude this activity by emphasizing that it is always important to be cautious about what you post on the internet. Some general prompts to guide how your students think through online safety include the following:

- Is this my image/photo to share?
- Do I have consent to post this image/photo?
- Who can see this post/photo and do I trust all of the people that might have access to it?
- What are the privacy settings and safety controls like on this particular tool that I am using? How much control do I have over who gets to see the content of my post/photo?
- Once posted, who owns the content?
- How would a friend, family member, and/or potential employer see this post/photo?
- What are the potential consequences of this post/photo if they got into the hands of people who did not know or did not like me?
- Does this post/photo reveal an aspect of me that I would not otherwise share with friends, family, and/or co-workers?

Activity 2 [2] [3]

Instructions

1. Have students work in pairs on **Social and Digital Media Scenarios**.
2. Ask students to analyze Scenario A and answer the questions by putting themselves into the mindset of both Beck and Beck's employer. Allot 5 to 7 minutes.
3. Change the pairings so that students are with a new partner. Have students work on Scenario B.
4. Change the pairings one more time for Scenario C.
5. As a large group, ask students what surfaced in the discussions that was compelling for them. What surprised them? Where were there agreements and disagreements between partners in terms of the scenario analysis? What are common themes in the scenarios? How could each of these scenarios have been prevented? What were some important lessons that emerged from the conversations between partners?

POSSIBLE MENTIONS OF SEXUAL VIOLENCE *(for more information on trigger warnings, see modules 1.3 and 1.6)*

Activity 3 3

Instructions

1. Ask students to choose a social/digital media platform that they find empowering for self-expression, self-representation, and/or community connection/engagement.

2. Ask students to individually brainstorm reasons why they find this form of social/digital media empowering. *Students can brainstorm by using writing, drawing, or some other visual representation/tool, such as a mind map.*

3. For homework, have students create a series of posts (or other content appropriate to the social media platform) that digitally represent why they find social media empowering. For instance, if a student finds using Instagram empowering because they are a vegan and do not know many other vegans at their school, they might consider creating a series of vegan food posts to share recipes and bring attention to the reasons why they are vegan.

4. As students work on their homework assignment, ask them to complete the **Social and Digital Media Safety Plan** and reflect on ways to protect themselves and their social/digital media content.

5. Optional: Ask students to present their social media content and safety plans to the rest of the class using a projector or Smart Board.

Wrap-up

Summarize the module with the following points:

- Social and digital media use is full of possibility, both positive and negative.
- Use social/digital media platforms wisely, cultivating awareness of the viral and long-lasting nature of consequences.
- If you have consent to take a photo and/or draw an image, you do not necessarily have consent to distribute it. Even if you obtain consent from all of those impacted, there may still be legal and/or social/emotional consequences.

QUICK TIP

If you do not have access to a projector or Smart Board, ensure that students hand in a written assignment outlining the goals of their social media project, why they chose to focus on the format and topic that they did and their Social/ Digital Media Safety Plan.

6.6 PORNOGRAPHY VS. REAL LIFE

Level 3

There are many different aspects of teaching media literacy specific to pornography that can potentially be addressed by educators seeking to promote sexual health. It is advisable for educators to assess their own comfort level in discussing pornography in the classroom and the social/emotional maturity of students.

Big Ideas in Module 6.6

- Pornography, like other forms of media, is more accessible to young people than ever before and developing media literacy skills includes a critical analysis of pornography.
- Mainstream pornography presents unrealistic portrayals of bodies, sexual interaction, and relationships. These unrealistic portrayals are based on gender norms and stereotypes that cause harm.
- A sensitive and nuanced treatment of the topic of pornography is necessary. Young people should not be shamed for watching pornography and the topic should not be ignored. Decreasing unrealistic expectations with conscious decision-making and critical awareness is key to reducing harm.
- While some pornography can present an unrealistic and potentially harmful picture of human sexuality, accessible sexual images can also provide an opportunity for young people to safely explore their sexuality.

Learning Objectives

Students will:

- Address the wide availability of pornography online and understand the reasons why some people choose to consume pornography.
- Have their feelings and reactions to pornography affirmed.
- Identify ways in which bodies, sexual interaction, and relationships in pornography may be unrealistic.
- Consider the effects of consuming a form of media that systematically skews reality.

Cross-Curricular
Connections
- Communications
  Studies
- English
- Equity Studies
- Gender Studies
- Media Studies
- Psychology
- Social Studies
- Sociology

Terminology
- Fetishize
- Marginalization
- Pornography

Materials
- Sticky notes of 2 different colours
  (3 to 4 per colour per student)
- Chalkboard or whiteboard for posting
  sticky notes
- Index cards (2 per student)

Background Information for Educators

Like most forms of media, **pornography** is not a representation of reality. Unlike some other types of media, in pornography, the purpose and intention is clear—it is the portrayal of sexual *fantasy* and exists for the purposes of sexual gratification. In this way, pornography is an extreme example of the ways in which reality can be distorted in the media. Knowing that there is a distinction between reality and the fantasy that pornography portrays is an essential part of learning media literacy skills.

Due to advances in digital and communication technologies, sexually explicit material is easily accessible to young people. Sexually explicit material comes in the form of all media, including television shows, movies, pornography, and hypersexualized advertising. This increased access increases the need for critical thinking and media literacy skills to sort through unrealistic expectations of bodies, relationships, and sexual interaction. It is extremely important in the context of sexuality education because part of media literacy skills is understanding the ways that gender norms and stereotypes influence the production of mainstream pornography and how these norms and stereotypes can cause harm (for more information, see modules 3.4, 3.5, 3.6, 3.7, and 3.8).

One of the manifestations of gender norms and stereotypes causing harm is in the way that female sexual response is portrayed in mainstream pornography. Female sexual response is portrayed as a performance for someone else rather than an experience that happens internally and is expressed out of pleasure. This can lead to an unrealistic, exaggerated, and distorted image of what female sexual response and pleasure is supposed to look (and sound) like. In mainstream pornography, there is little to no communication that happens between sexual partners. When communication does happen, it is unrealistic and does not address safer sex and consent.

While it is challenging to assess precisely how much content young people have access to, it is clear that young people do have increased exposure due to increased access to digital and communication technologies. Young people's increased exposure to online mainstream pornography raises many issues and questions. It is a difficult and challenging issue for educators to discuss in the classroom. The reality is that most, if not all, young people have accidentally encountered or actively sought out online pornography. One Canadian study found that over 70% of adolescents had accessed pornography at least once (University of Alberta, 2007).

While the topic of pornography could be addressed under multiple topics within sexuality education, including **human rights** and **consent** (in terms of compensation for labour and consent to the production, use, and public distribution), it is important to address the topic of pornography in the context of media because it is a form of media that young people access (either by accident or on purpose) in high numbers and it provides students with opportunities to use the literacy and critical thinking skills they developed in other modules to critically consider and distinguish between real life and fiction/fantasy.

A sensitive and nuanced treatment of the topic of pornography is necessary. Pornography is neither inherently good nor bad. Like other kinds of media, it exists on a spectrum of empowering/affirming to disempowering/harmful. Young people should not be shamed for watching pornography and the topic should not be ignored. Most young people will consume pornography at some point and they need to be given the skills to do so in ways that reduce harm, increase empowerment, and enhance sexual and mental health.

While some pornography can present an unrealistic and potentially harmful picture of human sexuality, accessible sexual images can also provide an opportunity for young people to safely explore their sexuality. This is especially the case for people whose sexualities have been marginalized (e.g., LGTBQ+ youth and youth with disabilities). Online pornography is sometimes the only place they can see their sexual selves reflected and this can feel empowering. At the same time, the ways that their sexual selves are reflected, like all mainstream media images, are unrealistic—it can distort and **fetishize** people's identities in ways that might reinforce **marginalization**. For instance, people of colour may see themselves reflected in pornography more often then other forms of media but they also might be portrayed in stereotypical, 2-dimensional ways that reinforce racist myths and **racism**. It is worth noting that although young people might not have easy access to feminist pornography, feminist pornography presents more realistic portrayals of sexual response and a diversity of bodies and sexualities. Feminist pornography can be empowering for anyone whose sexuality has been marginalized as it actively works to challenge fetishization and marginalization. Most young people are going to consume pornography; reducing unrealistic expectations through conscious decision-making and critical awareness are key to reducing harm.

Student Readiness

Before students engage with this lesson, ensure that safer space guidelines and group norms have been established (and revisited) within your classroom (for more information on how to establish safer space guidelines, see module 1.3). In order to effectively prepare for this activity, ensure students understand that:

- Media, including pornography, is not inherently good or bad. Pornography is a form of media that must be engaged with critically.
- Because pornography is widely available online, many young people are accidentally or purposefully exposed to sexually explicit imagery. This is nothing to feel ashamed about. Some people have never seen sexually graphic images and this is also nothing to feel ashamed or self-conscious about.
- There will be no pornography shown. The activities in this module help build media literacy skills specific to consuming pornography.
- The purpose of this module is to address the wide availability of pornography online, answer any questions, affirm anxieties and fears, and develop a critical awareness about pornography. *Reassure and manage students' expectations that they will not see any pornographic images as part of the class.*

Summary of Activities

Students will:

- Anonymously brainstorm reasons why someone would consume pornography and collectively discuss the effects of its consumption.
- Individually reflect on how representations in pornography are not realistic and on the consequences of believing that they are.

Activity 1 3

Instructions

1. Ask students to define pornography. *One way to ask is: You have probably heard people talk about "porn," "online porn," or "pornography," can anyone give me a definition of the term?*

2. Provide a clear and simple definition such as the *Beyond the Basics* definition.

3. Distribute 3 to 4 sticky notes of each of the 2 colours to each student.

4. Designate 1 colour as "Reasons" and 1 colour as "Reactions."

5. On the colour designated as reasons, ask students to write down reasons why someone may consume online pornography (students should write 1 reason per sticky note).

6. Ask students to come up to the board and place these sticky notes on the board and to sit back down once everything is placed.

7. Group the sticky notes into the following 5 categories: accidental, curiosity, sexual pleasure, peer pressure, other.

8. On the colour designated as reactions, ask students to write down possible reactions when viewing pornography.

9. Ask students to come up to the board and place these sticky notes on the board and to sit back down once everything is placed.

10. Summarize this activity by observing the many reasons why someone may consume pornography and the many different reactions to viewing pornography, including conflicting feelings.

11. Ask: Who are these images made for? Adults or young people your age?

EDUCATOR ANSWER KEY

While this can be a sensitive subject, it is important to affirm a diversity of experience while being both sex-positive and age-appropriate. One way to do this is to affirm that it is okay to not view pornography, to dislike pornography, or to react negatively to it. Affirm that these are common reactions. Affirm that there can also be feelings of pleasure, mixed-in with conflicting concerns about what is being viewed. Affirm that most pornography that is available online is made for adults and applying caution and a critical eye to anything found online is key to limiting the potential emotional/social consequences of viewing pornography.

Activity 2 3
Instructions
1. List the following 2 headings on the board: "Bodies" and "Bodies and Relationships."
2. Hand out index cards so that each student has 10 cards: 5 for "Bodies" and 5 for "Behaviours and Relationships."
3. Instruct students to start with the "Bodies" index cards and list ways that the bodies of pornography actors may be different from the average person. Give students a few minutes to complete the cards and then collect them.

   Ensure students know that this activity is to be completed individually and anonymously. Instruct students to not put their names on their cards and to turn them over when they are finished. Encourage everyone to flip over their card and write something, even if it is not an answer to the question asked.

4. From the collected index cards, list appropriate responses from the students on the board. *You can omit offensive or inappropriate responses.*

EDUCATOR ANSWER KEY
Answers can include: breast implants, surgical alterations, enlarged penises, no body hair, and fake finger nails.

5. Instruct students to complete the "Behaviours and Relationships" index cards by listing the ways that the behaviours and relationships shown in pornography are often unrealistic. Give students a few minutes to complete the cards and then collect them.
6. From the collected index cards, list appropriate responses on the board. *You can omit offensive or inappropriate responses.*

EDUCATOR ANSWER KEY

Answers can include: relationships are distorted; progression of sexual intimacy may be unrealistic; sexual advances and reactions are unrealistic; communicating about and practising consent is often not shown; sexual chemistry is sometimes absent; no conversation about safer sex or contraception; pleasing only one partner is often the goal; sex is focused on sexual intercourse; sexual interactions can seem more rough or violent than it needs to be in order to experience pleasure.

7. Ask: What do you think are the consequences of viewing unrealistic representations of bodies and sexuality while believing they are real? How could this affect someone's sense of their own body, their own sexuality? How will this affect what they expect from relationships and sexual interactions?"

EDUCATOR ANSWER KEY

Possible consequences include: believing that your body is not good/beautiful/sexy enough; that pleasing someone else is the number one goal in a sexual relationship; that if you do not have the same kinds of reactions to the sexual activities shown in pornography, there is something wrong with you; that sexuality is only about sex; that sexuality can only be expressed in a handful of ways; that intimacy must involve sex; that pleasure and sensuality are always tied to sexual activity; that sexual relationships must be exploitative, based on power, rough, and/or violent; that you do not need to ask for consent when engaging in sexual activity; that communication is unnecessary in sexual relationships; that asking for consent and constant communication throughout sexual activity is not sexy; and that you are not allowed to say no to sexual activity.

8. Ask: Are these consequences gendered? Do the consequences have different impacts depending on your gender identity and/or how closely your gender identity conforms to gender norms? If so, how?

EDUCATOR ANSWER KEY

The consequences are gendered because there are different messages for different genders contained in pornography, affecting gender identities differently. Mainstream available pornography upholds restrictive gender norms and the gender binary (for more information, see modules 3.4, 3.5, 3.6, 3.7, and 3.8). Girls/women are generally portrayed as passive, weak, and vulnerable. They are also often portrayed as victims and as sex objects for the pleasure of boys/men. Boys/men are often portrayed as strong, confident, aggressive, and entitled to receive sex from girls/women. These patterns of gendered sexual objectification in pornography can have lasting consequences on both boys/men and girls/women but the effects on girls/women can be more harmful, including increased sexual violence (McVeigh & Marsh, 2016).

Wrap-up

Summarize the module with the following points:

- A diversity of reactions to pornography are okay: some people enjoy watching pornography, some do not, and some have conflicted feelings. Some people find pornography confusing, disturbing, and/or exciting. Some people find pornography offensive and/or think it is harmful. Some people find pornography empowering if they cannot find their identities represented anywhere else.
- There are many reasons for watching pornography and many reasons not to. It is important for young people to understand that most pornography found online is unrealistic and made for an adult audience.
- Mainstream pornography unrealistically portrays bodies, sexual interaction, and relationships. There are many gendered consequences to thinking that these portrayals are realistic.

CHAPTER 7

Relationships, Peer Norms, and Decision-Making

7.1 INTRODUCTION

While learning to be in relationships is a life-long skill and learning process, relationships play a large role in many of the key developmental stages of adolescence. Young people are negotiating independence from parents, guardians, and family, while they navigate the possibilities of friendships and romantic and sexual connections with peers.

Adolescents learn about friendships and romantic and sexual connections through peer norms, media, popular culture, and experience. They negotiate physiological drives, emotional motivations, social dynamics, and responsibilities all the while being confronted by mixed messages about gender norms and sexuality from the media, peers, parents, school. They often receive conflicting messages between the need to fear and reject sexuality and the need to embrace and perform it.

Decision-making in adolescence is complicated by the physiological development of the brain during this period. Research shows that the adolescent brain goes through a period of growth similar in importance to that of the first couple of years of a child's life and that the brain does not reach maturation until young people reach their 20s (NIMH, 2011).

Because of this, young people are more likely to act on impulse, misread or misinterpret social cues and emotions, and engage in high-risk behaviour and are less likely to think before they act or pause to consider the potential consequences of their actions (American Academy of Child & Adolescent Psychiatry, 2011). These findings hold significant meaning for safer sex practises, contraceptive use, and STBBI prevention and testing among young people.

In light of these physiological and social factors, the *Canadian Guidelines for Sexual Health Education* (Public Health Agency of Canada, 2008) says that "effective sexual health education supports informed decision-making by providing individuals with the opportunity to develop the knowledge, personal insight, motivation and behavioural skills that are consistent with each individual's values and choices" (p. 25). Educators and other adult allies can help young people navigate this time of emotional change and growth by providing information that is supportive, affirming, and avoids condescension, shame, and embarrassment. There is also a comprehensive list of supports that can be accessed from across Canada in the **National Support Services** resource section.

The modules in this chapter support young people's emotional and social development by helping them to build critical thinking, relational skills, decision-making skills, communication skills, and the setting of personal boundaries.

Educator Reflection Questions

Relationships are what structure our world and learning how to be in relationships are skills that are developed and refined throughout a person's life. Beginning to develop communication, decision-making, critical thinking, and boundary-setting skills during adolescence sets the stage for creating behaviours and habits that will be useful across all of a person's relationships throughout their life. Think back to when you were your students' age and ask yourself:

- What was the most challenging aspect of developing and maintaining relationships as an adolescent? *These could be friendships, romantic and/or sexual relationships, or even the relationships you had with your family.*
- What skills do have now that you wish you had when you were an adolescent?
- If you could share one insight about relationships that you have gained with your adolescent self, what would it be?

- What kinds of pressures did you feel in your relationships when you were an adolescent? Have these pressures changed over the years? If so, how?
- How did the adults in your life react to the decisions and behaviours of you and your peers? How did these reactions make you feel and has this influenced how you interact with your students?
- In the context of relationships, what did "boundaries" mean to you? Did these change as you grew older?
- Was setting boundaries difficult? Why or why not?

What about now?
- What are the strengths that you bring to your current relationships?
- In what ways have your decision-making and communication skills improved since adolescence?
- How do you set boundaries within your current relationships?

Big Ideas in Chapter 7

- Adolescence is a time of massive social and emotional development and change; building the skills necessary to keep up with the pace of these changes is integral to supporting young people's mental, emotional, social, and physical well-being.
- Because of the ways that the adolescent brain develops, young people may be more likely to act on impulse, not consider all of the consequences of their actions, be more vulnerable to criticism, be less likely to read social and emotional cues, and be more likely to follow peer social norms without question. Helping young people navigate these behaviours and brain changes means giving them the tools to learn from their mistakes without shame and building confidence in this process.

7.2 FRIENDS AND RELATIONSHIPS

LEVEL  3

Big Ideas in Module 7.2

- Relationships (of all kinds) are complex and learning how to be in a relationship with another person is not always easy, obvious, or a linear learning process.
- Relationships are often not entirely healthy or unhealthy. They are a combination that must be evaluated on how they contribute to overall feelings of well-being and connection.
- Connections that young people make can be sources of support and sources of stress. Developing skills to navigate relationship stress and to ask for support are critical to increasing positive connections and building communication skills that will be useful throughout a person's life.

Learning Objectives

Students will:

- Identify what a healthy relationship feels/looks like.
- Critically evaluate their relationships in terms of what might promote or hinder connection.
- Learn how to articulate and negotiate their relationship needs and boundaries.

Cross-Curricular Connections

- English
- Equity Studies
- Gender Studies
- Psychology
- Social Studies
- Sociology

Terminology

- Boundaries

Materials

- Drawing and art utensils (crayons, markers, colour pencils, etc.)
- Construction paper or other large pieces of paper
- Printed copies of **Relationship Questionnaire**

Background Information for Educators

During adolescence, young people are learning to navigate different types relationships, including friendships. They are in a process of discovering who they want to be around and why; they are weighing the benefits of relationships, how some social connections feel really good and others, not so good. It is a process of learning by trial and error. While you cannot control the relationship choices of your students, you can provide them with the skills to evaluate and make decisions about the kinds of relationships that they want in their lives. You can provide skills that will help them cultivate more of the types of friendships that they want, while helping them set and communicate **boundaries**. You can also provide students with information to determine the ingredients for a healthy relationship.

Friendships, peer social dynamics, and relationships in general are significantly influential during adolescence. While this could be said of any point in life, the reality for young people is that they are experimenting with what it means to develop separately from family and to make stronger ties with peers (Hey Sigmund, 2016). The connections that young people make and maintain during this time are both sources of support and sources of stress. The ability to identify and critically evaluate these connections are important first steps toward articulating and negotiating relationship needs and boundaries.

The activities in this module are meant to help students see the complexity of relationships. Relationships are not black and white—they are not healthy or unhealthy—relationships often include both qualities. Identifying qualities of a relationship that feel positive and healthy, as well as identifying qualities that feel negative and unhealthy, can help determine which relationships you want in your life and which you do not. It is not always possible to entirely disconnect from a person/relationship (i.e., a sibling or a parent) but you can learn to communicate needs and develop boundaries to help navigate the relationship.

Learning how to communicate needs is different than expecting 100% of your needs to be met 100% of the time. Learning how to communicate your needs is about learning how to communicate expectations while listening to the other person's needs and expectations. Part of listening to the other person's needs is being aware that they may set a boundary that could lead to feelings of rejection and emotional pain (for more information, see module 4.6). Being in a relationship is about negotiating how you can best meet each other's expectations in ways that are mutually supportive, respectful, and fulfilling.

Student Readiness

Before students engage with this lesson, ensure that safer space guidelines and group norms have been established (and revisited) within your classroom (for more information on how to establish safer space guidelines, see module 1.3). In order to effectively prepare for this activity, ensure students understand that:

- Learning how to be in relationships that feel positive, affirming, and supportive can be a lifelong process—many adults do not have it all figured out!
- Building and maintaining healthy, positive, affirmative, fulfilling, and supportive relationships is not something that comes naturally. Like everything else in life, these are skills that need to be learned. Much of this skill building starts in adolescence.
- The activities in this module will be done individually and privately.
- The purpose of this module is not to shame anyone for engaging in unhealthy relationships. The purpose is to develop skills to identify qualities you want in relationships and to communicate your needs, expectations, and boundaries within relationships.

Summary of Activities

Students will:
- Individually reflect on and visually map the relationships in their lives.
- Individually reflect on and evaluate the quality of connection in their relationships by taking a quiz.

Activity 1 ☐2 ☒3

Before beginning this activity, remind students that this is a private, reflective activity. Students will not be asked to present their drawings.

Instructions
1. Provide art and drawing supplies and paper. Ask students to draw a circle and label it either "Me," their name, or draw in a caricature of themselves. You can demonstrate an example for them on the board.
2. Add other circles as per figure 7A. Ask students to use the whole page.

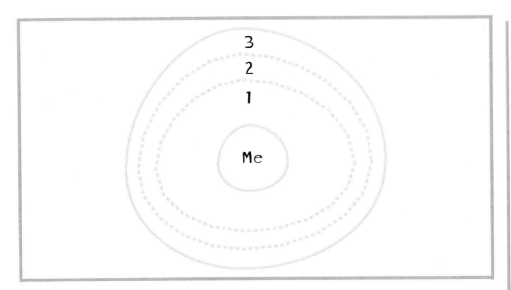

Figure 7A

3. Ask students to close their eyes and think about the most important people in their lives. With eyes still closed, ask them to reflect on who these people are and what makes them important.

4. Ask students to open their eyes and choose 4 to 8 people in their lives who they consider to be important. Explain that importance can be related to emotional closeness, their role (e.g., who they are to you), and/or time spent together. Importance does not always mean the people you feel the strongest connection to or the most supported by. *Emphasize that it is rare for one person to satisfy all of a person's relationship needs. That is why it is important to cultivate different kinds of relationships with different kinds of people (i.e., friendships, mentorships, etc.).*

5. Ask students to map each person in the drawing according to how close they are. Use a circle and an initial or a symbol (see figure 7B). *Emphasize that students should complete their drawings by thinking about how they are feeling today, recognizing that feelings about people and relationships can change day to day, month to month, etc.*

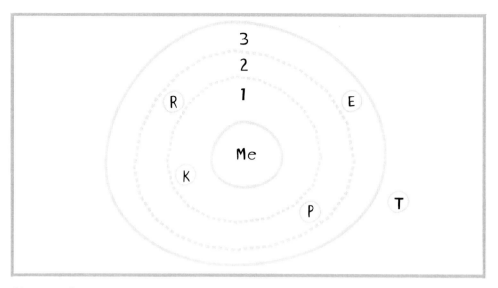

Figure 7B

Circle 1: Very close relationships
Circle 2: Close relationships but not as close as Circle 1
Circle 3: Impersonal relationships
Outside of solid line: People you do not trust and want strong boundaries with

6. Draw lines from "Me" toward each person on the map. The line can be solid (strong connection), dotted (weak connection) or zigzagged (conflicted connection). See figure 7C.

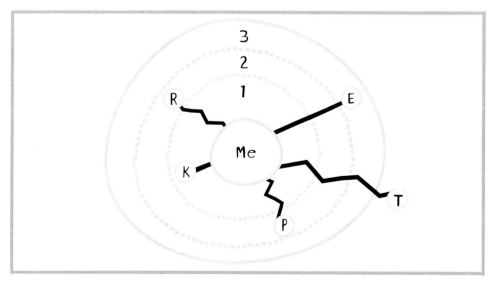

Figure 7C

7. Add a "+" and/or a "-" on each line to show whether the relationship is supportive or draining. Supportive relationships where you get care, insight, and feel safe are "+". Relationships where you give and feel depleted are "-". Some relationships are both. See figure 7D.

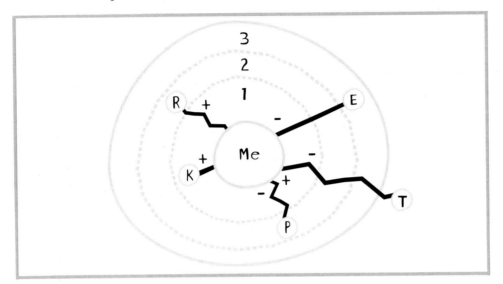

Figure 7D

8. Remind students that this is a snapshot of their relationships and relationship "orbit" today. It is not the past or the future. Give students some time to finish up their drawings. Then, ask students to privately reflect on their drawings/relationship orbits by turning over their paper and either writing or drawing their answers to the following questions:
   • What do you notice about your orbits today?
   • What do you like and what would you like to change?
   • Do your orbits reflect your values and who you are as a person?
9. ✦ Optional: Have students use the written or drawn reflections to create a poem about one of the relationships in their lives. The poem can be kept private or presented to the class (as long as there is no identifying information).
10. Debrief as a class using the following prompts:
   • What can we do to change distances with people in our orbits? How can we invite them closer? How can we make more distance?
   • Strong connections do not always feel supportive and weaker connections do not always mean there is no trust. What do you think that means?
   • How would it feel if everyone in your orbit was in Circle 1? What if they were all in Circle 3?

- What do you think might happen if you did this activity once every year?

EDUCATOR ANSWER KEY

- You can invite people closer by reaching out. You can do this by telling them that you would like to spend more time together. You could also talk with them more often, invite them to hang out with you, invite them to an event, and/or activity that you enjoy. You can create more distance by telling them that you would like to take some distance in the relationship. You could also hang out with them less often, and/or find activities to do that are not associated with them, and/or spend more time with other people who you want to bring in closer.
- There are many different kinds of connections that you can have and these might not always feel supportive. For instance, you can have a strong romantic connection with someone but you may not feel emotionally supported. Likewise, you could have a childhood friend whose connection has grown weak over the years and yet you trust them with your life. Trust is something that is often built and earned, not something that happens because you have a strong connection with a person.
- Everyone is different, meaning that people have different preferences when it comes to relationships. Some people might thrive if all of their connections are in Circle 1, while others might thrive if all of their connections are in Circle 3. People often thrive from a mix. It is important to cultivate different kinds of relationships and sometimes this means that the connections will be various degrees of strong or weak as is appropriate with the kinds of relationships being developed. Having every relationship in Circle 1 might seem great objectively but it can become difficult to sustain and draining to keep up close and strong connections with everyone in your life all of the time. It might feel draining to have everyone in Circle 1 and it might feel lonely or isolating to have everyone in Circle 3.
- You might be able to see how your relationships change year to year. You might be able to see which relationships stay relatively stable and which do not. You might be able to track how your relationships change and how they stay the same. This kind of reflection can be helpful to see if and how your relationships have grown and if you have succeeded in bringing in people you want closer and distancing yourself from people you want space from.

Activity 2 2 3

Instructions

1. Give students copies of the **Relationship Questionnaire**. Clarify that they can use this for friendship or dating relationships. *The indicators also apply to family and sibling relationships to some degree though power dynamics might be different.*

2. Ask students why they think that the same things that build friendships also build dating/romantic/sexual relationships.

EDUCATOR ANSWER KEY

Both kinds of relationships are based on connection, authenticity (i.e., being yourself), trust, respect, and communication. Whether long term (e.g., best friends for many years, long term couples) or short and casual (e.g., summer camp friends, casual dates, hookups), you can be real, honest, and clear.

3. Ask students to rate some of the relationships in their own lives.
4. Optional: Include rating into the chart from Activity 1.
5. Discuss what students have learned from these exercises.

EDUCATOR ANSWER KEY

Let students' answers guide the discussion. Encourage students to look for patterns instead of specific observations that might name people. These patterns could include:

- Most relationships are not all positive or all negative and are instead a combination of both. It can be helpful to figure out which relationships are more positive than negative and assess whether or not you want to bring those relationships closer into your "orbit."
- The value of reflecting on relationships is trying to figure out which relationships to invest in and which to ask for distance on/around.
- Relationships are constantly changing. Through reflection and evaluation, we can guide the changes that we want to make.

Wrap-up

Summarize the module with the following points:

- Relationships are not all positive or all negative, they hold aspects of both.
- Relationships keep changing. We always have some control in how they change.
- Reflection and evaluation are an important part of having relationships. They can help clarify how you feel, what you need, and how you want to be in the relationship.

7.3 FRIENDS AND RELATIONSHIPS: BOUNDARIES AND LIMITS

LEVEL ☐1☐ ☐2☐ ☐3☐

Big Ideas in Module 7.3

- Boundaries are a way of keeping space around aspects of yourself and your life. Boundaries are important to have in all relationships, whether they are with friends or family members, romantic, sexual, and/or dating relationships.
- One of the healthy foundations of relationships is setting boundaries. It is everyone's responsibility to learn about and set their own boundaries as well as communicate and respect other people's boundaries.
- In dating relationships, boundaries can be an important part of self-care. Without boundaries, you can easily let one aspect of your life and/or a relationship take over.
- Setting, maintaining, and communicating boundaries is a lifelong learning process. Like most processes, it is not linear and at times can feel unclear and messy. Building self-reflection and confidence through practise and experience are the only ways to develop and mature boundary setting skills.

Learning Objectives

Students will:

- Understand why limits and boundaries are useful in relationships.
- Explore noticing and practising how to set and communicate limits and boundaries.
- Identify situations where boundaries are not respected.

Cross-Curricular Connections

- Art (drama)
- English
- Equity Studies
- Gender Studies
- Psychology
- Social Studies
- Sociology

Terminology

- Boundaries

Materials

- Chalkboard, whiteboard, or flip chart
- Printed copies of **Boundary Setting Scenarios**
- **Educator Answer Key—Boundary Setting Scenarios**

Background Information for Educators

One of the healthy foundations of interpersonal connection is setting boundaries. Having healthy boundaries means knowing what kinds of relationships you want to engage in, how often you want to engage in those relationships, who you want to have relationships with, and when and where you make relationships a priority. In any relationship, it can be challenging to balance between closeness and space, attachment and independence. Balance between these qualities is key to building sustainable, resilient relationships that feel mutually supportive. Knowing what your boundaries are and having the courage to set and communicate them requires self-awareness and assertive communication skills.

"Hard" boundaries do not change very much over time. They could include not developing friendships with students, ensuring that professional relationships stay professional, or not engaging in sexual activity without consent (for more information, see chapter 8). Other boundaries might change as life circumstances, relationships, and people change. Boundaries can also change person to person—just because you have a particular set of boundaries with one friend, does not mean that you will have the same boundaries with another friend. These more flexible, adaptable boundaries might include how much time you spend supporting a friend in need, the kinds of details about your life that you share with family members, how much energy you put into making a dating relationship work, and whether or not you want to be hugged by an acquaintance.

Boundaries are sometimes discovered when violated either by ourselves and/or other people. Self-reflection is key to learning the kinds of boundaries we need and communication is essential in setting boundaries. Both of these skill sets can (and need to) be developed (regardless of age) in order to limit boundary violations of ourselves and others. In relationships of all kinds, it is everyone's responsibility to learn about and set their own boundaries as well as communicate and respect other people's boundaries.

Getting to know which boundaries are "hard" and which are more flexible can help students understand that boundaries are not all written in stone, they can change. Because boundaries are likely to change over time and throughout relationships, ongoing communication is necessary to clarify assumptions and/or expectations that can arise. Setting and respecting boundaries is not a one-time event, it is a constant process of communication, action, and reflection.

Boundaries can be especially challenging with deep, intense, and/or unfamiliar connections, like a "first love." The breaking of boundaries and sacrifice are, for example, often romanticized as symbols of love, commitment, and trust (Milhausen et. al., 2013). Dealing with feelings of rejection when boundaries are asserted is another challenge for people of all ages but with our "first love," feelings of rejection and pain can be intensified. Managing feelings of rejection and pain in constructive ways is a skill set that involves self-reflection, emotional intelligence, personal boundary setting, and communication. Educators can empower young people by providing them with tools to better recognize their motivations, investigate and get curious about where emotional pain comes from, develop communication skills, and make conscious, informed choices.

Student Readiness

Before students engage with this lesson, ensure that safer space guidelines and group norms have been established (and revisited) within your classroom (for more information on how to establish safer space guidelines, see module 1.3). In order to effectively prepare for this activity, ensure students understand that:

- Learning how to set and communicate healthy boundaries can be a lifelong process—many adults do not have it all figured out.
- Boundaries are not set in stone, they will change over time and throughout relationships.
- Sharing about specific relationships or people will not be tolerated.

Summary of Activities

Students will:

- Collectively reflect on what boundaries are and how to set them.
- Work in pairs to verbally practise boundary setting.
- Work out scenarios in small groups through role play.
- Individually reflect on their favourite television show/movie and rewrite a scene where a boundary violation has occurred.

Activity 1 ⬜1

Instructions

1. Write the word "boundaries" on the board. Discuss as a class what it means.
2. Ask: Who do we set boundaries with? List their answers.
3. Ask: How do we set boundaries? Point out that the answer are forms of communication.
4. Ask: How do we know someone is setting a boundary if they do not say, "No, I do not want that"? What are all the subtle ways that we know when someone does not want to do something? Or does not feel okay about something?

EDUCATOR ANSWER KEY

1. Boundaries are limitations a person establishes in a relationship (e.g. friendship, romantic relationship, family relationship, etc.) in order to protect and take care of themselves. Having healthy boundaries means knowing what kinds of relationships you want to engage in, how often you want to engage in those relationships, who you want to have relationships with, and when and where you make relationships a priority.

2. Every relationship has boundaries, whether it is a relationship with romantic or sexual partners, friends, family members, teachers, counsellors, doctors, spiritual or religious leaders, we have boundaries with everyone.

3. All of the ways that we set boundaries involve communication. This includes eye contact, facial gestures, verbal expressions, subtle body language, explicit physical cues, stating rules (e.g., body language like crossing arms could indicate a physical boundary, like not wanting to be touched and/or hugged).

4. Communication can happen in many ways. For instance, being able to pay attention to body language, hesitation, what they do not say, and their silence are important cues and moments to ask for clarification.

Activity 2 ☐1 ☐2

Instructions

1. Have students pair up. One student becomes "A" and the other "B."

2. A is to offer a fist bump to B three times and B is to refuse each time. *A fist bump is a friendly gesture where each person holds a fist and the two gently tap the flats of their fingers together.*

3. Give the student pairings specific instructions:
   - Round One: Both A and B are silent. B gestures refusal. A respects B's refusal and stops offering.
   - Round Two: B can speak. A respects B's refusal and stops offering.
   - Round Three: B can speak. A ignores B's refusal and keeps offering.

4. Ask students to switch positions and repeat.

5. Discuss the following questions as a class:
   - How did it feel to set a boundary? What were some of the words you used? What did you do when you could not set your boundary verbally? What kinds of strategies worked well? What was challenging about having limited communication?
   - How did it feel to have your boundary respected? How did it feel to have it crossed?
   - How did it feel to cross someone else's boundary?

- What are things that make it hard to set boundaries in real life?
- How does it feel to be rejected in real life? How do people usually react?
- What are some strategies you can think of to better cope with rejection?

EDUCATOR ANSWER KEY

- Affirm students' experiences of the activity and emphasize that setting boundaries can be challenging. Emphasize that it is not only up to the person setting boundaries to communicate them but also up to the other person to respect them.
- Affirm students' experiences of the activity and emphasize that setting a boundary can feel vulnerable. When a boundary is crossed, it can lead to mistrust and can make the experience of vulnerability feel even worse. At the same time, having a boundary respected can help build confidence and self-esteem as it becomes obvious that your needs are valued by the other person.
- Affirm students' experiences of the activity. Be aware that students might respond to this question with giggling and joking that it felt good to cross someone else's boundary. Validate that it can be funny in a structured exercise but that in real life, it can be very hurtful. Reinforce that we are all responsible for noticing the many different ways that people communicate their boundaries and for respecting them.
- Affirm students' responses and emphasize that setting boundaries in real life can be challenging (for people of all ages and maturity levels). Things that make this especially challenging are: power differences; not knowing that you can set a boundary; not knowing how; being scared of consequences; feeling guilty; not wanting to reject someone etc. Emphasize that even though it might sometimes feel like it is not socially acceptable to set boundaries, everyone has the right to set boundaries.
- People might respond by feeling bad, humiliated, disappointed, embarrassed, angry, and/or vengeful. Affirm students' responses and emphasize that rejection is a possible outcome of any request and that all people, regardless of age, need to learn how to manage that feeling. Point out that getting angry or vengeful when a request is denied, or when someone sets a boundary with you, is hurtful and can feel violent. Help students understand that vengeful anger or indignant retaliation are signs that we are not coping well with rejection. Managing the feeling of rejection is something that people will need to put into practise throughout their lives; adolescence is a great time to start practising. (For more information on coping with rejection and dealing with emotional pain, see module 4.6).

CONT'D NEXT PAGE

EDUCATOR ANSWER KEY CONT'D

- Let students lead this discussion and affirm that rejection can be dealt with and managed in healthy ways. Some of these strategies include walking away from a situation where you feel angry or vengeful; channelling anger, vengeance, and resentment into something like art, journaling, and/or playing a sport; taking responsibility for your reactions to rejection; and if it is appropriate, communicating those feelings in a way that avoids blame or manipulation. (For more information on coping with rejection and dealing with emotional pain, see module 4.6).

Activity 3 2 **3**

Instructions

1. Ask students to close their eyes and consider (to themselves) a situation where boundaries they set were not respected.
2. After 1 to 2 minutes have passed, write the following four steps on the board:
   - **Name it:** Make an observation about what is happening.
   - **Direct it:** Say what you want them to do.
   - **Repeat it:** Repeat the first two statements.
   - **End it:** If someone is not respecting your boundary while you are repeatedly trying to set it, recognize this and get yourself out of the situation.
3. Ask students to silently apply the formula to their situation.
4. Ask students to arrange themselves in small groups (3 to 4 people) and distribute copies of the **Boundary Setting Scenarios**.
5. Ask each group to work through the scenarios using the 4-step boundary setting formula.
6. Have each group present their scenario to the rest of the class.
7. ✦ Optional: If appropriate for your class, ask each group to either role play each scenario or create a dramatic skit (for more information on role playing readiness, see module 1.6). Emphasize that no matter what option your students decide, they must clearly articulate each of the 4 steps.
8. Debrief the activity using the **Educator Answer Key—Boundary Setting Scenarios** as a guide.

Activity 4

Instructions

Optional homework activity

1. Ask students choose their favourite "rom-com" (romantic comedy) and/or romantic drama movie and/or television show and watch it at home (they should choose an episode or movie that they have seen at least once before).

2. As students watch their chosen movie/television show, have them answer the following questions:
   - In what ways do the characters model healthy boundary setting within their relationships (can be friendships, family relationships, and/or romantic/dating/sexual relationships)? If characters do not model healthy boundary setting, in what ways do they model unhealthy boundaries?
   - Do the main characters model a balance between attachment and independence in their relationships? If not, how are attachment and independence portrayed?
   - In what ways are boundaries communicated? If boundaries are not communicated, are there any consequences that are shown?
   - When a boundary is communicated, how do the characters cope?
   - Are there any boundary violations that occur? If so, how are they dealt with? Is the breaking of boundaries associated with reward and/or romantic gestures?
   - If a character sacrifices and/or gives something up for someone else, are they seen as a hero?

3. After students have answered these questions, ask them to consider ways that they could have changed the storyline of the movie/television show. Specifically ask them to:
   - Choose a scene where a boundary violation either occurred or was romanticized (e.g., as heroic or an act of devotion, as "true love" etc.)
   - Rewrite the scene in a way that supports the successful setting, communication, and maintenance of a boundary.
   - Hand in the rewritten scene as an assignment and/or present the rewritten scene to the entire class.

4. Debrief the activity as a class.

QUICK TIP

To make this into an in-class activity, choose an applicable movie/television show to watch in class and follow instructions 2 to 4.

EDUCATOR PROMPTS
- Did you notice the boundary violations the previous times you watched the episode/movie?
- How did it feel to rewrite the scene?
- How has this movie/television show impacted your sense of relationships? Has this changed since rewriting the scene?

Wrap-up

Summarize the module with the following points:
- Boundaries are an important part of all relationships. Connection is a balance between attachment and independence.
- There are many ways to communicate boundaries. We are responsible for setting ours as well as respecting other people's.
- If the boundaries you have set are not respected, consider what actions you will take within the relationship and assess whether or not you need to create more space between you and the other person/the relationship. The relationship may need to end entirely. Do not rule this out.

7.4 DECISION-MAKING AND NEGOTIATING

LEVEL 2 [3]

Big Ideas in Module 7.4

- The adolescent brain assesses risks and makes decisions differently than the adult brain. Giving young people the tools to assess their decisions and risk-taking in terms of consequence and likelihood, as opposed to "good" or "bad" behaviour, is one way to support young people as they navigate the complicated terrain of adolescence.
- Decision-making involves skills that can be honed through experience. Adolescence is full of opportunities to evaluate consequences, negotiate needs and wants, and expand your understanding of options.
- It is important for young people to learn negotiation skills so that they can effectively communicate what they want and/or need as well as channel conflict and argument into effective dialogue.

Learning Objectives

Students will:

- Explore the concept of decision-making using the Consequence vs. Likelihood Chart.
- Identify the material, emotional, and relational consequences of decisions.
- Practise negotiation as an alternative to lying and arguing.

Cross-Curricular Connections	Terminology	Materials
• Art (drama)	• Consequence	• Chalkboard or whiteboard
• English	• Likelihood	• Paper and writing utensils
• Equity Studies	• Negotiation	• **Educator Resource—Consequence vs. Likelihood Chart Example**
• Gender Studies		• Printed copies of **Negotiation**
• Psychology		• **Educator Resource—Negotiation** (Scenarios A, B, C)
• Social Studies		
• Sociology		

Background Information for Educators

The adolescent brain goes through a period of growth only matched by the first couple years of a child's life and does not reach maturation until the young person is in their 20's (NIMH, 2011). This growth period is incredibly important in terms of the development of risk-assessment and decision-making skills. During this time, the adolescent brain assesses risks and makes decisions differently than the adult brain (Talukder, 2013). This is not to say that all adults have perfect decision-making or risk assessment skills but that adolescent brains work differently.

It is sometimes challenging for adults to understand the reasons why a young person might make a certain decision or take a certain risk. It is important for adults to remember that judging and/or condemning decisions and risks taken may not achieve the results they are hoping for. A more productive approach is to give young people the tools they need to assess their decisions and risk-taking in terms of consequence and likelihood as opposed to "good" or "bad" behaviour.

Just like decision-making and risk assessment, negotiating is a skill that is developed and does not come automatically. It is a powerful skill to learn and use at any point in life that can help build bridges in professional relationships and strengthen relationships when there is conflict and/or disagreement. It is important for young people to learn negotiation skills so that they can effectively communicate what they want and/or need as well as channel conflict and argument into effective dialogue.

Student Readiness

Before students engage with this lesson, ensure that safer space guidelines and group norms have been established (and revisited) within your classroom (for more information on how to establish safer space guidelines, see module 1.3). In order to effectively prepare for this activity, ensure students understand that:

- Learning decision-making, risk assessment, and negotiation skills is challenging life-long work and not all adults have it figured out or do a good job role modelling these skills.
- Building these skills in adolescence is ideal. The brain is hungry for this kind of learning as it grows and develops new neural pathways.
- Sharing personal examples with the whole class is not necessary.
- Sharing about specific relationships or people will not be tolerated.
- The purpose of this lesson is not to shame anyone for lying or arguing. The purpose is to develop skills to effectively communicate needs and wants.

Summary of Activities

Students will:

- Individually reflect on and visually map possible consequences of a challenging decision.
- Act out a negotiation scenario in small groups.

Activity 1  3

Instructions

1. Ask students:
    - How many decisions do you think you make on an average day?
    - What are some decisions that are automatic? What are ones you have to consider for longer?
    - What are some examples of difficult decisions that people your age may have to make? What makes them difficult?
    - What are things that we do to help make difficult decisions?

EDUCATOR ANSWER KEY

- Estimates for adults indicate that 35,000 conscious decisions are made each day.
- Deciding when and where to cross the street can be automatic. Decisions that are considered for longer are what school to attend, whether or not to go to a party, whether or not to join a sports team, etc.
- Difficult decisions that young people may have to make include: deciding whether or not to engage in sexual activity and with whom, deciding whether or not to get in a vehicle with someone who is intoxicated, and deciding whether or not to go to college/university. These decisions are difficult because there is a lot a stake. There are material, emotional, and relational consequences to consider.
- Ways to help make difficult decisions include: weighing the "pros and cons," consulting experts, practising through trial and error, tossing a coin, asking friends, changing the options to make it easier to decide, and weighing the risks and consequences.

2. Introduce the **Consequence vs. Likelihood Chart**:
    - A **consequence** is the possible outcome of a decision. For example, if you jump off a high place, a possible consequence is hurting yourself. Another possible consequence is landing perfectly.
    - **Likelihood** refers to the chances of a consequence happening. For example, if you jump off a high place onto a large area of grass, you are very likely to land on the grass. If you jump off a high place onto a small pillow, you are not as likely to land on the pillow.

3. Have students draw out the Consequence vs. Likelihood Chart (see figure 7E). Ask them to choose a challenging decision from their own lives and plot it on the chart. Have students map all possible consequences of the decision on the chart. *If it will help students, demonstrate an example using the **Educator Resource— Consequence vs. Likelihood Chart Example.*** Ask students to choose a challenging decision from their own lives and plot it on the chart. They can use this chart for any decision. Have them map all possible consequences of the decision they have to make.

Consequence vs. Likelihood Chart

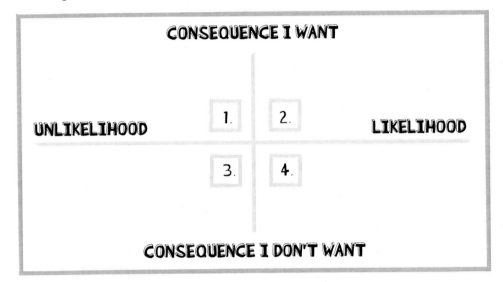

CONSEQUENCE I WANT

UNLIKELIHOOD   1.   2.   **LIKELIHOOD**

3.   4.

CONSEQUENCE I DON'T WANT

Figure 7E

EDUCATOR PROMPTS
Consider:
 • Material consequences: what will happen to things, places, people, bodies?
 • Emotional consequences: how will it feel? Immediately? Later?
 • Relational consequences: what will happen to your relationships?

4. Ask the class: Did you learn anything about your decision and its consequences by putting it on the chart? Did completing this chart help you make a decision?

EDUCATOR PROMPTS

Think about where on the chart most of the consequences are clustered. What does this clustering tell you about your decision? Were you surprised at where the clustering happened or did it just affirm what you already knew?

EDUCATOR ANSWER KEY

There are multiple consequences to any decision. It is important to consider how decisions will affect your emotions and relationships, not just material things. If a decision poses too many likely consequences that you do not want (e.g., making this decision means that you will be taking X risks) you can think of creative alternatives (e.g., talking to parents about going to the party by stating your needs and minimizing their concerns and talking to parents about going to the party and making a safety plan with them).

Activity 2 ☐2☐ ☐3☐

This activity is based on findings from a study on the reasons why teens lie, with the assumption that parents do not lie. It is important to be aware that students might learn lying behaviours from their parents. This activity assumes that parents will respond most effectively to negotiation (as opposed to lying or argumentation) but this is not always the case for every student. Because you will not always know the family dynamics of your students, it is important that students be encouraged to learn how to assess their individual risk in trying to redefine the relationship in favour of negotiation.

Instructions
1. Give students the following highlights from Ranard's 2009 article on *Teens and Dishonesty* (for more information, see the 7.4 resources):
    *   96% of teens say they sometimes lie to their parents.
    *   Teens do not just lie to avoid getting into trouble. They lie to protect their relationship with their parents, as an alternative to arguing and to avoid disappointment.
    *   Teens in this study think of arguing with their parents as a form of negotiation. Many parents think of arguing as harmful and destructive.

2. Ask: What do you think of these findings? Do they feel true for you and people your age?

3. Follow-up the questions with: Is it important for you to be able to negotiate with adults in your life? Is arguing useful? Does argument feel like a form of negotiation? What are ways to negotiate that work best?

4. Introduce the idea of **negotiation**. Give the definition: to reach an agreement or compromise by discussion with others.

5. Ask the class to brainstorm a list of human needs and write them on the board. The list could include: love, acceptance, fun, security, independence, touch, expression, understanding, privacy etc.

6. Divide students into small groups of 3 to 4 and distribute copies of the **Negotiation** handout.

7. Ask each group to pick a scenario on the handout (or pick the same scenario for the whole class). Have each group answer the questions in the chart as guided. For sample answers, see the **Educator Resource—Negotiation** (Scenarios A, B, C).

8. Once the **Negotiation** handout is completed, have students act out a negotiation in their group according to their worksheet.

9. Optional: Have each group present their role play on negotiation to the class.

10. Discuss as a class:
    - Did you come up with any solutions that were not obvious at first?
    - Teens are changing from kids to adults. What do you think it would take for people to take teens seriously in a negotiation?
    - Is there anything in your lives that is non-negotiable?

EDUCATOR ANSWER KEY

- Let students' answers guide the discussion.
- Being able to hear/acknowledge the other person's needs/wants/concerns and offering solutions that would address the other person's needs/wants/concerns.
- While the distinction between negotiable and non-negotiable is different from person to person, there are some things that are objectively non-negotiable. For instance, obtaining someone's consent about sexual activity is not something that can be negotiated in the same way that a disagreement can be negotiated (for more on consent and sexual assault, see chapter 8). Negotiation is not manipulation or coercion. Pressuring someone emotionally, socially, and/or physically into doing something that they do not want to do is coercion.

Wrap-up

Summarize the module with the following points:

- Decisions are sometimes challenging to make for adolescents and adults alike. Keep short and long term consequences and risks in mind as well as how they will affect your relationships.
- Instead of deciding to lie or argue, you have options to negotiate.
- Negotiation changes the way we look at problems and conflicts. Improving negotiation skills can help avoid unnecessary conflicts.

7.5 ASSERTIVE COMMUNICATION

LEVEL ☒1 ☐2

Big Ideas in Module 7.5

- Effective communication is assertive communication. It takes practise and is a lifelong skill. Learning how to communicate assertively will help foster healthy and intimate relationships throughout life.
- Assertive communication is considerate though not passive, confident though not aggressive. Assertive communication is direct and clear and at the same time, kind and respectful.
- An individual who communicates assertively values and expresses their needs without encroaching on the rights of other people

Learning Objectives

Students will:
- Discern between aggressive, passive, passive-aggressive, and assertive communication styles.
- Develop assertive communication skills.

Cross-Curricular Connections	Terminology	Materials
• Art (drama) • English • Equity Studies • Gender Studies • Psychology • Social Studies • Sociology	• Aggressive communication • Assertive communication • Communication • Passive communication • Passive-aggressive communication	• Chalkboard or whiteboard • Printed copies of **Communication Role Plays** • Optional: Printed copies of **Assertive Communication Homework**

Background Information for Educators

There are few communication role models in the media, in our public institutions, and in many families. Communication is more than words: it is about tone, body language, what is said and unsaid. Learning how to communicate effectively is a learned skill that many adults are still working on. It is often honed through trial and error throughout a person's life. Effective communication requires continual practise.

Effective communication is a skill that is foundational for all aspects of life: social, emotional, romantic, sexual, and professional. Relationships (including friendships) that are healthy and intimate are fostered by clear, kind, and firm communication, sometimes referred to as **assertive communication**. Assertive communication can help people navigate all types of relationships. Assertive communication is considerate though not passive, confident though not aggressive. A person who communicates assertively listens and values their needs as well as those of the people around them. They are able to directly and clearly state their feelings, needs, and opinions without encroaching on the rights of others.

YOU SHOULD KNOW

Assertive communication comes from an individualist framework, which assumes that every person represents only themselves and values directness and disclosure. While this may not match with all cultural values, assertive communication can still be used as a tool. It does not require specific values.

Student Readiness

Before students engage with this lesson, ensure that safer space guidelines and group norms have been established (and revisited) within your classroom (for more information on how to establish safer space guidelines, see module 1.3). In order to effectively prepare for this activity, ensure students understand that:

- Learning how to effectively communicate can be a lifelong learning process—not all adults have it figured out.
- Communication style is learned and assertive communication often takes practise; it can be more difficult as it is not many people's default communication style.
- This module teaches assertive communication as a tool for communicating within relationships of all kinds; it does not require specific values.

Summary of Activities

Students will:

- Collectively distinguish between passive, aggressive, passive-aggressive, and assertive communication styles.
- In pairs, work through a scenario that requires assertive communication using role play.

Activity 1

Ensure that students know this game is pretend and that one of the guidelines is that students cannot leave the circle with another student's toy.

Instructions
1. Ahead of this lesson, ask students to bring a favourite toy for show and tell. *Exceptions to the show and tell would be a device that can send and receive digital data/communications.*
2. Divide students up into Team A and Team B.
3. Ask Team A to stand in a circle with their toys and take a moment to think about why it is their favourite toy.
4. ✛ Optional: Have students share reasons with the entire class.
5. After you have given Team A a moment to reflect, ask them to put their toys on the ground, step outside of the circle and sit down.
6. Ask Team B to take one of the toys in the circle and to sit back down.
7. Ask Team A what they felt when a member from Team B took their toy away. *Prompt for annoyed, jealous, neutral, sad, angry, and frustrated.*
8. Ask students what they understand by the term **communication**.

> **EDUCATOR ANSWER KEY**
> Communication is an exchange of thoughts, ideas, and feelings; it is the sending and receiving of messages and meaning.

9. Ask what can get in the way of communication.

> **EDUCATOR ANSWER KEY**
> Some examples include not being clear, not listening, self-interest, no common language, feeling like you need to "win."

10. Explain that there are four basic types of communication styles: passive, aggressive, passive-aggressive, and assertive.
  - Passive response: You are annoyed but you do not say anything.
  - Aggressive response: You yell at them.

- Passive-aggressive response: You curse them under your breath and gossip about them with your friends.
- Assertive response: You respectfully and clearly stand up for yourself, say how their action of taking the toy made you feel and what action you want to see taken to correct the mistake. "Maybe you did not realize it but that is my toy and when you are done looking at it, I would like it back because I felt sad when you took it without asking."

11. Discuss the advantages and disadvantages of each kind of communication. Table 7F provides examples.

Table 7F

	Passive	Aggressive	Passive-Aggressive	Assertive
Advantages	• Avoids confrontation • Seems generous	• Releases tension • Seems powerful • Feels like you "win"	• Releases some tension • Seems nice on the surface • Avoids confrontation	• Takes responsibility for yourself and your needs (self-care) • Is open and honest • Gets some of your needs met • Maintains good relationships • Leads to increased self-confidence • Leads to increased connection • Reduces anxiety • Minimizes possible hurt to others and yourself

	Passive	Aggressive	Passive-Aggressive	Assertive
Disadvantages	• Does not feel heard • Feels resentful and taken advantage of • Does not solve the problem • Represses feelings and increases stress build-up that can lead to an emotional outburst • Leads to a loss of confidence (feeling unheard)	• Does not solve problem • Creates conflicts and enemies • Seems rude and abusive • Results in paranoia and long term fear • Leads to guilt and shame • Leads to negative relationships	• Seems "two faced" • Leads to distrust • Feels powerless • Creates resentment • Seems manipulative • Seems challenging to be honest • Feels like lying • Leads to loss of confidence (feeling unheard or not trusted)	• Requires work and practise • Feels scary to use at first • Lacks good role models

12. Write the following assertive response formula on the board: When X happens, I feel X, and I would like X to happen.
13. Ask each student from Team A to find the individual from Team B who has their toy. Ask Team A students to use the assertive response formula to communicate how they feel about Team B taking their toy.
14. Switch team roles so that Team A takes the toys of Team B.
15. ✦ Optional: As a class, work through the following hypothetical examples to further demonstrate assertive communication:
   • Your sibling opens the door and comes into your room without knocking.

EDUCATOR ANSWER KEY
When you come in like that without knocking, I feel really annoyed and I get so mad at you. I'd like you to knock, like we agreed, so that I can talk to you nicely.

   • Your best friend starts spending more time with someone else. You are not sure what is happening.

EDUCATOR ANSWER KEY

You have been spending a lot of time with X...I miss you and am worried that maybe you are spending less time with me on purpose. I'd like to talk about what might be happening.

Activity 2 [1] [2]

Before beginning this activity, assess whether it is appropriate to facilitate a role play activity. (For more information on what to consider in your assessment, see module 1.6).

Instructions

1. Place students in pairs and assign scenarios from the **Communication Role Plays** or allow pairs to pick.
2. Choose from the following options (you may choose more than one):
   - Have students prepare their scenario together and carry it out in front of the class.
   - Have students prepare the scenario individually. Without knowing the other person's directions, ask students to carry out the scenario in front of the class.
   - Have students act out the scenario. Ask for comments about whether the communication worked well or not.
   - Allow other students in the audience to stop the scenario, make comments, ask the participants questions (while in character), or replace one of the participants before carrying on the conversation.
3. Discuss each role play as an entire class. Emphasize how assertive communication can be used at any time, not only when something is "wrong" (e.g., Scenario 4 is advocating for yourself and Scenarios 5 and 6 involve taking responsibility and apologizing).
4. Optional Homework: Give students copies of the **Assertive Communication Homework** handout for more practise.

Wrap-up

Summarize the module with the following points:
- There are a number of ways to communicate: passive, aggressive, passive-aggressive, assertive. All have advantages and disadvantages but assertive communication produces some of the most positive results and can lead to more fulfilling relationships.
- Assertive communication takes practise but it allows us to be honest, respectful, and clear.
- Assertive communication is a tool that can be used for any situation.

7.6 PEER NORMS, HEALTHY RELATIONSHIPS, AND YOUTH SEXUALITY

LEVEL 2 [3]

Big Ideas in Module 7.6

- Peer norms can be powerful and are always changing. They can vary in different friend groups, different schools, different places, and across time. Many people do not follow and/or are an exception to peer norms.
- Clarifying and communicating values, wants, needs, and boundaries is important for cultivating healthier relationships and shifting peer norms of dating, love, intimacy, and sex.
- Peer norms are sometimes based on assumptions about the kinds of sexual activities young people are engaging in. Statistics can help clarify misconceptions that may lead to youth feeling inadequate or shame.
- Relationships (of all kinds) are complex. Learning how to be in a relationship with another person is not always easy, obvious, or linear. Knowing and articulating your own values is a helpful place to start the learning process.

Learning Objectives

Students will:

- Identify and articulate values and peer norms around relationships and sex.
- Compare assumptions about adolescent sexual behaviour with Canadian research findings.
- Reflect on their own desires and boundaries around dating, relationships, and sexual experience.

Cross-Curricular Connections

- English
- Equity Studies
- Gender Studies
- Psychology
- Social Studies
- Sociology

Terminology

- Cissexism
- Gender norms
- Heterosexism
- Peer norms

Materials

- 3 large signs to post on walls: AGREE, DISAGREE, and DEPENDS.
- **Educator Resource—Peer Norms, Healthy Relationships, and Youth Sexuality Statements**
- Printed copies of **Peer Norms and Relationships**

- Printed copies of **Everyone's Doing It. Right?**
- **Educator Answer Key—Everybody's Doing it. Right?**
- Printed copies of **My Healthy Relationship Plan**
- Printed copies of **My Sexual Health Plan**

Background Information for Educators

Students are exposed to values and ideas about intimate, romantic, and sexual relationships from their families, friends, school, and the media, all of which impact their perspectives (for more information, see modules 2.6, 2.8, 5.1, and 6.1). **Peer norms** are scripts, rules, and/or assumptions that are common to a specific age group and/or groups with other common social identifiers. Peer norms are based on a combination of influences, including media, family, school, and friends. Peer norms often reflect **gender norms**. Gender norms reinforce romantic and sexual relationship scripts that equate power struggles, jealousy, and control with intimacy and love (for more information, see modules 8.2 and 8.4). Providing the space for students to talk about their personal perspectives on relationships can help them clarify and communicate their values as well as debunk myths, make decisions, and shift peer norms—all of which lead to cultivating healthier relationships that are not based on power or control.

Everyone needs space and opportunity to practise clarifying and communicating values, wants, needs, and boundaries with friends, partners, and family members. It is important that the forum you provide as an educator is a safe and supportive one. It is up to you to take a leadership role in challenging and dissolving assumptions by using inclusive language and speaking to a wide variety of experiences and identities (for more information, see chapter 1).

While sexuality is often taboo shrouded in silence and mystery, it is also everywhere and commonly exaggerated within adolescent peer groups. Because of this, many young people are left to make assumptions about the actual sexual experiences of their peers. Peer norms are, in part, based on these assumptions that can lead to feelings of inadequacy, fear of missing out, vulnerability, self-consciousness, guilt, judgment, shame, and pressure. Learning about the actual experiences and statistics on adolescent sexual activity can help clarify assumptions and relieve many of these feelings.

Part of comprehensive sexuality education is to debunk the idea that sex and sexual expression is limited to partnered, penetrative sex. Expanding young people's perception of sexual options empowers them to make choices, express themselves, and connect with others in ways that are informed and appropriate for them. It can also reduce the risks involved with sexual activity by using appropriate safer sex methods (for more information on safer sex and contraception, see chapters 9 and 10).

Student Readiness

Before students engage with this lesson, ensure that safer space guidelines and group norms have been established (and revisited) within your classroom (for more information on how to establish safer space guidelines, see module 1.3). In order to effectively prepare for this activity, ensure students understand that:

- Peer norms exist across all age groups and everyone is influenced by peer norms. Adolescence is a time when peer norms might have more influence than other points in life.
- Peer norms can be powerful and are always changing. Students have the power to change norms by questioning and challenging them.
- The sexuality statistics presented in this module are presented in a way that is meant to help ease feelings of inadequacy or shame around sexual experience.
- Creating a healthy relationship plan and a sexual health plan are tools that can help to clarify your values and your needs, which can change over time and in different contexts.
- Sharing about specific relationships or people will not be tolerated. The personalized healthy relationship and sexual health plans will be done individually and privately.

Summary of Activities

Students will:

- Individually reflect on and collectively move their bodies throughout the room to indicate their opinions on different peer norms.
- ✛ Optional: Articulate the reasons for their opinions on different peer norms.
- Collectively discuss reactions to statistics on the sexual behaviours of youth in Canada.
- Individually work on a personal healthy relationship plan and a sexual health plan.

QUICK TIP

If there are concerns about anonymity, provide copies of the **Peer Norms and Relationships** handout and ask students to fill them out individually and anonymously. Ask students to crumple up and return completed handouts. Mix and redistribute the papers (one for each student). Students then move around the room according to the answers on the handout they were given.

Activity 1 2 3

Instructions

1. Clear the space as much as possible. Post AGREE and DISAGREE signs on walls opposite one another. Post the DEPENDS sign on the wall between both. *If space is limited, students can remain in their seats and show a thumbs-up or thumbs-down for AGREE and DISAGREE, and thumbs sideways for DEPENDS.*

2. Read each statement aloud from the **Educator Resource—Peer Norms, Healthy Relationships, and Youth Sexuality Statements.** Ask students to move to the part of the room that matches how they feel about each statement.

3. Optional: After students move to their chosen spot for each statement, invite those interested to talk about their choice. Make space for opinions from different areas of the room.

4. Debrief the activity with the following questions:

   - What did you notice when exploring your opinions around the room? Did it help to clarify or obscure your perspectives?

   - How did it feel to explore your perspectives on relationships with peers? Did it feel vulnerable or empowering? Did you feel like changing your perspective/place in the room when your peers were moving towards a different area?

   - [Anonymous Version] How did it feel to move around the room with opinions that were not necessarily yours? Did it help you see another different perspective or further entrench you in your own perspective?

EDUCATOR ANSWER KEY

There are no right or wrong answers. Key points to emphasize are that peer norms are powerful and it is important that individuals assess what their perspective is and what feels right for them when navigating the world of dating, romantic, sexual, and intimate relationships. Peer norms change and can be diverse even within one school.

Activity 2 2 3

Instructions

Part 1

1. Introduce the topic by explaining that sex is often a taboo subject that is exaggerated greatly when discussed. Ask students to give examples of both.

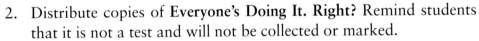

EDUCATOR ANSWER KEY

Allow students to guide and shape the responses. Emphasize that directly discussing sexuality is challenging for most people. Most people use symbolic language and euphemisms to talk about sex, sexuality, and reproduction. Even though the subject of sex is taboo, people are constantly exposed to sex and narrow definitions of sexuality (for more information, see modules 6.4 and 6.6). In our culture, emphasis is often placed on "virginity" and the consequences of "losing your virginity" are different depending on your gender identity. For young people, it can feel like sex is happening all around them and that "having sex" is the most important thing to their peer group.

2. Distribute copies of **Everyone's Doing It. Right?** Remind students that it is not a test and will not be collected or marked.
3. Take-up the questions as a class using the **Educator Answer Key—Everyone's Doing It. Right?**
4. Ask: Did you guess too low or too high? Why do you think this is the case? Why do you think chlamydia rates are increasing while pregnancy rates are decreasing and penile/vaginal intercourse rates remain the same?

EDUCATOR ANSWER KEY

There are a lot of misconceptions about what sex is, what "counts" as sex, and what young people in Canada are doing (or not doing) when it comes to sex. Chlamydia rates are increasing while pregnancy rates are decreasing and intercourse rates remained the same because while contraceptives (i.e., birth control) are being used at higher rates, only condoms prevent STBBIs (sexually transmitted and blood-borne infections).

Part 2 (extended debrief)

1. Reiterate that while 30% of 15 to 17-year-olds and 68% of 18 to 19 year-olds in Canada have had sexual intercourse (Rotterman, 2008 & 2012), a higher percentage claim to have had sexual intercourse when asked. Ask the class why they think that is.

2. Explain that pregnancy and STBBIs (e.g., HIV, chlamydia, gonorrhea, syphilis) can happen through the exchange of bodily fluids (seamen, vaginal mucus, breast milk, blood) and that some STIs can be transmitted through skin contact (e.g., herpes, crabs, pubic lice, genital warts). Ask the class to list ways to sexually express yourself without exchanging bodily fluids or penetration.

3. Ask the class to name some possible advantages of sending sexual messages, images, videos, and texts ("sexting").

4. Ask for the possible risks of "sexting" and how to minimize them.

EDUCATOR ANSWER KEY

Emphasize that sexual intercourse was not defined in the study. This means that there could have been multiple interpretations of the question. Sexual intercourse is often assumed as penis/vagina sex, an assumption that is rooted in **heterosexism** and **cissexism**. People are sexually active with each other through many means, including but not limited to: oral sex, anal sex, digital penetration, touching bodies, mutual masturbation, etc.

Emphasize that sexual expressing and/or intimacy can include many activities that do not involve the exchange of bodily fluids and/or penetration, including but not limited to: holding hands, kissing (some exchange of saliva), snuggling, hugging, "dry humping" (rubbing bodies together with clothes on), touching bodies (there could be some fluid exchanged depending on where you are touching), masturbation, mutual masturbation, sharing fantasies, phone sex (sexual phone calls), sexting (sexual text messages), etc.

Emphasize that while there are risks involved in sending and receiving sexual messages, images, videos, and texts (for more information, see module 6.5), there are also some advantages to this kind of sexual expression. These advantages include: no risk of STBBI or pregnancy, the ability to experiment with your sexual identity and expression, do not have to be in the same place, can view later, feel easily connected to someone across distance.

CONT'D NEXT PAGE

EDUCATOR ANSWER KEY CONT'D

The risks involved in sending and receiving sexual messages, images, videos, and texts include: privacy might be compromised, material might be used against you, it is challenging to delete material once it is online/shared through digital and communications technology, illegal if you are under 18 (with certain exceptions), there is a risk of being charged even if the exchange is consensual (for more information, see module 6.5). To minimize risk, ask yourself the following questions: can you 100% trust the person, even if you get in an argument and/or break up? Has everyone involved given their consent at every stage? Is there a way to not include identifying features in an image and/or message while keeping the integrity of what you want to express? Is someone manipulating you and/or forcing you to do something that you do not want to do? If you start to lose control of the ways images and/or messages are being shared, is there someone who you trust (ideally who is older than you) to help? Will you be able to permanently delete all concerning material on all the devices and networks it was shared on/with? Are your privacy settings activated on your social media accounts?

Activity 3 2 3

Instructions

1. Explain that just as we can plan important parts of our life (like reaching educational and career goals or physical fitness), we can make healthy relationship and sexual health plans. Planning helps us understand what we desire and feel ready for and where our boundaries are. It also helps to map out any questions and uncertainties we have.

2. Give students copies of **My Healthy Relationship Plan** and **My Sexual Health Plan**. Tell them not to put their names on the handouts and to keep their papers private. Emphasize that you do not have to be dating and/or sexually active to fill out the plan.

3. Give students a few minutes to work on their plans then discuss the following question: In which circumstances might relationship and sexual health planning be useful?

4. Give students resources about where to get their relationship and sexual health questions answered (for more information, see the 7.6 resources).

5. Optional: Encourage students to write any relationship and sexual health questions onto anonymous pieces of paper. Ask them to place their questions into a closed box near your desk. Review the questions and provide answers as appropriate. (For more information on the Question Box activity, see module 4.3 activity 3).

Wrap-up

Summarize the module with the following points:

- Like all norms, those related to relationships, dating, and sexuality can be challenged; they can vary in different friend groups, different schools, different places, and across time. Many people do not follow and/or are an exception to peer norms.

- Sex is often exaggerated and a taboo subject. Statistics on actual sexual activity are often surprising because of the assumptions we make.

- Some adolescents feel pressure regarding their sexual experience (what they have and/or have not done). It is okay to be different from others; everyone has their own path.

- There are many ways to express sexual feelings and curiosities besides penile-vaginal sexual intercourse.

- It is important to know your personal values and perspectives on relationships, dating, and sex. Creating your own relationship and sexual health plans can help to identify wants, needs, values, and boundaries.

- Your relationship and sexual health plans (like other aspects of sexuality) will likely change over time and context—this is okay!

- It is important to challenge stereotypes about relationships and people. Stereotypes can get in the way of seeing the many ways people relate to one another.

7.7 HEALTHY RELATIONSHIPS: IDENTIFYING STRENGTHS AND PREVENTING VIOLENCE

LEVEL ① 2 ③

Big Ideas in Module 7.7

- Relationships are complex. They are usually not entirely healthy or entirely unhealthy; they often have qualities of both.
- Having the information and skills to better amplify the positive, change the negative, and prevent abuse in relationships of all kinds is part of cultivating healthier relationships.
- Jealousy is a challenging but common feeling within relationships of all kinds. Jealousy is usually an indication of insecurity or self-consciousness about something unrelated to the target of jealousy.
- Intimate partner violence is a public health crisis that affects people of varying identities, social locations, backgrounds, and life experiences.

Learning Objectives

Students will:

- Explore concepts about relationships, love, jealousy, violence, and relationship strengths through performance.
- Evaluate relationship dynamics and strategize next steps using hypothetical scenarios.

Cross-Curricular Connections

- Art (drama)
- English
- Equity Studies
- Gender Studies
- Psychology
- Social Studies
- Sociology

Terminology

- Intimate partner violence
- Oppression
- Social determinants of health
- Stigma

Materials

- Open space to move around in
- Printed copies of **Satisfying Relationships Crossword**
- **Educator Answer Key—Satisfying Relationships Crossword**
- Printed copies of **How are they doing?**
- **Educator Answer Key—How are they doing?**

Background Information for Educators

Relationships are complex. They are usually not entirely healthy or entirely unhealthy; they often have qualities of both and exist somewhere along a spectrum between healthy and unhealthy. Identifying where on the spectrum the relationships in your life fall can help determine which relationships you want in your life, which might need to change, and which might need clearer boundaries. Identifying relationship qualities that feel positive and healthy as well as those that feel negative and unhealthy can help determine the kinds of relationships you want in your life and which you do not.

Jealousy is a challenging, yet common feeling in relationships of all kinds. When jealousy takes over a relationship it can feel negative and unhealthy (for all people involved) and can easily undermine a relationship.

Often people think that jealousy and envy are the same thing. Envy is a feeling of wanting something that you do not have, jealousy is a fear of losing something you already have. Jealousy often comes from feeling insecure. It can happen between friends, family/siblings, and in romantic/sexual relationships. You can manage jealousy by surrounding yourself with different hobbies/activities and people, doing things that affirm qualities you like in yourself, choosing friends or contacts who affirm your worth, getting support from a counsellor, social worker, therapist, and/or friends, being aware if/when you are blaming your jealousy on someone or something else, not bottling up feelings, and talking to the person you are jealous about if you can.

While you cannot control the relationship choices your students make, you can provide them with skills to evaluate the kinds of relationships they want in their lives. You can provide skills that will help them cultivate the types of relationships they want while setting and communicating boundaries. You can also provide young people with information to determine the ingredients for a healthy relationship. It is important for young people to learn relationship skills so that they can better amplify the positive, change the negative, and prevent abuse.

Intimate partner violence can include physical, sexual, emotional, psychological violence, and/or controlling behaviours by a current or former partner, spouse, or boyfriend/girlfriend. It is an issue that touches people of all ages from all different communities and regions. Although it can affect people of any assigned sex, gender identity, gender expression, or sexual orientation, there is a higher prevalence of male perpetrators and female survivors (WHO, 2012). It is important to note that while there is not a lot of data that separates trans and gender non-binary people from the existing research on intimate partner violence, we do know that transphobia puts people at higher risk.

Intimate partner violence has been described as a public health crisis with factors such as homophobia, transphobia, racism, ableism, and classism exacerbating experiences in different but overlapping ways. This does not mean that intimate partner violence only affects specific communities and/or regions, it means that intimate partner violence, like other public health issues, is not experienced equally. It is exacerbated and amplified by **oppression** and **social determinants of health** (for more information, see module 2.4). Violence perpetrated by an intimate partner is much more common than violence perpetrated by strangers but is underreported due to **stigma**, shame, and victim blaming. It is important to introduce young people to intimate partner violence to help identify if it happens in their own lives and end the shame and stigma around disclosing.

YOU SHOULD KNOW

It is not always safe for a person to disclose violence, especially when in close contact and/or reliant on the perpetrator. As an educator, you have a legal obligation to consider when a student discloses violence to you. (For more information, see modules 1.6 and 3.12).

Student Readiness

Before students engage with this lesson, ensure that safer space guidelines and group norms have been established (and revisited) within your classroom (for more information on how to establish safer space guidelines, see module 1.3). In order to effectively prepare for this activity, ensure students understand that:

- Learning how to be in relationships (including friendships) that feel positive, affirming, and supportive can be a lifelong learning process—not all adults have it figured out!
- Building and maintaining healthy, positive, affirmative, fulfilling, and supportive relationships is not something that comes naturally. Like everything in life, there are skills that need to be learned. Much of this skill building starts in adolescence.

- One of the activities involves creating a tableau with bodies. Students will be encouraged to ask for consent before physically coming into contact with anyone else. Students concerned about this level of physical contact can sit out of the activity but will be encouraged to engage in the debrief.
- The purpose of the lesson is to develop skills to identify the qualities you want in relationships and to communicate your needs, expectations, and boundaries within relationships. It is not to shame anyone for engaging in unhealthy relationships.

Summary of Activities

Students will:
- Individually or in pairs work on a crossword puzzle.
- Work in small groups to create a tableau based on themes.
- Work in small groups to evaluate relationship scenarios.

Activity 1

Instructions
1. Print and distribute copies of **Satisfying Relationships Crossword**
2. Allow students to work on the crossword individually or in pairs. Once completed, take up answers as a class using the **Educator Answer Key—Satisfying Relationships Crossword.**
3. Discuss as a class:
   - Which answers were the most obvious? Which were the most obscure?
   - Were there any surprising answers?

Activity 2

Instructions
1. Clear space in the classroom.
2. Place students into groups of 3 to 5 and give each group a different relationship theme from **Table 7G.**
3. Explain that they will be creating tableaus based on assigned themes. A tableau is a dramatic exercise that uses the body to create a still picture or a still scene. No words are used in the picture/scene but students can use words to organize themselves into the tableau. *The groups can artistically interpret the theme in any way. Encourage students to use their imagination.*
4. Remind students to ask for consent before touching or coming into physical contact with each other.
5. Give the groups approximately 5 minutes to come up with their tableau.
6. Ask each group to come up to the front of the classroom (one at a time) and present their tableau.

7. Ask the students watching the tableau to guess the relationship theme. Once students have been given a chance to guess, read the relationship theme and the theme summary from table 7G aloud.

8. After each group has presented, debrief with the following questions:
   - Could you relate to some themes more than others? Why or why not?
   - Was it challenging or easy to guess what the themes were? Why do you think this was?
   - How does witnessing an artistic interpretation change or influence the ways you understand a theme.

EDUCATOR ANSWER KEY

Allow the insights of your students to lead the debrief. Affirm that everyone might have different associations and interpretations of the themes based on their own relationship experiences. One interpretation is not more right than the other. Explain that artistic interpretations can deepen and/or expand an understanding of a theme, that relationships are complex, and that different interpretations reflect this complexity.

Table 7G

Theme	Theme Summary
Relationship	Every connection between two people is a relationship. We have many different relationships in our lives, including with friends, family members, classmates etc. Relationships are not simply "good" or "bad," "healthy" or "unhealthy." Most relationships have qualities of both. Relationship skills are about maximizing good aspects, changing the challenging ones, and ending those harmful to us if/when we can. What are some of the healthy qualities of a relationship?

Theme	Theme Summary
Jealousy	Jealousy often comes from feeling insecure. It can happen between friends, family/siblings, and in romantic/sexual relationships. You can manage jealousy by surrounding yourself with different hobbies/activities and people, doing things that affirm qualities you like in yourself, choosing friends or contacts who affirm your worth, getting support from a counsellor, social worker, therapist, and/or friends, being aware if/when you are blaming your jealousy on someone or something else, not bottling up feelings, and talking to the person you are jealous about if you can.
Falling in love	Falling in love can feel very intense for your heart and your brain. Brain chemicals drive you to want to constantly be with that person, put them up on a pedestal, and drop everything else in your life. The good news is that it feels amazing. The bad news is that this feeling and brain chemical activity does not last for long—it changes as a relationship matures. To get to the next level of intimacy and love, these intense feelings need to change.
Silent treatment	Silent treatment is a passive-aggressive way of being angry with someone. Sometimes people do not think much of it because there is no yelling or physically aggressive behaviour but it is a very unhealthy, ineffective way of expressing something that is important. If you are feeling angry or resentful, do your best to honestly and assertively communicate your feelings.

Theme	Theme Summary
Intimate partner violence	Intimate partner violence is any physical, sexual, emotional, psychological violence, and/or controlling behaviours by a current or former partner, spouse, or boyfriend/girlfriend. It affects people of all ages from all different communities and regions. Although it can affect people of any assigned sex, gender identity, gender expression, and any sexual orientation, there is a higher prevalence of male perpetrators and female victims/survivors. The rate of violence by dating partners is 42% higher than by strangers.
Independence	Independence is important in any relationship, including friendships. It allows you to have friends, hobbies, ideas, and aspects of life that are your own, separate, or private. A good relationship consists of independent individuals who are connected.

Activity 3 2 3

Instructions

9. Place students in groups of 2 or 3. Print and distribute copies of **How are they doing?**
10. Ask each group to discuss the scenarios, assign a green, yellow, or red flag to each, and record options for the individuals involved.
11. Debrief the scenarios by letting each group present one scenario, giving their reasoning for assigning their colour flag and the options for the individuals involved.
12. Ask for additional thoughts and/or other considerations from the rest of the class.
13. Use the **Educator Answer Key—How are they doing?** to add to the discussion already taking place and conclude the exercise.

Wrap-up

Summarize the module with the following points:

- Relationships are complex. They are neither all good or all bad, all healthy or all unhealthy. It is important to be able to promote the strengths, change the challenges, and identify abusive situations.
- Jealousy usually originates from insecurity. Building security, confidence, and self-esteem can be a gradual (and sometimes lifelong) process. It requires support, connection to others, and engaging with things that we feel confident and good about.
- Intimate partner violence and violence in relationships comes in many shapes and forms. Physical, verbal, or sexual aggression as well as demeaning, controlling, and coercive behaviours are all examples of violence.

7.8 HARM REDUCTION: THE SAFER USE OF DRUGS, ALCOHOL, AND DIGITAL MEDIA

LEVEL 1 2 3

Big Ideas in Module 7.8

- Harm Reduction is an effective, evidence-based public health strategy based on the recognition that adolescents are likely to engage in risk-taking behaviours.
- Harm reduction empowers the person by reducing social, physical, and economic harm without necessarily having to completely abstain.
- Harm reduction can be applied to any kind of behaviour that is addictive and as an addiction can cause potential harm, including substance use, shopping, digital/social media, television, gaming, pornography, and phone use.

Learning Objectives

Students will:

- Understand concepts and patterns of substance use and dependence.
- Identify and learn practical tools to evaluate and reduce harms of using substances, including digital media.

Cross-Curricular Connections

- Communications Studies
- English
- Equity Studies
- Gender Studies
- Media Studies
- Psychology
- Social Studies
- Sociology

Terminology

- Abstinence
- Addiction
- Dependence
- Drugs
- Harm reduction
- Intoxication
- Overdose
- Tolerance
- Withdrawal

Materials

- Printed and cutout sets of **Harm Reduction Activity Cards** (version for level 1 or 2, as appropriate)
- **Reduction Student Activity Cards** (level 1 or level 2)
- Printed copies of **Harm Reduction Small Group Scenarios**
- **Educator Answer Key—Harm Reduction Small Group Scenarios**
- Printed copies of **Safer Digital Media Use**
- **Educator Answer Key—Safer Digital Media Use**
- Printed copies of **My Substance Safety Plan**

Background Information for Educators

Alcohol and drug use is common for many adolescents. Some may use alcohol and/or drugs out of experimentation, pleasure, to fit into peer culture, or to cope with anxiety, sadness, boredom, or stress. These are similar to some of the reasons why young people use digital and social media. It is possible that overusing any of these substances, including digital and social media, can lead to **addiction**.

The differences between recreational use, abuse, and addiction are not always obvious or clear. The "abuse" label creates unnecessary stigma and can deter many people from seeking help. For this reason, many prevention and support organizations refer to "substance use" instead of "substance abuse." When substance use becomes out of control, you might hear it referred to as "binging" or "chaotic use."

Abstinence is one of the strategies used to control substance use. While abstinence is useful for some users, it is unrealistic for many. **Harm Reduction** recognizes that young people are likely to engage in risk-taking behaviours and offers a solution that works with users to identify ways to reduce harm within risky activities. Harm reduction is a health promotion strategy that has been proven effective at increasing positive health outcomes; it is increasingly being adopted by public health organizations. Harm reduction empowers the substance user to reduce the social, physical, and economic harm in using without having to completely abstain. Harm reduction is not necessarily the opposite of abstinence. Harm reduction offers choice in dealing with substance use; abstinence is one of these choices.

Harm reduction can be applied to any kind of behaviour that potentially causes harm, including substance use, shopping, social media, television, gaming, pornography, and phone use. Harm reduction is a way to have the conversation about substance and digital media use with adolescents in a way that is relevant to their lives and realities.

Student Readiness

Before students engage with this lesson, ensure that safer space guidelines and group norms have been established (and revisited) within your classroom (for more information on how to establish safer space guidelines, see module 1.3). In order to effectively prepare for this activity, ensure students understand that:

- Adolescence is an important time in human brain development; risk-taking behaviour is common at this stage and not necessarily a bad thing if harms associated with risk are minimized.
- This module will be covering alcohol, drugs (both legal and illegal), and digital media use.
- The purpose of this module is to empower young people to develop strategies to reduce harms associated with using these substances and media, not to shame people for using alcohol, drugs, or digital media.

Summary of Activities

Students will:

- Work in pairs to match terminology related to substance use with definitions using a card game.
- Work in small groups to evaluate pros and cons using a hypothetical scenario.
- Individually, or in small groups, fill out a handout that reflects how alcohol and drug use, dependence/addiction, and harm reduction are related to digital media use.

Activity 1 ☐1 ☐2

Instructions

1. Give students this dictionary definition of a **drug**: a substance other than food intended to affect the structure or function of the body.
2. Ask students to list drugs that they have heard of.
3. Ask students for the reasons that people might use legal drugs.
4. Now, ask students for the reasons why young people might use illegal/recreational drugs and alcohol.

EDUCATOR ANSWER KEY

1. Allow the students to list as many as possible but be sure to include prescription and pharmaceutical drugs, recreational and illegal drugs, steroids, caffeine (found in coffee and pop/soft drinks), nicotine (found in cigarettes), and alcohol.
2. To ease pain (physical, emotional, and/or mental pain); to ease symptoms of a behavioural issue (e.g., ADHD); to help you feel less tired; to help you fall asleep; to ease stress, anxiety, sadness, and/or fear.
3. To have fun; to fit in; to stay awake; to relax; to experience altered realities; to ease boredom; to escape reality/violence; to ease pain (physical, emotional, and/or mental pain); to ease symptoms of a behavioural issue (e.g., ADHD); to help you feel less tired; to help you fall asleep; to ease stress, anxiety, sadness and/or fear.

5. Group students into pairs and provide each with a set of the **Harm Reduction Student Activity Cards**. *There are two different card decks, one for level 1 and one for level 2. Use your discretion and knowledge of your class to determine which cards are appropriate for your students. You can use the full deck or pick and choose.*

6. Ask students to place the cards face down. Taking turns, each person in the pair will turn over two cards at a time. When someone turns over a term and definition that match, that person gets to put the cards aside. The person with the most pairs of cards put aside "wins."

7. After students have finished matching their cards, take up the correct answers with the whole class. Ensure students have a basic understanding of how drug use works:

   - Tolerance goes up over time, user requires more for same high/effect.
   - Dependence happens at a different time and amount for each drug and each body.
   - Dependence is when it is difficult or impossible to quit. This is also called addiction.
   - **Withdrawal** symptoms from quitting can be physically, mentally, and emotionally hard to withstand.
   - **Overdose** often happens accidentally because it depends on the amount of drug ingested, the purity of the drug, and how it interacts with the body. The more you know about a drug (where it comes from, what else is in it, the concentration of the drug, etc.) and how it interacts with your body, the less likely you are to accidentally overdose and the safer you will be. (For more information, see activity 4 of this module).

Activity 2 $\boxed{2}$ $\boxed{3}$

Instructions

1. Place students into groups of 3 to 4. Give each group a copy of **Harm Reduction Small Group Scenarios**.

2. Ask students to work through each scenario and record their discussions.

3. Have each group present their answers to the class.

4. Conclude the activity by using the **Educator Answer Key—Harm Reduction Small Group Scenarios** to fill in any blanks from the student presentations.

QUICK TIP

For level 1, students can turn over all the cards at once and work collaboratively to pair up the terms. Another option is to match the terms and definitions as a class.

Activity 3 2 **3**

Instructions

1. Remind students of the definition of **dependence:** when someone has trouble cutting down their substance use even if they want to or when a person feels like they need a substance to function regularly or feel normal. It is sometimes referred to as addiction.

2. Students can work individually or in small groups. Give each group/ student a copy of the **Safer Digital Use** handout to complete.

3. Discuss answers as a class using the **Educator Answer Key—Safer Digital Media Use.**

Activity 4 2 **3**

Instructions

1. Explain that just as we can plan important parts of our life (like educational and career goals or physical fitness), we can come up with a plan to stay safe if experimenting with substances such as drugs and alcohol. Creating a plan can help to understand the risks and how to minimize harm if choosing to take those risks.

2. Give students copies of the **My Substance Safety Plan.** Tell them not to put their names on the handouts and to keep their paper private. Emphasize that they do not have to be using drugs or alcohol to fill this out.

3. Give students a few minutes to work on their plans, then discuss the following question: Under which circumstances might a substance use safety plan be helpful?

4. Debrief by ensuring students know that preventing accidental overdose is easier the more you plan in advance and the more you know about a substance you ingest. *It is easier to prevent accidental overdose of substances that are legal and regulated by the government (like alcohol) than it is with substances that are illegal and with less information and/or misinformation. Make sure students have the resources they need (for more information, see 7.8 resources).*

5. Optional: Ask students to write their substance use questions onto anonymous pieces of paper and place them in a closed box near your desk. Review the questions and provide answers as appropriate (for more information on the Question Box activity, see activity 3 in module 4.3).

Wrap-up

Summarize the module with the following points:

- Substance use and addiction follow certain patterns (use, tolerance, dependence, withdrawal).
- Harm reduction is an approach that helps reduce the harms caused by substance use. Harms can include social, physical, and financial. Harm reduction offers choice and safer ways to continue to use a substance; choice includes abstinence.
- Evaluating pros and cons and making a substance use safety plan can help in deciding what to do going forward while reducing associated harms.

CHAPTER 8

Sexual Violence, Rape Culture, and Consent

8.1 INTRODUCTION:

Sexual violence refers to behaviours that exist on a continuum and are experienced as violence. The continuum of sexual violence includes normalized behaviours and criminalized behaviours (that are socially recognized as violence). The behaviours that are normalized are not legally defined or enforced, even though the impact is still experienced as violence. What is most helpful to students are the knowledge and skills to practise consent and recognize sexual violence, the empowered permission to end sexual violence, and support in disclosing and seeking help. It is also important that students know where to access sexual assault crisis lines. For a comprehensive list, see the **National Support Services** resource.

SEXUAL VIOLENCE
(for more information on trigger warnings, see modules 1.3 and 1.6)

Sexual violence occurs for many different reasons and in many different forms; it can happen between anyone. Shame and stigma surrounding sexuality, significant power differences between people, and habits of being manipulative or aggressive in relationships are some factors that make sexual violence more likely. Discussing sexual violence is an opportunity to debunk myths, clarify rights, and help students avoid coercive behaviours and develop resilience and resistance against them.

Interpersonal power difference as well as larger social power differences affect our risk for sexual harm. People who have less social power are more likely to be sexually violated. People with more social power or who are in positions of authority are more likely to be the perpetrators of sexual violence. Sexual violence is not about sexual desire; it is about the abuse of power.

Systemic power and oppression have a direct influence on the ways individuals experience health, risk, and social identity. It is important to make the connections between systemic forces and the ways that health and risk are experienced individually. For instance, it can be empowering to know that risk of sexual assault has nothing to do with anything you do or do not do, that risk is determined by systemic oppression such as sexism and transphobia. It is equally important that as educators, you do not assume that because someone belongs to a social identity, they will automatically fall into the category of "victim" or "perpetrator." Educators can take a leadership role in ensuring that everyone, regardless of social identity, is empowered to prevent and end sexual violence. Anyone could be a perpetrator, a "victim," and/or a bystander of sexual violence. Empowering bystanders to take action to stop sexual violence is one tangible way that educators can take a leadership role in preventing sexual violence.

In 2011, over 21,800 sexual assaults were reported (Brennan, 2012), a number representing only about 10% of sexual assaults that actually took place (roughly 90% of sexual assaults go unreported) (CWHN, 2013). Most of the data on sexual assault indicates that cisgender girls/women are at the highest risk but cisgender boys/men also experience sexual assault. Although freedom from sexual violence is a human right, it is estimated that one in three women and one in six men in Canada will experience sexual violence in their lifetime (StatCan, 2006). Trans and gender non-binary people are often lumped into national data with cisgender people making it challenging to determine how many trans and gender non-binary people are sexually assaulted but research from Ontario suggests that 20% of trans people have experienced physical and sexual violence because of transphobia (Bauer & Scheim, 2015). Research from the United States estimates that transgender individuals are 21 times more likely to be sexually assaulted than cisgender men and 5 times more likely than cisgender women (Grant et al, 2011).

In 80% of sexual assault cases, a person knows the perpetrator (Canadian Women's Foundation, 2016). It is therefore important to challenge the myth that sexual violence only happens in dark alleys or secluded parks, or that aggressors are strangers. In truth, they are often partners, ex-partners, dates, friends, or family members.

The term **rape culture** refers to the social environment in which sexual violence is prevalent and goes unpunished. Rape culture describes how dominant ideas, gender norms and stereotypes, the media, and social institutions all normalize, trivialize, and eroticize sexual violence, especially male violence against women and other forms of **gender-based violence**. **Misogyny, sexism,** and other forms of systemic oppression all feed into and support rape culture in different but intersecting ways.

Victim blaming and **slut shaming** are both manifestations of and tools that support rape culture. Victim blaming assumes that rape is inevitable and natural and faults "victims" for putting themselves in harm's way. Victim blaming also places the blame on "victims" in gendered ways, often in the form of **slut shaming**. For instance, a cisgender girl/woman may be blamed for an assault because of the clothes she wears and whether or not she flirted. A transgender girl/woman may also be blamed for an assault because of the clothes she wears and whether or not she flirted but for a trans girl/woman, transphobia might be further used to justify the violence. People who dress and/or behave in gender non-conforming ways (regardless of their gender identity) may be blamed because they "needed to be taught a lesson" based on their non-conformity. Victim blaming also obscures, enables, and encourages the behaviours of perpetrators in gendered ways. For instance, a boy or man may be excused for the assault because aggression and dominance are integral to upholding gender norms of masculinity.

The justice system is a social institution that is heavily influenced by rape culture and perpetuates rape culture by victim blaming during sexual assault trials. The behaviour of survivors leading up to and after the assault is often challenged and the behaviour of perpetrators excused. In order for sexual violence prevention to work, rape culture needs to be challenged so that perpetrators are held accountable, instead of victims being blamed.

One way to challenge rape culture is through **consent culture.** Consent culture is a resistance movement to rape culture. It strives to create a culture where consent is never assumed. In its most basic form, **consent** is something that is asked for and then given fully and freely without coercion or manipulation. Consent is something that has legal definitions and implications but it is also something that has social meaning and nuance (for introductory information about the legal definition of consent and implications in the Canadian context, see 8.1 resources). In terms of the social meaning of consent, it is something that we practise everyday—we practise asking, refusing, giving, and receiving in a variety of contexts in ways that are sometimes even unconscious.

Consent in the context of sexuality is necessary whenever engaging with another person but can be difficult to navigate without the necessary skills. Everybody is responsible for learning the skills necessary to navigate and communicate consent before any physical and/or sexual contact. As sexuality educators, it is your responsibility to teach these skills. Access to comprehensive sexuality education in every school ensures that young people are being taught and learning how to practise consent.

Consent culture is a way of challenging the continuum of sexual violence. It is about teaching consent from an early age. It is about making clear that consent to anything involving your body is consistent with your right to bodily autonomy (no matter your gender identity). It is about teaching that consent is not only the absence of a "no" but requires an enthusiastic "yes." Consent is active and clear verbal and physical communication. It is communication throughout physical, sexual, and intimate contact that needs to be asked for every time you engage in sexual activity, even if you have engaged in that particular sexual activity before. Consent can also change throughout sexual activity; even if you consented to something, you can change your mind and withdraw your consent. Consent for one kind of sexual activity does not mean consent for other sexual activity. Consent cannot be obtained if someone is asleep, intoxicated, or otherwise unable to clearly communicate (for more information, see modules 8.3 and 8.4).

Educator Reflection Questions

- Before reading this module, who did you assume were perpetrators of sexual violence and who did you assume were at risk? Have your assumptions changed? Why or why not?
- In what ways have you seen and/or experienced rape culture?
- Has there ever been a time where you challenged someone's ideas about sexual violence?
- In what ways have gender norms and/or stereotypes influenced how you experience rape culture? (E.g., do you feel you would be blamed if you were sexually assaulted because of your gender identity? Or do you feel you would be protected if you committed a sexual assault because of your gender identity?).

- What does consent look like to you? Has your understanding of consent changed over time? If so, how?
- Are you surprised by the idea that people could be blamed for being sexually assaulted because of their gender identity?
- Have you ever witnessed sexual violence as a bystander (could be anything from street harassment or sexual cyberbullying to a sexual assault)? If so, how did you respond? What skills do you wish you had in that moment to take action and respond? How would you respond differently now?
- What concerns about sexual violence and consent might be unique to the generation that your students are growing up in and what concerns might be similar to what you experienced growing up?

Big Ideas in Chapter 8

- To live free from sexual violence is a human right; yet, sexual violence is common in Canada.
- Sexual violence is not about sexual desire; it is about the abuse of power.
- Interpersonal power difference as well as larger social power differences affect our risk for sexual harm. People with more access to social power or who are in positions of authority are more likely to be the perpetrators of sexual violence. Social power cannot be separated from gender norms and stereotypes and systemic oppression.
- Sexual violence occurs for many different reasons and in many different forms. It can happen between anyone. In the majority of sexual violence cases, a person knows their perpetrator.
- The majority of sexual assault cases go unreported because of victim blaming and the associated shame and stigma.
- Consent can never be assumed. It is not the absence of "no," it is the enthusiastic and continuous verbal and physical communication of "yes."
- Rape culture describes the pervasiveness and normalization of gender-based sexual violence. Consent culture is part of the resistance to rape culture.
- Sexual violence exists on a continuum and encompasses a broad range of behaviours and impacts. Bystanders have a responsibility to intervene if they witness any form of sexual violence along the continuum.

8.2 SEXUAL VIOLENCE, GENDER NORMS, AND RAPE CULTURE

LEVEL 2 [3]

SEXUAL VIOLENCE *(for more information on trigger warnings, see modules 1.3 and 1.6)*

Big Ideas in Module 8.2

- Sexual violence encompasses a broad range of behaviours and impacts, including forms of violence that are not explicitly stated within Canada's *Criminal Code* and enforced by law.
- Sexual violence is not about sexual desire; it is about the abuse of power.
- Sexual violence is supported and reinforced by **systemic oppression** and **gender norms**.
- Rape culture describes the pervasiveness and normalization of sexual violence.
- Rape culture is informed by gender norms. The impacts of sexual violence disproportionately depend on gender identity and expression.

Learning Objectives

Students will:

- Understand the scope and prevalence of sexual violence.
- Articulate opinions on topics related to sexual violence.
- Critically examine myths around sexual violence.
- Be introduced to the concept of rape culture and ways to oppose it.
- Consider the complexities of systemic oppression, sexual violence, and gender norms in relationship to rape culture.

Cross-Curricular Connections

- Communication Studies
- Equity Studies
- Family Studies
- Gender Studies
- Law
- Media Studies
- Psychology
- Social Studies
- Sociology

Terminology

- Coercion
- Consent
- Gender norms
- Rape culture
- Sexism
- Sexual violence
- Survivor
- Systemic oppression

Materials

- Printed copies of the **Rape Culture Graphic** or a projector and screen to project the graphic
- Printed copies of the **Sexual Violence Continuum** or a projector and screen to project the graphic
- **Educator Answer Key—Sexual Violence Continuum**
- Three differently coloured paper clips (e.g., red, blue, and yellow) for each student
- Printed copies of **"Don't ~~Get~~ Raped!"** or a projector and screen to project the image
- Printed copies of **Resisting Rape Culture**
- Three large signs to post on walls: "AGREE," "DISAGREE," and "DEPENDS."
- Printed copies of **Is it Wrong?**
- **Educator Answer Key—Is it Wrong?**

Background Information for Educators

Sexual violence can happen between any two or more people. Sexual violence is not about sexual desire; it is about the abuse of power. It occurs for many different reasons and in many different forms; it can happen between anyone. Sexual violence refers to behaviours that exist on a continuum and are experienced as violence. The continuum of sexual violence includes behaviours that are often normalized within society and behaviours that are criminalized and socially recognized as violence. The behaviours that are normalized are not legally defined or enforced, even though the impact is still experienced as violence.

Not all violence is experienced equally. In the same way, the range of sexually violent behaviours should not be conflated as the same thing. It is important to explain the relationship between sexually violent and coercive behaviours in order to demonstrate how the normalization of behaviours contributes to the permissiveness and prevalence of other more extreme behaviours. Sexual violence does not exist inside a social vacuum; it is supported and reinforced by **systemic oppression** and **gender norms**. Seeing sexual violence as behaviours that exist on a continuum (supported and reinforced by systemic oppression and gender norms) helps bust the myth that sexual violence is only the most extreme, legally defined examples we see in the media. It helps to understand the variety of aggressive, violating, coercive, and harmful behaviours that all have a violent impact and do not exist in isolation of one another.

QUICK TIP

Any student may be a **survivor** and/ or witness of sexual violence. Discussions on this topic can be upsetting, overwhelming, or triggering. Acknowledge this at the beginning of every activity and allow students to take space if they need. Do your best to keep discussions focused, open, and respectful to everyone.

Sexually violent behaviours are all symptoms of and exist within **rape culture**. Rape culture refers to the assumption that sexual violence is normal and inevitable. This assumption is informed in part by **sexism** (and other forms of systemic oppression) and **gender norms** that position sexual violence as an acceptable extension of masculinity that is aggressive and entitled to sex and femininity that is passive and asking for sex. Rape culture cannot be separated from the very narrow rules and limited scripts gender norms prescribe to masculinity and femininity. These rules and scripts limit everyone from expressing and being their full selves.

In the context of rape culture, gender norms affect different gender identities and expressions in disproportionate ways. For instance, cisgender women are painted as passively "asking for it" because of what they wear or how friendly they are. Similarly, people who do not adhere to the gender binary (including trans and gender non-conforming people) are seen as "asking for it" because they do not conform to dominant expectations, unwritten rules, and assumptions of gender. For cisgender men, masculinity teaches them that in order to be "real men" they have to be aggressive and that it is acceptable to display this aggression in the form of sexual violence. They are also taught that it is unacceptable to be seen as weak, passive, and emotionally vulnerable, which makes it challenging to disclose sexual assault as survivors.

Rape culture, like gender norms, is a cultural phenomenon. It is as pervasive as it is invisible; what people think, feel, and do constitute and influence it. Developing critical analysis through knowledge sharing and reflection is an important step in increasing awareness, empowering action, and beginning to shift culture. Part of shifting culture means teaching consent to everyone at a very young age, instead of victim blaming and slut shaming. Critical awareness of the ways rape culture operates and permeates every facet of society can empower students to identify, stop, and heal from sexual violence.

The continuation of rape culture relies on **victim blaming**, **slut shaming**, the protection of perpetrators, and antiquated ideas of **consent**. Promoting **consent culture** is one way of actively challenging rape culture. Consent culture challenges victim blaming and actively opposes sexual violence across the full continuum. Consent culture is about teaching consent from an early age. It teaches that regardless of gender identity and other social identities, consenting to anything involving your body is consistent with your right to bodily autonomy.

Consent is something that is asked for and then given freely and fully without coercion. **Coercion** refers to the use of intimidation or manipulation to get someone to do something. Subtle forms of coercion include leveraging existing power imbalances and social and gender norms to get someone to do something they may not otherwise do, in order to fit in or avoid consequence. Consent is not only the absence of a "no." It is an enthusiastic and ongoing "yes." It is agreeing to physical, sexual, and intimate contact through verbal and physical communication that needs to be asked for every time you engage in sexual activity even if you have engaged in that particular sexual activity before. It also needs to be ongoing throughout sexual activity; if it is not ongoing, the sexual activity is no longer consensual. An example of this is "stealthing," removing a condom during sex without your partner's knowledge and consent. If partners communicate with each other about condom use and it is established that a condom will be used during sexual activity, removing the condom without consent means that the sexual activity is no longer consensual and no longer safe. Stealthing is a form of sexual violence and a violation of bodily autonomy (Brodsky, 2017).

Consent cannot be obtained if someone is asleep, intoxicated, or otherwise unable to clearly communicate.

Student Readiness

Before students engage with this lesson, ensure that safer space guidelines and group norms have been established (and revisited) within your classroom (for more information on how to establish safer space guidelines, see module 1.3). In order to effectively prepare for this activity, ensure students understand that:

- This module addresses sexual violence, rape culture, and consent.
- In this module, the term survivor refers to people who have survived sexual violence.
- All human beings have the right to bodily autonomy and to be free from sexual violence.
- Sexual violence is more common than most people realize; it is underreported and most often perpetrated by someone who is known to the survivor.
- If you experience sexual violence, it is never your fault.
- There are supports available to students who are survivors. *Ensure that you have identified these supports ahead of time. Before starting the activities, inform students what these supports are and where they can find them.*

Summary of Activities

Students will:

- Collectively discuss the scope, prevalence, and root causes of sexual violence.
- In small groups, visually depict sexual violence statistics and challenge myths about perpetrators.
- Work in small groups to discuss and then individually reflect on ways to challenge rape culture and promote consent culture.
- Work in small groups to critically analyze a news story about sexual violence and then rewrite the news story to promote consent culture.
- Individually articulate opinions and practise listening to one another on topics related to sexual violence by moving around the classroom.
- Collectively analyze and discuss how gender norms impact whether someone is convicted of sexual assault.

Activity 1 2 3

If you sense that it is not safe for students to speak honestly and openly about sexual consent in your class, make the exercise anonymous using the **Is it Wrong?** chart. Students fill the chart out anonymously, fold it, and return to you. Mix and redistribute the papers, one to each student. Then each student moves according to the answers on the paper they now have. (For more information on facilitating sensitive activities and disclosure, see module 1.6).

Instructions

1. Clear the space as much as possible. Post "AGREE" and "DISAGREE" signs on opposite walls and "DEPENDS" on the wall between them.
2. Read each statement found in **Is it Wrong?** and ask students to move to the part of the room that matches how they feel.
3. After students move to their chosen spot in the room for each statement, invite a few students to talk about their choice. Make space for opinions from different parts of the room and encourage different students to speak (without forcing anyone).
4. After giving students a chance to speak, read the corresponding educator prompts found in the **Educator Answer Key—Is it Wrong?**

QUICK TIP

If space is limited, or students have accessibility needs, students can remain in seats and show a thumbs-up for "AGREE," thumbs-down for "DISAGREE," and thumbs sideways for "DEPENDS."

Activity 2 [3]

Instructions
Part 1

1. Show the **Sexual Violence Continuum** to students (hand out copies to each student or project graphic onto screen). *This graphic is not meant to be exhaustive of every form or detail of sexual violence that exists. It is also not meant to create a hierarchy of experiences of sexual violence. It is meant to situate sexual violence along a continuum of experiences. While some forms of sexual violence are socially normalized and others are legally enforced, all sexually violent behaviours are related but not the same, and resulting in different impacts. Illustrating that behaviours are related (without conflating them) can help question why some forms of sexual violence are normalized and others are punished.*

2. Explain: Sexual violence refers to behaviours that exist on a continuum. The behaviours range from socially normalized to criminalized. Socially normalized behaviours are not legally defined or enforced, even though the impact is still experienced as violence.

3. Ask students to name sexually violent behaviours and place them on the **Sexual Violence Continuum**. For an example see **Educator Answer Key—Sexual Violence Continuum.**

4. Discuss the following:
   - What does it mean that sexually violent behaviours exist on a continuum?
   - Why is it important to show the relationship between behaviours that are normalized and ones that are legally defined?
   - Why is the context (i.e., background) of the continuum rape culture?
   - What kinds of sexual violence are most often portrayed in movies and television? (Ask students to indicate on the **Sexual Violence Continuum**) How does this portrayal influence your perception of what may be experienced as violence and what is not?
   - What do you think would happen if more people intervened in and challenged sexual violence that is normalized by society?

EDUCATOR ANSWER KEY

   - There is a wide array of behaviours that are sexually violent, not only behaviours that are legally defined and enforced. These behaviours are all about asserting power (not about sexual desire) and all exist within rape culture. Seeing sexual violence on a continuum helps bust the myth that sexual violence is only the most extreme examples that media tends to pick up on and that are legally enforced.

CONT'D NEXT PAGE

EDUCATOR ANSWER KEY CONT'D

- Placing sexual violence that is normalized on the same continuum as behaviours that are legally defined and seen as violent by society demonstrates that the more extreme forms of sexual violence are related to (but not the same as) the less extreme examples and that the less extreme examples are often invisible (as a problem) because the social reactions to them are normalized.
- The context of the continuum is rape culture because sexually violent behaviours exist within and are symptoms of rape culture. The normalization of sexual violence is an integral part of rape culture, which affects the ways that sexually violent behaviours are dealt with across the continuum. For instance, if someone is on the receiving end of hateful speech, humour might be used as a tool to normalize the behaviour, even though the behaviour is experienced as violence. On the other end of the continuum, if someone is charged with sexual assault, the reaction to the behaviour might be sentencing but the normalization of sexual violence will influence the legal, judicial proceedings in terms of how facts of the case are presented and perceived, which influences the severity and duration of a sentencing.
- Most sexual violence that is shown on television and in movies is graphic sexual assault. It is the kind of sexual assault that is more towards the legally defined side of the continuum. This reinforces the myth that sexual violence is always graphic, usually committed by "deranged strangers," and that there is always physical injury present afterward.
- If more people intervened and challenged socially normalized sexual violence, we might begin to stop more extreme forms of sexual violence from happening before they begin. In changing our reactions to/interrupting socially acceptable behaviour, we might also begin to change the ways that behaviour is experienced.

Part 2

1. Show the **Rape Culture Graphic** to students (hand out copies to each student or project graphic onto screen). Explain any terms that students may not understand using the terminology definitions.

2. Discuss the following:
   - Why is it important to show the interrelationship between sexual violence, systemic oppressions (e.g., racism, classism, homophobia, transphobia, ableism, etc.), and gender norms? Why do you think rape culture is on the outside of the graphic?
   - Why is systemic oppression part of the middle triangle?
   - Why do you think "power" is in the middle of the graphic?
   - Optional: Ask students to provide examples of cultural, institutional, and individual behaviours that are a part of rape culture.

EDUCATOR ANSWER KEY

- Sexual violence, systemic oppression, and gender norms are all expressions of power. They reinforce and uphold each other, which affects the outcome of cultural, institutional, and individual behaviours. The confluence of systemic oppression, gender norms, and sexual violence create the rape culture in which we live. Rape culture feeds back into these expressions of power, which helps to justify the cultural, institutional, and individual behaviours that impact people in harmful, violating, and violent ways.

- Systemic oppression interacts with sexual violence and gender norms in mutually reinforcing ways. Systemic oppression is one way to maintain power and control over a social group; sexual violence and gender norms are one of the tools that systemic oppression uses to maintain control and assert dominance. Various systemic oppressions do not work in isolation and instead influence the forms, severity, risk, and harms of sexual violence, as well as the ways gender norms impact people (e.g., masculinity norms impact black cisgender men in a different way than white cisgender men because of racism).

- Placing power in the middle illustrates that systemic oppressions, gender norms, and sexual violence are all expressions of power that are used to assert power and maintain dominance and control over groups of people. Rape culture is created by these expressions of power and is the context in which these expressions of power operate. It also helps illustrate that sexual violence is not about sex or about desire; it is an expression of the abuse of power.

- Examples include: victim blaming, slut shaming, rape "jokes," police not taking sexual assault seriously, especially if it happened between intimate partners, judges protecting perpetrators and giving them light sentences, online forums about "stealthing" (how to non-consensually remove a condom during sex without your partner finding out), normalizing sexual and gender-based violence, sexual violence in media, sexual cyberbullying and internet trolling, "cat calling" (street harassment) under the assumption that it is a form of flattery, etc.

Activity 3 ☐2☐ ☒3☒

Instructions

1. Before facilitating this activity, take note of the number of students in your class and divide that number by three. Put aside that number (1/3 of class) in paper clips from one colour (red) to be handed out to that many students. Ensure that 80% of the red paper clip students also receive a yellow paper clip. The remaining 2/3 of students (without any paper clips) will receive a blue paper clip. (E.g., if you have a total of 30 students in your class, 10 students will receive a red paper clip, 8 of those 10 will receive a yellow paper clip, and 20 students will receive a blue paper clip).

2. Ask all students to come to the front of the class and arrange themselves in a line. Ask them to close their eyes and extend one hand. Place the paper clips in each student's hand. Once they receive the paper clip(s), ask them to close their hand and open their eyes. Ask the students to take a moment to discreetly look at what colour paper clip(s) are in their hand.
3. Ask students with a red paperclip to silently take three steps forward.
4. Read the following statement aloud: It is estimated that one in three women/girls are sexually assaulted in their lifetime.

QUICK TIP

This visual activity can be modified and repeated to include statistics about men/boys. The statistic for men/boys is that one in six men/boys will be sexually assaulted in their lifetime. To know how many red paper clips to handout, divide the number of students in your class by six. The number of yellow paper clips will be 80% of the red paper clips.

5. Ask students with a yellow paper clip to take three more steps forward and read the following statement aloud: It is estimated that 80% of sexual assault survivors know the perpetrator.
6. Discuss: Did these statistics surprise you? Why or why not?

EDUCATOR ANSWER KEY

Allow students' answers to guide the discussion. Affirm that surprise is a common response because of the ways that sexual assault is portrayed and because of the fact that we often do not talk about the multiplicity of ways that sexual violence is experienced in real life even though we are exposed to lots of sexually violent content. Despite exposure to sexually violent content, shame, stigma, and fear of being blamed surround the topic and often prevent survivors from openly talking about their experience and/or reporting the violence.

7. Place students into small groups and provide the following information: Most people are sexually assaulted by an acquaintance, a family member, a spouse, a partner, a date, or a friend but we often talk about sexual assault as committed by strangers lurking in dark alleys or parks.

8. Have students discuss the following in small groups, record answers, and report back to the entire class: How do you think the myth about perpetrators as strangers affects all of us and what are some ways that we could challenge this myth?

EDUCATOR ANSWER KEY

The myth makes us less aware of what the risk of sexual violence looks like and how to best minimize it. It contributes to survivors feeling alone or blaming themselves. This myth often allows perpetrators to keep sexual violence hidden; it is harder to hold them accountable because they seem so "normal," "trustworthy," or "nice."

Activity 4 2 3
Instructions
Part 1
1. Hand out or project the **"Don't ~~Get~~ Raped!"** image onto a screen.
2. Collectively discuss: What message does this image convey?

EDUCATOR ANSWER KEY

This image conveys that the response to people disclosing and/or reporting sexual violence is often to blame the survivor of violence. This image challenges the common response by pointing out that it is perpetrators who are responsible for sexual assault and it is crucial that we stop blaming sexual assault on survivors and hold perpetrators accountable.

3. Define rape culture and victim blaming with the following: Victim blaming is the idea that if someone is sexually violated, it is their fault. Victim blaming is a part of a bigger set of ideas that make up rape culture. The "Don't ~~Get~~ Raped!" sign changes the rape culture message into one that opposes it. In rape culture, it is assumed that sexual violence is normal and inevitable. It perpetuates the idea that violence is sexy and that sexuality is violent. Rape culture includes jokes, television, music, and advertising that make light of sexual assault or conflate sex with sexual violence.
4. Introduce the idea of consent culture. Explain: One way to challenge rape culture is through consent culture. Consent culture is a resistance movement to rape culture. It strives to create a culture where consent is never assumed and always asked for.

5. Divide students into small groups and distribute a copy of **Resistance to Rape Culture** to each group. Explain that each of these actions resists rape culture and works towards a culture of consent. Ask each group to pick one statement that they think is easy to do and one that is challenging. *Assure students that choosing one action that is challenging does not mean that they are perpetrators or bad people. It indicates that we all live and are socialized within rape culture. To unlearn the assumptions, norms, and stereotypes within rape culture, we need to identify what is challenging to unlearn and then take steps to intentionally and actively unlearn.*

6. In their groups, have students discuss how they made their choice and then present their choices (and the reasons for their choices) to the entire class.

7. Ask students to individually reflect (privately) on situations in their own lives where they can choose between perpetuating rape culture or challenging it.

Part 2

This activity can be adapted to be video and drama based. Instead of written news stories/articles, each group can choose a video news clip from those curated ahead of time. Students then rewrite the news clip and perform/film it as if they were a news anchor reporting the story. This version of the activity may require students to complete as homework.

Instructions

1. Ahead of the activity, curate a series of written news stories, and/or magazine articles about a sexual violence case anywhere along the continuum.

2. Place students into small groups and give each group one news story/article.

3. Explain: Many people who have experienced sexual violence use the term "survivor" instead of "victim" because words matter. Survivor focuses on the person's strengths and resilience; victim focuses on something that happened to them. Survivor also implies that it takes hard work to survive sexual violence and not all people who have experienced sexual violence survive. Using the term survivor can help lessen the stigma and shame that is associated with experiencing sexual violence and helps shift the shame, stigma, and blame onto the perpetrators instead of the "victims." Some people find that using the term survivor feels empowering, whereas others may find it disempowering.

4. Ask students to critically consider and discuss the following questions in their groups:
   - What kind of language does the news story use? Do they refer to the survivor as a "survivor" or as a "victim"?

- How does the news story portray the survivor?
- How does the news story portray the accused?
- Does the news story individualize the experience of sexual violence or is it contextualized within a larger picture?
- If the news story involves the criminal justice system, is the news story critical and/or questioning of the way the case was handled by the criminal justice system?

5. Based on their discussions, ask each group to rewrite the news story in a way that presents the facts of the case in a way that challenges rape culture and promotes consent culture.

6. Have students present the rewritten news story to the entire class.

Activity 5 3

Instructions

Part 1

1. Share either the article, the study, or the findings below with students:
   - Article introducing 2002 study on rape: www.upworthy.com/whoa-4-questions-that-got-120-rapists-to-admit-they-were-rapists-5
   - 2002 Study on rape: www.innovations.harvard.edu/cache/documents/1348/134851.pdf
   - Findings related to rape: In 2002, 120 men denied they had ever committed sexual assault or rape. When the same men were asked four questions that fit within the legal definition of sexual assault, all of them admitted to at least one.

2. Share the 4 questions that were asked in the study:
   - Have you ever been in a situation where you tried, but for various reasons did not succeed, in having sexual intercourse with an adult by using or threatening to use physical force (twisting their arm, holding them down, etc.) if they did not cooperate?
   - Have you ever had sexual intercourse with someone, even though they did not want to, because they were too intoxicated (on alcohol or drugs) to resist your sexual advances (e.g., removing their clothes)?
   - Have you ever had sexual intercourse with an adult when they didn't want to because you used or threatened to use physical force (twisting their arm; holding them down, etc.) if they didn't cooperate?
   - Have you ever had oral sex with an adult when they didn't want to because you used or threatened to use physical force (twisting their arm; holding them down, etc.) if they didn't cooperate?

3. Explain: None of the men in the study were ever convicted of sexual assault.

4. Ask: Why do you think this is the case, even when every one of the acts they admitted to is punishable by law?

5. Place students into groups of 3 to 4 and ask them to prove how each one of these statements is against the law. Students must use at least 3 legal concepts from the following articles to argue their point:
   - Ontario Women's Justice Network. (2016). *Sexual Assault and Consent*. Retrieved from: http://www.owjn.org/2016/08/sexual-assault-and-consent/
   - SexAssault.ca. (n.d.) *Sexual Assault Criminal Process, Canada*. Retrieved from: http://www.sexassault.ca/criminalprocess.html

6. Discuss as a class:
   - Why do you think they denied committing sexual assault but then answered yes when asked these specific questions?
   - How could a lawyer/legal expert make the connections and build a case against them?
   - What gets in the way of justice for sexual assault survivors?

EDUCATOR ANSWER KEY

- Sexual assault is mistakenly thought of as only penis-vagina penetrative sex when in fact it refers to any kind of non-consensual sexual activity. Sexual assault also includes trying and "not succeeding" or not finishing the sexual activity. Often people do not think of rapists as being everyday people and they do not think of themselves as rapists. People do not think of themselves as rapists partly because they might believe that rapists are only rapists if they are convicted of rape. Perpetrators might also so firmly believe that they are not a rapist that they create a story of their victim enjoying it despite reluctance, that they only resisted because they needed to maintain an image of propriety, and/or that their victim secretly enjoyed rough sex. All of these myths/beliefs are created, held-up, and perpetuated by rape culture.

- A lawyer/legal expert could build a case against them by arguing that they have admitted to a state of mind and an action that constitutes assault under Canada's criminal code, namely that assault happens when:
  - Someone without the consent of another person applies force intentionally to that other person, directly or indirectly.
  - Someone attempts or threatens, by an act or a gesture, to apply force to another person.

- Rape culture gets in the way of justice for sexual assault survivors by normalizing sexual assault and blaming victims based on restrictive, sexist ideas of masculinity and femininity. Consent is assumed based on markers of femininity that rape culture has coded as "asking for it," including wearing revealing clothing and past sexual history. Sexual assault survivors often do not get justice because they are put in the position of trying to prove why they were not "asking for it" instead of the accused being asked about why they did it.

Part 2

1. Continue with the same small groups and distribute the following news articles to each group:
   - Hasham, A. and Donovan, K.(2016). *Jian Ghomeshi acquitted on basis of 'inconsistencies' and 'deception.'*
   - The Globe and Mail. (2017). *Ghomeshi acquitted: Read the verdict and catch up on what you missed.*
   - CBC News. (2016). *Jian Ghomeshi's trial's not guilty decision triggers outrage, march to police headquarters.*

2. Ask each group to read through the articles and identify 2 to 3 examples of gender norms that the Ghomeshi verdict used to reinforce rape culture and victim blaming.

EDUCATOR ANSWER KEY

Each of these articles discusses the ways that the judge in the ruling used the complainant's inconsistencies to question her credibility and ability to tell the full truth. What has been considered as inconsistencies in the case were linked to the complainant's sexuality through a "love letter," flirtation, and a photograph sent to the defendant by the complainant wearing a red bikini. In the case of the "love letter" and red bikini photograph, femininity was framed as something that is treacherous and purposefully manipulated to seduce the defendant. The result is that consent is framed as something that is assumed based on the ways that the complainant dressed and acted outside of the context of the reported assaults. A person's character and the ability to tell the truth becomes tied to their femininity and sexuality. The complainant's femininity and sexuality is on trial instead of the accused's masculinity. The Ghomeshi verdict shows how gender norms contribute to normalizing sexual violence and rape culture by focusing on the survivor's character and blaming the survivor for bringing it on herself and "consenting" by wearing provocative clothing, sharing the picture, flirting, and being "confused" about her feelings. This narrative positions consent as "asking for it" through performing femininity and sexuality in certain non-desirable ways, which leads to victim blaming, stigma, and the reinforcing of rape culture.

Wrap-up

Summarize the module with the following points:

- Sexual violence includes a range of behaviours, not all of which are legally defined or enforced.
- Sexual violence is connected to larger power dynamics, gender norms, and systemic oppression.
- Rape culture and victim blaming is commonplace; we all have a role in opposing it and promoting consent culture.
- Systemic oppression, gender norms, and sexual violence are integral parts of rape culture.
- Rape culture, systemic oppression, and sexual violence are pervasive and invisible.
- Like gender norms and stereotypes, rape culture hurts everyone by limiting who we are and what we can be.

8.3 COMMUNICATION AND CONSENT: GETTING AND GIVING IT

LEVEL ☐1 ☐2

{TW}

SEXUAL VIOLENCE
*(for more information
on trigger warnings,
see modules 1.3 and
1.6)*

Big Ideas in Module 8.3

- Consent relies on effective verbal and non-verbal communication. Consent is not only about asking for permission, it is also about listening to the answer.
- Consent is given and received comfortably in a variety of everyday contexts but there tends to be a discomfort in communicating about sexual consent. This is due to stigma, a lack of boundary-setting skills, gender norms, and unrealistic romantic and sexual relationship scripts.
- Consent needs to be clear. Consent is not only the absence of a "no," it is an enthusiastic "yes." If it is unclear, reluctantly given, and/or coerced, it is not consent.

Learning Objectives

Students will:

- Identify consent skills and knowledge they already have.
- Apply consent skills and knowledge to sexuality.
- Discern between coercive, manipulative behaviour and requests for consent, as well as between clear and unclear consent messages.

Cross-Curricular Connections

- Equity Studies
- Family Studies
- Gender Studies
- Psychology
- Social Studies
- Sociology

Terminology

- Coercion
- Consent
- Rape culture
- Stigma

Materials

- Open space for students to move around in
- Flip chart paper
- Markers
- Duct tape
- String or twine
- Chalkboard or whiteboard
- Printed copies of **Consensual and Non-Consensual Phrases**
- **Educator Answer Key—Consensual and Non-Consensual Phrases**

Background Information for Educators

*Any student may be a **survivor** and/or witness of sexual violence. Discussions on this topic can be upsetting, overwhelming, or triggering. Acknowledge this at the beginning of every activity and allow students to take space if they need. Do your best to keep discussions focused, open, and respectful to everyone.*

Communication is an essential part of getting and giving **consent**. No one is always bad at or always good at communication, it is a skill that is developed over time in a variety of contexts. Communication skills might be easier to develop in some contexts because they have become habit (e.g., asking to go to the washroom during class or asking your friends if they want to hang out over the weekend). In other contexts however, communication skills might be more challenging to develop because they are less practised, the context is stigmatized and taboo, and/or the relationship is socially nuanced (social nuance in a relationship includes not wanting to disappoint the other person, liking the other person, having a physical reaction to the other person that is contradictory to your emotional feelings about them, etc.). It is often the stigmatized and taboo situations where consent becomes even more important. It is these sexual and physically intimate situations that require extra attention and practise to develop habits around intentional, clear communication.

Consent is not only the absence of a "no." It is an enthusiastic and ongoing "yes." Consent is about paying attention to how a partner is feeling: asking open ended questions, listening, and respecting your partner's response. It is important to consider more than words because consent may be withheld in different ways. Sometimes saying no directly might feel uncomfortable. Sometimes it feels easier or safer to say "let's just cuddle" or "I want to go to sleep." Sometimes lack of consent may look like someone turning away, moving the other person's hands or stopping any participation in the activity. Some people may freeze if they feel threatened or uncomfortable. It is important to pay attention, silence or the absence of "no" should never be interpreted as a "yes."

We practise consent (asking, giving, receiving, and refusing) daily. What makes good sexual consent difficult is not necessarily a lack of understanding but the **stigma** and discomfort in talking about sexuality itself, a lack of boundary-setting skills (for more information, see module 7.3), gender norms, and unrealistic romantic and sexual relationship scripts. It is important for everyone to learn about sexual consent from a young age because knowing how to get and give consent is one of the most practical tools in preventing sexual assault and challenging **rape culture.**

Preventing sexual assault and challenging rape culture is everyone's responsibility.

Student Readiness

Before students engage with this lesson, ensure that safer space guidelines and group norms have been established (and revisited) within your classroom (for more information on how to establish safer space guidelines, see module 1.3). In order to effectively prepare for this activity, ensure students understand that:

- This module addresses sexual violence, consent, and coercion.
- All human beings have the right to bodily autonomy and to be free from experiencing sexual violence.
- If you experience sexual violence, it is never your fault.
- There are supports available to students who are survivors. *Ensure that you have identified these supports ahead of time. Before starting the activities, inform students what these supports are and where they can find them.*

Summary of Activities

Students will:

- Collectively discuss the components and nuances of consent.
- In large groups, act out everyday consent scenarios.
- In small groups, work towards finishing a challenging task as a team through communication.
- In small groups, match common phrases related to consent with appropriate titles to discern between coercive and consensual sexual scripts.

Activity 1 ☐1 ☐2

Instructions

1. Open the activity with the following discussion questions:
    - What does the word consent mean (in everyday non-sexual contexts)?
    - In what areas of life (other than sex) do we need permission to do something?
    - How does someone get consent in these situations?
    - How do we know when we have someone's consent in these situations?
    - ☐2 Optional: In what ways are these situations and practising sexual consent the same? In what ways are they different?

EDUCATOR ANSWER KEY

- Permission to do something, allowing something, being informed and then choosing to go ahead with a plan based on the information (e.g., a consultation with a doctor).
- Going on a field trip (permission form), borrowing someone's things, going onto private property, having surgery done, being in a movie or on television (signing a media release form).
- They provide a form to sign, they ask, they check with the owner, they talk about what the surgery involves and then choose whether or not to continue.
- The owner says "yes," they invite us, a form is signed, they understand what is involved and are given the space to ask questions then decide "yes" or "no."
- International human rights law lays out two different standards of consent that are applied in different contexts. Informed consent is applied to decision-making on medical procedures by learning the benefits, drawbacks and risks of something. This is different from the free and full consent that is necessary to engage in relationships and sexual activity with others. Free and full consent refers to consent that is free of violence and coercion; it is affirmative and about desiring to be involved in something. Free and full consent mirrors the kind of affirmative and enthusiastic consent around sexual activity that is talked about socially in Canada.

2. Make sure that there is an open, clear space for students to move around in. Divide the class into 3 large groups.
3. Provide each group with one of the following components of consent and ask each group to think about an everyday, non-sexual scenario to act out and present to the other groups:
   - Consent is not just the absence of "no." You cannot take something out of someone's bag just because they did not stop you. You cannot walk into someone's home just because they have not said "do not come in."
   - Consent has to be particular to the activity. It is not consensual if you ask to "see" someone's apple but then you bite into it. They handed it to you with the understanding that you would look and give it back. If your friend lends you their flute to play, you cannot use their flute as a baton/weapon.
   - Consent has to be active and expressed. You do not have consent to park your car if the attendant is asleep. You do not have consent to take someone's food if no one is looking.
4. After each group presents their scenario, the other groups have to try and guess what the scenario is and which component of consent it illustrates.

Activity 2 1️⃣ 2️⃣

Instructions

1. In preparation for the activity, make a station for groups of 4 to 6 students that consists of a table, flip chart paper, and a marker (cap removed) with 4 to 6 pieces of string taped onto it.
2. Place students into groups of 4 to 6 and assign them to a station.
3. Instruct each student to hold onto one piece of string with one hand.
4. Position the felt tip of the marker onto the piece of paper.
5. Once each student is holding onto a piece of string and the groups have their markers positioned, inform them that each group will have to communicate and work together to draw a five-pointed star.
6. ✛ Optional: Inform students that each group is a team and that the teams are racing each other to see who can complete the drawing first.
7. Once all the groups have completed the drawing and/or a winning team has been declared, facilitate a debrief with the students using the following prompts:
   - What kinds of communication did you notice happening within your groups/teams? Were there some types of communication that worked better than others?
   - What was the most and the least challenging aspect about completing this activity?
   - How would your communication have changed if you had to communicate with someone you had a crush on and/or someone you were rejected by?
   - How would your communication have changed if you had to communicate about something that was taboo/stigmatized?

EDUCATOR ANSWER KEY

Let the students' experiences of the activity lead the debrief. You can help guide the discussion by highlighting that communication worked best when everyone was listening as well as talking and then acting based on what was communicated. There are sometimes social dynamics and nuance in relationships that make communication more challenging, including if you have a crush on someone, have been rejected by someone, or are communicating about sex and sexuality. This activity provides a basic lesson in communication. It is important to develop these basic skills so that when faced with social/relationship dynamics that are challenging and/or topics that are taboo/stigmatized (like sex and sexuality), communication can happen with more ease.

Activity 3 [2]

Instructions

1. Read the following statement:

    The Criminal Code of Canada defines consent as voluntary agreement to a sexual activity. This agreement has to be clearly, fully, and freely expressed by words and/or actions. There is no consent if someone is not capable of consenting. This includes if they are drunk, drugged, asleep, or unconscious. No one can give consent on behalf of another person. If someone agrees to a sexual activity and then does not want to continue, there is no longer consent. You do not have consent to continue.

2. Post the following titles on the wall or write them on the chalkboard. Explain that the first column asks about the process of consent and the second assesses whether consent was given.

Is there a request for consent?			Is consent given?		
Yes: Seeking consent	Unsure/ Subtly coercive	No: Not seeking consent and coercive	Yes: Enthusiastic consent	Unsure/ Unclear consent	No consent

3. Place students into groups of 3 to 4.
4. Print and cut out the phrases from **Consensual and Non-Consensual Phrases**. Distribute a few phrases to each small group and ask them to consider where each phrase belongs. Each group posts their phrases under the appropriate title.
5. Collectively discuss the phrases that are challenging to place and why. Discuss:
    *   Coercion comes in many forms, it can be forceful/violent AND softly spoken.
    *   Coercion looks like manipulative, pestering, and/or threatening behaviours. Coercion can also look like using social power and norms to your advantage and/or to get what you want.
    *   Many common sexual, romantic, and relationship scripts are actually coercive. If coercion is present, there is no consent. If you are unsure about whether or not the request for consent is coercive and/or if consent is unclear, you do not have consent. Consent must be freely and fully given, it must be enthusiastic. *Use the points in step 6 to help students distinguish between coercion and consent.*

6. Lead the discussion using the **Educator Answer Key—Consensual and Non-Consensual Phrases.** You can also use the following three points to help guide the analysis:
   - Consent is not just the absence of "no."
   - Consent has to be particular to the activity.
   - Consent has to be active and expressed.
7. Look at the phrases under "Yes: Seeking consent" and "Yes: Enthusiastic Consent." Ask: What does it take to ask for consent this directly? What does it take to give or refuse consent this directly?

EDUCATOR ANSWER KEY

Trust, communication skills, feeling safe, confidence, knowing what to say, a sense of care for the other person.

Wrap-up

Summarize the module with the following points:
- We already know and use consent skills every day. Sexual consent requires similar skills.
- Communication skills are a necessary component of consent.
- Consent is a skill set that we can practise. Practising consent also requires confidence, feeling safe, communication, care for the other person, and trust.
- Consent needs to be clear. Consent that is unclear, reluctantly given, and/or coerced is not consent.
- Coercion comes in many forms. No matter how subtle or overt, coercion is not consent.

8.4 POWER AND CONSENT: YES, NO, AND EVERYTHING IN BETWEEN

LEVEL 2 3

SEXUAL VIOLENCE
(for more information on trigger warnings, see modules 1.3 and 1.6)

Big Ideas in Module 8.4

- Consent relies on effective verbal and non-verbal communication. Consent is not only about asking for permission, it is also about listening to the answer.
- Consent needs to be clear. Consent is not only the absence of a "no." It is an enthusiastic "yes." If it is unclear, reluctantly given, and/or coerced, it is not consent.
- No one can make assumptions about what someone wants to do sexually, the only way to know for sure is to ask and pay attention to whether an affirmative answer is given. If there is any doubt, assume that you do not have consent.
- Practising consent is about communication and requires paying attention to power differences. The line between consent and coercion becomes less clear when there are power differences between the people involved.

Learning Objectives

Students will:

- Explore the challenges of saying "no" as well as saying "yes" in a sexual context.
- Identify the challenges that are based on skills and ones anchored in social expectations and power differences (e.g., gender, age, economic power, etc.).
- Strategize ways to overcome the challenges of practising consent.
- Examine the dynamics and nuance of sexual assault through story.
- Strategize how to prevent sexual assault and support those involved.

Cross-Curricular Connections

- Equity Studies
- Family Studies
- Gender Studies
- Psychology
- Social Studies
- Sociology

Terminology

- Coercion
- Consent
- Sex positive
- Survivor

Materials
- Large pieces of paper
- Markers
- Printed copies of **Terri's Story**
- Printed copies of **Zach's Story**
- Printed copies of **Survivor Effects**

Background Information for Educators

*Any student may be a **survivor** and/or witness of sexual violence. Discussions on this topic can be upsetting, overwhelming, or triggering. Acknowledge this at the beginning of every activity and allow students to take space if they need. Do your best to keep discussions focused, open, and respectful to everyone.*

A decade ago, sexual **consent** was assumed on the absence of a "no." Today, sexual consent goes beyond a lack of disagreement, it includes voluntary agreement. Consent is therefore not only the absence of a "no," it is also an enthusiastic "yes." This is an important change in popular thought because refusals in everyday life, including in sex, can be nuanced and subtle (for more information, see module 8.3). This change leaves more room for consent to be taught from a **sex positive** perspective where young people are empowered to discover, make decisions, and communicate about what they want in sexual relationships, not only what they do not want. Teaching consent from a sex positive perspective empowers young people to avoid unwanted sexual experiences and **coercion** and to make informed decisions about their bodies and be clear about wanted experiences. Sexuality education can promote a culture where we respect all forms of "no" and enjoy all forms "yes."

Consent is something that is necessary when engaging in any kind of sexual activity. Consent requires communication as well as power analysis. Power (systemic and individual) influences the context of sexual relationships and can obscure the lines between coercion and consent. There are some situations where the line between coercion and consent is clear and has legal consequences (e.g., if the sexual relationship is between an adult and a child or a teacher and a student) (for more information see, module 8.1 and 8.2). The line becomes less clear when the difference in power is not illegal but still meaningful in terms of the ways that it influences social interactions. It is important for students to develop the skills to analyze what is influencing a decision about sexual activity and to become empowered to clearly and firmly say no and to enthusiastically say yes.

Acquaintance sexual assault is the most common form of sexual assault, whether it takes place among youth or adults. In some cases, there is deliberate and intentional predation leading to sexual assault (e.g., drugging someone's drink and assaulting them). In other cases, miscommunication and preconceived notions about sex lead to unwanted, non-consensual sexual activity (sexual assault). In both of these scenarios, the outcome is the same: sexual assault. "Yes" and "no" are more nuanced when put into the context of real life. It is important to develop clear and assertive community skills to practise consent.

Student Readiness

Before students engage with this lesson, ensure that safer space guidelines and group norms have been established (and revisited) within your classroom (for more information on how to establish safer space guidelines, see module 1.3). In order to effectively prepare for this activity, ensure students understand that:

- This module addresses power, sexual violence, consent, and coercion.
- Activity 2 presents a fictional story about sexual assault. The details of the story, although fictional, are based on common sexual assault stories that happen between acquaintances in the context of dating and relationship scripts.
- All human beings have the right to bodily autonomy and to be free from experiencing sexual violence.
- If you experience sexual violence, it is never your fault.
- There are supports available to students who are survivors. *Ensure that you have identified these supports ahead of time. Before starting the activities, inform students what these supports are and where they can find them.*

Summary of Activities

Students will:

- Work in small groups to list reasons why saying "no" or saying "yes" in a sexual context can be challenging. Continue working in these small groups to categorize the challenge as either a lack of skill/knowledge or a social power imbalance.
- Work in small groups to analyze one side of a fictional story about sexual assault, then collectively discuss the differences in perspectives about the event and the ways that social power informs the way the event unfolded and the potential impacts to each character.

Activity 1 2 ☐3☐

Instructions

Part 1

1. Explain: Consent is the absence of disagreement ("no means no") AND the presence of voluntary agreement ("yes means yes"). Remember that saying yes is not limited to responding to someone else's question. It can include proposing activities and asking for consent. For example, questions like "do you want to kiss me?" or statements like "I would like to be kissed by you."

2. Place the students into small groups of 3 to 4. Provide each group with a large piece of paper and markers to take notes.

3. Give half the groups the question: In a sexual situation, why might it be challenging to say NO when you want to? Give the other half of the groups the question: In a sexual situation, why might it be challenging to say YES when you want to? Remind the YES group that saying "yes" includes giving consent as well as asking for consent.

4. Ask all groups to present. Have the "NO" groups go first.

5. After all groups have presented, discuss and validate the challenges students identified using the Educator Answer Keys. Add to their lists if anything is missing. Draw students' attention to reasons that appear in both answer keys.

EDUCATOR ANSWER KEY—NO GROUPS

In a sexual situation, it might be challenging to say NO when you want to because of...

Fear of violence	Not knowing how/what to say
Guilt	Pressure or threat
Fear of rejection	Feeling bad rejecting someone
Fear of speaking up	**Feeling confused, unsure what you want**
Not knowing this is an option	Feeling obliged or like you "have to"
Not wanting to cause a scene	**Fear of getting a bad reputation**
Feeling unsafe	Not wanting to lose the relationship
Feeling triggered from the past	**Pressure surrounding gender norms**
Feeling shy or embarrassed	Feeling frozen or overwhelmed
Having never said no before	Fear that saying no to one thing would stop everything
Being unsure of what you want	
Liking the other person	

CONT'D NEXT PAGE

EDUCATOR ANSWER KEY—YES GROUPS CONT'D

In a sexual situation, it might be challenging to say YES when you want to because of…

Fear of violence
Feeling bad or dirty
Fear of rejection
Not knowing you can ask
Feeling unsafe
Feeling shy or embarrassed
Having never said yes before
Being unsure of what you want

Not knowing how/what to say
Fear of being foolish/being ridiculed
Feeling confused, unsure what you want
Fear of getting a bad reputation
Pressure around gender norms
Fear of being labelled as overly sexual, desperate, or easy
Fear that initiating something might stop everything else

6. Ask: Did any reasons surprise you when you realized that they were in both the YES and NO groups? If so, why were you surprised?
7. ✚ Optional: In personal notebooks, ask students to individually reflect and write down some ways that you can challenge yourself to better communicate (actively asking and actively listening) in sexual situations? What might get in the way of your ability to communicate?

Part 2
1. Consider the lists made in Part 1. Have students pick out a few that relate to a lack of skill or knowledge.
2. Ask: How can you develop sexual consent communication skills and knowledge?

EDUCATOR ANSWER KEY

Challenges: Skills and knowledge	Sample strategies
Not knowing how/what to say	Talking about it with friends, family, at school
Not knowing you can ask	Watching videos and reading blogs about consent
Not knowing you can say yes/no	Practising in low-stress, non-sexual situations
Not have said it before	Talking to partner(s) about it
Being unsure of what you want	Talking about sex when you are not being sexual
Feeling shy or embarrassed	Using movies or blogs as conversation starters

3. Consider the lists made in Part 1. Ask the class to pick out a few examples that relate to power differences and social expectations.

EDUCATOR ANSWER KEY

Fear of violence, feeling unsafe/threatened, fear of being labelled, fear of bad reputation, pressure of gender norms, feeling bad rejecting someone, not knowing you could say yes/no.

4. Ask students what kinds of situations create power differences that make it harder to practise consent.

EDUCATOR ANSWER KEY

Any kind of systemic oppression such as sexism, transphobia, homophobia, racism, classism, and/or ableism make it more challenging and complicated to practise consent. More specifically, gender norms and the relationship, romantic, and sexual scripts that are based on restrictive gender norms, stereotypes and the gender binary (for more information, see modules 3.4, 3.5, 3.6, 3.7, 3.8, and 8.2); economic power, especially when one person relies on the other for economic security and/or housing; age differences; physical size and strength; social isolation; and difference in access to social power/capital.

5. Affirm that power differences are real and effectively challenging them needs to be strategic and conscious. The first step is to notice them. Ask students to strategize how to work with unavoidable power differences.

EDUCATOR ANSWER KEY

Avoid gender stereotyping your partner and yourself; be vigilant about not stepping into relationship, romantic, and sexual scripts that are based on restrictive gender norms; stay connected to others that you enjoy spending time with; have multiple sources of support while in a relationship.

Activity 2 ☐2 ☐3

Instructions

1. Explain that even though explicit sexual consent is possible and necessary, many people communicate about consent in unclear and indirect ways. Especially when they are feeling shy, embarrassed, unsure, nervous, or if they are not experienced with consent skills.

2. Remind the class of the definition of consent in the context of sex: Consent means voluntary agreement to a sexual activity. This agreement can be expressed by words or actions. There is no consent if someone is not capable of consenting. For example, if they are drunk, drugged, asleep, or unconscious.

3. Preface the exercise by saying that sexual non-consent can happen between any two people (any assigned sex, gender identity, age, length of relationship, sexual orientation etc.). Let students know that they will be reading a story about two people who happen to be a young cisgender woman and a young cisgender man.

4. Divide the class into groups of 3 to 5 students. Distribute **Terri's Story** to half of the groups and **Zach's Story** to the other half. Ask one person from each group to read it out loud to their group.

5. Post the following questions on the board for students to discuss within their groups:
   - What does the main character think happened?
   - How does the main character feel about what happened and why?
   - What does the main character think should happen now?
   - What kinds of social power are at play in this story and must be taken into consideration?

6. After the groups have finished discussing the questions, lead a large group discussion based on the Educator Answer Key. Invite students to share both Terri and Zach's sides of the story.

EDUCATOR ANSWER KEY

A.

Terri: Some may think she was sexually assaulted, some may be unsure.

Zach: Some may say he thought they had sex, some may think that he sexually assaulted her, some may be unsure.

CONT'D NEXT PAGE

EDUCATOR ANSWER KEY CONT'D

B.

Terri: Possibly upset, angry, confused, vulnerable, taken advantage of, ashamed, hurt.

Zach: Possibly good, some doubt, unsure, confused, hopeful, shocked.

C.

- They should talk about it
- They should get support
- They should consider the risk of pregnancy and whether it is possible
- They should consider the risk of sexually transmitted infections and where they can get tested

D.

Terri: Might be feeling like she will not be believed and/or that she will be blamed if she reports the sexual assault because she is a young woman who was wearing revealing clothing and was drinking. She may also be feeling that if she tells people what happened, she will be called "easy" or a "slut."

Zach: Might be feeling like the police will take his side if he tells them his truth because in the movies and on television, sexual assault is committed by older, strange, evil men, it also looks violent, bloody, and physically dangerous, all things that he is not, nor is he capable of doing.

7. Read both stories out loud and tell students to look for the differences in perspectives on what happened. On the board, brainstorm differences as a class under the headings "Terri" and "Zach."

EDUCATOR ANSWER KEY

Terri:

- Thought that it was a date from the beginning.
- Borrowed her friend's party clothes because she was going to a party and wanted to look nice.
- Did not mean to get drunk but had not eaten and the beer affected her more than she thought.
- Got uncomfortable because people were watching them kiss on the dance floor and fell deeper into Zach's arms from feeling unsteady on her feet.
- Needed to go to the washroom and just wanted to lie down and rest.

CONT'D NEXT PAGE

EDUCATOR ANSWER KEY CONT'D

- Wanted to kiss some more and thought that Zach locked the door because there were coats in the room that people might want to get (locking the door would ensure that they would knock first).
- Was shocked when Zach put his hand under her skirt.
- Tried to push him away but could not because he was stronger.
- Loved kissing and wanted to sit down on the bed because of dizziness.

Zach:

- Did not necessarily think that it was a date from the beginning.
- Thought that Terri's clothing was hot and a signal that she wanted to dance with him.
- Thought that Terri was really thirsty.
- Thought that Terri snuggled into him.
- Thought that Terri wanted privacy.
- Interpreted Terri falling into him as wanting to lay down on the bed and being really into it.
- Thought that Terri was shy about wanting to be touched under her skirt.
- Thought that Terri was play wrestling with him, which got him more excited.

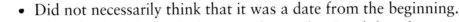

8. Read to the class: The next day, Terri was very upset, stayed in her room, and could not stop crying. After her Mom left for work, her older sister kept asking her what was wrong. Finally, Terri told her what had happened. She blamed herself and begged her sister not to tell, especially because she had lied about where she was going that night and that she had been drinking. Her sister insisted on calling their Mom at work. They took Terri to a sexual assault care centre. Because of her age, the police were called. They gave her Emergency Contraceptive Pills and offered her antibiotics in case of an STI. She was told she needed to come back for STI testing in a week and to come back for an HIV test in three months. They set her up with a counsellor and offered her a "rape-kit." The police interviewed her and she ended up giving them Zach's name. When the police came to Zach's door, he was surprised to hear they were investigating a sexual assault.

YOU SHOULD KNOW

A person who is offered a "rape kit" after a sexual assault should never feel pressured to get one. It is entirely that person's choice. A "rape kit" is more accurately a forensic exam and while it can determine if sexual activity occurred, it cannot determine whether or not the sexual activity was consensual. The exam is intensive and invasive, must happen soon after an assault, and can be re-traumatizing. While a "rape kit" might be used as evidence if a case goes to court, the exam is often not evidence enough to lead to conviction.

9. Ask the class how Terri might have blamed herself. Remind students that it is part of rape culture that survivors often blame themselves.

EDUCATOR ANSWER KEY

Terri might be thinking: I should not have gone to the party; I should not have worn those clothes; I should not have had those drinks; I should not have danced so close; I should not have gone into the room; I should not have let him kiss me.

10. Ask the class why Zach would have been surprised to see the police at his door.

EDUCATOR ANSWER KEY

Zach was confused by Terri's reaction but did not think he had done anything wrong.

11. Ask: Objectively, can you determine what happened and what the impact on both characters will be, considering the social power in this situation?

EDUCATOR ANSWER KEY

Terri was sexually assaulted by Zach. Terri could be impacted in multiple ways for many years to come (for more information, see **Survivor Effects**). While Zach will also be impacted in terms of possible charges, Zach needs to be held responsible for his actions. From a restorative perspective, the best way to do this might be for him to learn about what the impact of his actions are and for him to take responsibility for the harm that his actions caused. Part of taking responsibility is learning how to practise consent and then actively practising consent as he moves forward in his life. The long term emotional, social, mental, and physical well-being of Terri (the survivor) needs to be central because more often than not, the judicial system and rape culture favour the word and well-being of the accused. Due to the ways that sexism, misogyny, gender norms, and stereotypes inform rape culture, women who are sexual assault survivors are put on trial for their behaviours, actions, and clothing choices leading up to and including the assault as opposed to the actions of the men who have committed the assault. (For more information, see the Stanford Rape Case in 8.4 resources).

12. Ask: How could this situation have been prevented and what could Zach have done differently at every stage of their interaction?

EDUCATOR ANSWER KEY

If sexual consent skills were taught and challenging rape culture, systemic oppression, and gender norms were a part of their education from a young age, this situation could have been prevented before it started. General ways that this situation could have been prevented include:

- Not initiating sexual activity with someone who is intoxicated (and making sure they get home safely).
- Clearly and actively asking the other person what they want and do not want sexually before and during sexual activity. Checking in throughout sexual activity is key to practising consent!
- Paying attention to all types of communication, including body language. If you are unsure about something that is being communicated, ask.
- Respecting a person's "no" right away, regardless of how it is expressed.

CONT'D NEXT PAGE

EDUCATOR ANSWER KEY CONT'D

Ways that the situation could have been prevented by Zach at every stage of their intervention include:

- Asking Terri what she expected and if she thought it was a date.
- Asking Terri if she wanted to dance with him.
- Asking Terri if she wanted water since she seemed really thirsty.
- Asking Terri if she wanted help since she looked a bit unsteady on her feet.
- Asking Terri if she wanted him to find the friend she came with and/or to call someone she trusted to come and pick her up.
- Asking Terri if she wanted to go home.
- Asking Terri if she wanted to lay down by herself in a quiet room since she looked out of it and unsteady.
- Asking Terri if she wanted to be touched (before touching her) and if her communication was unclear, stopping.
- Asking Terri if she wanted to have sex (before having sex) and if her communication was unclear, stopping.

Wrap-up

Summarize the module with the following points:

- True consent is the absence of "no" and the presence of "yes."
- "Yes means yes" refers to giving consent as well as asking for consent.
- Consent is a skill you can develop. There are strategies to overcome the challenges of practising consent both related and unrelated to sexuality.
- Power differences can make it harder to identify the line between consent and coercion. Being aware of power differences and having support systems can help.

8.5 INTERVENING IN SEXUAL VIOLENCE AS EMPOWERED BYSTANDERS

LEVEL [1] [2] [3]

SEXUAL VIOLENCE
(for more information on trigger warnings, see modules 1.3 and 1.6)

Big Ideas in Module 8.5

- Sexual violence exists on a continuum and encompasses a broad range of behaviours. Empowered bystander action can have a big impact in stopping and challenging sexual violence anywhere on the continuum.
- Sexual violence is not about sexual desire; it is about the abuse of power.
- All bystanders have a responsibility to intervene if they witness sexual violence. Those with more access to power have an opportunity to challenge rape culture by shifting the way sexually violent behaviours are normalized.
- There are many ways to intervene in sexual violence, strategies include: direct, distract, delegate, and delay.

Learning Objectives

Students will:
- Examine the role of the bystander in sexual violence.
- Use empathy to challenge the idea of "tattling."
- Explore the challenge of intervening as a bystander.
- Consider the many options to intervene on sexual violence.

Cross-Curricular Connections
- Art (drama)
- Communication Studies
- Equity Studies
- Family Studies
- Gender Studies
- Media Studies
- Psychology
- Social Studies
- Sociology

Terminology
- Misogyny
- Rape culture
- Sexism
- Sexual violence
- Survivor
- Systemic oppression

Materials
- Flip chart, chalkboard, or whiteboard and appropriate writing utensils
- A computer with projector and large screen or a Smart Board to show online videos to class
- **Educator Answer Key—Bystander Impacts**
- Printed copies of **Bystander Intervention Scenarios**
- **Educator Answer Key—Bystander Intervention Scenarios**

Background Information for Educators

*Any student may be a **survivor** and/or witness of sexual violence. Discussions on this topic can be upsetting, overwhelming, or triggering. Acknowledge this at the beginning of every activity and allow students to take space if they need. Do your best to keep discussions focused, open, and respectful to everyone.*

Sexual violence refers to behaviours that exist on a continuum and are experienced as violence. The continuum of sexual violence includes behaviours that are normalized within society and behaviours that are criminalized and socially recognized as violence. The behaviours that are normalized are not legally defined or enforced, even though the impact is still experienced as violence.

Sexual violence can happen between any two or more people. Sexual violence is not about sexual desire, it is about the abuse of power. It occurs for many different reasons and in many different forms; it can happen between anyone. It can be long term or a one-time occurrence. It can happen between two people or involve many people. It can happen between people who know each other well or people who do not. It can happen to people of any demographic and it may or may not involve physical force. Sexual violence can happen in public or private spaces and with the hushed, often unspoken, knowledge of family or friends. Empowered bystander action can stop sexual violence.

Just as not all violence is experienced equally, the range of sexually violent behaviours should not be conflated as the same thing. The relationship between sexually violent and coercive behaviours needs to be considered so that students can learn how the normalization of certain behaviours contributes to the permissiveness and prevalence of other more extreme behaviours. Bystander intervention can challenge reactions that contribute to the normalization of sexually violent behaviours, stopping the permissiveness and prevalence of behaviours all along the continuum.

Sexual violence is supported and reinforced by **systemic oppression** and **gender norms**. Seeing sexual violence as behaviours that exist on a continuum within rape culture helps bust the myth that sexual violence is only the most extreme, legally defined examples portrayed by the media. It helps to understand the variety of aggressive, violating, coercive, and harmful behaviours that all have a violent impact and do not exist in isolation of one another. It also helps to understand the relationship between systemic oppression, gender norms, and sexual violence.

While it is important to challenge the systems that support and reinforce sexual violence (i.e., systemic oppression and gender norms), it is equally important to empower individual bystanders to take action to stop and challenge sexual violence that they witness. Having access to social power is something that can be used to take positive action as a bystander—if you have power in a situation, it is important to use that power to intervene when you witness sexual violence. If you have social power, you can set an example for others to follow. All bystanders have a responsibility to intervene if they witness sexual violence but those with more power have an opportunity to challenge rape culture by shifting the way sexually violent behaviours are normalized. People with less access to power who are the targets of sexual violence will feel the impacts of bystander inaction the most because of the added impacts that come with being socially isolated, ostracized, stigmatized, and discriminated against.

Student Readiness

Before students engage with this lesson, ensure that safer space guidelines and group norms have been established (and revisited) within your classroom (for more information on how to establish safer space guidelines, see module 1.3). In order to effectively prepare for this activity, ensure students understand that:
- This module addresses sexual violence, rape culture, bystander intervention, and consent.
- All human beings have the right to bodily autonomy and to be free from experiencing sexual violence.
- Sexual violence is more common than most people realize; it often happens in public spaces, is underreported, and mostly perpetrated by someone who is known to the survivor.
- If you experience sexual violence, it is never your fault.

- Despite how uncomfortable it may feel, bystanders have a responsibility to challenge and/or stop sexual violence that they witness.
- There are supports available to students who are survivors. *Ensure that you have identified these supports ahead of time. Before starting the activities, inform students what these supports are and where they can find them.*

Summary of Activities

Students will:

- Individually imagine a scenario and privately think about how they would respond as a bystander.
- Collectively brainstorm the different choices each character has within the scenario.
- Collectively watch a public education campaign and discuss the idea of bystander intervention across the continuum of sexual violence.
- Work in small groups to create their own public education campaign.
- Work in small groups to determine different ways of intervening in sexually violent scenarios and the role of social power in each.

Activity 1 □1

Instructions

1. Ask students to close their eyes. Read the following scenario to the class: Harley and Darci recently became friends and are both popular at their school. They are working on a project together with another student named Ro. Ro was really excited to get paired with Harley and Darci because Ro really looks up to both of them and wants to become their friend. They have class time to work on the project and they are all having a lot of fun laughing and talking. Harley excuses themselves to go to the washroom. After they leave, Darci reaches into Harley's bag, takes out Harley's phone, and starts going through it. At first, Ro is surprised and doesn't know what to think or feel about what Darci is doing. Darci then looks at Ro and says, "Don't worry, Harley gave me their password last week, so it's cool, but don't tell anyone. You don't want to be a snitch, do you?"

2. With their eyes still closed, say to the class: Imagine being in Ro's place. With your eyes still closed, raise your hand if you know for certain that you would intervene. Everyone can put their hands down. Now, raise your hand if you would feel unsure about intervening.

3. Ask the class to open their eyes and brainstorm a list of choices that Ro has. For each choice that Ro has, list the impacts to Harley, Darci, and Ro. See the **Educator Answer Key—Bystander Impacts** for an example.

4. Ask the class to close their eyes again and think about Ro's decisions and the impacts that each would have on the people in the scenario. With their eyes still closed, ask the class: Who would change their answer to the question about whether or not to intervene?

Activity 2 2 3

Instructions

Part 1

1. Pre-screen the following YouTube videos about bystanders to sexual violence and select the one most suitable for your students. *For each video, it is important that you pre-screen and provide trigger warnings to students. (For more information on trigger warnings, see modules 1.3 and 1.6).*
    *   **Ontario Campaign #WhoWillYouHelp (1:00), 2015** 2 3
        Campaign to promote intervening on sexual harassment and assault. Perpetrators look at the camera to say, "thanks for not saying anything."
    *   **CARE Norway Campaign #DearDaddy (5:00), 2015** 2 3
        Campaign that personalizes the impacts of sexual violence across the continuum. It makes links to rape culture, sexism, gender norms, and how you might be a bystander to sexual violence without even realizing it.
    *   **New Zealand Campaign *Who Are You?* (8:06), 2015** 3
        Campaign that portrays a night of partying and drinking leading to sexual assault, then retraces the evening with possible points of bystander intervention.

2. After screening the video, discuss as a class:
    *   In what kinds of situations are there bystanders?
    *   What does it feel like to be a bystander?
    *   What are some reasons that bystanders do not intervene?
    *   What message does silence send to perpetrators? To survivors?

EDUCATOR ANSWER KEY

- Fights, bullying, intimate partner violence, accidents, attacks on social media, name-calling, street harassment, workplace harassment, cyberbullying, sexist jokes.
- Scary, indifferent, helpless, angry, worrisome, confusing, wanting to do something, self-conscious, invisible.
- Social and peer norms, gender norms, scared for their own safety, fear of becoming victims, belief that it will not help, preserving relationships and or social status, do not know what to do, feel frozen, belief that "it is none of my business," fear of being a snitch or tattletale, belief that someone else will step in, belief that it betrays friendship of perpetrator.
- The message that silence sends to perpetrators is that violent behaviour is acceptable, condoned, and okay to continue. The message it sends to survivors is that they are alone, without support, unsafe, and deserve it.

Optional: Part 2

1. In small groups of 3 to 6, ask student to create a script for their own public education campaign on bystander intervention.
2. Homework: Have each group turn the script into a 2 to 8 minute campaign video with a social media hashtag. Videos can be screened in class for feedback. If the content is suitable and you have permission from parents/guardians of students under 16, have students post to social media.

Activity 3 [3]

Instructions

1. Explain: Sometimes bystanders do not intervene because they mistakenly think that there are only two options: to intervene in a drastic way or to do nothing. There are actually other options, you can remember them as the 4Ds (Fox, 2013).
2. Write the following on the board as you explain:
   - **Direct**: Address specifically and directly use words like "Stop!" "This sucks." "No more!" "I see what you're doing."
   - **Distract**: Indirectly change the focus of attention using distractions like "Who wants to go for pizza?" or "Hey, a teacher is coming!"
   - **Delegate**: Find other people to help and assign them tasks.
   - **Delay**: Get more information from the person being impacted. Find a chance to check in with them or send a private message asking, "Are you ok?" "Do you need help?"
3. Divide students into small groups of 4 to 6. Give each group a scenario from the **Bystander Intervention Scenarios.**

4. Ask each group to record their discussion using the following questions as a guide. *You can write the questions on the board or project onto a screen.*
   - Who has the most access to power in this scenario? Who has the second most access power? Who has the least access? Why? (For more information on social power and consent, see module 8.4).
   - How can they make it clear that this kind of behaviour is unacceptable? Consider in-the-moment ways and ways before or after; humorous and creative ways; and distracting ways that can interrupt the situation without huge personal risks. Use as many of the 4Ds as possible (Direct, Distract, Delegate, Delay).
5. Come back together as a class to discuss. Use the **Educator Answer Key—Bystander Intervention Scenarios** to urge the discussion towards the responsibility of bystanders to intervene, especially those with social power in a situation. (For more information on social power and consent, see module 8.4).

Wrap-up

Summarize the module with the following points:
   - The scenarios were examples of sexual violence. Bystanders play an important role in stopping sexual violence.
   - Bystanders can be passive or active, condoning or engaged in intervention. Even inaction and silence is a choice with consequences. People with less access to social power will feel the impact of those consequences most of all.
   - There are many ways to intervene on an unjust, sexually violent situation, strategies include: direct, distract, delegate, and delay.

CHAPTER 9

Safer Sex, Contraception, and Pregnancy Options

9.1 INTRODUCTION

Safer sex is a term that most young people hear at some point during their adolescence. It is a term that is usually used in reference to prevention of pregnancy through the use of **contraception** (i.e., birth control) and/or prevention of **Sexually Transmitted and Blood Borne Infections** (STBBIs). *Beyond the Basics* takes a comprehensive, holistic view of sexuality and the meaning of safer sex. Educating young people about contraceptives and STBBIs needs to be placed in the social, political, and economic contexts of access, healthy relationships, **consent**, power, **oppression**, and choice.

Choice, access, **empowerment**, and autonomy are essential in upholding the sexual and reproductive rights of young people. Access to contraception, family planning, and unintended pregnancy options (**abortion**, **adoption**, and parenting) is a **human right** that is part of the right to bodily autonomy, to freedom from torture, to the enjoyment of the highest attainable standard of physical and mental health, and to decide the number and spacing of children (for more information, see modules 2.2 and 2.3). Access is about affordability, geography, skilled health care professionals, information, and education. It needs to be in place for there to truly be choice.

Chapters 0 to 8 focus on the social and emotional aspects of practising safer sex, including how to set boundaries, deal with painful emotions, communicate consent, challenge **gender norms**, identify power imbalances within relationships, and ensure safety in an increasingly digitally connected age. Chapters 9 and 10 provide more information on the physical and biological aspects of practising safer sex and the practical aspects of avoiding unintended pregnancies and STBBIs from a **sex positive** perspective.

Teaching from a sex positive perspective acknowledges that sexual activity among young people is normal, expected, and healthy. Sex positivity counters the fear, shame, and stigma that is often linked to youth sexuality and perpetuated through curricula that overemphasize the risks of sex and underemphasize the joys, pleasures, and discovery of sex and sexuality. Sex negative and fear-based approaches to contraception and safer sex have proven ineffective at reducing **unintended pregnancies** **and STBBIs**. A more effective approach is empowering young people to enhance their sexual health through sex positive teaching approaches that do not stigmatize sex and instead value pleasure for all partners (Oliver et al, 2013). Emphasizing pleasure for all partners is effective at reducing unintended pregnancies and STBBIs, essential for fostering mutual respect between partners, and key in teaching the skills necessary for practising consent.

Recognizing that young people are sexually active and equipping them with information to make empowered decisions about safer sex effectively reduces unintended pregnancies and STBBIs while increasing healthy, satisfying, pleasurable sexual relationships that are based on the **human rights** principles of equality, empowerment, autonomy, agency, choice, and mutual respect. Young people of all gender identities and sexual orientations are engaging in sexual activities and 66% of youth aged 15 to 24 have had sexual intercourse (Rotermann, 2012). Equipping young people with education and information about how to be safer when engaging sexually and how to prevent pregnancy are essential in ensuring that the **sexual rights** of youth are being respected and realized, and that they feel empowered to enhance their sexual health.

Safer sex, contraception, and pregnancy options are important to discuss together because using contraception and practising safer sex is the best way to prevent unintended pregnancy and STBBIs. While access to information, education, and contraceptives is key to preventing unintended pregnancy, unintended pregnancy happens for a variety of different reasons. It is important for young people to know all of their options and the resources available to them when it comes to making decisions about pregnancy. Knowing their options and available resources includes information about abortion (surgical and medical), parenting, and adoption. Both surgical abortion and medical abortion are legal in Canada and standard procedures that are mostly provided under provincial health insurance. Access to abortion is a human right and although it is legal in Canada and covered under provincial health insurance, access to abortion services is unevenly distributed across the country with limited procedures and medication available outside of urban centres.

YOU SHOULD KNOW

All provinces and territories cover the cost of surgical abortion in a hospital setting through public health insurance. Provinces and territories with clinics also cover the cost of surgical abortion in clinic settings (with the exception of New Brunswick). In most provinces, the highest standard of medical abortion costs between $300 to $450. At the time of publication, not all provinces/territories cover the cost of the highest standard of medical abortion. For more information on abortion services and referrals, call the Action Canada for Sexual Health and Rights 24-hour toll-free Access Line at 1-888-642-2725.

As an educator, it is important to challenge your own assumptions about the kinds of information related to safer sex, contraception, and pregnancy options that young people need and want. Sexuality education is often taught from a risk-management and fear-based approach that fails to recognize curiosity and the exploration of sexual pleasure as central to adolescent sexuality (for more information, see modules 0.3 and 1.2). Teaching also tends to be **heterosexual** and **cisgender** focused, where the experiences of heterosexual adolescents are centred and the experiences of **LGBTQ+** youth are marginalized and made invisible. One of the ways that this occurs in teaching safer sex is the almost exclusive focus on penis-vagina sexual intercourse.

Safer sex is something that everyone, regardless of **sexual orientation** or **gender identity,** needs to practise to prevent pregnancy and STBBIs. The importance of this cannot be underestimated; pregnancy rates among adolescents who identify as LGBTQ+ are currently higher than rates among heterosexual adolescents (Corinna, 2016). One way to engage the whole class and challenge assumptions about who has what kind of sex is to ask students how they define sex and use non-gendered language when talking about safer sex. Another way is to refer to the sexual activities that people participate in as opposed to their sexual orientation. For instance, referring to people who engage in anal sex as "having anal sex" rather than "having gay sex." Sex is not gay or straight, people are, and a whole list of other sexual orientations. (For more information on gender neutral ways of teaching about pregnancy options, see table 9B in module 9.5).

Comprehensive sexuality education recognizes that human sexuality is holistic—it encompasses the social, political, economic, emotional, psychological, physical, and spiritual dimensions of a person's life. Teaching young people about safer sex, contraception, and pregnancy options from a comprehensive sexuality education approach recognizes that individual choice is influenced by social norms, political landscape, economic and geographical access, and education/accurate information. Comprehensive sexuality education also recognizes that sex happens within the context of social norms and relationships, even if those relationships are fleeting or purely sexual.

Gender norms are one of the most powerful kinds of social norms in the context of sexual and relationship scripts. Because of these norms, contraception is assumed to be the primary responsibility of the person assigned female at birth and socialized as a girl/woman. As educators, it is important that you teach safer sex, contraception, and pregnancy options to all genders in a way that promotes **equity**, sex positivity, shared responsibility, and respect. Educators must lead by example and ensure that all genders are equally and fully engaged in classroom discussions on contraception.

Educator Reflection Questions
- What assumptions do you have about the sexuality of young people? Do you assume that young people are not sexually active? Do you assume that they are engaged in all types of sexual activities or just some?
- What do you assume young people consider as sex? Do you assume they are only concerned about risk? Do you think they are concerned about pleasure too?
- Do you try not to think about young people's sexuality? Why or why not?
- Do you believe that young people's sexuality is something to be hidden or denied?
- Do you believe that young people should have control over every aspect of their sexual and reproductive lives? Why or why not?

- Were you surprised by any statistics from this module? Why or why not?
- What do you believe is the most effective way to teach young people about safer sex? Why do you have this belief and where does it come from? Is this belief based in evidence, your personal experience, and/or a feeling that you have?
- Have you ever thought about access to contraception as a human right?
- Have you ever thought about access to all pregnancy options (including abortion) as a human right?
- What are your assumptions about teen pregnancy? What are your values related to the choices that young people make when faced with an unintended pregnancy? Do you assume that just because someone is young, they would want an abortion, or that they are not ready to parent?

Think back to when you were the age of your students...
- Did you consider yourself a sexual being?
- Were you thinking about sex?
- Were you having sex? If so, what kinds of sex were you having? If not, were your peers having sex?
- Were you able to access the kinds of contraception that you wanted and/or needed at the time? What barriers (if any) existed for you in terms of being able to access this contraception?
- What kinds of information, education, and/or resources did you wish you had access to?

Big Ideas in Chapter 9
- Educating young people about contraceptives and STBBIs needs to be placed in the social, political, and economic contexts of access, healthy relationships, consent, power, oppression, and choice.
- Choice and access are essential in upholding the sexual and reproductive rights of young people.
- Teaching safer sex, contraception, and pregnancy options from a sex positive perspective acknowledges that sexual activity among young people is normal, expected, and healthy.
- Healthy adolescent sexuality includes curiosity and the exploration of sexual pleasure.
- Access to safe and effective contraception, emergency contraception, and pregnancy options (abortion, adoption, and parenting) is a human right.

- Regardless of sexual orientation or gender identity, safer sex is something that everyone needs in order to help prevent pregnancy and STBBIs.
- Comprehensive sexuality education recognizes that individual choice is influenced by social norms, political landscape, economic and geographical access, education, and access to accurate information.

9.2 EDUCATOR RESOURCE: CONTRACEPTION METHODS

This module provides information on available contraceptive methods in order to equip and empower young people to select the methods that best match their specific circumstances. Providing young people with information on a variety of contraceptives gives them the opportunity to thoughtfully engage with the most commonly used methods of **contraception** (condoms and oral contraceptives) and consider other contraception options and their efficacy. It also ensures they are aware of their choices and the best methods that suit their individual needs. Giving young people accurate information and trusting that they will make the choices that are best for them is one way to empower them to cultivate behaviours that contribute to their sexual health and well-being.

The groundwork for consistent and correct use of contraception begins with the acceptance that many students are or will soon be sexually active. It is important to equip them with information about STBBIs, unintended pregnancy, and how contraceptives can play a role in practising safer, consensual, and pleasurable sex. It is equally important to encourage a **dual protection** approach that emphasizes safer sex that reduces the chance of STBBI transmission and unintended pregnancy. In discussing the potential risks of sexual activity and the risks and side effects of contraception methods, ensure that information is framed in the context of sex positivity (for more information, see modules 0.3 and 1.2). Emphasize and encourage contraceptive planning as a normal and expected aspect of healthy living for young people.

Part of contraceptive planning for young people is knowing how and where to confidentially access effective and affordable contraception. Although young people have the right to access health care (including **contraception, STBBI** testing, and **abortion**) that is confidential and without parental permission, these rights are not always respected. Young people need to know their rights (for more information, see 9.1 resources, and modules 2.2 and 2.3) in order to recognize the standard of care they deserve from health care providers when it comes to sexuality and sexual health.

When teaching the modules in this chapter, students should leave the class feeling well informed about how and where to access effective and affordable contraception. You and/or your students might have further questions about contraception, STBBIs, and safer sex. The 9.2 resources, **National Support Services** resource, and the **Educator Resource—Frequently Asked Questions** can help navigate these questions from reliable, accurate sources.

Trends in Current Contraception Use Among Youth

Condoms are the most commonly used contraceptive method among adolescents in Canada, followed by oral contraception and the withdrawal method (Black et al., 2009). It is important to provide information on these three methods as well as other options, especially emergency contraception options (i.e., the "morning after pill" and copper IUD insertion) so that sexually active youth are adequately prepared for all sexual outcomes, including contraception failure and unprotected sex. The **Contraception Options** handout provides a comprehensive list of contraception options available in Canada (at the time of publication) along with the advantages and disadvantages of each.

Most sexually active youth in Canada (80% of 15 to 17 year-olds and 74% of 18 to 19 year-olds) reported using condoms the last time they had sexual intercourse (Rotermann, 2012). Youth also reported that they primarily use condoms to prevent pregnancy rather than reduce STBBI risk (Milhausen et al., 2013). Sexual health educators need to emphasize the continued importance of dual protection, pregnancy prevention as well as assessing STBBI risk, by continually encouraging behaviours such as condom use or STBBI testing as part of contraception.

YOU SHOULD KNOW

Condoms (both external and internal) are the only method of contraception that provide dual protection against STBBIs and pregnancy when used properly. The exceptions to this are external lambskin condoms and novelty condoms, which have not been approved for STBBI protection.

Perfect Use vs. Typical Use

Practising safer sex and using contraceptives happens in the context of everyday life where mistakes happen and things do not always go as planned. This means that the effectiveness of contraception tested within a lab setting is not affected by the everyday habits of the person using the contraceptive. Differentiating between perfect use and typical use is one way of recognizing that effectiveness partially depends on the method chosen and partially on the user.

Perfect use refers to using the contraceptive exactly as directed in a controlled setting (i.e., a lab). Typical use refers to the more realistic use of a contraceptive, where it may not be used consistently or correctly. Among 100 sexually active individuals taking oral contraception exactly as directed, 0.3% will become pregnant within a year. Thus, under perfect use conditions, the pill is 99.7% effective. Typical use however is 91% effective (Hatcher, 2011); it reflects the fact that not everyone will take their oral contraceptive exactly as directed (e.g., some may occasionally forget to take their pill on schedule).

Activities in modules 9.3, 9.4, and 9.6 balance information sharing with skill building on how to properly use contraceptive methods and practise **safer sex**. In talking to young people about perfect vs. typical use, it is important to emphasize that oral contraceptives can be 99.7% effective if they are consistent about how and when they take their pills. If students are interested in oral contraceptives but concerned about remembering to take the pill at the same time every day, let them know that here are smart phone applications that can help keep them on schedule and other contraceptive methods that do not require remembering to take a pill every day. It is also important to emphasize that contraception is not the sole responsibility of the person preventing their own pregnancy, it is the responsibility of anyone who is sexually active.

Overview of Contraception Methods and Access

There are six main types of contraception methods: hormonal, **intrauterine**, barrier, surgical, natural, and emergency. Hormonal methods use low doses of synthetic **hormones** (either combined **estrogen** and **progestin** or just progestin) to regulate the menstrual cycle in such a way to prevent pregnancy. Hormonal methods prevent pregnancy either by supressing **ovulation**, thickening the **cervical mucus**, and/or thinning the **endometrium** (lining of the uterus), and slowing egg and sperm transport. Barrier methods use a physical barrier to prevent pregnancy by preventing **sperm** from entering either the **vagina** or the **cervix**. Surgical methods (also known as sterilization) are performed by medical professionals to permanently inhibit reproduction. When teaching young people about safer sex and contraception methods, it is extremely important to emphasize that the only kinds of contraception that prevent both pregnancy and STBBIs are external and internal condoms (with the exception of lambskin and novelty condoms).

Each contraceptive method comes with its own advantages, disadvantages, and effectiveness. What works best for one person may not work as well for another, just as one person's contraception preference may change throughout the lifespan. The **Contraception Options** handout provides a user friendly guide to help young people make the contraceptive choices that are best for them. The **Educator Resource—Frequently Asked Questions** provides answers to some common questions that students may have.

Oral contraceptive pills require a prescription and can be found at local pharmacies or sexual health clinics. On average, a package of pills costs around $20 per month ($240 annually) for those without private insurance (Phillips, 2016). Local sexual health clinics can sometimes offer subsidized and less expensive rates for youth. Other hormonal methods differ greatly in cost, approximately $30 per month for the hormonal ring or patch, $40 every 3 months for a Depo-Provera shot, $60 to $80 for a copper IUD lasting between 5 and 10 years, and $350 to $400 for a hormonal IUD/IUS lasting for 3 to 5 years (costs currently based on Ontario rates at time of publication). Costs should be weighed against an individual's sexual health needs, financial situation, medical history, and preferences. Educators can direct students to the Action Canada for Sexual Health and Rights online directory of service providers to locate nearby sexual health clinics that are youth friendly and **sex positive** (for more information, see 9.1 resources and **National Support Services**).

YOU SHOULD KNOW

Different combined hormonal methods and brands have similar side effects and risks. It is important for individuals to meet with their health care provider to discuss their medical history prior to beginning any hormonal contraceptive method.

A prescription is required for all hormonal methods of contraception except the progestin-only emergency contraception pill. The exception to this is Quebec, where accessing the emergency contraception pill requires a prescription. In Saskatchewan, you will have to ask the pharmacist for the emergency contraceptive pill and they will ask you some questions before giving it to you. In every other province and territory, you have the right to access the emergency contraceptive pill over the counter. Students have the right to receive contraception from doctors without permission from their parents/guardians (for more information, see modules 2.2 and 2.3). The emergency contraceptive pill can be found at most pharmacies and sexual health clinics and does not require a prescription. Emergency contraception costs approximately $35 to $40 depending on the individual pharmacy. At sexual health clinics, emergency contraception is often available at a significantly reduced cost.

Educator Reflection Questions

- Were there any types of contraceptive methods that you did not know about before reading this module and looking at the **Contraception Options** handout?
- Do you have a preference towards any of the methods discussed? If so, how will you teach the information in a way that does not show your own preference?
- Which information do you wish you had access to as a young person? How will this inform the way you teach?

9.3 SEX AND CONTRACEPTION: WHICH METHODS TO USE WHEN?

LEVELS  2 3

Big Ideas in Module 9.3

- Sex and intimacy can mean different things to different people, there is no universal definition. When communicating about being intimate and safer sex, it is important for partners to clarify how they want to be intimate, what kinds of sexual activities (if any) they want to engage in, and how they want to protect themselves from unintended pregnancy and STBBIs.
- Safer sex is something that everyone, regardless of sexual orientation or gender identity, needs to practise in order to prevent pregnancy and STBBIs.
- The circumstances in which young people negotiate contraception are impacted by socio-economic status, discrimination, and potential experiences of coercion and violence.
- Young people have the right to access contraception without parental permission, just as they have the right to privacy if accessing contraceptives from a health care provider.

Learning Objectives

Students will:

- Consider the multiple meanings of sex and intimacy.
- Learn which sexual activities can lead to pregnancy and which can lead to STBBIs.
- Learn about contraceptive options, including the advantages and disadvantages of each.
- Challenge common myths associated with the emergency contraception pill.

Cross-Curricular Connections

- Biology
- Equity Studies
- Family Studies
- Gender Studies
- Psychology
- Social Studies
- Sociology

Terminology

- Asexual
- Cisgender
- Coercion
- Contraception
- Discrimination
- Emergency contraception
- Gender identity
- Sexual orientation
- Stigma

Materials
- Chalkboard, whiteboard, or interactive Smart Board
- Sticky notes in 2 different colours
- Tape
- Printed copies of **Contraception Options**
- Printed copies of **Contraception Card Deck**
- Printed copies of **Emergency Contraception Quiz**
- **Educator Answer Key—Emergency Contraception Quiz**
- Printed copies of **Who Am I? Cards**
- Printed copies of **Contraception Case Studies**
- **Educator Answer Key—Contraception Case Studies**

Background Information for Educators

Definitions of sex, sexual activity, and intimacy vary widely from person to person and can change over time. It is important for partners to clarify and communicate how they define "sex" (for more information, see modules 2.7 and 4.4). This is a first step in practising safer sex and consent. Providing students with the skills to communicate with each other about taboo subjects can help them clarify with their partners what kinds of sexual activities they want to engage in, practise consent, and figure out how to most effectively protect themselves from unwanted pregnancies and STBBIs.

Be sure to challenge your own assumptions about the kinds of information that young people need and want. There is no right age at which individuals should start having sex—it depends on their comfort level, emotional and social preparedness, and circumstances. Some young people may be very interested in sexual activity and other young people may not. As an educator, it is up to you to not place judgement on students' levels of interest or disinterest in sexual activity. Instead, affirm that interest, disinterest, and everything in between is a healthy part of adolescent sexuality.

There tends to be a significant focus on teaching sexuality education from a **heterosexual, cisgender** perspective, where the experiences of heterosexual adolescents are centred and the experiences of **LGBTQ+** youth are marginalized and made invisible. One of the ways that this occurs in teaching about safer sex is the almost exclusive focus on penis-vagina sexual intercourse. What is considered to "count as sex" often privileges penis-vagina sexual intercourse over other sexual activities. Safer sex is something that everyone, regardless of **sexual orientation** or **gender identity,** needs to practise to prevent pregnancy and STBBIs. The importance of this cannot be underestimated as there are currently higher rates of pregnancies among adolescents who identify as LGBTQ+ than among heterosexual adolescents (Corinna, 2016). One of the ways to engage all students and challenge assumptions about who has what kind of sex is to ask students how they define sex and to use non-gendered language when talking about safer sex. Another way to engage all students and challenge assumptions about who is having what kind of sex is to refer to the sexual activities people participate in as opposed to people's sexual orientation. For instance, people who engage in anal sex are having anal sex, as opposed to "having gay sex." Sex is not gay or straight, people are, among a long list of other sexual orientations. (For more information on non-gendered ways of teaching about pregnancy options, see table 9B).

Accessing and using contraception happen within a social context. For young people, their social context can affect access to a prescription (for hormonal methods), availability, **stigma**, income and affordability, communication, and assumptions around responsibility for **contraception**. The circumstances in which young people negotiate contraception use are impacted by socio-economic status, **oppression, discrimination,** and potential experiences of **coercion** and violence. For instance, students living in poverty may not have the money to purchase certain types of contraception; discussions around where to locate free and subsidized contraception are imperative to ensure that all students have access to the contraceptive method that is best for them. It is also important that young people know their rights when it comes to accessing contraception. Even if the contraceptive they want requires a prescription, young people, including those under 16 years, have the right to access contraception without parental permission. Just as it is important for students to know their rights, it is important for cisgender boys/men to understand contraception (and how contraceptive choices relate to pleasure for all partners) to instill a sense of shared responsibility so that the burden does not always fall to the person who could become pregnant. Students might also be afraid to consult their family doctor, so it is extremely important that they know where to find sexual health clinics that are youth friendly, sex positive, and non-stigmatizing. (For a list of clinics, see the Action Canada for Sexual Health and Rights directory in 9.1 resources and **National Support Services**).

Student Readiness

Before students engage with this lesson, ensure that safer space guidelines and group norms have been established (and revisited) within your classroom (for more information on how to establish safer space guidelines, see module 1.3). To effectively prepare for this activity, ensure students understand that:

- Sex does not have a universal meaning. Not everyone defines sex as penis-vagina intercourse.
- People engage in a variety of sexual activities regardless of their gender identity and sexual orientation (e.g., it is not only gay men who have anal sex, straight people also have anal sex).
- Contraception helps protect against unintended pregnancy and STBBIs and is important for everyone to learn about, regardless of sexual orientation and gender identity.
- Sexual activity among young people is normal, expected, and healthy.
- There is no right age at which individuals should start having sex. It depends on their comfort level, emotional and social preparedness, and circumstances. Some young people may be very interested in sexual activity and other young people may not be.

Summary of Activities

Students will:

- Individually write down what they consider sex and intimacy and collectively discuss as a class.
- Work in small groups to create and present a lesson, jingle, song, or skit on contraception methods.
- Work in pairs to match contraception methods with facts using a card game.
- Collectively match types of contraception methods with whether they protect from pregnancy and STBBIs.
- Take a quiz on emergency contraception and compare their answers with facts.

Activity 1 2 3

Instructions

Part 1

1. Explain: Sex and intimacy can mean different things to different people. There is no universal definition of sex or intimacy. When communicating about being intimate and having safer sex, it is important for sexual and intimate partners to each clarify how they want to be intimate, what kinds of sexual activities (if any) they want to engage in, and how they want to protect themselves from unintended pregnancy and STBBIs.

(For more information on how build the communication skills necessary for navigating these nuanced conversations, see modules 2.7, 4.4, 7.3, 7.4, 7.5, 8.3, 9.4, and 10.4).

2. Hand out two different colours of sticky notes (4 to 6 notes per colour) to each student.

3. Write "Sex is…" on one large piece of paper and "Intimacy is…" on another. Place both on the wall.

4. Assign each paper to a different colour of sticky note (e.g., sex is… = blue, intimacy is… = yellow) and ask students to finish the sentence on the corresponding colour of sticky note.

5. Once students have finished writing down their answers, ask them to post their answers onto the corresponding paper. Let students know that they are not required to post every answer, only the ones they feel comfortable sharing.

6. Collectively take up and discuss the answers posted under each heading. If some answers were missed, write them down on the appropriate colour sticky note and place under the corresponding paper.

EDUCATOR ANSWER KEY

Sex is…

intimate, fun, pleasurable, oral sex, anal sex, penis-vagina intercourse, digital penetration ("fingering"), dry humping, masturbation, mutual masturbation (masturbation with another person), skin-to-skin genital rubbing, stroking, using sex toys, virtual sex, "sexting."

Intimacy is…

pleasurable, closeness, being naked together, being sexual, emotional connection, physical connection, sexual connection, spiritual connection, oral sex, anal sex, penis-vagina intercourse, digital penetration ("fingering"), dry humping, masturbation, mutual masturbation (masturbation with another person), skin-to-skin genital rubbing, stroking, using sex toys, virtual sex, "sexting."

7. Write the following three lines on the board. Leave lots of space between each.
   a) Pregnancy could happen from…
   b) STBBIs could happen from…
   c) Ways to experience pleasure that are low risk (in terms of risk of pregnancy and STBBIs) are…

8. Ask students to finish the sentences using the "sex" and "intimacy" sticky notes. Let them know that they can move any sticky note around, not just the ones they originally created, and that not all the sticky notes belong in the sentences.

9. Ask: Were there any sticky notes that belong in all the sentences? Which ones? *As you take up the answers, ensure students understand which sexual activities can lead to pregnancy, which can lead to STBBIs, and which can lead to both, as well as which activities are low risk and pleasurable.*

EDUCATOR ANSWER KEY

a) Pregnancy could happen from…
    penis-vagina intercourse where ejaculation happens inside the vagina. Though it is less likely, pregnancy could also happen from penis-vagina intercourse where pre-ejaculate "pre-cum" is released into the vagina, and from mutual masturbation onto the vulva or skin-to-skin genital rubbing that results in ejaculation onto the vulva.

b) STBBIs could happen from…
    oral sex, anal sex, penis-vagina intercourse, digital penetration ("fingering"), mutual masturbation with contact to skin and/or fluids, skin-to-skin genital rubbing, stroking, using sex toys.

c) Kissing, kissing with tongue ("French kissing" or "deep kissing"), mutual masturbation without contact to skin and/or fluids, sharing fantasies and desires, "sexting," touching and stroking external genitals, rubbing bodies together over clothing ("dry humping").

10. Keep the sticky notes where they are because part 4 of the activity comes back to them.

Part 2

1. Explain: Contraception or "birth control" prevents pregnancy. There are many different types of contraception. It is important to know all your options so that you can choose what works best for you. Some types of contraception also protect against STBBI transmission but usually more than one type is used to prevent both pregnancy and STBBIs.

2. Place students into small groups of 2 to 3.

3. Give each group a copy of the **Contraception Options**. Have each group create a short lesson (between 3 to 6 minutes) on a different contraceptive method. The lessons should touch on the following points:
   - A description of the method (a drawing or verbal description of how it works)
   - When it is most useful (for whom and during which acts)
   - Limitations of the method
   - Whether it can be used alongside other methods
   - Whether it protects against pregnancy and/or STBBIs
   - Where you can find it
   - Whether it requires a prescription
   - How much it costs
   - Side effects, risks, advantages, and disadvantages

4. Optional: Ask students to create a song, jingle, and/or skit about the method as a way of communicating about the method and helping students remember key points.

Part 3
Instructions
1. Place students in pairs and provide each pair with a **Contraception Card Deck**.
2. Ask students to shuffle the cards and place them face down. Taking turns, each student in the pair will turn over 2 cards at a time. When a picture/name is turned that matches the "facts at a glance" turned, that person gets to put the matching cards aside. The person with the most matching cards wins.
3. After students have finished matching their cards, take up the correct answers with the whole class using a projection of **Contraception Options** handout.

Part 4
1. Draw students' attention back to the sticky notes from part 1 of the activity.
2. Explain: Now that you understand different contraceptive methods, you have a chance to match contraceptive methods with whether they prevent pregnancy and/or STBBIs.
3. Ask: Which contraceptive methods could be used to prevent pregnancy? Which methods could be used to prevent STBBIs? Which methods prevent both?

EDUCATOR ANSWER KEY

Prevent Pregnancy	Prevent STBBIs	Prevent Pregnancy and STBBIS
Oral contraceptive pill		
Transdermal patch		
Depo Provera shot		
Vaginal ring		
Hormonal IUD/IUS		
Copper IUD		
External condom	External condom	External condom
Internal condom	Internal condom	Internal condom
Emergency contraceptive pill		
Fertility awareness method		
Withdrawal method		
Sterilization (vasectomy or tubal ligation)		
Diaphragm and cervical caps		
Lactation amenorrhea method		
Abstinence	Abstinence	Abstinence
Spermicides		

Activity 2 2 3

Instructions

1. Explain: There are many myths about emergency contraception. This activity will help dispel those myths. Emergency contraception can be used to prevent pregnancy in situations where no contraception was used or a contraception method failed (e.g., missed birth control pills, condom broke).

2. Distribute copies of **Emergency Contraception Quiz** to each student.
3. Give students between 5 to 10 minutes to fill out the quiz. Reassure students that the quiz is private and they will not be marked on their answers.
4. Take up answers as a class making sure to elaborate on each answer as provided in the **Educator Answer Key—Emergency Contraception Quiz.**

Activity 3 2 3
Instructions
1. Print the **Who Am I? Cards**
2. Divide the class in half.
3. Give one half of the class the set of cards that contain the description of the contraceptive methods. Allow them a chance to read their method but ask them not to share their method with anyone else.
4. For the remaining students, ask for their consent to tape the contraceptive name cards on their back (1 per student) without them looking at the card.
5. Have students circulate around the classroom.
6. Explain: If you have a description card, try to locate the person with your corresponding contraceptive method without saying the name of the method. The person with the contraceptive method taped on their back should correctly guess the name of the method by asking questions to those with description cards.
7. Once they have correctly identified the method and found their partner, the pair gets to sit down where they are.
8. After each pair has found each other and is sitting down, have each pair describe their method without naming it and get the class to collectively guess which method they are.

Activity 4 2 3
Instructions
1. Explain: Contraception is more than just the birth control pill. There are many different types of contraception.
2. Place students into small groups of 3 to 5. Distribute a copy of the **Contraception Case Studies** to each group.
3. Assign each group a case study and ask students to brainstorm the best contraception method(s) for the scenario.
4. Have each group present their case study and suggested contraception method (and explain why they made that decision).

5. Wrap up the activity by affirming that while the case studies were an exercise in debating which choice might be best for each scenario, in real life, you cannot choose which contraceptive method is best for someone else. At the same time, the responsibility of contraception should not always fall on the person who could get pregnant, contraception needs to be communicated about between sexual partners.

Wrap-up

Summarize the module with the following points:

- Sex means different things to different people and it is important to learn about STBBI and pregnancy prevention no matter your sexual orientation or gender identity.
- Choosing a contraceptive method that is right for you depends on several emotional, social, bodily, and economic factors.
- Contraception choices will likely change over your lifespan—knowing all your options can be helpful in assessing what works best, when.
- Dual protection is important if you want to prevent STBBIs and pregnancy.
- The emergency contraception pill is available without a prescription (except for Quebec, where a prescription is required).

9.4 CONDOMS AND COMMUNICATION

LEVELS 2 3

Big Ideas in Module 9.4

- All sexual activity requires communication between partners. Communication is essential for practising consent and safer sex and increasing pleasure and comfort.
- Condoms are the only form of contraception that provide dual protection from pregnancy and STBBIs.
- Knowing the mechanics of how to use a condom properly and the communication skills necessary in negotiating their use are essential to having safer sex.

Learning objectives

Students will:

- Debunk myths associated with condom use.
- Learn how to properly use external condoms.
- Reflect on the importance of communication in safer sex.

Cross-Curricular Connections

- Art (drama)
- Biology
- Communications Studies
- Equity Studies
- Family Studies
- Gender Studies
- Psychology
- Social Studies
- Sociology

Terminology

- Contraception
- Dual protection
- Gender norms
- Vulva

Materials

- Printed copies of **Condom Statement Sets**
- Printed copies of **Condom Cards**
- **Educator Answer Key—Condom Cards**
- Condoms
- Water-based lubricant samples (found at sexual health clinics and/or local public health units)
- Bananas

Background Information for Educators

All sexual activity requires communication between partners. Communication is one of the central ingredients to ensure the sexual pleasure and safety of all partners. While communicating about sex can feel awkward or uncomfortable, it can make sex more physically, emotionally, mentally, and socially comfortable before, during, and after sexual activity. Communication is key for practising consent and it is essential in establishing how to have safer sex.

Consent is also a key part of practising safer sex. Consent is not just the absence of "no;" it is an enthusiastic "yes." If partners communicate with each other about condom use and it is established that a condom will be used during sexual activity, removing the condom without consent means that the sexual activity is no longer consensual and no longer safe. This form of sexual violence is called "stealthing" and is a violation of bodily autonomy (Brodsky, 2017). Like all forms of sexual violence, **systemic oppression** and **gender norms** support and reinforce these behaviours. Ongoing communication is essential for practising consent and safer sex.

Gender norms that feed into sexual and relationship scripts place the sole responsibility of **contraception** with the person who could become pregnant. If this assumption is not talked about between sexual partners, the risks associated with sexual activity are heightened because it is assumed that pregnancy prevention is covered and STBBI prevention is often not talked about.

Condoms (both external and internal) are the only form of contraception that provide **dual protection** (protection from pregnancy and STBBIs). External condoms are one of the most frequently used contraception methods by young people. If used properly, external condoms are 98% effective but typical use significantly decreases effectiveness to 82%. In terms of STBBI protection, no barrier method is 100% effective but condoms are a useful risk-reduction strategy (SOGC, 2015). Knowing the mechanics of how to use a condom properly and the communication skills necessary in debunking condom myths (how to negotiate their use and increase pleasure for all partners) are important when striving towards perfect use and maximum effectiveness.

YOU SHOULD KNOW

Internal condoms are sometimes referred to as "female condoms." Referring to them as internal condoms can help make your classroom a safer space for gender non-binary and trans students who may not identify with the term "female."

Condoms significantly reduce the risk of pregnancy and STBBI transmission for a variety of sexual activities, including: penis-vagina intercourse (reduces risk of pregnancy and HIV, HPV, herpes, gonorrhea, chlamydia, syphilis, hepatitis B, etc.); oral sex on a penis (reduces risk of HPV, herpes, gonorrhea, chlamydia, and syphilis, etc. in and around the mouth and throat); oral sex on a **vulva** and anus (reduces risk of HPV, herpes, hepatitis B (anus), and syphilis etc. in and around the mouth when cut open down the side and used as a dental dam).

While the uses of lubricant or "lube" are numerous, it is an essential component of good condom use. Places that offer free external condoms like sexual health clinics and community health centres often offer free lube as well. For condoms, it is important to use water-based lubricant as opposed to oil-based lubricant, which can break down the integrity of the condom. While some condoms come pre-lubricated, additional lubrication should still be applied to the outside of the condom when available to avoid condom breakage during vaginal and anal intercourse. Extra lubrication on the outside of the condom can increase pleasure and comfort during penis-vagina and anal intercourse for all partners. For extra pleasure, one or two drops of water-based lube can be applied inside the condom before placing the condom on the penis.

Talking about condoms and other forms of contraception is an important part of communicating about the sexual activities that you are interested in trying, how to use protection specific to each act, and how to increase pleasure for all partners.

Student Readiness

Before students engage with this lesson, ensure that safer space guidelines and group norms have been established (and revisited) within your classroom (for more information on how to establish safer space guidelines, see module 1.3). In order to effectively prepare for this activity, ensure students understand that:
- Sex does not have a universal meaning even though many assume it only refers to intercourse with a penis and vagina.
- Sexual intercourse most often refers to penis-vagina sex but can sometimes mean anal sex.
- People engage in a variety of sexual activities regardless of their gender identity and sexual orientation.
- Contraception helps protect against unintended pregnancy and STBBIs and is important for everyone to learn about, regardless of sexual orientation or gender identity.

Summary of Activities

Students will:

- Work in small groups to decipher between myths and facts about condoms, contraception, and sex.
- Work in larger groups to figure out the order of how to properly use a condom.
- Work in small groups to creatively demonstrate how to properly use a condom.
- Learn how to put on a condom using a banana.

Activity 1 2 3

Familiarize yourself with the information contained in modules 9.1 and 9.2 and the **Educator Resource—Condom Statement Sets** before facilitating this activity.

Instructions

1. Introduce the lesson by drawing on the following points:
   - People often believe a number of myths about condoms, contraception, and sex and may hold on to particular myths depending on what they hear from their social group, family, and what media they consume.
   - It is important to discern between myths and facts about condoms, contraception, and sex because it is part of being able to make informed decisions about sexual health.
   - Identify places, websites, hotlines, and people that students can go to for more information (for ideas, see 9.4 resources and **National Support Services**).
2. This activity is modeled after the game "Two Truths and a Lie." Each set of 3 statements will contain 2 statements that are true and one that is false. Print and cut out the **Condom Statement Sets**. Have small groups of 2 to 5 students work on 1 or multiple sets of statements. *Depending on your students and the amount of time, you can have multiple groups working on the same statement sets or only one group working on each set.*
3. Debrief the statements as a class using the **Educator Resource— Condom Statement Sets** and information contained in modules 9.1 and 9.2. *After students have worked through the activity, you can give them the Educator Resource as a handout, if appropriate.*

Activity 2 2 [3]

Instructions

Part 1

1. Divide the class into 2 groups and print 2 sets of the **Condom Cards.**
2. Give 1 set of cards to each group and ensure that everyone in the group is holding at least 1 card.
3. Without speaking to one another, ask students to arrange themselves in the order of how to properly and successfully put on and take off an external condom.
4. Take up the answers as a class using the **Educator Resource— Condom Cards.**
5. Debrief the activity with the following prompts:
   a) What kinds of communication did you use to arrange yourselves?
   b) Why is communication important throughout using a condom and having sex?
   c) What are communication strategies we can use before, during, and after sex?

EDUCATOR ANSWER KEY

Communication is key when engaging in any kind of sexual activity. Communicating with sexual partners before, during, and after sex is important to ensure that sex is consensual, safe, and pleasurable for all partners. Communication can be verbal and non-verbal, use as many communication strategies and skills when talking about and throughout sex. Some of these strategies and skills include: body language, gestures, tone of your voice, being assertive. (For more on communication, see modules 7.5 and 8.3).

Part 2

1. Divide students into groups of 3 to 5.
2. Explain: The best way to learn how to use a condom is to practise. Now that you know the proper order and steps of how to put on an external condom, each group will demonstrate using a banana, a condom, and water-based lube samples.
3. Ask each group to come up with a creative way to demonstrate to the rest of the class with a banana, a condom, and lube.
4. Provide the following ideas to students for creative ways to demonstrate:
   • Musical
   • Social media campaign
   • Drama skit

- Television advertisement
- YouTube video

5. Have students present their demonstrations to the rest of the class.
6. ✦ Optional: Make it into a competition and explain that the demonstration gets more points for the more creative it is but that everyone has to demonstrate all steps clearly and appropriately in order not to be disqualified.

Wrap-up

Summarize the module with the following points:

- All sexual activity requires communication between partners.
- Communicating with sexual partners before, during, and after sex is key to ensuring that sex is consensual, safe, and pleasurable for all partners.
- Condoms provide protection from pregnancy and STBBIs; communication is essential in ensuring their effectiveness.

9.5 EDUCATOR RESOURCE: PREGNANCY OPTIONS

Easy access to information about contraceptives and affordable options are an important part of upholding young people's basic human rights, including the right to bodily autonomy. This is also true in terms of choice between all options (adoption, abortion, parenting) when faced with an unintended pregnancy. Pregnancy is initially confirmed by a pregnancy test and possible examination by a health care provider. The date that the pregnancy starts is the first day of the person's last period. The sooner pregnancy is confirmed and dated, the sooner a person can consider their options. A health care provider can help date the pregnancy and an ultrasound might be used to get a more accurate dating.

The person who is pregnant has the right to choose whether to make the decision on their own and how much or little to inform their sexual partner. You are not legally required to tell your sexual partner about a pregnancy. If you want to make a confidential decision without the partner's input, that is okay. If you are pregnant and choose to communicate and discuss options with your partner, legally the decision is still entirely yours. This module provides information on all options a pregnant person can choose (parenting, abortion, and adoption).

No decision is morally better than the other and a person's decision on how to navigate an unintended pregnancy should be made freely and without judgement from others. "Teen pregnancy," in general, is highly stigmatized, as is getting an abortion, as is deciding to parent as a young person, as is adoption (to a certain extent). It is this stigma and judgment that causes the most harm. Being mindful of language use is crucial—it is one way to ensure that all pregnancy options are discussed in ways that are not moralizing or stigmatizing (for more information, see module 1.4). When discussing options, the terms embryo and fetus should be used instead of baby. Follow the lead of the pregnant person in terms of the language that they use. In discussing options, avoid phrases like "keep the baby," use "continuing the pregnancy" or "choosing to parent" instead. When abortion is being discussed, use "terminating the pregnancy." Similarly, **adoption** should not be referred to as "giving up the child."

There is no "right" or "wrong" emotional response to pregnancy decisions. As an educator, it is important that you follow your student's lead when offering support. Young people have the right to access all up-to-date information about all pregnancy options. One of the ways that you can identify yourself as an ally is to teach all pregnancy options in a way that is affirming, empowering, non-judgmental, and respectful of youth agency and resilience (for more information, see module 1.7). This will help young people get connected with the resources and health care services to pursue the choice that is best for them.

Abortion

While abortion is legal in Canada, it is not always easy to access. Factors like where you live in Canada and gestational limits (how long into a pregnancy you can access abortion) can impede access. Clinics and hospitals providing abortions are often disproportionately located in big cities and urban centers. This leaves many rural areas underserved and forces many individuals to travel far distances for their appointments. Abortion services are also disproportionately spread across the provinces and territories—Quebec, Ontario, and British Columbia offer the most services with more of a range in gestational limits. Still, even in big cities, wait times can be long. Because of the many barriers that exist, if a person decides to have an abortion, they should make an appointment as soon as possible.

YOU SHOULD KNOW

All provinces cover the cost of surgical abortion in a hospital setting and most provinces cover the cost of surgical abortion in clinic settings. The exception to this is New Brunswick, which only covers abortions performed in hospital settings. In most provinces, medical abortion currently costs between $40 and $450 depending on the province and which abortion pill is available. For more information on abortion services, call Action Canada for Sexual Health and Rights 24-hour toll-free Access Line at 1-888-642-2725.

Young people face specific barriers rooted in stigma and myth when it comes to abortion. Even though young people have the right to patient-doctor confidentiality, they still might not feel comfortable talking to their family doctor for fear of their parents/guardians finding out. They also might not know who to reach out to for non-judgmental support and are more likely to stumble across anti-choice counselling services online. All of these barriers make it more challenging for youth to access abortion right away, even if they have already chosen the option. It is important for young people to be able to identify people in their life who can and will support them regardless of the decision they make.

There are two types of abortion: medical and surgical. In Canada, medical abortions are performed up to 7 weeks using a combination of medications. The World Health Organization gold-standard created specifically for abortion and more effective than other medications on the market is a combination of mifepristone and misoprostol. In Canada, the combination of medications is known under the brand Mifegymiso. This can be used up to 10 weeks but at the time of publication is only offered in Canada up to 7 weeks. Mifegymiso is newly approved in Canada and still challenging to access, even though it has been standard practise for decades in medical abortion throughout the world. There are multiple regimens available for medical abortion but the regimen of choice in Canada is a combination of Mifepristone and Misoprostol (i.e., Mifegymiso). The other regimen available is a combination of Methotrexate and Misoprostol. Some people prefer medical abortion while others will prefer surgical. It is a matter of personal choice that varies from person to person.

Medical abortion can feel more discreet because it mimics a miscarriage. It can also be performed earlier than surgical abortion and may offer a sense of control during the process. For many different reasons (i.e., discrimination, transphobia, and trauma) some may have a strong desire to avoid surgery or to be in a hospital or clinic setting that is unknown.

The first medication is usually taken at a doctor's office and this is the medication that terminates the pregnancy. The second medication is often taken at home and empties the uterus of all pregnancy tissue, which results in bleeding (more than a period) and cramping. Because of the time needed in between medications and the length of time necessary for the **uterus** to empty completely, medical abortion takes between 3 to 5 days.

Surgical abortion is the most common type of abortion. It can be performed up to 23 weeks and 6 days in Canada (but gestational limits vary by provider and by province). The majority of abortions in Canada are performed during the first trimester (12 weeks). For this common procedure, local or general anesthetic is given, a **speculum** (like the ones used in a **Pap test**) is inserted into the **vagina**. This is followed by the dilation of the **cervix** and removal of the pregnancy tissue through aspiration (a small vacuum-like device). The doctor will often run a small instrument around the inside of the uterus to ensure that all the pregnancy tissue has been removed, a procedure called **curettage**. The entire procedure, for a first trimester abortion, takes between 5 to 10 minutes. Often when people hear the word "surgical" they assume that the procedure is more involved, lengthy, and complicated than it is. While with any medical procedure there are possible risks and complications, this is an opportunity to dispel the myth and decrease stigma around what is a common, safe, and effective procedure.

With both forms of abortion, doctors will usually require an **ultrasound** to date the pregnancy. An ultrasound is not mandatory but it is required by many doctors; individuals have the right to not see the ultrasound (the technician can turn the screen around). Medical abortion procedures require a follow-up appointment to ensure that everything has gone smoothly, whereas surgical abortions do not. In rare cases after a medical abortion, an appointment might reveal that the medical abortion was not successful. If this is the case, a surgical abortion is necessary.

Normal side effects for abortion can include cramping and bleeding (more pronounced in the medical abortion process). There can also be a wide range of emotions. The emotions that are experienced are varied, personal, and can be linked to the shift in hormones. There is no "right" or "wrong" emotional response to having an abortion—and often it is not just one feeling that someone experiences but a range of complex, and at times, seemingly contradictory ones. It is also very common to need some time to emotionally process the procedure regardless of the types of feelings that surface. This is normal and individuals should be encouraged to look up pro-choice counselling resources. (For toll-free pro-choice counselling, see **National Support Services** in the resources section) Watch out for "pregnancy crisis centres" that offer counselling; these centres are anti-choice. Many abortion clinics offer excellent pre- and post-abortion counselling so that individuals can discuss how they are feeling before and after their appointment.

Abortion is a safe and common medical procedure. Like any medical procedure, there is a small risk of complications, including hemorrhaging (heavy bleeding), infection, or injury to the uterus or cervix. These risks are uncommon (1% or less) and doctors will tell you how to identify any of these so that you can receive proper follow-up care in the event of any complications (Upadhyay et al., 2015).

Adoption

Adoption is a legal process that gives permanent custody of a child to someone other than the birth parent(s). It is a permanent and legal agreement where an individual gives birth and then permanently places their child in the care of a different person or family. There are two types of adoption, public and private.

Public adoptions occur through the Children's Aid Society. Private adoptions occur through an adoption agency and licensee. Private adoptions generally require a fee to be paid by the potential adopting parents, public adoptions do not.

Adoptions can be either open or closed (sometimes referred to as confidential adoptions). Open adoptions allow birth parent(s) and the adopting parent(s) to meet and get to know one another and choose whether or not to continue to build a relationship that works for them. In closed adoptions, birth parent(s) and the adopting parent(s) have no information about each other and do not remain in contact after the adoption process. In Canada, open adoptions are becoming more and more common.

All pregnancy options come with their own set of complex emotional responses, the range of which is often similar, and the decision to pursue adoption is no different. Continuing a pregnancy can be a physically challenging and an emotional task. If a person chooses adoption, it can be helpful to create a birth plan and identify people who will support them regardless of the decision they make. Individuals can choose to share this process with the adoptive parents or not.

Parenting

Like adoption and abortion, the decision to continue parenting a child is complex. It is informed by individual circumstances and comes with a possible range of emotions, including joy, fear, relief, grief, worry, excitement, etc. No matter the decision that the pregnant person makes, there is no one right way to feel. While the decision to parent a child, particularly in the case of an unintended pregnancy, is never a light one, supports such as adolescent-focused pregnancy (antenatal) care, social assistance, neo-natal support, food, housing, and child care exist. These supports vary across Canada and so it is important to research resources in the relevant province or territory. It is also important for individuals to be able to identify people in their life who can and will offer non-judgmental support regardless of the decision made.

Many young parents provide a wonderful parenting experience for children. Unfortunately, there is still stigma around the idea of "teen parenting," which can cause harm to both parents and children in the long term. As educators, it is important that you challenge myths and your own assumptions about "teen parenting," including the assumption that teens do not want to be parents or that they cannot be "good" parents. In reality, anyone, regardless of age or other identity, can be a "good" or a "bad" parent (and everything in between). Encourage students to seek out adolescent-focused pregnancy (antenatal) care and support groups for individuals in similar situations as soon as their decision is made. These support groups can help with practical support and the emotional and social issues that come up when parenting.

Unintended Pregnancy

While unintended pregnancies are very common (51% of pregnancies in North America are unplanned), many continue to be surrounded with shame and stigma (Guttmacher, 2014). Part of this shame and stigma comes from **sex negative** social norms that create myths and assumptions about unintended pregnancies. These myths and assumptions carry power unless actively and purposefully challenged. Here are some common myths and ways to challenge them:

- **Myth: Those facing unplanned pregnancies were irresponsible.**
  Even when using contraception perfectly, there can be a chance of pregnancy. Do not shame people, make assumptions, or ask about how their unintended pregnancy happened. There are a variety of circumstances beyond not using contraception or contraceptive failure that can result in unintended pregnancies, including sexual assault and coercion.

- **Myth: If they cannot handle being pregnant, they should not be having sex in the first place.**
  For many, sex is a normal, healthy, and pleasurable part of adolescent and adult life. While everyone should be given accurate information about how to minimize the potential for unintended pregnancy and STBBIs, a readiness or desire to parent a child should not be a precondition to engaging in sexual activity.

If a student is navigating an unintended pregnancy and finding it overwhelming, many services exist for free pregnancy options counselling. Local Planned Parenthood and sexual health clinic locations often provide free counseling either in-person or over the phone (for a directory of service providers, see 9.1 resources). (For toll-free pro-choice counselling, see **National Support Services** in the resources section)

If they choose to have an abortion, students can access non-judgmental, confidential information on where and how to access abortion services by calling the Action Canada for Sexual Health and Rights 24-hour toll-free Access Line at 1-888-642-2725. You can also reassure the student that it is up to them to decide whether they inform their partner, parents, friends, or family. Only the person who is pregnant can decide if it is safe or desirable to do so, just as they are the only ones who can decide what option is best for them.

Before You Begin: Teaching Pregnancy Options in a Non-Gendered Way

Be mindful that some students may already have experienced or supported a friend or partner through an unplanned pregnancy or abortion. Avoid making assumptions about the experiences of your students. In the same way, avoid making assumptions about the **gender identity** of people who are (or could become) pregnant. See table 9A for examples of how to use non-gendered language.

Table 9A

Instead Of...	Try...	What's the reason?
Both genders	All genders	"All genders" captures genders that do not fall under the binary system of male and female and promotes thinking about genders as a spectrum rather than two opposing choices.
Pregnant women	Pregnant people, pregnant individuals, or people with uteruses	These options reflect the fact that cisgender women have uteruses and not only ciswomen become pregnant.

When discussing sexual activity, contraception, pregnancy, and STBBI risk, avoid using language that reinforces the **gender binary**. It is not only cisgender women who become pregnant. People who identify as transgender, gender non-binary, agender, etc. can also become pregnant. Always using she/her pronouns when referring to pregnant people assumes that everyone who is pregnant uses she/her pronouns when in fact, people can use he/him and they/them pronouns. It is possible to teach this material without gendering experiences and the information people need in order to take care of themselves. Using non-gendered terms and language when talking about pregnancy can help avoid assumptions about people's identities and pronouns while ensuring that students of all gender identities are equipped with sufficient knowledge to navigate a variety of sexual activities and outcomes.

In the same way, avoid dividing STBBI symptoms by gender. Instead, discuss them in terms of "penis symptoms" and "vagina/vulva symptoms." This ensures that transgender students who may not identify as the gender that corresponds with their genitals can receive the most from their education and avoid feeling shame or stigma in the classroom.

Never assume that transgender students are not in your class simply because you cannot identify them. This replicates harmful ideas about what transgender individuals should look and act like. The modules in chapter 9 are purposely not separated according to assigned sex, the language used focuses on information that is relevant to everyone. (For more information on language use, gender identity, and assigned sex, see modules 1.4, 3.1, 3.8, 3.9, and 3.10).

Educator Reflection Questions

- Was there any content in this module that surprised you? Why or why not?
- Have you or someone close to you ever experienced an unintended pregnancy? If so, what support did you or the person close to you seek out? Was it helpful? Why or why not?
- Do you hold one of the pregnancy options above the others? If so, how can you ensure that this bias does not interfere with how you present this information? What are some practical things you can do before the lesson to practise teaching the information in a non-judgmental way?
- Have you ever assumed that young people always want to get an abortion when faced with an unintended pregnancy because they are young?

QUICK TIP
Avoid making assumptions about who is in your class. Gender identity and sexual orientation cannot be read from the body. Ensure your lessons apply to all genders by consciously avoiding gendered language.

- Have you ever made the judgment that young people should not be parents because they are young?
- When you were your students' age, did you believe any of the common myths about unintended pregnancies? How about now? If your belief changed between then and now, what influenced that decision?
- What does the idea of choice in the context of pregnancy mean to you?
- What are some tangible ways that you can practise being an ally in the context of unintended pregnancy to the young people that you teach?

9.6 UNINTENDED PREGNANCIES: OPTIONS AND DECISION-MAKING

LEVEL 3

Big Ideas in Module 9.6

- Access to and accurate information about all pregnancy options is a basic human right.
- "Teen pregnancy" and "teen parenting" is highly stigmatized, as is getting an abortion. It is this stigma and judgment that ends up causing the most harm.
- In Canada, abortion is a legal and safe medical option for people facing unintended pregnancy.
- The only person that has the right to make the decision about which option is best for them is the person who is pregnant.
- There is a mixture of social, emotional, and practical considerations that often go into the decision-making process when navigating an unintended pregnancy.

Learning Objectives

Students will:

- Identify the options that someone has when navigating an unintended pregnancy.
- Learn skills to help navigate decision-making.

Cross-Curricular Connections

- Art (visual)
- English
- Equity Studies
- Family Studies
- Gender Studies
- Psychology
- Social Studies
- Sociology

Terminology

- Abortion
- Contraception
- Human rights
- Unintended pregnancy

Materials

- Chalkboard, whiteboard, or flip chart and appropriate writing utensils
- Printed copies of **Options Scenarios**
- **Educator Answer Key—Options Scenarios**
- Drawing and painting supplies with appropriate paper

Background Information for Educators

Part of discussing safer sex and contraception with students includes complete information on all options. When faced with an **unintended pregnancy**, young people have the option of parenting, **adoption**, and **abortion**. The only person that has the right to make the decision about which option is best for them is the person who is pregnant. They also have the right to choose who they inform and when—only the pregnant individual can decide if it is safe or desirable to do so. it is up to them whether they inform their partner, parents, friends, or family about the pregnancy and their choice.

For some people, deciding what to do when faced with an unintended pregnancy is extremely tough, for others, it is not. For some people, the choice is clear, for others, it is murky and unclear. Regardless of whether the decision-making process is tough or clear, there are a mixture of social, emotional, and practical considerations that often go into the decision-making process. The person facing the pregnancy might consider:

- Whether they want to be pregnant or continue the pregnancy at this time.
- Whether they have a support network in making this decision, regardless of what the decision is.
- Whether they are coping with negative feelings related to the pregnancy, like shame, sadness, worry, anxiety, or embarrassment.
- What kinds of material support and resources might be available to them.
- Whether their family, their partner, and/or their partner's family is supportive, coercive, or abusive.
- Whether they are at a time and place in their life where continuing a pregnancy is desirable for them.
- Whether they have identified the personal factors that are important to them and that might impact their decision-making process (including, but not limited to, personal beliefs, intuition, spirituality, cultural, and/or religious backgrounds).
- Whether their gut feeling aligns with other considerations.

Information available to support young people in making decisions about unintended pregnancies is generally difficult to find. This is compounded by the fact that evidence-based information on abortion can be challenging to find because abortion is stigmatized and politically debated. Regardless of personal opinion, access to safe, legal abortion is a basic **human right**. In Canada, abortion is a legal and safe medical procedure; the misinformation that exists stigmatizes what is a standard medical practise and shames those who seek abortions. Students should be made aware that they have the right to choose and access abortion when facing an unintended pregnancy.

Choice and access are essential in upholding the sexual and reproductive human rights of young people. Access to **contraception**, family planning, and unintended pregnancy options (abortion, adoption, and parenting) is a human right that is consistent with the right to bodily autonomy, to freedom from torture, to the enjoyment of the highest attainable standard of physical and mental health, and to decide the number and spacing of children. Access is about affordability, geography, skilled health care professionals, and information/education; it needs to be in place for there to truly be choice.

YOU SHOULD KNOW

While abortion is largely stigmatized, it is often encouraged as the only option for youth, people with disabilities, people living in poverty, Indigenous, black, and other racialized people of colour. This is part of a continuing history of forced and coerced sterilization in Canada based on systemic oppression (ableism, classism, colonialism, classism, etc.) and ideas of social "desirability." (For more information, see modules 2.1, 2.2, and 2.3).

Those who choose to have an abortion have the option of medical abortion or surgical abortion. Medical abortion is done by taking a combination of medications and is available for pregnancies up to 7 to 10 weeks gestation in Canada. First trimester surgical abortions involve either manual or vacuum aspiration of the uterus and are available up to 23 weeks in Canada (varies by province/territory).

While abortion is entirely legal in Canada, it is not entirely accessible. Not all hospitals or clinics provide abortions and abortion providers tend to be concentrated in urban centers and major cities, which leaves many rural areas underserviced. Different abortion providers also have different gestational limits, meaning that individuals may have to travel further to find an abortion provider that accommodates them, depending on gestational age.

There are many abortion myths that expand the internet and social spheres of life and political influence. These myths are not based in evidence and usually come from anti-choice sources. It is important for educators to be equipped with evidence-based information to help challenge any abortion myths that students have (for more information, see module 9.5 and 9.6 resources). Educators need to make it clear that individuals experiencing an unintended pregnancy have a legal right to abortion services. It is your responsibility to provide students with accurate information about abortion and how to access abortion services. (For non-judgmental, confidential information on where and how to access abortion services, refer students to the Action Canada for Sexual Health and Rights 24-hour toll-free Access Line at 1-888-642-2725).

Student Readiness

Before students engage with this lesson, ensure that safer space guidelines and group norms have been established (and revisited) within your classroom (for more information on how to establish safer space guidelines, see module 1.3). To effectively prepare for this activity, ensure students understand that:
- Half of pregnancies are unintended pregnancies and no matter how it happened, it does not make you a bad or irresponsible person.
- Unintended pregnancies happen regardless of gender identity or sexual orientation.
- This module does not moralize, stigmatize, or hold one pregnancy option above the other.
- Sexual activity among young people is normal, expected, and healthy.
- They will be presented with all pregnancy options, including information on abortion access in Canada.

Summary of Activities

Students will:
- Work in small groups to navigate various pregnancy options using scenarios.
- Individually reflect with a writing and drawing exercise on decision-making processes.

Activity 1 ③

Before facilitating this activity, familiarize yourself with the information contained in module 9.5 and the **Educator Answer Key—Options Scenarios**.

Instructions

1. Provide an overview of all pregnancy options available in Canada from the information contained in module 9.5. *You can write the key points from each option on the board or on chart paper and place around the classroom.*

2. Place students into groups of 3 to 4. Give each group a copy of **Options Scenarios.**

3. Ask students to work through each scenario and record their discussions.

4. Have each group present their answers to the class.

5. Conclude the activity by using the **Educator Answer Key—Options Scenarios** to fill in any blanks from the student presentations.

Activity 2 ③

Before facilitating this activity, remind students that this is a private, reflective activity. Students will not be asked to present their drawings.

Instructions

1. Provide art and drawing supplies and paper. Ask students to draw a circle in the middle of their page and label it "gut feelings." *You can demonstrate an example for them on the board.*

2. Add 3 more circles around the first circle (see figure 9B for an example). Ask students to use the whole page.

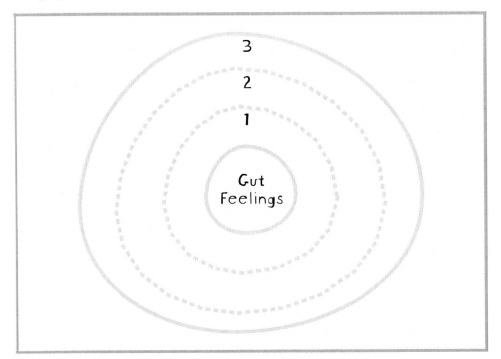

Figure 9B

3. Ask students to close their eyes and think about a big decision that they have made in their life. With eyes still closed, ask them to reflect on why that decision was big and what elements and considerations went into making that decision.

4. Ask students to place the headings "hopes," "fears," and "practical considerations" into the 3 remaining circles (see figure 9C for an example). *Emphasize that students should complete their drawings by thinking about how they are feeling today, recognizing that feelings about decisions can change.*

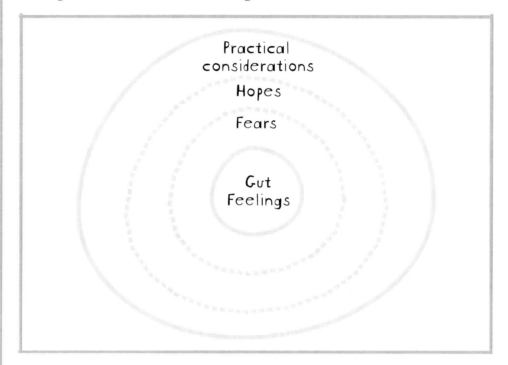

Figure 9C

5. Ask students to categorize all the things they felt and considered when making their big decision within the relevant circle. If something applies to more than 1 of the circles, students can indicate this with lines and/or arrows

6. Ask students to take a minute, step back and look at their circles and categories. Have them indicate which considerations feel in their control with a   and which feel outside of their control with a   .

7.   Optional: Have students interpret all the considerations and feelings from their decision as a drawing and/or painting.

8.   Optional: Have students write a letter to their future selves at any point after the decision was made and followed through with.

9. Once everyone has finished the exercise, explain: Decision-making has many different layers. Sometimes we give one layer more importance than the others. It can be helpful to write down these different layers to see them more clearly and notice where we are placing all our energy for deciding. When considering a decision, it can be helpful to notice what is in our control and what is not in our control. Asking ourselves if there is anything that seems out of our control but is actually in our control can help provide a new perspective on the situation. It can help to let go of what we cannot control and take responsibility and action of what we can. There is no right or wrong "layer" in decision-making. Most often, decisions are made from a place of balancing all the layers; however, your gut feelings can be a good grounding force, a place to return to and a navigator in the middle of all the other layers that you are thinking and feeling your way through.

Wrap-up

Summarize the module with the following points:
- Decision-making is a challenging skill to learn, no matter what the decision.
- When faced with an unintended pregnancy, even if the decision is clear and straightforward, it can be a difficult and emotionally challenging situation.
- It is important to know all pregnancy options and receive accurate, non-judgmental information about each.
- The right decision for you might not be the right decision for someone else—respect everyone's decision-making process.

Safer Sex and Sexually Transmitted and Blood-Borne Infections

CHAPTER

10

10.1 INTRODUCTION

Safer sex is a term that most young people hear at some point during their adolescence. It is a term that is usually used in reference to **contraception** (i.e., birth control) and/or **Sexually Transmitted and Blood Borne Infections** (STBBIs) prevention. *Beyond the Basics* takes a comprehensive, holistic view of sexuality and the meaning of safer sex. Educating young people about contraceptives and STBBIs needs to be placed in the social, political, and economic contexts of access, healthy relationships, **consent**, power, **oppression**, and choice.

YOU SHOULD KNOW

Students may be familiar with the older terms: sexually transmitted infections (STIs) and sexually transmitted diseases (STDs). Using "sexually transmitted and bloodborne infections" (STBBIs) is more inclusive; It considers infections transmitted sexually or through blood.

CONT'D NEXT PAGE

YOU SHOULD KNOW CONT'D

Using the word "infection" rather than "disease" acknowledges that someone with an illness may not necessarily feel sick but can still transmit the infection. There is also less stigma around the word infection and it reflects the reality that most STBBIs can be cured if detected early and treated with appropriate medications.

Sex negative and fear-based approaches to contraception and safer sex are ineffective at reducing **unintended pregnancies** and STBBIs. A more effective approach is empowering young people through sex positive teaching approaches that value pleasure for all partners and do not stigmatize sex (Oliver et al, 2013). Teaching from a **sex positive** perspective acknowledges that sexual activity among young people is normal, expected, and healthy. Sex positivity counters the fear, shame, and stigma that is often linked to youth sexuality and perpetuated through curricula that overemphasize the risks of sex and underemphasize the potential joys, pleasures, and discovery of sex and sexuality.

Risk is a normal part of life. We take risks all the time, including every time we get in a car, cross the street, get on a bus, etc. We also assess risk every time we take a risk. Whether physical, emotional, or social, we consciously or unconsciously calculate risk and benefit. Overemphasizing risk does not teach young people how to assess risk—risk is something to be informed about, not afraid of. Learning the skills to assess and then reduce risk is essential to finding pleasure in being alive rather than living in fear. Informing young people about possible risks in ways that reduce fear and emphasize sex positivity can help in assessing risk with clarity and creating strategies to reduce possible risks that come with being sexually active. Chapter 10 focuses on STBBI transmission, STBBI risk assessment, and how to practise safer sex that provides **dual protection** from STBBIs and unintended pregnancy.

Being aware of ways to reduce the risk of STBBI transmission significantly reduces the chances of contracting an STBBI. While STBBIs are common among youth, the **stigma** attached to STBBIs make them challenging to communicate about with sexual partners, including having one and the importance of testing and receiving any required sexual health care. Part of teaching safer sex is actively working to reduce stigma associated with STBBIs by using scientific evidence to challenge assumptions.

The most common viral STBBIs among youth are chlamydia and the human papillomavirus (HPV). HPV can result in genital warts or precancerous changes to the cervix. There are over 100 different strains of HPV. Many are benign and pose low risk but there are some less benign strains that have been linked to cervical and anal cancers. Most people will clear HPV from their body within two years.

In most cases, chlamydia and HPV are asymptomatic (there are no symptoms). Many STBBIs do not have symptoms but can be passed onto partners and cause eventual complications if not identified and treated right away, which makes STBBI testing an integral part of a person's sexual health plan. Learning how to communicate with partners about STBBIs, testing, and safer sex is part of learning how to normalize safer sex and reduce STBBI stigma.

Having one STBBI can put you at higher risk for other (potentially more serious) STBBIs. This is another reason why making STBBI testing a part of your normal health routine is important. If detected early, most STBBIs can be cured altogether, others can be effectively managed using treatment.

Part of encouraging young people to get STBBI testing is ensuring that they know where to access youth friendly care, how to identify if they are receiving youth friendly care, and how to advocate for care that does not stigmatize them for being sexually active and/or for any part of who they are (e.g., sexual orientation, gender identity, ability, race, socio-economic status, immigration status, etc.) or what they do (e.g., have unprotected sex, use drugs, self-harm, self-pierce/tattoo, trade sex for money or goods, etc.).

Young people have the right to have all their sexual health questions answered in non-judgmental, non-stigmatizing ways with the most up-to-date scientific evidence (for more information on how to advocate for sexual health care, see module 10.7). These are part of our basic human rights. Equipping young people with education and information about safer sex and how to advocate for youth friendly, stigma free health care is essential in ensuring that their **sexual rights** are respected and that they feel empowered to enhance their own sexual health.

Comprehensive sexuality education recognizes that human sexuality is holistic; it encompasses the social, political, economic, emotional, psychological, physical, and spiritual dimensions of a person's life. Teaching young people about safer sex from a comprehensive sexuality education approach recognizes that individual choice is influenced by social norms, political landscape, economic and geographical access, education, and accurate information. Comprehensive sexuality education also recognizes that sex happens within the context of social norms and relationships, even if those relationships are fleeting or purely sexual. Addressing STBBIs in the classroom will be most effective if it occurs within comprehensive sexuality education and addresses issues such as **self-concept**, healthy relationships, media literacy, **consent**, **sexual orientation**, and **gender identity**.

Sexuality education that is not comprehensive often fails to provide information that is relevant for the diverse social contexts in which youth live and the intersections of their identities. Young people need to be equipped with the knowledge of STBBIs and their symptoms as well as how to communicate and negotiate safer sex within the social contexts they live. The modules in chapter 10 prioritize evidence-based STBBI information, sex positive risk reduction strategies, and the necessary behavioural skills to practise safer sex. The **National Support Services** and chapter 10 resources provide additional information on sexual health, STBBIs, and safer sex.

Educator Reflection Questions

- What assumptions do you have about the sexuality of young people? Do you assume that young people are not sexually active? Do you assume that they are engaged in all types of sexual activities or just some types?
- Do you consider yourself a risk averse person or someone who likes taking risks? Why or why not?
- What kinds of risks do you take daily? (Try to come up with at least five risks, they can be emotional, social, intellectual, and/or physical).
- Do you feel differently about risk related to sexual behaviour than you do about your list of daily risks? Why or why not?
- What do you believe is the most effective way to teach young people about practising safer sex? Why do you have this belief and where does it come from? Is this belief based in evidence, your personal experience, and/or a feeling that you have?
- Have you ever thought about access to accurate information and education on safer sex and STBBI risk reduction (beyond abstinence) as a human right?
- Have you ever thought about access to stigma free sexual health care as a human right for adults? Have you ever thought about access to youth friendly, stigma free sexual health care as a human right for youth?

Think back to when you were your students' age and ask yourself...

- If you were having sex, were you practising safer sex and thinking about how you could reduce your risk of STBBIs?
- Were you able to access the kinds of sexual health care that you wanted and/or needed at the time? What barriers (if any) existed for you in terms of being able to access this sexual health care?

Big Ideas in Chapter 10

- Educating young people about contraceptives and STBBIs needs to be placed in the social, political, and economic contexts of access, healthy relationships, consent, power, oppression, and choice.
- Access to information, education, and youth friendly, stigma free health care is essential in upholding the sexual and reproductive rights of young people.
- Risk is a normal part of life; we take risks all the time. Overemphasizing risk does not teach young people how to assess risk.
- While sex does involve risk, these risks are not something to be afraid of, they are something to be informed about.
- Teaching safer sex and STBBI risk reduction from a sex positive perspective acknowledges that sexual activity among young people is normal, expected, and healthy.
- Everyone, regardless of sexual orientation or gender identity, needs to have information about safer sex and STBBI risk reduction and the social and emotional skills to practise it.
- Comprehensive sexuality education recognizes that individual choice and behaviours are influenced by social norms, political landscape, economic and geographical access, education, and accurate information.

10.2 EDUCATOR RESOURCE: SEXUALLY TRANSMITTED AND BLOOD-BORNE INFECTIONS

Youth Trends

Many people find **Sexually Transmitted and Blood-Borne Infections (STBBIs)** difficult to talk about but they are more common than most people think; 75% of adults will have had at least 1 type of **human papillomavirus (HPV)** in their lifetime (SOGC, 2017). The **stigma** and fear associated with STBBIs makes communication about them challenging. If peers and sexual partners are not talking to each other about STBBIs, they may seem less common than they actually are.

The most common viral STBBIs among youth in Canada are **chlamydia** and HPV. Not only are both common but the majority of cases are also asymptomatic (there are no symptoms). Asymptomatic STBBIs can be passed onto partners and cause eventual complications if not identified and treated right away. Knowing how to identify symptoms, assess risk, communicate, get tested, and have safer sex is part of learning how to normalize safer sex and reduce STBBI stigma.

Transmission and Risk

We assess risk every time we take one. While a person's perception of and comfort with different risk levels might change over the course of their life, we are constantly consciously or unconsciously calculating physical, emotional, and/or social risk and benefit. Having the skills, information, and resources to assess risk and make decisions over time and with changing circumstances is important in all aspects of life, especially in practising safer sex and making choices we are comfortable with.

Although the most likely transmission routes can vary somewhat among different STBBIs, the highest risk for transmission occurs with unprotected penetrative sex (i.e., penis-vagina intercourse and anal intercourse with a **penis**). STBBIs can also be transmitted through oral-genital contact, oral-anal contact, skin-to-skin contact with genitals (with or without penetration), genital-genital contact, digital-vaginal intercourse ("fingering"), and digital-anal intercourse.

YOU SHOULD KNOW

The term "unprotected sex" has different meanings depending on the context. In chapter 10, "unprotected sex" means not using anything to protect yourself from STBBIs. This often means not using condoms during penetrative sex but can also mean not using dental dams and in the context of HIV, not using condoms or any other form of HIV prevention (i.e., PrEP, treatment as prevention, and/or the maintenance of an undetectable viral load).

Risk is a part of everyday life and not something to fear; it is something to be informed about. Correct and consistent use of condoms and/or **dental dams** or gloves will reduce the risk of STBBI transmission for the body parts that are covered. It is important that young people know the **transmission routes** of STBBIs, the symptoms to look for, and the available treatment to prevent complications. The **STBBI Chart** from module 10.3 provides information for each STBBI.

Having access to accurate information is one part of practising safer sex. The other is making STBBI testing a part of your normal health routine—this is especially important since two of the most common STBBIs among young people are often asymptomatic. Having an STBBI can put you at higher risk for other, potentially more serious, STBBIs like HIV. If found early, most STBBIs can be cured altogether, others can be effectively managed using treatment. Educating young people and equipping them with information about safer sex, where to find sexual health care, and how to advocate for sexual health care that is youth friendly and stigma free is essential in ensuring that the **sexual rights** of youth are being respected and that they feel empowered to enhance their own sexual health.

Bacterial and Viral STBBIs

Most STBBIs are either bacterial or viral. Bacterial infections are caused by bacteria; viral infections are caused by viruses. Bacteria are single-celled microorganisms that thrive in different types of environments. Most bacteria cause no harm to people. Viruses are even smaller than bacteria and require living hosts (such as people) to multiply and survive.

The most important distinction between bacteria and viruses is that antibiotic drugs usually kill bacteria but are not effective against viruses. Bacterial STBBIs can be treated and cured with antibiotics if detected early. Many viral STBBIs can be effectively managed with medication and other kinds of treatment but most are not curable. Of course, there are exceptions. HPV is an example of a virus that is often cleared by the body naturally and new treatments for Hepatitis C (HCV) offer a cure.

Human Papilloma Virus (HPV)

Some STBBIs are easier to understand and explain to students than others. Even though HPV is the most common STBBI in Canada and the world, there is considerable confusion and fear surrounding it. It is important to approach the confusion and fear with a mixture of caution and calm. While HPV **incidence** is highest in adolescents and young adults, (particularly among 15 to 24 year-olds) about 90% of people with a strong immune system will clear the virus within two years (WHO, 2016). There is also no conclusive evidence that the presence of a latent virus in the body causes subsequent symptoms.

There are approximately 100 known types of HPV that can infect the genital, anal, and reproductive tract (CATIE, 2016). Less than half (40 strains) are linked to genital warts and cancer (SOGC, 2017) and only about 15 strains have been known to cause cancer of the **cervix**, anus, mouth, throat, **vulva**, **vagina**, and/or penis (SOGC, 2017). The most common type of cancer caused by HPV is cervical and the second most common is anal (Canadian Cancer Society, 2017). Since 2007, students across the country have been offered an HPV vaccine that covers 4 strains: 6 and 11, which cause the majority of warts, and 16 and 18, which are responsible for the majority of cancers (CATIE, 2016; Canadian Cancer Society, 2017; SOGC, 2017). The vaccines do not prevent cancer but do prevent the HPV infections that can cause it. They originally targeted people with a cervix but since 2010, vaccines have also been available for those with penises.

YOU SHOULD KNOW

The HPV vaccine is not publicly funded for all people in Canada though the vaccine is free of charge to some populations through provincial and territorial voluntary immunization programs. Girls between ages 9 and 13 can receive a free HPV immunization through school programs. Alberta, Manitoba, Ontario, Nova Scotia, British Columbia, and P.E.I. currently offer the vaccine to boys as well.

The HPV vaccine does not cover all strains but does protect against several of the highest risk strains. Discussion of the vaccine should emphasize the need to practise safer sex and get regular STBBI and **Pap tests** (both cervical and anal in the case of receptive anal intercourse). Pap tests are the main HPV screening tool for cervical cancer. The most recent guidelines suggest those who are sexually active begin routine Pap tests at age 25 every 3 years until age 70, unless there are symptoms or early signs of cervical cancer (SOGC, 2013).

It is important to keep in mind that having HPV does not mean that you have cancer. The majority of people will clear the virus. Like many other STBBIs, people often do not have (or cannot tell if they have) any signs or symptoms of HPV. Regular Pap tests are the best way to ensure early detection and effective treatment (if necessary). It is the fear and stigma surrounding HPV diagnosis that causes the most distress and harm.

The Pap test allows cells from the cervix or anus to be collected and tested to look for any cellular changes that may indicate abnormal, pre-cancerous, or cancerous cells. Abnormal Pap test results are also called **dysplasia** and do not equal cancer. Even though these terms seem scary, it is estimated that 40% of people with a cervix will have an "abnormal" Pap test result in their life and in 80% of cases, dysplasia does not turn into cancer (Our Bodies Ourselves, 2017). If a Pap test indicates cervical or anal dysplasia, the body will often heal itself if the dysplasia is mild (low-grade) and the individual is under 30 and has a functioning immune system. In this case, a follow-up Pap or other tests are often recommended until it can be confirmed that the dysplasia is gone. If the dysplasia is of a higher grade, the individual is over 30, or their immune system is compromised, treatment may be required to remove the abnormal cells.

Pap tests are not the same as other STBBI tests, although some STBBI tests can be done at the same time as a Pap test. Students should be aware that they can and should still be tested for STBBIs as soon as they become sexually active.

Educator Reflection Questions

- Did anything about this module surprise you? Why or why not?
- How has STBBI stigma affected you in terms of how you approach your own sexual health? Has this changed throughout your life? Why or why not?
- What were your assumptions of STBBIs before reading this module and have those assumptions changed?
- Did you know that HPV was so common?
- Are there any aspects of HPV that have confused you in the past? If so, did this module help clarify HPV for you?

10.3 UNDERSTANDING STBBI TRANSMISSION AND ASSESSING RISK

LEVEL 2 3

Big Ideas in Module 10.3

- Like sexuality, risk is a normal part of life.
- We assess risk every time we take one. Accurate information about STBBI transmission is necessary to effectively assess risk related to sexuality.
- A person's perception of and comfort with different risk levels might change over the course of their life. Having the skills, information, and resources to assess risk and make decisions over time and with changing circumstances is important in all aspects of life, especially in practising safer sex.
- A sex positive approach to risk recognizes that there are benefits of being sexually active, including sexual pleasure, curiosity, intimacy, exploration, and expression. Risk assessment is weighing these benefits with accurate information about possible risks in order to make choices we are comfortable with.

Learning Objectives

Students will:

- Learn how to identify and distinguish STBBIs and the difference between viral and bacterial STBBIs.
- Identify STBBI transmission risk on a scale from "commonly passed on" to "not passed on."
- Compare STBBI risk assessment to every day activity risk assessment.
- Apply a framework for risk assessment and decision-making.

Cross-Curricular Connections

- Biology
- Equity Studies
- Family Studies
- Gender Studies
- Psychology
- Social Studies
- Sociology

Terminology

- Immune system
- Sex positive
- Transmission routes

Materials
- Chalkboard, whiteboard, or interactive Smart Board
- Open space to move around in
- Masking tape
- Printed copies of **STBBI Identification Cards** (cut so that names and descriptions are separate)
- **STBBI Chart**
- **Daily Tasks Risk Chart** (projected or written on board)
- **STBBI Transmission Risk Chart** (projected or written on board)
- **Educator Answer Key—STBBI Transmission Risk Chart**
- Printed copies of **Risk Cards**
- **Educator Answer Key—Daily Tasks Risk Chart**
- Printed copies of the **Consequence vs. Likelihood Chart**
- **Educator Resource—Consequence vs. Likelihood Chart Example**
- Drawing and other art supplies
- Optional: Projector and screen

Background Information for Educators

Risk is a normal part of life. We take risks all the time: when we get in a car, cross the street, get on a bus, etc. We also assess risk every time we take a risk. Whether physical, emotional, or social, we often unconsciously calculate risk and benefit.

When engaging in sexual activity there are social, emotional, and physical benefits as well as risks. The risks of being sexually active can be managed by accurate information and informed decisions about the level of risk a person wants to take at any given moment.

Like most things in life, a person's comfort with and perception of different risk levels might change, be dependant on sexual partners, and/or life circumstances. Having the skills to assess risk and make decisions over time and with changing circumstances is important in all aspects of life, especially in practising safer sex.

This module focuses on the information necessary to assess the physical risks of being sexually active and how to move knowledge and assessment into decision-making and action for risk management. Understanding the **transmission routes** of STBBIs is an important part of assessing physical risk, making decisions, and applying appropriate safer sex practises (risk management).

The language used in this module recognizes that STBBI transmission is made up of common and uncommon transmission routes. What is considered "risky" is not automatically linked to a sexual activity. We discuss "risk" as a gradient or continuum that ranges from activities where STBBIs are "commonly passed on" to activities where STBBIs are "not passed on." This kind of language accurately describes transmission and risk while counteracting the fear and **stigma** supported by terms like "high risk" or "no risk." When teaching young people about STBBI risk, it is important that the information is relatable as well as accurate. "Commonly passed on" does not mean a 100% chance of getting or passing on an STBBI if protection is not used, it means that the likelihood of STBBI transmission is higher than in other cases. A **sex positive** approach to risk assessment recognizes that there are benefits of being sexually active, including sexual pleasure, curiosity, intimacy, exploration, and expression. Weighing these benefits with accurate information about possible risks is what risk assessment is. Almost everything in life has risk and benefit, learning how to make decisions based on accurate, balanced information is a skill applicable to all aspects of life.

Student Readiness

Before students engage with this lesson, ensure that safer space guidelines and group norms have been established (and revisited) within your classroom (for more information on how to establish safer space guidelines, see module 1.3). To effectively prepare for this activity, ensure students understand that:

- People engage in a variety of sexual activities regardless of their gender identity and sexual orientation.
- Being at risk for an STBBI is not related to sexual orientation or gender identity. It is related to unprotected sex.
- There is no perfect calculation for risk assessment. Comfort levels can change moment to moment, partner to partner, and that is okay. It is important for partners to communicate risk and changing comfort.
- It is everyone's responsibility to practise safer sex and STBBI prevention.
- Most STBBIs can be cured and/or managed, especially if detected and treated early.
- Sexual activity among young people is normal, expected, and healthy.
- Many people have sex for pleasure. Part of risk assessment in being sexually active is weighing the risks with benefits like pleasure.
- We take risks everyday. Having accurate information about STBBI transmission can help make informed decisions about the level of risk you feel comfortable taking.
- There is no right age to start having sex. It depends on comfort level, emotional and social preparedness, and circumstances.

Summary of Activities

Students will:

- Collectively work together to physically match STBBI names to descriptions, then categorize STBBIs as bacterial or viral.
- Work in small groups to compare risk as it relates to sexual activities, with risk as it relates to daily activities.
- Individually reflect on how they make decisions related to sexual activities and health by charting and/or drawing.

Activity 1 2 3

Instructions

1. Create enough space in the classroom for students to comfortably walk around and draw a line down the middle of the open space using masking tape. Designate one side of the room as "bacterial" and the other side as "viral."

2. Explain: Bacterial STBBIs like chlamydia, gonorrhea, and syphilis can be eliminated from the body if they are treated with antibiotics. Viral infections like herpes and HIV can be treated and managed but not eliminated. While most HPV infections are cleared by the body's **immune system** without any symptoms, strains with symptoms like genital warts can be treated but might require several treatments before there are no more symptoms.

3. Divide the class evenly in half and provide one half of the room with the name cards and the other half with the description cards from the **STBBI Identification Cards.**

4. Ask students to mingle throughout the room and try to find their counterpart, not worrying just yet about whether they are bacterial or viral infections.

5. Once students have found their counterpart, have them choose (based on the description card) if they are a bacterial or a viral infection and move to that side of the room. If they are unsure, tell them to stand outside of the space.

6. Have each pairing present their name, description, and why they chose bacterial, viral, or unsure. Check their answers against the STBBI Identification Cards and the **STBBI Chart.** Correct any mismatched pairings or incorrect placements.

7. For the students that were unsure whether they were bacterial or viral, explain that there are some STBBIs that do not fall into either category and are infestations and/or parasites that can be cured with proper treatment.

8. Debrief as a class using the following prompts:
   - Was it challenging to find your counterpart?

- How did you and your counterpart decide what kind of infection you were?
- Did anything surprise you about the STBBI descriptions?

Activity 2 2 3

Instructions

1. Introduce this activity by asking students to raise their hand if they consider themselves a risk-taker. Now ask students to raise their hand if they consider themselves risk adverse.
2. Explain that risk is a very normal part of living in the world and that we take risks all the time, often without even realizing it. We take social, emotional, physical, and intellectual risks daily but the degree to which we notice these risks often depends on our perception and comfort levels.
3. Project or draw the **Daily Tasks Risk Chart** on the board. Ask students to:
   - Raise their hand if they have ever thought about any of these daily activities as risky.
   - Share which activities they think of as risky and why.
   - Come up with some of the benefits of "risky" activities.
   - Identify ways to reduce possible risks or harms while still gaining the benefits of these activities.

EDUCATOR ANSWER KEY

Students will likely have a variety of perspectives about what could be classified as risky and why. Use this as a learning opportunity—the variety in risk assessment demonstrates how subjective and fluid the idea of risky can be and how it can change depending on life experiences, personalities, identities, peer group norms, and the social/cultural context in which you live. Emphasize that most daily activities carry some kind of risk, whether emotional, physical, and/or social. Sometimes, the benefits outweigh the risks and sometimes, the risks outweigh the benefits. Give the example of driving to school. Sometimes the convenience might outweigh the physical risk. This risk calculation (or assessment) is always changing and dependant on many factors, some of which are outside of our control (like weather) and some of which are within our control (like wearing a seatbelt). Having all of the information about risk and benefit can help clarify risk assessment and the decision-making process. Knowing how to reduce possible risks and/or harms is a part of decision-making. For instance, while driving to school might bring benefit in terms of saving time, there is a risk of getting physically injured in a car; wearing seatbelts and driving sober are ways to reduce potential risks and harms.

4. Project or draw the **STBBI Transmission Risk Chart** on the board. Ask students to:
   - Raise their hand if they have ever thought about any of these sexual activities as risky.
   - Share which activities they think of as risky and why. Come up with some of the benefits of "risky" activities.
   - Identify was to reduce possible risks or harms while gaining the benefits of these activities.

EDUCATOR ANSWER KEY

Most sexual activity carries some kind of risk, whether emotional, physical, and/or social. Sexual activity also carries benefits like pleasure, emotional intimacy, and/or feeling like you fit in with your peers. Sometimes the benefits outweigh the risks and sometimes the risks outweigh the benefits. For example, herpes is commonly passed during oral sex but the benefit of physical pleasure could also be high. This risk calculation (or assessment) is always changing and dependant on many other factors, some of which are outside of our control (like a sexual partner with **asymptomatic viral shedding**) and some of which are within our control (using a **dental dam**). Having all of the information about risk and benefit can help clarify assessment and the decision-making process. The chart focuses on specific physical risks (STBBIs) and demonstrates that there is a gradient of risk—not all unprotected sexual activity commonly passes all STBBIs all of the time. Even with activities where particular STBBIs are commonly passed, actions can be taken to lower or eliminate the risk of transmission. Knowing how to reduce possible risks and/or harms is a part of decision-making. For instance, one of the biggest benefits of sexual activity is pleasure but there can be potential risks and/or harms related to STBBIs. Using protection (e.g., condoms, dental dams, and/or HIV pre-exposure prophylaxis medication) during sexual activity can reduce potential risks and harms.

5. Divide students into groups of 3 to 4 and give each group a mixture of **Risk Cards** and tape (ensure that all cards are distributed and split up evenly between the small groups).
6. Ask students to work in their groups to figure out where to place their cards on the two charts. *There are only enough spaces as there are cards. Ensure that they are working with both charts. Cards can be placed with tape directly on the board within the chart.*

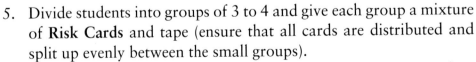

7. Take up the answers for both charts using the **Educator Answer Key—Daily Tasks Risk Chart** and the **Educator Answer Key—STBBI Transmission Risk Chart**. For additional information, consult the **STBBI Chart**. *The risk levels contained in the Educator Answer Key—STBBI Transmission Risk Chart are based on the most up-to-date evidence at time of publication on STBBI transmission of the major bacterial and viral STBBIs.*

8. Debrief the activity by asking:
   - Were there any activities you had trouble labelling?
   - Were there any activities whose risk levels surprised you?
   - Which activities do you (or would you) actively assess risk for? Which activities do you think you assess risk for in an unconscious way? Is your active risk assessment based on accurate information about risk level or something else?
   - How can you more consciously assess risk about sexual activity based on the information you have? How can you reduce risk?

9. Wrap up the activity by explaining: Almost everything in life has risks and benefits, learning how to make decisions based on accurate, balanced information is a skill applicable to all aspects of life.

Activity 3

Instructions

1. Ask students:
   - What kinds of risks do you take on an average day?
   - What are some risks that you assess subconsciously? What are ones you consciously assess?
   - What are examples of risk assessment required when making a difficult decision? What makes this assessment and decision difficult?
   - What kinds of information do we need for the assessment and decision to be made easier?
   - What can we do to make the risks involved in these difficult decisions safer and less risky?

EDUCATOR ANSWER KEY

- Students will come up with their own risks but examples include leaving your house, getting to know a new person, eating a new type of food, riding your bike, getting in a car, crossing the street, sharing an opinion in class, posting a photo to social media, texting with friends, asking someone out on a date.

CONT'D NEXT PAGE

EDUCATOR ANSWER KEY CONT'D

- Assessing when and where to cross the street can be subconscious. For some people, sharing their opinion in class can be a subconscious risk assessment, for others this can feel like a bigger decision and a more conscious assessment or calculated risk. More conscious risk assessments might include assessing when, where, and with whom to have sexual intercourse, whether to go to a party, whether to have unprotected sex, whether to try a new sports activity, etc.

- Examples of risk assessment required for a difficult decision include whether to engage in sexual activity and with whom, to send a "sext" and/or intimate selfie, to get in a vehicle with someone who is intoxicated, to go to college/university and/or which one, to "come out" to your family and friends. These decisions are difficult because there could be a lot at stake. There are physical, emotional, and social risks and benefits to consider.

- We need as much evidence-based, accurate information about risk as possible. We also need to be able to name the factors that we can control and recognize what we cannot. We also need to understand that although we can try and make the best decisions based on the best available evidence and information, nothing is ever 100% without risk, especially in relationships.

- We can minimize risk by consulting experts, doing research and gathering accurate information, having a back-up plan, learning about what to do and ways to protect ourselves in an emergency or crisis situation, trusting ourselves and our gut instincts/feelings, and taking action to minimize risk if we can.

2. Introduce the **Consequence vs. Likelihood Chart** to help with risk assessment and decision-making by stating the following:
   - A **consequence** is the possible outcome of a decision. It can be positive, negative, or neutral. For example, if you jump off a high place, a possible consequence is hurting yourself. Another possible consequence is landing perfectly.
   - **Likelihood** refers to the chances of a consequence happening. For example, if you jump off a high place onto a large area of grass, you are very likely to land on the grass. If you jump off a high place onto a small pillow, you are not as likely to land on the pillow.
   - Calculating consequence vs. likelihood is risk assessment. It is one way to consider the positive and negative consequences and likelihood. Weighing consequences and likelihood can help to make a decision and move knowledge into action.

3. Give students a copy of the **Consequence vs. Likelihood Chart**. Ask students to privately choose a risk that they are considering in their own lives that has to do with sex and sexuality. Have them plot it on the chart with all the possible consequences. Remind students that this is an individual, reflective activity. They will not be asked to present their charts.

4. Ask students to consider the following questions. *If it will help students, demonstrate an example on the board (see the Educator Resource—Consequences vs. Likelihood Chart Example for a completed chart).*
   • Physical consequences: What will happen to your body, the body of the other person/people, and/or the physical environment?
   • Emotional consequences: How will it feel? Immediately? Later?
   • Social consequences: What will happen to your relationships?

5. Ask: Did you learn anything about risk assessment by putting it on the chart? Did completing this chart help you make a decision? Is there anything that can be done to minimize negative consequences and increase positive or neutral consequences? *If students are having difficulty with the questions, ask them to think about where on the chart most of the consequences are clustered. What does this clustering tell you about your decision? Were you surprised at where the clustering happened or did it just affirm what you already knew?*

EDUCATOR ANSWER KEY

There are multiple consequences to any decision. It is important to consider how decisions will affect your physical, emotional, and social health. If a decision poses too many likely consequences that you do not want, ask yourself what actions you can take to minimize the negative consequences and risk. In the example of unprotected sex, you could ensure that you and your partner get STBBI testing before but if you are having penis-vagina sexual intercourse, there is still a risk of pregnancy (unless using another form of **contraception**). Other factors can be considered, such as whether you are monogamous or non-monogamous and what safer sex looks like in these various relationship configurations. In this example, many of the positive consequences would exist even if the decision is to have safer sex with **dual protection**. Having safer sex by using dual protection and getting tested are the best ways to minimize physical risk when sexually active, without decreasing the physical benefits, such as pleasure.

Wrap-up

Summarize the module with the following points:

- STBBIs can be bacterial, viral, and/or infestations and parasites.
- STBBIs can often be cured and/or effectively managed if detected and treated early.
- Most sexual activity carries some risk, whether it be emotional, physical, and/or social. Sexual activity also carries benefits like pleasure, emotional intimacy, and/or fitting in with your peers. Sometimes the benefits outweigh the risks and sometimes the risks outweigh the benefits.
- Learning how to make decisions based on accurate, balanced information is a skill applicable to all aspects of life.

10.4 SAFER SEX: COMMUNICATION AND NEGOTIATION

LEVEL 2 [3]

Big Ideas in Module 10.4
- Communicating about and negotiating safer sex practises includes how to reduce risk and increase pleasure at the same time.
- All sexual activity requires communication between partners. Communication is key for practising consent, increasing pleasure for all involved, and establishing how to have safer sex.
- Distinguishing between supportive and coercive communication within sexual relationships can be challenging and takes practise. Knowing how to set boundaries and communicate assertively is a good place to start.
- Condoms protect against STBBIs and pregnancy. They have uses in a variety of sexual activities, including oral sex, anal intercourse, and vaginal intercourse. Despite the benefits, condom negotiation can be challenging.

Learning Objectives
Students will:
- Identify solutions to better communicate about safer sex.
- Distinguish between communication that is coercive/manipulative and mutually supportive/affirming.
- Challenge negative assumptions around condom use with the benefits of condom use.

Cross-Curricular Connections
- Biology
- Equity Studies
- Family Studies
- Gender Studies
- Psychology
- Social Studies
- Sociology

Terminology
- Consent
- Dual protection
- Gender norms
- Negotiation
- Safer sex
- Stigma

Materials
- Chalkboard or whiteboard
- **Educator Resource—Safer Sex Negotiation Scenarios**
- **Educator Resource—Condom Negotiation**
- **Educator Resource—STBBI Role Play Scenarios**

Background Information for Educators

Communicating about and negotiating **safer sex** practises includes how to reduce risk and increase pleasure at the same time. While communication and **negotiation** can be challenging because of the **stigma** that surrounds sex and sexuality, learning the necessary skills is essential for safer, more pleasurable sexual lives. Distinguishing communication and negotiation that is supportive and mutually affirming from communication and negotiation that is manipulative and coercive is challenging and takes practise. Knowing how to set boundaries and communicate assertively is a place to start. (For more information on communication and boundary setting, see modules 7.3, 7.4, and 7.5).

All sexual activity requires communication between partners. Communication is one of the central ingredients to sexual pleasure. While communication about sex can feel awkward or uncomfortable, it can make sex more physically, emotionally, mentally, and socially comfortable before, during, and after sexual activity. Communication is key for practising **consent** and is essential for establishing how to have safer sex. (For more information on consent, see modules 8.1, 8.3, and 8.4).

Consent is not just the absence of "no;" it is an enthusiastic "yes." If partners communicate with each other about condom use and it is established that a condom will be used during sexual activity, removing the condom without consent means that the sexual activity is no longer consensual and no longer safe. This form of sexual violence is called "stealthing" and is a violation of bodily autonomy (Brodsky, 2017). Like all forms of sexual violence, **systemic oppression** and **gender norms** support and reinforce these behaviours. Ongoing communication is essential.

Communicating about safer sex includes practising consent, condom negotiation, communicating about STBBIs, testing, and contraceptive methods being used, boundaries and comfort levels, desire, pleasure, **gender norms** and sexual scripts, and whether one or both partners are monogamous.

Condoms are the only safer sex supply/contraception that provides **dual protection** from STBBIs and pregnancy. Condoms also have uses in a variety of sexual activities—avoid framing condoms solely in terms of penis-vagina intercourse. There are many ways to use a condom for safer sex, including during oral sex on a penis, vulva, or anus (as a dental dam), and during anal intercourse.

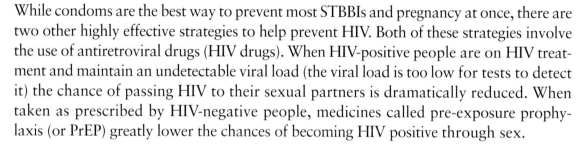

YOU SHOULD KNOW

While condoms are the best way to prevent most STBBIs and pregnancy at once, there are two other highly effective strategies to help prevent HIV. Both of these strategies involve the use of antiretroviral drugs (HIV drugs). When HIV-positive people are on HIV treatment and maintain an undetectable viral load (the viral load is too low for tests to detect it) the chance of passing HIV to their sexual partners is dramatically reduced. When taken as prescribed by HIV-negative people, medicines called pre-exposure prophylaxis (or PrEP) greatly lower the chances of becoming HIV positive through sex.

While condoms can significantly decrease STBBI risk, it can be challenging to negotiate their use. This is partly due to the myth that safer sex supplies like condoms and dental dams reduce pleasure and that once you are in a long-term relationship, you do not have to worry about STBBIs and can discontinue their use. If expectations are communicated, partners are honest with one another, trust exists, and there is mutual agreement/consent to discontinue condom use, it is still important that all people involved are aware of potential STBBI transmission risks and are considering harm reduction strategies, including regular STBBI testing and using PrEP as prescribed (if relevant). Gender norms, stereotypes, and sexual scripts about who should be responsible for acquiring condoms and what it means to carry them can also make it challenging to negotiate their use (e.g., gender norms create different social meanings for cisgender boys/ men carrying condoms and girls/women carrying condoms). Learning the communication skills to negotiate condoms and other safer sex practises is integral to comfort and pleasure.

Student Readiness

Before students engage with this lesson, ensure that safer space guidelines and group norms have been established (and revisited) within your classroom (for more information on how to establish safer space guidelines, see module 1.3). To effectively prepare for this activity, ensure students understand that:

- Sex does not have a universal meaning even though many assume it only refers to intercourse with a penis and a vagina.
- People engage in a variety of sexual activities regardless of their gender identity and sexual orientation.
- It is everyone's responsibility to practise safer sex and STBBI prevention.
- Sexual activity among young people is normal, expected, and healthy.
- There is no right age at which individuals should start having sex. It depends on their comfort level, circumstances, and emotional and social preparedness and circumstances. Some young people may be very interested in sexual activity and others' may not be.
- Assertive communication and boundary setting skills are developed with practise.

Summary of Activities

Students will:

- Work in small groups to identify potential solutions to communication problems.
- Collectively brainstorm the positives and negatives of condom use.

Activity 1 2 3

Instructions

1. Introduce the activity by explaining: Distinguishing communication and negotiation that is supportive and mutually affirming from communication and negotiation that is manipulative and coercive can be challenging and takes practise. It can be challenging because sexual and relationship scripts, which are informed by gender norms, normalize and romanticize manipulative and coercive behaviours as signs of love and devotion.

2. Explain: Coercion can be challenging to identify (especially when it is subtle, passive aggressive, and/or softly spoken) and can include manipulative, pestering, and/or threatening behaviours. Coercion can also look like using social power and norms to your advantage and/or to get what you want. Many common sexual, romantic, and relationship scripts are actually coercive. If coercion is present, there is no consent. If you are unsure about whether or not the request for consent is coercive and/or if consent is unclear, you do not have consent. Consent must be freely and fully given, it must be enthusiastic. *(For more information, see modules 8.2, 8.3, and 8.4).*

3. Ask students to brainstorm different lines people might use to pressure someone into having sex and/or sex without a condom. If appropriate, students who feel comfortable can raise their hands and offer their suggestions to the class.

EDUCATOR ANSWER KEY

Some answers might include:
- If you loved me you would.
- I don't have a condom on me.
- I just can't keep an erection if I wear a condom.
- It doesn't feel as good if I wear a condom.
- I don't have an STBBI.
- You're on the pill, so condoms are unnecessary unless you think I'm dirty.
- Don't you trust me?

4. Ask students for a definition of negotiation.

EDUCATOR ANSWER KEY

A mutual discussion and arrangement of the terms of a transaction or agreement.

5. Ask: What determines the outcome of a negotiation?

EDUCATOR ANSWER KEY

Determining factors could include individual and social power dynamics, communication styles, knowledge of the subject matter under negotiation, how well you know the other person/people you are negotiating with, etc.

6. Place students into small groups of 3 to 5. Provide each group with one problem from the **Educator Resource—Safer Sex Negotiation Scenarios**.
7. Instruct groups to indicate whether there were any coercive and manipulative behaviours at play and to provide potential solutions to the problems.

8. Have each group present their problem and potential solution scenarios. Add in any information using the **Educator Resource—Safer Sex Negotiation Scenarios.**
9. Wrap up the activity by asking: What can get in the way of negotiating safer sex?

EDUCATOR ANSWER KEY

Power dynamics, lack of communication, miscommunication, being in the heat of the moment, not challenging assumptions, using euphemisms to talk about sex, different definitions about what "safer sex" means, dislike of condoms, coercion, manipulation, stealthing, passive-aggressive communication styles, etc.

Activity 2 2 3
Instructions
1. As a class, ask students to brainstorm all the positives they have heard about condom use. Write these on the board in a list.
2. Ask students to brainstorm all the negatives they have heard about condom use. Write these on the board next to the list of positives.
3. Ask students to use the positive statements to counter the negative statements by matching them up.
4. Use the **Educator Resource—Condom Negotiation** to add to the answers already on the board.
5. Wrap up the activity by explaining: Condoms are a versatile and effective safer sex supply. Sometimes negotiation of their use can be challenging because there are many negative assumptions about their use. For every common negative assumption, there is a positive. Having this information can help to make decisions about and negotiate condom use and safer sex.

Activity 3 3

Role playing sensitive subject matter with students offers rich learning by "placing yourself in someone else's shoes" and at the same time, requires a keen understanding of the social dynamics and personalities of your students. (For more information and tips about how to facilitate role play effectively and safely, see module 1.6).

QUICK TIP

If you are nervous about facilitating the role play scenarios, you can divide the chalkboard into thirds and write "COERSIVE" on one side, "SUPPORTIVE" on the other, and in the middle write "UNSURE." Divide the class into two groups and give each group 16 pieces of construction paper. Read out the first scenario (both A and B's parts) and ask each group to come up with ways to communicate that are assertive, supportive, and mutually affirming, instead of passive aggressive, manipulative, and/or coercive. Each group will write down 4 suggestions (1 suggestion per paper). Once both groups are done writing, they will switch papers and decide as a group which heading the paper should be placed under on the board. Continue with other scenarios.

Instructions

1. Cut out each role play scenario from **Educator Resource—STBBI Role Play Scenarios** ahead of facilitating the activity.
2. Explain that discussing safer sex and STBBIs can be challenging and sometimes uncomfortable or awkward. Ask students what needs to be part of such a conversation between partners or potential partners.

EDUCATOR ANSWER KEY

Suggested answers include: honesty, openness, kindness, and non-judgment. Point out that in many cases, people may be unaware of having an STBBI.

3. Ask: What might make it challenging for people to have honest, open, kind, non-judgmental conversations about safer sex, STBBIs, and condom use?

EDUCATOR ANSWER KEY

Suggested answers include: stigma, taboo, fear of rejection, uncertainty, feeling uninformed, gender norms and stereotypes, peer norms, unrealistic sexual scripts, and assumptions.

4. Make space at the front of the classroom.
5. Explain that this activity is a version of a role play exercise where the whole class participates.
6. Ask for two volunteer "actors" who will each have to read their "role" in front of the class.

7. Place actor A on one side of the classroom and actor B on the opposite side. Have them turn away from each other and give each actor their role (both A and B).

8. Ask actor A to read their role, then ask actor B to read their role.

9. Explain: Coercion can be challenging to identify (especially when it is subtle, passive aggressive, and/or softly spoken) and can include manipulative, pestering, and/or threatening behaviours. Coercion can also look like using social power and norms to your advantage and/or to get what you want. Many common sexual, romantic, and relationship scripts are actually coercive. If coercion is present, there is no consent. If you are unsure about whether or not the request for consent is coercive and/or if consent is unclear, you do not have consent. Consent must be freely and fully given, it must be enthusiastic. *(For more information, see modules 8.2, 8.3, and 8.4).*

10. Ask the class to provide suggestions on how to communicate through the scenario in ways that are assertive, supportive, and mutually affirming and are not passive aggressive, manipulative, and/or coercive. Ask the class to provide specific suggestions for actor A and specific suggestions for actor B.

11. Every time a student gives a suggestion about communication that is assertive, supportive, and/or mutually affirming, whichever actor (A or B) it is aimed towards will start by turning around to face the other actor and take steps towards them. *The more assertive, supportive, and/or mutually affirming the suggestion, the more steps the actor can take forward.*

12. ✦ Optional: Every time a student gives a suggestion about communication that is passive-aggressive, manipulative, and/or coercive, whichever actor (A or B) it is aimed towards will take a step backward. *The more passive aggressive, manipulative, and/or coercive the suggestion, the more steps the actor can take backward.*

13. Once both actors have taken an even number of steps towards one another and are almost face-to-face, stop the role play, debrief, and/or move onto the next role play scenario with two new actors.

14. Debrief the activity using the following questions:
    *   What was it like to watch the actors physically move closer to and/or further away from one another?
    *   For the actors, what was it like to evaluate the suggestions from the rest of the class and decide whether to stay still, move forward, or move backward?
    *   Did communication suggestions get easier or harder to think of as they got closer to each other? What do you think that this means in a real life context?

- How were you able to distinguish communication that was coercive and manipulative from communication that was supportive?
- What did you learn about safer sex communication?

EDUCATOR ANSWER KEY

a) and b) There are no right or wrong answers to these question as they are based on the students' experiences of witnessing and participating in the activity. Possible answers might include: it was uncomfortable; became clear that communication about safer sex takes practise; unclear when communication was supportive versus coercive even when partners want the same thing, it can be difficult to communicate; when partners want different things, there is a fine line between compromising to make one partner happy/not disappointed and coming to a mutually agreed upon and mutually affirming place that satisfies both partners.

c) Communication, like other skills, gets easier with practise. Practising communication that is assertive, supportive, and mutually affirming will help you gain confidence in yourself, increase pleasure, and become closer to your sexual partner(s).

d) A statement is coercive and manipulative when you craft your message in order to make sure you get your way or to make someone feel guilty or like they have done something wrong. A statement is supportive when you are genuinely trying to understand what would make someone most comfortable, without compromising your own comfort and safety.

e) Being manipulative, coercive, and/or unclear about intentions can create doubt, distrust, and resentment in relationships, which can make communication and connection between partners more challenging. When communication and connection is challenged, sexual activity can become less emotionally, socially, and physically safe, which increases risk and decreases pleasure for all involved.

Wrap-up

Summarize the module with the following points:

- All sexual activity requires communication between partners.
- Communicating before, during, and after sex is key to ensuring that sex is consensual, safe, and pleasurable for all partners.
- Many different factors impact safer sex communication and negotiation but with practise, everyone can become more comfortable with negotiating and asserting their wants, desires, and needs.
- Communication, like other skills, gets easier with practise. Practising communication that is assertive, supportive, and mutually affirming will help you to gain confidence in yourself, increase pleasure, and become closer to your sexual partner(s).

10.5 OVERCOMING BARRIERS TO SAFER SEX: CHALLENGING STBBI STIGMA

LEVEL [3]

Big Ideas in Module 10.5
- Stigma surrounding STBBIs is one of the biggest barriers to practising safer sex.
- Stigma is exacerbated by systemic oppression.
- STBBIs are common but stigma makes them seem less common.
- Sex negative social norms contribute to STBBI stigma.
- Stigma can be challenged with sex positive communication that counters systemic oppression but this stigma is what most often impedes communication about safer sex and STBBIs.

Learning Objectives
Students will:
- Identify factors that promote safer sex practises.
- Identify barriers that impede practising safer sex.
- Critically analyze how stigma impedes safer sex.
- Strategize ways to challenge stigma.

Cross-Curricular Connections
- Biology
- Equity Studies
- Family Studies
- Gender Studies
- Psychology
- Social Studies
- Sociology

Terminology
- Prejudice
- Sex negative
- Stereotype
- Stigma
- Systemic oppression

Materials
- Chalkboard or whiteboard
- Two containers, receptacles, or bowls to place small pieces of folded paper into
- Small pieces of paper
- Printed copies of **STBBI Stigma Case Studies**
- **Educator Resource—STBBI Stigma Case Studies**

Background Information for Educators

Being aware of ways to reduce STBBI risk significantly decreases the likelihood of contracting an STBBI. While STBBIs are common, STBBI **stigma** can make it challenging to communicate about having one and/or the importance of testing and receiving any required sexual health care. STBBI stigma creates assumptions regarding who or what "type" of person gets STBBIs. This makes STBBIs seem less common than they actually are.

STBBI stigma is exacerbated by **systemic oppression** and the **stereotypes, prejudice,** and assumptions that oppression uses to uphold social power and privilege. For instance, homophobia exacerbates HIV stigma by obscuring who is at risk for HIV and preventing communication between partners who either do not identify as gay or are worried about being labelled gay. It is not social identity that puts you at risk for STBBIs, it is the harmful impacts of stigma and systemic oppression that do. Teaching safer sex includes actively working to challenge systemic oppression and reduce STBBI stigma with scientific evidence that debunks misconceptions.

Part of STBBI stigma comes from **sex negative** social norms that create myths and assumptions about who gets STBBIs and why. In reality, anyone who is sexually active is at risk of contracting and transmitting STBBIs. Practising safer sex significantly minimizes this risk but does not eliminate it entirely. These myths and assumptions about STBBIs carry power unless actively and purposefully challenged.

Student Readiness

Before students engage with this lesson, ensure that safer space guidelines and group norms have been established (and revisited) within your classroom (for more information on how to establish safer space guidelines, see module 1.3). To effectively prepare for this activity, ensure students understand that:

- STBBIs are common and do not make you a bad, dirty, irresponsible, or untrustworthy person.
- Sexual activity among young people is normal, expected, and healthy.
- Practising safer sex can significantly minimize STBBI risk but does not eliminate the risk entirely.
- Risk is a normal part of life. We take risks all day, everyday.

Summary of Activities

Students will:

- Collectively brainstorm factors that may lead young people to practise safer sex and factors that might cause barriers to safer sex.
- In teams, communicate how to use an external condom and a dental dam without being able to say certain words.
- Work in small groups to answer questions about STBBI stigma scenarios and then present these scenarios to the rest of the class.

Activity 1

Instructions

1. Introduce the activity by acknowledging and affirming that most young people (70%) practise safer sex and that practising safer sex is often an indication of comfort and experience. *This can be affirming and reassuring to students who may be wary about whether encouraging safer sex will make them seem inexperienced.*

2. Ask students why they think some people do not consistently practise safer sex.

EDUCATOR ANSWER KEY

Lack of preparedness, being in the heat of the moment, no condoms or other safer sex supplies at hand, pressure, manipulation, coercion, and being afraid to talk about safer sex.

3. As a class, brainstorm at least 3 positive factors that influence safer sex. Write them on one side of the board.

EDUCATOR ANSWER KEY

Some positives might include: knowledge about STBBIs; preparedness (e.g., having condoms, lube, dental dams, etc. on hand); communication skills to negotiate safer sex; access to advice and knowledge from teachers, parents, peers (including peer educators), staff at sexual health clinics, etc.; knowing sex is better when you do not have to worry as much about STBBIs or unplanned pregnancy; confidence, boundary setting, and assertive communication skills; an equal, mutually respectful relationship; etc.

4. Now brainstorm at least 3 negatives that reduce the likelihood of safer sex and write them on the other side of the board.

EDUCATOR ANSWER KEY

Some negatives might include: lack of information about STBBIs and pregnancy; differing attitudes and assumptions about condoms; an unhealthy relationship or power dynamic; low self-confidence; too embarrassed, shy, or awkward; not knowing how to and/or being afraid to bring up and discuss condom use with partners; intimate partner violence; prior sexual assault; sexual, emotional, or physical abuse; alcohol and other substance use; etc.

Activity 2 3

Instructions
1. Divide the class equally into 2 teams (Team A and Team B).
2. Ask each team to choose an "actor" to act out a scenario.

    Team A scenario:
    The actor must verbally communicate to the rest of the team how to put an external condom on a penis but is not allowed to say the following words: condom, penis, ejaculation, or sex.

    Team B scenario:
    The actor must verbally communicate to the rest of the team how to use a dental dam but is not allowed to say the following words: oral, sex, vulva, vagina, or dental dam.

3. Before the actors start, have each member of Team A and Team B write down 4 random (non-sexual) words on pieces of paper.
4. Fold up each paper and place into 2 different receptacles. Switch Team A and Team B's receptacles.
5. Give the following instruction: Every time either actor says one of the words that they are not allowed to say, they must reach into the receptacle and pull out a word to substitute the forbidden word with (e.g., if they say "vulva" and pull out a paper with "sky scrapper" written on it, they must use the word sky scrapper when referring to vulva).
6. It is up to the rest of the team to guess what their actor is trying to demonstrate. The team to do this first wins.

7. Debrief the activity using the following questions:
   - Why could the actors not use certain words? What does this represent?
   - How does stigma act as a barrier to safer sex?
   - How could you challenge this stigma?
   - How might this stigma be exacerbated by other social factors?

EDUCATOR ANSWER KEY
- The actors could not use certain words to illustrate the stigma that is attached to these words. It represents how stigma can complicate talking about sex and safer sex in accurate, practical ways.
- Stigma acts as a barrier to safer sex by breeding assumptions and preventing communication about those assumptions. This often increases risk through less safe sexual practises. Without proper communication, it becomes difficult to seek and/or grant consent. Without proper communication, pleasure, comfort, and intimacy are also reduced.
- The only way to challenge stigma is to talk about it. Topics that remain unspoken, remain stigmatized. This can lead to embarrassment, shame, and/or fear, which inform people's choices and actions. To challenge stigma, talk about safer sex with your friends and with your partners. The more that you talk about safer sex with your peer group, the more chance you have of challenging and eventually changing social norms surrounding safer sex and STBBIs.
- Stigma around sexuality and STBBIs can be exacerbated by other social identities that are stigmatized and stereotyped. For people whose social identities are often stereotyped in a sexualized and/or gendered way, they may be more hesitant to communicate about safer sex for fear of being stereotyped and discriminated against. Communicating about a topic that is stigmatized can also make us feel vulnerable but this vulnerability is not experienced equally. People who experience systemic oppression might experience this vulnerability in more pronounced ways or ways that have social and material consequences (such as losing economic security and housing or being slut shamed at school).

Activity 3 ③

Instructions
1. Place students into small groups of 3 to 4.
2. Provide each group with one case study and the corresponding questions from the **STBBI Stigma Case Studies.**
3. Give the groups 15 to 20 minutes to discuss the scenarios and come up with answers to the questions.

4. Have each group present their scenario and answers to the rest of the class. Fill in any missing aspects using the **Educator Resource—STBBI Stigma Case Studies.**

Wrap-up

Summarize the module with the following points:

- Communication is an essential part of practising safer sex but stigma can get in the way of effective, honest, and timely communication.
- STBBIs are common but stigma makes them seem less common.
- Many people do not know that they have an STBBI; regular testing is a normal part of maintaining and ensuring your sexual health and wellness.

10.6 TATTOOING AND BODY PIERCING: STBBI RISK AND HARM REDUCTION

LEVEL 3

Big Ideas in Module 10.6

- Young people often seek out affordable and accessible tattooing and piercing options, including "do it yourself" tattoos and piercings. These options come with STBBI risks that young people need to be informed about in order to feel empowered to ask the right questions, minimize risk, and tattoo/pierce as safely as possible.
- Harm reduction is an effective evidence-based public health strategy, which recognizes that adolescents are likely to engage in risk-taking behaviours.

Learning Objectives

Students will:
- Identify safer tattooing and piercing practises and how to apply harm reduction principles.

Cross-Curricular Connections
- Biology
- Equity Studies
- Gender Studies
- Social Studies
- Sociology

Terminology
- Harm reduction

Materials
- Printed copies of **Tattoos and Piercings Quiz**
- **Educator Answer Key—Tattoos and Piercings Quiz**
- Printed copies of **Safer Tattooing and Piercing**

Background Information for Educators

Tattoos and piercings are becoming more common and less stigmatized. This is especially the case with young people. Young people might get tattoos and/or piercings for a variety of reasons, including esthetics, fitting into peer/social norms, exploring identities, experimentation, boredom, and/or artistic expression. Like safer sex, students need to be informed of the risks and learn strategies of how to minimize risk and reduce potential harm. For tattoos and piercing, there is physical risk from unsterilized equipment. Equipment that has not been properly sterilized can transmit blood-borne viral infections such as HIV, Hepatitis C, and Hepatitis B.

YOU SHOULD KNOW

Information about sterilized equipment could be applied to any equipment that comes into contact with blood, including (but not limited to) equipment for the purpose of tattoos, piercings, self-harm or "cutting," and drug uses, which include needles used for hormone and steroid injections.

Being informed about the risks and knowing the right questions to ask in order to prevent transmission of blood-borne infections can be empowering for young people. This is part of taking a harm reduction approach to piercing and tattoos. It recognizes that young people will find ways to pierce and tattoo themselves despite age restrictions and money. **Harm reduction** is an approach to public health and infection prevention that begins with the recognition that it may not be possible, desirable, and/or realistic for everyone to stop participating in activities and behaviours labelled as "risky." From this recognition, evidence-based strategies to mitigate the risk associated with certain behaviours are promoted.

Young people should learn how to identify sterile conditions at tattoo and piercing shops and how to be safer when giving or receiving piercings and/or tattoos from friends. Tattoo and piercing shops are required to follow public health codes regarding their equipment in order to avoid the transmission of STBBIs. While this makes professional tattoo and piercing shops preferable, students should be aware of how to reduce STBBI transmission risks with "do-it-yourself" tattoos (stick and poke tattoos).

Stick and Poke Tattoos

Stick and poke tattoos are "do-it-yourself" tattoos that involve the sticking of a needle into the skin followed by the pushing of ink into that needle opening. This technique is generally done using a pencil with a sewing needle attached to it that is wrapped in thread but stick and poke tattoos are also commonly done using individual tattoo needles. This technique is rising in popularity, with many engaging in the trend with their friends at gatherings and parties.

A few things students should know about stick and poke tattoos:
- The tattoos may be less precise. Every individual dot has to be poked in rather than a tattoo machine that lays down solid lines. The design will most likely be shakier and less professional looking.

- Ideally, the needles need to be new and clean. At minimum, ensure the needle has been sterilized by holding it over a flame until it is red hot, boiling for 10 to 30 minutes, or with rubbing alcohol (soak in rubbing alcohol for at least 20 minutes). Even with these methods, there is not a 100% guarantee that all bacteria and/or viruses will be killed. It is always best to use a new needle.
- You need to remove bacteria from the skin. Wipe the area about to be tattooed down with rubbing alcohol. This will avoid poking the bacteria into the skin.
- Use bottled "India ink" or tattoo ink only. Ink from pens and other inks can be toxic and cause infection and a poor tattoo. "India ink" is available at art stores, stationary stores, etc.
- Use disposable gloves.
- Avoid stick and poke tattoos while intoxicated with alcohol. Alcohol thins your blood, makes you bleed more, and can impair judgment.
- Use a new container of ink. If many people are getting tattoos in the same sitting, ensure that a new container of ink is poured out for each individual. Otherwise, the needle from each person will be dipped into the same container, thereby sharing bacteria and potential viruses.
- If all of these steps are not followed, you may want to get tested for STBBIs such as HIV, Hepatitis C, and Hepatitis B (if not already vaccinated).
- Take good care of your stick and poke tattoo until it heals. It is open flesh that has the ability to transmit and/or receive bodily fluids and bacteria. Avoid baths and submerging the tattoo until it is completely healed. Showers are okay.

YOU SHOULD KNOW

There is a specific way to safely wipe an area of skin: Apply a 60% to 70% alcohol-based solution (isopropyl alcohol or ethanol) on a single-use swab or cotton-ball. Do not use methanol or methyl-alcohol as these are not safe for human use. Wipe the area from the centre of the injection site working outwards, without going over the same area. Apply the solution for 30 seconds then allow it to dry completely.

Student Readiness

Before students engage with this lesson, ensure that safer space guidelines and group norms have been established (and revisited) within your classroom (for more information on how to establish safer space guidelines, see module 1.3). In order to effectively prepare for this activity, ensure students understand that:

- Adolescence is an important time in human brain development. Risk-taking behaviour is common at this stage and not necessarily a bad thing if harms associated with risk are minimized.
- This module will be covering STBBIs as they relate to tattoo and piercing practises.
- The purpose of this module is to empower young people to develop strategies to reduce harms associated with tattoos and piercings, not to stigmatize the practise.
- Adults also have tattoos and piercings.

Summary of Activities

Students will:

- Collectively discuss the practise of tattooing and piercing.
- Individually fill out a quiz on safer piercing and tattooing practises.

Activity 1 [3]

Instructions

1. Reminding students not to mention any names, ask them to raise their hand if...
   - They know someone who has any kind of piercing, including pierced ears.
   - They know someone who did it themselves or with a friend.
   - They know someone who got a piercing without parental permission.
   - They know someone who has any kind of tattoo.
   - They know someone who did it themselves or with a friend.
   - They know someone who got a tattoo without parental permission.
2. Point out that piercing and tattooing are very common among a range of ages, especially ear piercing.
3. Ask students the following questions:
   - Are there any risks involved in piercing?
   - What factors might those risks depend on?
   - Are there any risks involved in getting a tattoo?
   - What factors might those risks depend on?

EDUCATOR ANSWER KEY
- There are risks involved in piercing, such as local bacterial infections, loss of sensation, and blood-borne viral infections (Hepatitis B, Hepatitis C, and HIV).
- Piercing risks depend on whether or not equipment is new or properly sterilized, whether a piercing needle is used as opposed to a piercing gun (less trauma to the skin with a needle), and where the piercing is located. Some areas of the body pose more risk than others. For instance, ear lobe piercings have less risk than tongue or lip piercings.
- There are risks involved in getting a tattoo, such as blood-borne viral infections (Hepatitis B, Hepatitis C, and HIV) and local bacterial infections.
- The risks involved in getting a tattoo are dependant on whether the equipment is new or properly sterilized, including whether or not new ink is used.

4. Hand out copies of the **Tattoos and Piercings Quiz.**
5. Take up answers as a class using the **Educator Answer Key—Tattoos and Piercings Quiz.**
6. Distribute copies of **Safer Tattooing and Piercing.**
7. Optional: As homework, students can call their local public health units and ask whether they have harm reduction piercing and tattooing kits. If students discover through their research that harm reduction piercing and tattoo kits are available, consider inviting a harm reduction public health nurse into your school to do a presentation on how to be safer and reduce harm from "do-it-yourself" piercing and tattooing.

Wrap-up
Summarize the module with the following points:
- Piercing and tattooing are both common; learning how to reduce harms will help everyone remain healthy.
- While piercing and tattooing can (under some circumstances) transmit STBBIs, there are ways to ensure they are as safe as possible.
- If seeking out tattoos and/or piercings in a shop, there are rules about who can perform them and who can obtain them (i.e., age of consent, which varies across provinces and territories).
- Some provinces/territories require parental consent for minors to receive tattoos.
- Lots of people do tattoos and piercings by themselves and/or their friends. There are ways to make this process safer and reduce harms, including the use of new needles and new ink every time.

10.7 SEXUAL HEALTH AND CLINIC VISIT

LEVEL 2 [3]

Big Ideas in Module 10.7

- Having access to sexual health services is a basic human right for all people, including young people.
- Young people have the right to privacy and confidentiality from their health care provider(s) on topics related to safer sex, contraception, and STBBIs. These are part of young people's sexual rights.
- Knowing what to expect, how to prepare, and what questions to ask regarding a sexual health appointment can help young people feel more at ease and empowered to access sexual health services such as STBBI testing.

Learning Objectives

Students will:

- Discover local sexual health services.
- Learn how to prepare for a visit to a sexual health care provider.
- Become empowered to use these services as a regular part of their health routine.

Cross-Curricular Connections

- Biology
- Equity Studies
- Family Studies
- Gender Studies
- Psychology
- Social Studies
- Sociology

Terminology

- Human rights
- Sexual health
- Sexual rights
- Sexuality
- Stigma

Materials

- Printed copies of **Clinic Visit**
- Printed copies of **Appointment Checklist**

Background Information for Educators

Sexual health is an important part of everyone's health, including young people. Having access to sexual health services is a basic **human right** for all people, including young people. Human rights include **sexual rights**.

There is often taboo around youth **sexuality** and **stigma** attached to sexual health care and services such as STBBI testing. Normalizing such health care services can help empower young people to take care of their sexual health. Students may not always wish to access sexual health services from their family doctor and/or ask their family doctor sexual health questions. It is important that they know about sexual health care services offered by their local clinics and where they can access youth-friendly sexual health care services. (For more information, see modules 2.2 and 2.3).

Clinics that offer sexual health services, like family doctors and other health care providers, are bound by their professional regulations to maintain confidentiality. Young people also have the right to privacy and confidentiality. They might be empowered to know that they can assert this right, even with their family doctor. The only exception to this is if a young person is under the age of 16 and if they are at risk of abuse, hurting themselves, and/or hurting others. This module will encourage students to locate their local sexual health clinic services while informing them of their right to receive proper sexual health care.

If there is a local sexual health clinic, youth clinic, and/or community health centre near your school, arrange for a field trip. Discuss expectations beforehand with clinic/centre staff. If possible, arrange to visit at a time when the clinic/centre is closed to the public. Staff can provide a tour to familiarize students with the examining room, procedures like STBBI and pap testing, and answer any questions. This familiarity can significantly help reduce anxiety and nervousness around accessing these services. Students will be able to visualize the clinic and will already be familiar with where it is located and how to access it.

Student Readiness

Before students engage with this lesson, ensure that safer space guidelines and group norms have been established (and revisited) within your classroom (for more information on how to establish safer space guidelines, see module 1.3). In order to effectively prepare for this activity, ensure students understand:
- What human rights and sexual rights are and why they are important (for more information, see modules 2.2 and 2.3).
- That sexuality and sexual health are experienced and influenced by individual and social factors.
- That sexual activity among young people is normal and healthy.

Summary of Activities
Students will:
- Walk around the room and individually consider and answer general questions about sexual health clinics.
- Either as a class or individually visit a sexual health clinic.
- Individually complete a worksheet about their sexual health clinic visit.

Activity 1 2 3
Instructions
1. Place 4 large pieces of chart paper around the room and write the following questions on each:
   - What are some reasons young people might visit a sexual health clinic?
   - If you can get many of the same services and resources from your family doctor, why might it be helpful to seek out a sexual health clinic?
   - What are the different resources offered by sexual health clinics?
   - Where can you go in your town/city/region to access sexual health care?
2. Provide each student with markers and ask them to consider each question, then walk around the room and place at least one answer per page.
3. Discuss the answers as a class.

EDUCATOR ANSWER KEY
- There are many reasons to visit a sexual health clinic. Some of these reasons include: to get contraceptives; to access STBBI testing; to access abortion (not all sexual health clinics provide abortion services but many can refer you to the right place); to ask questions about sexual health; etc. Some people like the anonymity of a sexual health clinic rather than their family doctor and it can also be a faster way to get the services you need (e.g., visiting a rapid-testing site for HIV).

- Sometimes sexual health clinics will be able to provide free contraceptives, where your family doctor may not. Because many people visit the same family doctor as members of their family, they might enjoy the anonymity of a sexual health clinic. They may not want their family doctor to know all of their sexual history and that is perfectly okay. Doctors are bound by confidentiality but going to a clinic can be a comforting way to ensure anonymity and confidentiality. *One thing to keep in mind is that while a sexual health clinic may provide more anonymity than your family doctor, you might have to wait in a room with everyone else, where it is clear you are all there for sexual health matters.*

CONT'D NEXT PAGE

EDUCATOR ANSWER KEY CONT'D

- Sexual health clinics are likely to offer the following: STBBI testing; contraceptives (sometimes for free); information on different contraceptives; youth-friendly care; advice on healthy relationships; resources on consent and places to receive support if you have been sexually assaulted (see the **National Support Services** resource); resources related to sexual orientation and gender identity (or at least referrals to appropriate services); pro-choice options counselling and abortion services (not all locations but they should be able to refer you to the closest clinic or hospital); and harm reduction resources.
- Sexual health services will vary by location. Seek these out ahead of time and discuss them with students so they are well aware of where they can access sexual health services. The Action Canada for Sexual Health and Rights directory of service providers can be a good starting place to locate services, as can provincial health bodies and community health centres. (For more information, see **National Support Services** and 10.7 resources).

Activity 2  ③

Instructions

1. 🌐 Field Trip: If possible, make arrangements for your class to visit the nearest sexual health clinic.
2. Give each student a copy of **Clinic Visit** and have students fill it out during the field trip/clinic visit.
3. ✚ Optional: Provide students with the **Appointment Checklist** and ask them to take this to the clinic visit and/or their next appointment with a doctor/health care provider.

Wrap-up

Summarize the module with the following points:

- Visiting the local sexual health clinic and asking questions can be an empowering experience for young people.
- Many people do not know that they have an STBBI; regular testing is a normal part of maintaining and ensuring your sexual health and wellness.
- Young people have human rights, including sexual rights. Part of these rights is the right to access youth-friendly, confidential sexual health care.

QUICK TIP

If a class field trip is not possible, encourage students to go in pairs outside of school time. You can help your students arrange a visit by calling ahead and explaining the situation to the medical receptionist.

DEFINITIONS

Ableism: the structural/systemic oppression of people living with disabilities, including the presumption that living with an able body is expected, normal, and fixed in time/space.

Aboriginal Status: refers to section 35(2) of Canada's 1982 Constitution, which includes under Aboriginal, "the Indian, Inuit and Métis peoples of Canada." While it has legal implications in the context of Canada, it is also commonly used as an umbrella term. Indigenous is another umbrella term that more accurately captures the fact that Indigenous nations and peoples lived (and continue to live) on the land that we now call Canada from time immemorial (pre-European contact). The term also holds more significance globally; it has been used to organize in solidarity with a diversity of Indigenous cultures from around the world for the universal recognition of human rights (Apihtawikosisan, 2011).

Abortion: a medical procedure that terminates pregnancy and empties the uterus of products of conception. Abortion can be either surgical or medical. Surgical abortion involves an emptying of the uterus using different surgical technique (depending on gestation) under local or general anesthetic; medical abortion involves the emptying of the uterus through a combination of prescribed medication.

Abstinence: completely refraining from doing something. In the case of sex, abstinence refers to not engaging in any type of sexual activity. In the case of substances, abstinence refers to not using substances, stopping substance use, and being substance-free.

Addiction: sometimes called dependence, addiction refers to the challenge of limiting substance use even if you want to or when a person feels like they need a substance to function regularly or feel normal.

Adoption: a legally binding decision to permanently place a child in the care of another person or family.

Ageism: a form of system discrimination based on age. Ageism mostly affects young people and elderly people but manifests differently depending on the context. For instance, young people are often stereotyped as unmotivated, lazy, unreliable/untrustworthy, unpredictable, only influenced by immediate gratification, sexually deviant, etc. (for more on the ageism that young people experience and how you can be a youth ally, see module 1.7). Elderly people experience ageism when others assume they are senile and treat them as children and/or as incompetent. They are often also viewed as non-sexual.

Agender: people who identify as not having a gender or being genderless. They can exist outside of the gender binary, be gender non-conforming, and/or identify as trans.

Aggressive communication: a style of communication that is rooted in anger. It is forceful and direct but not necessarily clear. It usually involves angry outbursts and can be abusive.

Androgens: a group of hormones produced by the ovaries and adrenal glands. The primary and most well-known androgen is testosterone.

Androgynous or Androgyne: a person whose gender expression and/or identity is between, across (both), or outside of the binary and/or does not conform to gender norms.

Anti-oppression: the recognition and active dismantling of systems of oppression. Anti-oppression includes a recognition of the ways that oppression and privilege based on dominant forms of power structures affect the lives of everyone. Anti-oppression rejects the idea that most people are either oppressed or privileged and instead recognizes that different aspects of our identity overlap and intersect to create experiences of both having access to power and being oppressed by power.

Areola: refers to the pigmented area surrounding the nipple.

Aromantic: a person who generally does not feel romantic attraction or desire to any group of people, either within or outside of a relationship.

Asexual: commonly referred to as Ace, a person who generally does not feel sexual attraction or desire to any group of people, either within or outside of a relationship.

Assertive communication: a style of communication that is direct, clear, and respectful. It allows individuals to clearly and firmly state their feelings, needs, and opinions, while respecting those of other people.

Assigned sex: the word assigned is used because doctors will usually determine a baby to be either male or female at birth. Doctors assign sex based on characteristics such as chromosomes and genitals. The ways that these sex characteristics can manifest in individuals' bodies is diverse and not as definite or binary as the categories of male and female suggest. Therefore, sex is not only assigned but the binary sex categories of male and female are socially constructed.

Asymptomatic viral shedding: when the herpes virus travels from the nerve cells (where it lives) up to the surface of the skin and can be transmitted without visible symptoms.

Autonomy: broadly refers to having independence. In relationship to human rights, sexual rights, and within *Beyond the Basics*, autonomy refers to bodily autonomy and the right to control decisions about your own body, free from coercion.

Bias: refers to the ways that perspective and subjectivity influence how an issue is presented. Media bias in the news refers to the ways that perspective and subjectivity influence the reporting of events and issues, including what is and is not reported.

Bicurious: a person who may not identify as bisexual or bi but is open to or curious about having sexual and/or romantic relationships with someone whose gender differs from their usual attraction.

Biphobia: a range of negative attitudes, feelings, and fears towards bisexual people or bisexuality, which may include negative stereotyping or denial of the existence of bisexuality.

Bisexual: commonly referred to as bi, a person who is attracted to more than one gender.

Body image: the way that individuals feel and think about their bodies. It is what they believe, perceive, and how they evaluate their bodies.

Boundaries: limitations a person establishes in their life and relationships in order to protect and take care of themselves. They are part of a healthy foundation in life and relationships.

Breast: the glandular organs on the chest. These organs often have the potential to secrete milk.

Bullying: early definitions defined bullying as a pattern of negative behaviour being carried out repeatedly by individuals against other individuals. More recently however, bullying is being thought of as representing larger systems of oppression that are manifested in repeated actions by an individual (or groups of individuals) who are exercising power against another individual (or groups of individuals) (Meyer, 2014).

Cervical mucus: produced by the cervix, it changes in amount and consistency throughout the menstrual cycle. It can look like a sticky or egg white like matter and/or a clear slippery fluid.

Cervix: the lower part of the uterus that opens into the vagina.

Chlamydia: a common bacterial STBBI that can be transmitted through unprotected oral, vaginal, and/or anal sex.

Chromosomes: structures in cells that carry genetic information. The building blocks of that genetic information is DNA.

Circumcision: the removal of the foreskin (or prepuce) so that the glans (or head) of the penis is exposed.

Cis man: a person who identifies as cisgender and as a man.

Cis woman: a person who identifies as cisgender and as a woman.

Cisgender: a person whose gender identity and assigned sex are the same (e.g., someone who was assigned male at birth and identifies as a man).

Cissexism: systemic or individual behaviours, assumptions, and rules that grant preferential treatment to cisgender people.

Classism: systemic oppression of people based on access to money and wealth. This systemic oppression manifests in institutions and in individuals (presenting as prejudice) and in implicit and explicit acts of classist discrimination. Classism is experienced differently depending on the other identities that an individual holds and their social circumstances.

Clitoris: a sensitive part of the vulva (external genitalia) that is made up of highly concentrated nerve endings. The clitoris also consists of erectile tissue that extends internally into a wishbone shape surrounding the vagina. Its function is sexual pleasure.

Closeted: a figure of speech used to describe a person who is keeping their sexual orientation and/or gender identity a secret from others. It is often used in a derogatory or disempowering way (someone who believes they know others' sexual orientations better than the person themselves).

Coercion: using intimidation or manipulation to get someone to do something that they would otherwise not do. Subtle forms of coercion include leveraging existing social norms and power imbalances to fit in and avoid consequences.

Colonialism: a historical and on-going process of colonial powers (who originated in Europe in the case of Canada) taking and occupying already inhabited land and imposing laws, religion, and governance structures onto the inhabitants of the land. The stealing and occupation of entire territories on what is now known as Canada happened (and continues to happen) through violence, coercion, and oppression. Part of this violence was the forced and coerced removal of children from communities into residential schools and the child welfare system during the sixties scoop. Indigenous children continue to be taken from communities and placed in the child welfare system at disproportionate rates, which is part of the failure of settler governments to remedy past and ongoing human rights violations in a meaningful way.

Coming out: a figure of speech that refers to communicating your sexual orientation and/or gender identity to yourself and others.

Communication: an exchange of thoughts, ideas, and feelings. It is the sending and receiving of messages and meaning.

Comprehensive sexuality education: an approach that recognizes sexuality as an integral part of being human and includes the ways that sexuality is expressed, manifested, and impacted by emotional, social, cultural, physical, psychological, spiritual, political, and economic aspects of an individual's life (UNESCO, 2009). Comprehensive sexuality education considers sexual health in relationship to human rights, gender norms, emotional, psychological, and spiritual well-being, civic engagement, and the social determinants of health (environmental, political, and economic) (ISHC Working Group, 2011).

Conception: when fertilization (of the egg and sperm) and implantation have been achieved.

Consent culture: a resistance movement to rape culture. It strives to create an environment in which consent is never assumed and always asked for.

Consent: in terms of sexual consent and Canadian law, consent is defined as ongoing voluntary agreement to a sexual activity. This agreement can be expressed by words or actions. A person who is incapacitated (e.g., drunk, drugged, asleep, or unconscious) is unable to consent.

Contraception: a variety of methods (hormonal, barrier, intra-uterine, etc.) used to prevent unintended pregnancy. Contraception is often colloquially referred to as birth control. Most contraception methods can only prevent pregnancy but some (e.g., condoms) can prevent pregnancy and STBBIs.

Criminalization: the process of turning behaviours into a crime and creating rules, policies, and laws around certain behaviours that will lead to punishment under the law.

Curettage: part of a surgical abortion procedure (and sometimes done after a miscarriage) that removes products of conception from the uterus with a surgical instrument called a curette.

Cyberbullying: bullying that happens online. Cyberbullying can originate online and still affect someone in other areas of life. It often seeps into (and/or is amplified by) a student's life at school.

Cyberstalking: stalking that happens online. Stalking is non-consensual, inappropriate, threatening, and/or aggressive behaviour directed at a specific person that is repeated over a period of time. Cyberstalking primarily happens online but can still affect a person in other areas of life.

Demiromantic: a person who only feels romantic attraction to people with whom a close emotional bond has been formed.

Demisexual: a person who only feels sexual attraction to people with whom a close emotional bond has been formed.

Dental dam: a thin piece of latex or polyurethane that is placed over the vulva or anus during oral sex to protect against STBBIs.

Dependence: in reference to substance use, when a person feels like they have to use a substance to perform regularly or feel normal. It includes the challenge of cutting down use, even if a person wants to. Also called addiction.

Discrimination: actions or decisions that are based on prejudice and negatively affect other people. Discrimination can happen on an individual level, for example, getting fired from a job because of a pregnancy or HIV status, being refused an apartment, experiencing verbal abuse, inappropriate jokes, or harassment, being offered a lower salary, being bullied, or being rejected by your family. It can also happen on an institutional level. This occurs when laws and policies are inadequate, inequitable, and fail to protect all people equally.

Diversity: the state of having many different forms, possibilities, types, ideas, etc. For instance, a box of crayons with 30 different colours is diverse in colour. A box of 30 crayons that are all red is not diverse.

DNA: the form that genetic information is stored in for all living organisms, including human beings. DNA is housed in chromosomes.

Drug: a substance, other than food, intended to affect the structure or function of the body.

Dual protection: using contraception during sexual activity that prevents both pregnancy and STBBIs.

Egg: large gamete cell that contains genetic material and is found in the ovary. It is often referred to as "the female gamete."

Embryo: a collection of cells that have resulted from the process of fertilization (the joining of sperm and egg).

Emergency contraception: contraception used to prevent pregnancy after penis-vagina intercourse. There are currently two main methods, hormonal oral emergency contraceptives and the copper IUD.

Empowerment: a process of becoming aware and acting on available information and resources that lead to opportunities to determine and control your own life (Grose, Gabe & Kohfeldt, 2013).

Endometrium: the inner lining of the uterus, which is partially shed during menstruation.

Epididymal hypertension: commonly known as "blue balls," it is an achy sensation in the testicles from blood being built up and retained in the testicles and penis through sexual arousal.

Epididymis: a set of coiled tubes that are part of the spermatic duct (within the scrotum, behind each testicle) that stores and then transports sperm between the testes and the vas deferens.

Equity: in the context of health, equity is closely related to the social determinants of health and refers to the decrease or removal of systemic barriers (such as racism, poverty, homophobia, etc.) that prevent particular populations from achieving positive health outcomes (Wellesley Institute, 2016; WHO, 2008). In the context of education, equity refers to fairness and inclusion in access to education, regardless of gender, socio-economic status, race, etc. (OECD, 2016). In other disciplines, such as law, equity is sometimes known as substantive equality.

Erogenous zones: places on and in the body that are pleasurable to touch and stimulate. These places can be very different from person to person.

Estrogen: a hormone that occurs in the body to regulate and control different kinds of growth and bodily development, including the menstrual cycle, endometrium, breast development, and armpit and public hair. Everyone has some estrogen but people whose assigned sex is female have higher levels of estrogen than males. Estrogen is mostly found in the ovaries but small levels are also found in the adrenal glands.

Euphemisms: indirect words that substitute the true meaning of something.

External genitals/genitalia: sexual organs that are external to the body.

Fallopian tubes (oviducts): two tubes leading from the ovaries to the uterus; it is where the ovum (egg) is usually fertilized by the sperm during fertilization.

Family: any combination of two or more individuals bound together over time by ties of mutual consent, choice, birth, adoption, or placement.

Fatphobia: the systemic and individual oppression of people who have more fat than what is considered socially desirable/beautiful. Fatphobia encompasses the subtle and overt forms of discrimination, fear, harassment, stigma, prejudice, and aversion to people who are fat and perceived to be "over-weight."

Female genital mutilation: also known as female genital cutting, a non-consensual surgery that ranges from removing all or part of the external female genitalia (including the clitoris, labia minor, and labia majora) to completely or partially closing the vaginal opening. It is an invasive surgery that has no health benefits and poses significant health risks.

Female: one of the categories that babies are assigned at birth based on sex characteristics such as hormones, chromosomes, and genitalia.

Femmephobia: the fear, aversion, hatred, and de-valuing of anything and anyone that is considered feminine, regardless of gender identity.

Fertilization: the union of the egg and sperm. It usually occurs in one of the fallopian tubes.

Fetishize: the process of making something the object of a sexual fetish. A fetish is a form of sexual desire in which pleasure is obsessively connected to a particular object or representation.

Food In/Security: the access or inaccess to healthy, safe, affordable, and nutritious food. It refers to physical access as well as economic and environmental/ecological access.

Forced/coerced sterilization: also known as compulsory sterilization, non-consensual medical and surgical interventions to render women infertile and limit reproductive choice. In Canada, forced and coerced sterilization were performed regularly by doctors on marginalized women (particularly Indigenous women, women of colour, and women with disabilities) in the 1970s and still today.

Foreskin: a fold of skin that covers the head of the penis.

Gamete: the sexual (germ) cells (the egg and sperm).

Gay: a person who is primarily attracted to people of the same gender. Although it can be used for any gender, it is most often used for men who are attracted to men.

Gender binary: the system in which a society classifies all people into one of two categories (men and women), each with associated stereotypes and norms.

Gender confirming surgeries: a surgery that aligns a person's physical body with their gender identity (formerly known as sex reassignment surgery).

Gender creative and gender independent: terms often used to describe children who do not conform to binary constructions of gender. Children who are gender creative or gender independent may or may not grow up to identify as transgender.

Gender expression: how a person publicly presents their gender. This can include behaviour and outward appearance, such as how someone dresses, wears their hair, if they use make-up, their body language, and their voice.

Gender fluid: a term to describe someone who moves between binary constructions of gender and whose gender identity and expressions vary over time.

Gender identity: an internal sense or awareness that all people have. For most, it can be described as a kind of "man-ness" or "woman-ness" but gender is not limited to two; it is not binary.

Gender non-binary and gender queer: umbrella terms used to describe a person whose gender identity and/or expression does not conform to the socially constructed gender binary.

Gender normativity: the social scripts that construct the gender binary of woman/man as "normal" and anything that exists outside of this binary as abnormal, unnatural, and/or deviant.

Gender norms: the mostly unwritten rules, scripts, and roles prescribed by socially constructed binary ideas of masculinity and femininity that are reinforced by the dominant culture.

Gender stereotypes: a stereotype is a belief or assumption about the characteristics of different groups or types of people based on prejudice. A gender stereotype is a rigid belief about how men and women typically behave based on sexist prejudice. Gender stereotypes, like all stereotypes, are limiting and can cause harm.

Gender: the ways that masculinity and femininity have been socially constructed and reinforced by the dominant culture through norms, scripts, and stereotypes. Gender is socially constructed as a binary (usually through classifications of woman or man), even though this is not the reality of how gender is experienced internally (gender identity) and expressed externally (gender expression).

Gender-based violence: violence that is rooted in gender-based power relations that manifest as systems of oppression, including sexism, misogyny, transphobia, and/or homophobia.

Gestation: the period of time it takes from when the two gamete cells become one and the cells start to divide inside the uterus. Eventually, there are millions of cells and a baby mammal is made.

Glans: otherwise known as the head of the penis, it can be a source of sexual pleasure.

Gray-asexual: a person who experiences sexual attraction but either not very often or only to a minimal extent.

Gray-romantic: a person who experiences romantic attraction but either not very often or only to a minimal extent.

Harassment: can be intentional and/or unintentional but is always biased and targeted towards an individual who belongs to (or is perceived to belong to) a particular social group or environment. It can include any pattern of behaviour that creates an intimidating, demeaning, or hostile environment. This can be verbal, physical, and/or emotional.

Harm reduction: a public health strategy used to minimize physical and social risk when abstinence is not always possible.

Harm reduction: an approach to public health and disease prevention that begins with the recognition that it may not be possible or realistic for everyone to stop using substances or to stop participating in other activities and behaviours labelled as "risky." From this understanding, evidence-based strategies are promoted to mitigate risk associated with certain behaviours. Some of the most well-known and effective harm reduction initiatives are supervised injection sites and needle exchange programs.

Heterosexism: behaviors, assumptions, and rules that grant preferential treatment to heterosexual people. Heterosexism reinforces the idea that heterosexuality is somehow better or more "right" than homosexuality or queerness and/or ignores the existence of homosexuality or queerness.

Heterosexual: a clinical term for people who are attracted to people of a different gender, often referred to as "straight."

HIV: stands for Human Immunodeficiency Virus. HIV is a virus that attacks the body's immune system, making individuals susceptible to other infections and disease. Anyone can acquire HIV through activities that pose a transmission risk. Although HIV does not currently have a cure, with access to the latest forms of anti-retroviral therapy, the virus can be managed and people can live long lives. Acquired Immunodeficiency Syndrome (AIDS) is the most serious stage of the virus, when people become sick with life threatening infections (CATIE, 2015).

Homophobia: the systemic and individual oppression of people whose sexual orientation does not conform to heterosexuality (and/or of people perceived to be LGBTQ+). This includes a range of negative attitudes and feelings, such as prejudice, fear, discrimination, harassment, and bias towards people whose sexual orientation does not conform to (or is not perceived to conform to) heterosexuality.

Homosexual: a clinical term for people who are attracted to the same gender. Some people find this term offensive because it was historically used to describe queerness as a disease that could be cured.

Hormones: refer to chemical substances that occur in the body and act like messenger molecules to regulate and control different kinds of growth and bodily development.

Human papillomavirus (HPV): a common viral STBBI that can be transmitted through skin to skin contact with genitals and oral, vaginal, and anal sex. HPV can cause genital warts and/or certain types of cancers. It can also go away on its own.

Human Rights: a set of freedoms and entitlements that belong to every individual simply by virtue of their being human. Human rights are universal; they apply to everyone regardless of who they are and where they live. Human rights are rooted in the notion that every human being is fundamentally equal and as valuable to society as every other. Thus, they are all equally deserving of being treated with respect and dignity and should be provided equal opportunity, free from discrimination. Human rights are interdepending and interrelated to one another, they involve and touch every aspect of life.

Hypersexualization: the process of inappropriately imposing a sexual image onto someone or something for the purposes of objectification and/or selling a product.

Hypothalamus: a part of the brain that produces hormones, houses the pituitary gland, and is responsible for maintaining the body's internal balance.

Immune system: a main system in the body that helps fight off infections.

Incarcerated people: people who are in prison. This includes people in pre-trial detention and immigration detention.

Incidence: in the context of STBBIs, refers to the number of new infections within a population over a period of time. Incidence is a rough indicator of the risk of a certain infection within a population.

Infantilization: the process of perceiving, representing, and/or treating someone as a child/infant.

Infantilized: being thought of and treated as a child and/or with less maturity than you actually have.

Intersex: an umbrella term used to describe people who have chromosomes, hormonal profiles, or genitals that do not typically fit into binary medical and social constructions of male and female. Biological sex, like gender, is not binary. Between 0.05% and 1.7% of people are born with intersex traits, although not everyone with intersex traits identifies as intersex (Free & Equal, 2015).

Intimate partner violence: include physical, sexual, emotional, psychological violence, and/or controlling behaviours by a current or former partner, spouse, or boyfriend/girlfriend.

Intoxication: when a person takes a psychoactive substance that results in behavioural and/or physical changes and/or becoming less able to think and act in ways normal for them.

Intrauterine: the inside of the uterus. In the context of contraceptive methods, intrauterine refers to types of contraception that are placed inside of the uterus.

Labia majora: the outer lips of the vulva.

Labia minora: the inner lips of the vulva.

Labia: folds of skin of the vulva that surround the vaginal and urethra openings.

Lesbian: a person who is primarily attracted to people of the same gender. It is most often used for women who are attracted to other women.

LGBTQ+: an acronym that includes gender identities as well as identities related to sexual orientation. Fully spelled out, the acronym contains lesbian, gay, bisexual, transgender, and queer, with the plus indicating more identities, such as asexual, intersex, pansexual, two spirit, and questioning.

Male: one of the categories that babies are assigned at birth based on sex characteristics such as hormones, chromosomes, and genitalia.

Marginalization: a term used to describe a process that limits people's access to power, opportunities, services, programs, or decision-making, based on social location, identities, and experiences.

Marginalized: a term used to describe people who have limited power and may not have access to opportunities, services, programs, or decision-making, due to their social location, identities, and experiences. Sometimes the term "vulnerable" is used in place of "marginalized."

Menstruation: commonly known as a period. It usually starts between 12 and 13 years of age but can begin earlier or later. Menstruation is a part of puberty. Puberty begins when hormones are released from the pituitary gland to stimulate the ovaries to produce other hormones called estrogen and progesterone. Right before ovulation (egg being released from an ovary), estrogen sends a signal to the uterus to build up its lining (endometrium) with extra tissue and blood. The lining of the uterus contains nutrients that help an egg (ovum) and sperm grow (if fertilized). This lining is shed approximately once a month, unless a fertilization and implantation has occured (conception). Once the lining has been shed, another one starts to grow. While menstruation typically occurs once a month, this can fluctuate to greater or lesser degrees throughout the life cycle.

Monoromantic: a person who has romantic feelings for one gender.

Monosexism: behaviors, assumptions, and rules that grant preferential treatment to monosexual people. Monosexism reinforces the idea that monosexuality is somehow better or more "right" than bisexuality or pansexuality and/or ignores the existence of bisexuality and pansexuality.

Monosexual: a person who is sexually attracted to one gender.

Negotiation: a mutual discussion and arrangement of the terms of a transaction or agreement.

Neutrois: a person who identifies as gender neutral. They may see themselves as fitting under the gender non-binary and/or trans umbrellas.

Nipples: a large concentration of nerves attached to breast/chest tissue from which milk can be secreted. They can be very sensitive to pleasure and pain.

Non-consensual surgeries: surgeries and medical interventions that are performed on someone without their consent and/or on someone that is not able to give consent.

Normative: the social construction of one thing as normal and everything outside of this as abnormal.

Objectification: the process of perceiving, representing, and/or treating someone as an object.

Oppression: the systemic exercise of power based on prejudice and perceived (or real) social differences. Oppression privileges one social group at the expense of another through institutional discrimination and social, cultural, and ideological domination (Anti-Oppression Network, 2014). Oppression negatively affects the individual lives of the oppressed group, while positively impacting the privileged group.

Orgasm: a pleasurable sexual feeling that usually comes at the height of sexual excitement. Orgasm is a nervous system event that often (but not always) happens in response to stimulation of the genitals and often (but not always) physically manifests as a series of muscle contractions in the pelvic area and genitals followed by a feeling of release and/or ejaculation.

Outing (someone): when someone reveals another person's sexual orientation or gender identity to an individual or group, often without the person's consent or approval. Not to be confused with "coming out."

Ovaries: internal sex organs that store and release eggs and produce the estrogen hormone.

Ovaries: internal sex/reproductive organs that produce, store, and release eggs and produce estrogen and progesterone hormones.

Ovulation: the release of an egg (ovum) from the ovary. Usually one egg is released per menstrual cycle (but sometimes more than one is released). When the egg is released, it travels through the fallopian tubes to the uterus. Fertilizaton occurs in the fallopian tubes and the embryo will travel to the uterus to implant. If the egg is not fertilized (by sperm), it dissolves.

Pansexual: a person who experiences sexual, romantic, physical, emotional, and/or spiritual attraction to members of all gender identities/expressions.

Pap test: a screening tool that collects cells from the cervix or anus to look for any cellular changes that may indicate abnormal, precancerous, or cancerous cells that are frequently associated with HPV infection. Pap tests are the main screening tool for cervical cancer.

Passive communication: a communication style that is avoidant, protective, and unclear. Individuals who use passive communication avoid expressing their feelings, needs, and opinions; they often feel unheard or disrespected.

Passive-aggressive communication: a communication style that is rooted in anger but expressed in ways that are avoidant, subtle, indirect, and unclear. Individuals who use passive-aggressive communication often feel powerless and resentful because they are unable to identify and/or state their feelings.

Peer norms: the unwritten scripts, rules, and/or assumptions that are common to an age group and/or group that shares other social identifiers.

Penis: an external sex organ made up of the shaft and the glans.

Ph balance: maintenance of the natural occurring balance of acidity and alkaline (basic) in the body.

Pituitary gland: a gland at the base of the brain that releases hormones that instruct the body in growth and development and initiate the process of puberty and other endocrine functions.

Polyamorous: a person who desires intimate partnerships with more than one person. This identity can take many different forms and can include people who identify across different sexual orientations.

Polyromantic: a person who is romantically attracted to multiple genders.

Polysexual: a person who is sexually attracted to multiple genders. This term can have different meanings to different people and often positions itself as different from bisexuality, pansexuality, and polyamory.

Pornography: sometimes called porn, sexually graphic/explicit images intended to cause sexual arousal.

Pregnancy: what happens after a fertilized egg implants (conception).

Prejudice: beliefs that someone holds about a group of people, usually based on stereotypes, misconceptions, and assumptions.

Pre-Menstrual Syndrome (PMS): symptoms that can occur in the time leading up to the menstrual cycle (often the week before). Although this manifests differently from person to person and month to month, common symptoms include intensified feelings/emotions, intensified mood swings, breast/chest tissue tenderness, abdominal bloating, acne, increased hunger and thirst, fatigue, and constipation or diarrhea.

Progestin: the synthetic version of the progesterone hormone. Progesterone is released by the ovaries and prepares the uterus for a fertilized egg to implant. Elevated progesterone levels inhibit the LH hormone surge, which inhibits ovulation.

Prostate gland: a gland that surrounds the ejaculatory ducts at the base of the urethra and secretes a whitish fluid that makes up part of semen (sperm is the other part). The prostate gland can also be stimulated for pleasure.

Puberty: a time of immense social, emotional, mental, and physical change initiated by the secretion of hormones from the hypothalamus and pituitary gland.

Queer Platonic: commonly referred to as QP, a very intimate friendship. It describes a kind of partnership that does not fit the traditional romantic coupling but can nonetheless be intense, emotionally intimate, and even romantically intimate.

Queer: an umbrella term to describe many different kinds of sexual orientations. Queer was historically used as a derogatory term for people who either were or were perceived to be LGBTQ+. In recent years, it has been reclaimed by some people within the LGBTQ+ community as a way of self-identifying and as a political statement against the oppression to which they have been subjected.

Questioning: for some, the process of exploring and discovering their sexual orientation.

Racism: the systemic oppression of people who are not white. This systemic oppression can be carried out by institutions and individuals in the form of prejudice and by implicit and explicit acts of racist discrimination. Racism is experienced differently depending on other identities that an individual holds and their social circumstances.

Rape culture: the environment in which sexual violence is prevalent and goes unpunished. Rape culture describes how dominant ideas, gender norms and stereotypes, the media, and social institutions normalize, trivialize, and eroticize sexual violence, especially male sexual violence against women and other forms of gender-based violence.

Representation: the ways that issues, ideas, groups, communities, and events are portrayed in the media. Representation is based on a certain perception that is ideological or values-based (whether those are visible/obvious or invisible/subtle).

Resilience: commonly refers to a person's ability to "bounce back" in the face of adversity and challenge. A more robust definition from The Resilience Research Centre highlights an individual's capacity to navigate challenge, change, and upheaval as well as their capacity to collectively negotiate for the resources needed to sustain their well-being (Ungar, 2016).

Rights holders: in the context of human rights, this refers to all human beings. All human beings are inherently rights holders and are entitled to human rights as outlined in the *Universal Declaration of Human Rights*.

Romantic orientation: the ways that people can experience romantic and emotional attractions. These may be separate from or connected to sexual and/or physical attraction. Sexual orientation and romantic orientation are not necessarily distinct identities; they are interrelated.

Safer sex: the use of contraception methods in order to prevent pregnancy and STBBIs. The word "safer" is used instead of "safe" to recognize that there is always some risk when engaging in sexual activity—that risk can be emotional, social, physical, and/or psychological.

Scrotum: the sac of skin that houses the testicles and epididymis.

Self-acceptance: the process of learning how to accept, love, and care for yourself. Self-acceptance is part of the process of developing a healthy self-concept.

Self-care: the action of caring for oneself beyond physical survival needs. Part of self-care is figuring out what feels like an affirming and supportive practice unique to each person. Self-care strategies are ways of loving, supporting, affirming, and caring for the whole of who you are and usually do not depend on another person.

Self-concept: the way that individuals think about themselves (what they believe, what they perceive, and how they evaluate themselves). It includes self-esteem, self-worth, self-image, and what a person considers their ideal self (McLeod, 2008).

Semen: a milky-white fluid made up of sperm and seminal fluid from the prostate gland and seminal vesicles that is discharged from the urethra of the penis during ejaculation.

Seminal fluid: the part of the semen produced by the prostate gland and the seminal vesicles.

Sex negativity: the view that sex is harmful, shameful, disgusting, and/or something to be feared. Sex negativity devalues sex and the experiences a person has in relation to sexuality. It promotes the belief that "non-conforming" sexual expression is not valuable and erases honest expression of sexualities and authentic connection between people. Sex negativity often leads to people feeling shame and fear related to sex.

Sex positivity: the view that the only relevant concerns when it comes to a sexual act, practice, or experience are the consent, pleasure, and well-being of the people engaged in it or the people affected by it. Sex positivity places no moral value on different sexualities or sexual acts. It helps in setting aside judgments and making room for the diversity of human sexuality.

Sex work: a form of labour that includes the sale and purchase of sexual services.

Sexism: the systemic oppression of women, non-binary people, trans people, or people who do not conform to gender norms. This systemic oppression can be carried out by institutions and individuals in the form of prejudice and by implicit and explicit acts of sexist discrimination and misogyny. Sexism is experienced differently depending on other identities that an individual holds and their social circumstances.

Sexual assault: any kind of non-consensual sexual activity between adults. Legal categories in the Canadian criminal code that define different kinds of sexual assault according to severity are categorized as levels 1, 2, and 3.

Sexual expression: the variety of ways a person expresses their sexuality, including the kinds of sexual activities they like to participate in. It is not the same as sexual orientation; someone may identify as heterosexual and express their sexuality in ways interpreted by others as queer.

Sexual health: defined by the World Health Organization as "a state of physical, emotional, mental and social well-being in relation to sexuality; it is not merely the absence of disease, dysfunction or infirmity. Sexual health requires a positive and respectful approach to sexuality and sexual relationships, as well as the possibility of having pleasurable and safe sexual experiences, free of coercion, discrimination and violence. For sexual health to be attained and maintained, the sexual rights of all persons must be respected, protected and fulfilled" (WHO, 2006a).

Sexual orientation: a person's emotional, romantic and/or physical and/or sexual attraction to others. Sexuality is complex and attraction can manifest very differently for different people. Categories are commonly used to understand our attractions, though are by no means inclusive of the vast variety of expressions that make up human sexuality.

Sexual response: how someone responds to sexual stimuli (physically, mentally, and emotionally).

Sexual rights: existing human rights that are applied to sexuality and sexual health (2006a, updated 2010). Sexual rights include the right to have full control over and to freely decide upon all aspects of your own sexuality, reproduction, and gender identity, free from violence, discrimination, coercion, and harassment.

Sexuality: an integral part of being human. It is a complex set of personal, social, and spiritual experiences that go beyond sexual activity. Sexuality is not just about what our body does and what we do with our bodies, it is how thoughts, fantasies, desires, beliefs, attitudes, values, behaviours, practices, roles, and relationships are experienced and expressed (WHO, 2006a).

Sexually Transmitted and Blood Borne Infections (STBBIs): sometimes called STIs, they refer to infections that are sexually transmitted or transmitted through blood. STBBIs can be bacterial, viral, protozoan, or microscopic bugs. With early detection and treatment, some can be cured while others can be effectively managed.

Skene glands: also called periurethral or paraurethral glands, empty prostatic fluid into the urethra. They are located on the vulva, near the urethra.

Slut shaming: shaming people (most often cis and trans girls/women) based on indicators that have been socially constructed as "slutty." In recent years, slut shaming has been linked to rape culture as a form of gendered victim blaming, where survivors are blamed for being sexually assaulted based on whether their behaviour and clothing choices are/were "slutty," "revealing," and/or "provocative."

Social determinants of health: factors such as income, race, immigration status, gender, sexual orientation, housing, access to social services and supports, education, social exclusion, and access to health services, among others, that are important in determining the health of a population (Raphael, 2009; WHO, 2008).

Social justice: a term used to describe the redistribution of power and justice in society. Social justice works from the understanding that there are significant power imbalances in society and that these power imbalances make access to justice dependant on many factors that are related to social locations and identities. It is the understanding that every person's struggles for social change are interconnected and dependant on one another and need to be adequately and equitably addressed.

Social movements: when people come together on a large scale to create social change. A social movement is most often a timely, action-oriented response (informal and/or organized) to an injustice that is happening at a large scale. The foundation of most social movements is rooted in social justice.

Speculum: an instrument used to open the vaginal canal to see and reach the cervix. This is one of the main instruments used in a Pap test.

Sperm: a small gamete cell that contains genetic material and is produced in the testicles/testes. It is often referred to as "the male gamete."

Stereotypes: beliefs or assumptions about the characteristics of different groups or types of people. Stereotyping is the action of ascribing a stereotype to someone based on a perception of them belonging to a certain social group.

Stigma: a broad term used to describe the negative and stereotypical thoughts, attitudes, and feelings people may hold about another individual or community on the basis of specific identities and health behaviours. Stigma has been used to label certain groups as less worthy of respect than others. These attitudes are spread by ignorance, prejudice, and discrimination. They are perpetuated when a community and/or health behaviour is represented in a way that is inaccurate by the media, in popular culture, and/or in formal institutions like our educational system.

Strengths-based perspective: a view that recognizes young people as resilient, strong, and capable, with contributions and experiences worth listening to.

Survivor: a person who has survived sexual violence. Identifying as a survivor is a way of reclaiming the experience of passive victimhood.

Systemic discrimination: discrimination refers to actions based on prejudice. Systemic discrimination specifically refers to discrimination that is created and perpetuated by systems of power (i.e., institutions).

Testicles (testes): organs that produce and store sperm.

Third/3rd gender: an umbrella term used to describe people who exist outside of the gender binary. For some people, it means the construction of a new gender.

Tolerance: in relation to substances, when a person's body adjusts and a higher amount is required to cause the same effect as before.

Trans man: a person who identifies as transgender and as a man.

Trans woman: a person who identifies as transgender and as a woman.

Trans: an umbrella term to describe people whose gender identity and assigned sex are different. It can be used for a range of identities and experiences; every community and individual may define trans differently. Trans is a term that someone chooses to describe their own identity. It is not something you can tell or determine in others.

Trans-feminine: a perons who identifies as transgender and feminine.

Transgender: a person whose gender identity and assigned sex are different. Transgender (like all gender identities) is internal and not something you can tell or determine in others.

Trans-masculine: a person who identifies as transgender and masculine.

Transmisogyny: the intersection of transphobia and misogyny. It is misogyny directed at trans women, trans people, and gender non-conforming feminine people. This includes a range of negative attitudes and feelings (such as prejudice, fear, discrimination, harassment, and bias) towards trans and gender non-conforming people who either identify as women and/or identify as femme/feminine. Transmisogyny comes from outside and within the LGBTQ+ community.

Transmission routes: the ways infections are passed from person to person.

Transphobia: the systemic and individual oppression of people whose gender identity and gender expression do not conform to cisgender identities. This includes a range of negative attitudes and feelings (such as prejudice, fear, discrimination, harassment, and bias) towards transgender people and gender non-binary, gender creative, and gender non-conforming people.

Trigger Warning: a way of notifying people that the content of a discussion, class, activity, video, etc. contains material, images, words, ideas, and/or concepts that may set off a memory of a traumatic event.

Trigger: something that sets off a memory of a traumatic event. There are multiple ways that someone who has experienced trauma can be triggered. Triggers can happen through sight, sound, smell, and taste (U of Alberta Sexual Assault Centre, 2015).

Two spirit (or 2 spirit): a term used by some Indigenous people to self-identify. It is an Indigenous specific term that can only be used by Indigenous people to identify themselves. While the term itself is Anishinaabe based, it has been taken up by different Indigenous nations to describe complex experiences and identities as well as cultural roles and responsibilities. Two spirit can sometimes refer to sexual orientation and at other times to gender identity, depending on the individual and/or their particular nation. It can also describe roles and responsibilities specific to different Indigenous nations that may or may not be tied to sexual orientation and/or gender identity. Like any other term that people use to self-identify, do not assume that just because someone is Indigenous and identifies as LGBTQ+ they will use the term two spirit to identify themselves.

Ultrasound: an imaging system used to assess the internal organs of the body.

Unintended pregnancy: becoming pregnant when that was not the reason for engaging in sexual intercourse.

Urethra: the tube that carries urine from the bladder out of the body. For people with vulvas, the urethra opening can be found between the vagina and the clitoris. For people with penises, the urethra opening can be found at the tip of the glans (penis head) and is the same tube that semen travels out of the body.

Uterus: a pear-shaped fibromuscular hollow organ with muscular walls and an inner lining (endometrium) where the fertilized egg becomes embedded and the fetus grows and is nourished. The uterus is situated between the bladder and the rectum, with the cervix at the bottom.

Vagina: a hollow canal that runs from the cervix (inside the body) to the vulva (outside the body).

Vas deferens: the tube that transports sperm from the epididymis on each testicle to the urethra.

Victim blaming: the notion that if someone is sexually violated, it is in some way their fault. Victim blaming is a part of rape culture.

Vulva: a collection of external sex organs (genitalia) that includes the clitoris, mons pubis, labia minora, labia majora, vaginal and urethra openings, vestibule, vestibular bulbs, bartholin, skene, and paraurethral glands.

Withdrawal: in relation to substances, refers to stopping or reducing heavy or lengthy use. Withdrawal is usually accompanied by a set of symptoms ranging from mild to severe, depending on the person and the substance.